Advances in Simulation

Volume 4

Series Editors:

Paul A. Luker
Bernd Schmidt

Advances in Simulation

Volume 1 *Systems Analysis and Simulation I: Theory and Foundations*
Edited by A. Sydow, S.G. Tzafestas, and R. Vichnevetsky

Volume 2 *Systems Analysis and Simulation II: Applications*
Edited by A. Sydow, S.G. Tzafestas, and R. Vichnevetsky

Volume 3 *Advanced Simulation in Biomedicine*
Edited by Dietmar Möller

Volume 4 *Knowledge-Based Simulation: Methodology and Application*
Edited by Paul A. Fishwick and Richard B. Modjeski

Paul A. Fishwick   Richard B. Modjeski
Editors

Knowledge-Based Simulation

Methodology and Application

With 78 Illustrations

Springer-Verlag New York Berlin Heidelberg
London Paris Tokyo Hong Kong Barcelona

Editors

Paul A. Fishwick
University of Florida
Department of Computer
and Information Science
Gainesville, FL 32611, USA

Richard B. Modjeski
U.S. Army Operational Test
and Evaluation Agency
Alexandria, VA 22302-1458, USA

Series Editors

Paul A. Luker
California State University, Chico
Department of Computer Science
Chico, CA 95929-0410, USA

Bernd Schmidt
Universität Erlangen-Nürnberg
Institut für Informatik
Erlangen, FRG

Library of Congress Cataloging-in-Publication Data

Knowledge-based simulation : methodology and application / Paul A. Fishwick, Richard B. Modjeski, editors.
p. cm. – (Advances in simulation ; v. 4)
Includes bibliographical references and index.
1. Computer simulation. 2. Expert systems (Computer science)
I. Fishwick, Paul A. II. Modjeski, Richard B. III. Series.
QA76.9.C65K65 1990
003′.3633—dc20 90-9926

Printed on acid-free paper.

Typeset using TEX by The Bartlett Press, Somerset, New Jersey, using authors' files.
Camera-ready copy prepared by TEXSource, Houston, Texas.
Printed and bound by R.R. Donnelley & Sons, Harrisonburg, Virginia.
Printed in the United States of America.

9 8 7 6 5 4 3 2 1

ISBN 0-387-97374-5 Springer-Verlag New York Berlin Heidelberg
ISBN 3-540-97374-5 Springer-Verlag Berlin Heidelberg New York

Series Preface

Simulation is a discipline or, as some would say, a collection of disciplines that has proved to be of vital importance to progress in all fields of endeavor. Modeling, as opposed to simulation, has a much longer history, but mathematical modeling, fundamental though it is, has a limited utility if the models do not yield to analytical solution. Even if analytical solutions do exist, the execution of those models by some "simulation engine" can impart an understanding that the models alone cannot provide. I still remember that thrill, some 25 years ago, when I first saw differential equations come to life on an analog computer. It was, of course, the advent of the computer in the 1940s that made simulation possible. As the complexity of our world increases, then our dependence—that is not too strong a word—on simulation also increases. Consequently, we are ever more demanding of our simulations, or, in other words, we are constantly seeking advances in simulation. It was from a desire to document, share, and encourage these advances that this series was created.

The last decade has witnessed a number of developments that have led to great advances in simulation methodology and technology. First, consider the evolution of hardware, which has become so powerful, small, and cheap that we can all enjoy the power of yesterday's mainframe on a small portion of our desks. As a result, many simulations, which hitherto had been prohibitively expensive to execute on the sequential von Neumann digital computer, now run in an acceptable time. Of course, many high-performance machines, employing a number of different architectures, have also been built for highly complex simulations. On the software front, the 1980s saw the simulation language gradually being edged out by the simulation environment, which typically makes use of multiple windows, menus, and icons, thereby providing the user with a more application-oriented interface than the raw language.

Another phenomenon of the 1980s was the upsurge of interest in artificial intelligence (AI). Thanks largely to the widespread application of expert systems, AI has become a commercial commodity. Nobody could (or should) claim that expert systems are the answer to all our prayers.

However, they do provide an interesting collection of paradigms that can be applied to solve certain classes of problems. A key component of all AI systems is the "knowledge base," which contains a codification of the system's "knowledge" about the world. The system has to interpret and manipulate this knowledge in order to interact with its environment.

Particularly exciting for me, as someone with a long interest in both simulation and AI, are the opportunities that arise from combining the two fields of endeavor. The marriage is a perfectly natural one. After all, AI can be viewed as a simulation of some aspect(s) of human intelligent behavior, whereas simulation can be viewed as the manipulation of a codification of our knowledge about some real world system. The relationship is clearly symbiotic. In many ways, simulation can help us with AI and AI can help us with simulation. But first a word of caution. We are deluding ourselves if we think that the task of combining AI and simulation is going to be easy. One of the reasons that AI has stagnated in the past is because too much had been promised too soon by too many. However, if we are realistic, the prospect is that we are now in a position to produce computer systems that will be more useful to society than ever before. As we make progress with simulation and AI, however slowly, we gradually gain a better understanding of ourselves and the world (and universe) in which we live.

This volume and its successor, *Qualitative Simulation Modeling and Analysis*, document some of the work that is currently in progress in combining simulation and AI. As can be seen from the table of contents of this volume, the scope is wide and varied and the results are very interesting.

On behalf of both series editors, Bernd Schmidt and myself, I would like to thank the editors of this volume, Paul A. Fishwick and Richard B. Modjeski, for the hard work that I know they have put into the compilation. And, of course, another big thank you goes to the authors of the individual chapters.

One person I would like to single out for his endless patience and for his faith in and commitment to the series is Gerhard Rossbach of Springer-Verlag.

Now, to sum up, and let the reader enjoy the book. In this series, we would like to cover all aspects of advances in simulation, whether theoretical, methodological, or related to hardware or software. An important part of publishing material that constitutes an advance in some discipline is to make the material available while it is still of considerable use. Gerhard and the production staff at Springer-Verlag see to it that this is the case. I urge anybody who is eager to share their advances in simulation to contact Bernd Schmidt or myself. We would love to hear from you.

Paul A. Luker
Chico, California, April 1990

Preface

What is knowledge-based simulation? We first define the concept of simulation, and then discuss the "knowledge-based" qualification. Computer simulation is the use of either an analog or digital computer to model and analyze complex artificial and natural systems. Systems operate over time and often contain many interacting sub-parts; thus, there are concepts such as local behavior and emergent global behavior of the system.

Computer simulation has been an active field of research since World War II. Simulation has been used in a variety of areas such as computer aided circuit design, factory automation, ecological systems, engineering and urban dynamics. Simulation has a huge number of possible applications and it is only just beginning to grow in terms of being one of the major thrusts of the next decade.

Computer simulation can be divided into two sections: methodology and application. In methodology, one is primarily concerned with the vast number of modeling and analysis methods that can be devised; one is not concerned, particularly, with one application. In the application section, we are concerned with a specific application, and how simulation can be utilized to do real world problem solving. Methodology and application are both essential, and we have chosen to divide the book into two parts based on these somewhat broad categories.

We define "knowledge-based" simulation as the application of knowledge-based methods within artificial intelligence (AI) to the field of computer simulation. As with any hybrid approach to research there is a two way street when considering the relationship between AI and simulation. That is, simulation techniques can often be seen to also have an effect on AI research. The reader might now ask: "Well, aren't all simulations knowledge-based?" We reply in the affirmative, but add that the recent interest in the bridge area between AI and simulation has suggested many new avenues of research such as 1) studying how heuristic and fuzzy knowledge might be used in traditional simulation languages, and 2) studying how many of the qualitative, mental models in AI can be improved by noting that discrete systems simulation methods (such as discrete time and discrete event) can serve as a fertile foundation.

This book is a representative cumulation of research within the bridge area of AI and computer simulation performed in government, industry and academia over the past years. Much of the research discussed in this text was presented in whole or in part at the Artificial Intelligence and Simulation workshops which were held in conjunction with the annual meetings of the American Association for Artificial Intelligence (AAAI) and the International Joint Conference on Artificial Intelligence (IJCAI).

The first AI and Simulation workshop was proposed by Richard B. (Dick) Modjeski in the spring of 1986. Marilyn Stelzner of IntelliCorp chaired the first workshop which was held at the University of Pennsylvania's Wharton Hall in conjunction with AAAI 86. Drs. Arthur Gerstenfeld, Dick Modjeski, and Y.V. (Ramana) Reddy served as cochairs. The first AI and Simulation workshop brought together some of the best ideas of computer scientists, cognitive psychologists, physicists, engineers, and practitioners from all disciplines. Lively discussions were given about the boundaries of AI and simulation, what one area could do for the other, and how the intersection of concepts from all these disciplines might form a unique composite which was useful to everyone.

The second AI and Simulation workshop, held in conjunction with AAAI 87 at the University of Washington in Seattle, enlarged on the concepts of the first workshop. Chairperson Malcolm R. Railey, led a discussion on the value added by combining AI and simulation and where do we go from here. Cochairs Marilyn Stelzner, Paul A. Fishwick, Dick Modjeski, Bernard P. Zeigler, and Ramana Reddy provided timely input into the growing awareness that the interplay of disciplines in AI and simulation is a process occurring over time rather than an immediate product.

In the third AI and Simulation workshop, held during AAAI 88 in Minneapolis, Minnesota, chairperson Paul A. Fishwick highlighted many of the achievements that had taken place in the area during the past few years. Cochairs Dick Modjeski, Norman R. Nielsen, Ramana Reddy, Lawrence Widman, and Bernard P. Zeigler encouraged the participants to think beyond their disciplines in order to achieve more robust applications from AI and simulation tools and technologies.

Jerzy W. Rozenblit chaired the fourth AI and Simulation workshop to consolidate and focus the use of AI techniques in simulation modelling around general paradigms and methodologies that focused on: 1) reasoning about physical systems with simulation-based approaches and qualitative methods; 2) the interplay of simulation with planning and scheduling; and 3) methodologies to achieve new applications. Cochairs Paul A. Fishwick, Dick Modjeski, Bernard P. Zeigler, Norman R. Nielsen, and Tuncer I. Ören wrote position papers that focused much of the discussion of the workshop. Steven Bankes, of the Rand Corporation, provided an insightful keynote address on simulation science and intelligence engineering.

Many of the notions of AI have been refined in the crucible of application. It is the intent of the editors to present a sampling of the methodological notions that represent current thinking in AI and simulation within a broad spectrum of applications. It is our contention that experimental design and rigorous testing of theoretical notions provides the next generation of theory builders a more solid foundation. The movement away from conjecture and guess toward a more systematic set of theoretical relationships will be useful for both AI and simulation.

The first editor, Paul Fishwick, would like to thank the National Science Foundation (under grant IRI-8909152) for partial support during the research period when this book was being prepared. The second editor, Richard Modjeski, has donated his portion of the royalties from this text to the Army Emergency Relief organization. Army Emergency Relief helps the children and families of soldiers killed and wounded defending the United States. Richard Modjeski would like to acknowledge the following individuals who encourage his efforts in AI and simulation while working for the United States Army: Honorable Mr. Walter W. Hollis, Deputy Under Secretary of the Army for Operations Research, The Pentagon, Washington DC. Mr. E.B. Vandiver III, Director, United States Army, Concepts Analysis Agency, Bethesda, Maryland. Lieutenant General Jerome B. Hilmes, United States Army, Deputy Chief of Staff of the Army for Command, Control, and Computers, The Pentagon, Washington, D.C. Major General Ennis C. Whitehead, United States Army (Retired), Burdeshaw Associates LTD, Bethesda, Maryland.

The editors are indebted most of all to every author who was involved in writing a chapter for this book. We hope that the book will serve as a springboard for future research in the areas of knowledge based approaches in artificial intelligence and computer simulation.

Paul A. Fishwick
Gainesville, Florida

Richard B. Modjeski
Alexandria, Virginia

References

Gerstenfeld, A., Modjeski, R., Reddy, Y.V., & Stelzner (Eds.). (1986). *Proceedings of the American Association for Artificial Intelligence Workshop on Artificial Intelligence and Simulation.* (NTIS No. AD-A174053). Washington DC: National Technical Information System.

Fishwick, P.A., Modjeski, R.B., Zeigler, B.P., Reddy, R., Stelzner, M., & Railey, M.R. (Eds.). (1987). *Proceedings of the American Association for Artificial Intelligence Workshop on Artificial Intelligence and Simulation* (NTIS No. AD-A183-736). Washington, DC: National Technical Information System.

Fishwick, P.A., Modjeski, R.B., Nielsen, N.R., Reddy, R., Widman, L., & Zeigler, B.P. (Eds.). (1988). *Proceedings of the Third Artificial Intelligence and Simulation Workshop.* Menlo Park, CA: American Association for Artificial Intelligence.

Rozenblit, J. W., Fishwick, P.A., Modjeski, R.B., Zeigler, B.P., Nielsen, N.R., & Ören, T.I. (Eds.). (1989). *Proceedings of the American Association for Artificial Intelligence Workshop on Artificial Intelligence and Simulation.* Menlo Park, CA: American Association for Artificial Intelligence.

Contents

Contributors

Norman I. Badler
Department of Computer and Information Science
University of Pennsylvania
Philadelphia, PA 19104-6389, USA

Arie Ben-David
Information Systems Department
School of Business Administration
The Hebrew University of Jerusalem
Mount Scopus, Jerusalem 91905, Israel

Albert Clarkson
ESL Incorporated
Advanced Intelligence Analysis Technology Laboratory
495 Java Drive
Sunnyvale, CA 94088–3510, USA

Jeffrey Esakov
Department of Computer and Information Science
University of Pennsylvania
Philadelphia, PA 19104-6389, USA

Paul A. Fishwick
Department of Computer and Information Science
University of Florida
Gainesville, FL 32611, USA

Andrew Gelsey
Department of Computer Science
Yale University
New Haven, CT 06520-2158, USA

Jhyfang Hu
Department of Electrical Engineering
Tulane University
New Orleans, LA 70118, USA

Stephen H. Kaisler
DARPA/NTO
1400 Wilson Boulevard
Arlington, VA 22209, USA

Tag Gon Kim
Department of Electrical and Computer Engineering
University of Kansas
Lawrence, KS 66045, USA

Douglas B. Lenat
Microelectronics and Computer Technology Corporation
P.O. Box 200195
Austin, TX 78720, USA

Richard B. Modjeski
United States Army
Operational Test and Evaluation Agency
Technical Support Directorate
Policy and Review Methodology Division
Park Center IV, 4501 Ford Avenue
Alexandria, VA 22302-1458, USA

Norman R. Nielsen
Intelligent Systems Laboratory
SRI International
333 Ravenswood Avenue
Menlo Park, CA 94025, USA

Tuncer I. Ören
Simulation Research Group
Department of Computer Science
University of Ottawa
Ottawa, Ontario K1N 6N5, Canada

Colleen M. Oresky
ESL Incorporated
495 Java Drive
Sunnyvale, CA 94088-3510, USA

Richard E. Reynolds
Naval Training Systems Center
Human Factors Laboratory
Orlando, FL 32826, USA

Jeff Rothenberg
The RAND Corporation
1700 Main Street
Santa Monica, CA 90406-2138, USA

Jerzy W. Rozenblit
Department of Electrical and Computer Engineering
University of Arizona
Tucson, AZ 85721, USA

Kent E. Williams
Institute for Simulation and Training
University of Central Florida
P.O. Box 25000
Orlando, FL 32816-0544, USA

Ben P. Wise
McDonnell Douglas Research Laboratories
Department 225, Building 105
P.O. Box 516
St. Louis, MO 63166, USA

Bernard P. Zeigler
Department of Electrical and Computer Engineering
University of Arizona
Tucson, AZ 85721, USA

Part I

Methodology

CHAPTER 1

Application of Artificial Intelligence Techniques to Simulation

Norman R. Nielsen

Abstract

Although the fields of artificial intelligence (AI) and simulation are both concerned with the development and use of models, these fields evolved almost independently until relatively recently. Now, the potential contributions of AI to the development and application of simulation models are being considered more widely. AI techniques can play a variety of roles in the simulation process, including:

- Knowledge representation in a model
- Decision making within a simulation
- Rapid prototyping of models
- Data analysis of simulator-generated outputs
- Model modification and maintenance.

Determining how well AI techniques can play these roles in practice was the subject of two experiments conducted at SRI International. A model development experiment demonstrated that the inclusion of AI-related techniques in the developer's toolkit can result in more rapid development, improved user interfaces, and lower required skill levels for users. A model maintenance experiment showed that six of ten identified classes of modifications could be assisted by generic intelligent support capabilities built into a model development tool. The potential benefits, and their practicality, are beginning to be recognized, and greater "AI content" is being built into tools.

1 Introduction

Scientists have long resorted to models—abstractions of reality—to test ideas and conduct experiments. In some cases machine efficiency considerations have motivated modeling activities; it is much less costly to work with a model of a system than with the actual system itself. In other cases simple necessity has motivated these activities, for example when the system under study does not exist or when modifying or otherwise experimenting with the actual system is impossible (e.g., testing that might cause catastrophic consequences).

The advent of analog computers allowed modelers to transform some types of physical models to analog representations. Digital computers offered much more extensive modeling capabilities, with a broad range of models being represented in logical rather than physical form. Although digital simulation was feasible, taking advantage of the opportunity was often tedious. Over time, various languages and tools were developed to facilitate the development of computer-based simulation models. Some languages, such as GPSS (IBM, 1965), were developed specifically to support simulation analyses. Others, such as the original Simscript language (Markowitz, 1963), were developed as a set of extensions to existing languages (in this case Fortran).

After more extensive usage, these tools and languages were enhanced. Simscript, for example, evolved into Simscript II.5, becoming a language in its own right and losing its tie to Fortran. Further, more powerful representational capabilities were incorporated into modeling languages—a particularly important development because the match between the representation form and the characteristics of the knowledge significantly affects model understandability and computational efficiency. Historically, the development of discrete-event modeling tools has focused on procedural representations and capabilities, although there have been exceptions (e.g., the object-oriented programming capabilities of Simula) (Dahl, 1966).

The field of discrete-event simulation developed somewhat independently. It borrowed, and took advantage of, developments in general computing technology, but not in other fields such as artificial intelligence. Although the modeling of knowledge (knowledge representation) and the modeling of the use and application of knowledge (reasoning) have been fertile areas of AI research, for many years this type of modeling was of interest only to other AI researchers. Yet, the modeling of knowledge and the modeling of systems have much in common (Bobrow, 1986), and various aspects of AI technology related to knowledge-based systems, including a variety of tools to aid in the construction of knowledge models, have now become commercializable, both because software reached a point of critical functionality and because hardware capabilities had evolved sufficiently to support the demands of that software.

Publicity surrounding this commercialization activity has stimulated interest in the potential that some AI-related tools and techniques might have for traditional modeling activities. This interest has arisen in both the simulation and the AI communities. The Society for Computer Simulation, for example, now sponsors an annual AI and Simulation Conference. Other simulation conferences have had sessions devoted to the topic of AI and simulation. "Simulation" vendors, such as CACI, are beginning to incorporate capabilities developed in the AI community into their simulation products (Andes, 1986). The AI community also has an interest in applying some of its developments to traditional simulation activities. The American Association for Artificial Intelligence (AAAI), for example, has been sponsoring an AI and Simulation Workshop at each of its annual conferences since 1986. "AI" vendors, such as IntelliCorp, are developing discrete-event simulation tools based on their knowledge-based system tools (IntelliCorp, 1985a).

The influence of the AI and simulation domains on each other is not unidirectional, however. Analysts are now investigating the use of simulation techniques to improve the reasoning capabilities of expert systems. Further, interest in these approaches is growing. During the recent AI and Simulation Workshop (Rozenblit, 1989) at the 1989 International Joint Conference on AI (IJCAI), a number of papers covered the use of a simulation model in the knowledge-based reasoning process. Tentative conclusions from the reasoning process would be applied to the model to confirm their effectiveness and to match modeled outputs with the state of the real world. Model outputs would also be used to support further reasoning.

2 Applicability of AI Techniques

AI techniques can play a variety of functional roles in the simulation process, including:

- Knowledge representation in a model
- Decision making within a simulation
- Rapid prototyping of models
- Data analysis of simulator-generated outputs
- Model modification and maintenance.

The following discussion of these functional roles focuses on their value and benefit. Unless these techniques can provide significant advantages to simulation model developers and users, the potential contributions from the AI community will be of little practical benefit.

2.1 Knowledge Representation

A variety of techniques can be used to represent and manipulate knowledge. Three techniques offered by the AI community that are of particular relevance to simulation are:

- Object-oriented programming
- Frames and inheritance
- Graphics-based editing.

2.2 Object-Oriented Programming

In one sense object-oriented programming may be viewed as a contribution of simulation to AI rather than vice versa. Many of the object-oriented programming concepts in SmallTalk™ (Goldberg, 1983), which subsequently have been applied in developing such knowledge-based system tools as Loops™ (Stefik, 1983) and KEE™ (IntelliCorp, 1985b), were originally derived from the object-oriented capabilities of Simula. In another sense, though, object-oriented programming should be considered a contribution of the AI community. The simulation community did little to capitalize on the object-oriented capabilities of Simula (Dahl, 1966), while the the AI community evolved and enhanced the concept. Thus, an improved technique is being given back to the simulation community (Cox, 1986; Shriver and Wegner, 1987).

The entities of a discrete-event simulation can be considered as objects in an object-oriented formulation. Two types of knowledge are associated with each entity (object)—factual and behavioral. An object's factual data can be viewed as the attributes of the entity, characterizing its capabilities, current state, or parameters. The object's behavioral data are essentially procedural functions that characterize how the entity is to behave in certain circumstances. Messages sent to an object result either in the provision of selected factual data or the initiation of a specific behavior (e.g., calling a function to log the object's current status and the current value of simulated time).

This type of representation and processing offers advantages to the program developer. Keene (1989) suggested that the independence and separation of functions lead to a cleaner design and the more rapid combination of program pieces. This capability supports rapid prototyping, in that particular model functions can be changed or replaced with minimal impact on other sections of the model. This capability also facilitates the modification and maintenance of models, as discussed below.

Object-oriented programming offers modelers a number of system capabilities; for example:

- Consistency checking—Each entity in the simulation would carry with it the mechanism necessary to check whether the other entities in the system were consistent or compatible with it; that is, each object can check that every other object can indeed provide each of the facts or behaviors required.
- Monitoring—Each entity controls access to its factual data; hence, run-time checks can easily be instituted to test data values either upon storage or retrieval. This feature enables various alarms to be set or displayed when particular values are stored, data collection to be initiated on state changes, and events to be scheduled or activated on the occurrence of specified conditions.

- Image-triggered activities—Placement of the cursor on a screen image can trigger the sending of a message to the entity (object) associated with the image. This feature permits users to initiate actions graphically and to set factual data (e.g., by moving the dial on a gauge).

The object-oriented approach can also be used within a model (Fox, 1987) to provide a variety of model-specific capabilities. Consider a model of a factory, for example. Various parts and components enter the factory, circulating from one machine to another. At each stage the parts are further processed and/or combined until a completed item is produced. An object-oriented approach would enable a decentralized routing procedure to be used. Each part would carry with it a list of the functional processing steps required to convert it into a product, and each machine would have a list of the functional processing steps it could perform. An algorithm could then be provided to each part, permitting it to seek out the appropriate next machine to provide service. This feature enables the modeler to adjust the types and numbers of equipment available in the factory without having to modify any of the workload descriptions.

2.3 Frames and Inheritance

Frames provide the structure that supports object-oriented programming (Minsky, 1975; Fikes and Kehler, 1985). Each frame can be viewed as containing slots. An object's factual data items can be placed in these slots, as can references to the functions that provide the desired behaviors for the object. The power of frame-based representation arises from the inheritance capabilities, the manner in which frames can be related to one another.

Frames can be related hierarchically (as in parent to child); slots and/or slot values can be inherited downward from parent to child to grandchild, etc. Frames can be viewed as representing a class of things, a subclass of things, and so forth until a frame represents a specific instance of something. A variety of other frame relations can be defined. In a machine shop, for example, each frame (machine) might be an instance of a parent machine class (frame). In addition, these same frames might also be related to each other in an upstream/downstream manner, depending on whether processing by one machine preceded another in the normal production flow.

The frame concept fits very naturally into the structure of discrete-event simulation, offering the modeler a number of capabilities; for example:

- Library development—New entities can be specified as members of a particular class with certain differences. These differences may relate to the addition or subtraction of slots, to the modification of slot values, or to the adjustment of relationships. New entities, whether actual or class representations, can be specified much more efficiently this way.
- Construction via component assembly—Systems can be assembled by selecting components from a library and then connecting those entities

with various relations. Each entity is thus created fully formed, complete with data, relations, and necessary procedures.

- Component representations—Component representations can be used efficiently to manipulate subcomponents. Consider three frames representing a machine, an input buffer, and an output tray, for example. The subcomponents can be linked to the machine by "has-a" and "belongs-to" relationships. Then, if an instance of machine is created at run time, the associated input buffer and output tray instances will also be created and properly linked. Thus, the frame relationships can provide the modeler with considerable power.

2.4 Graphics-Based Editing

Graphical editing is another technique that may appear to be related more to computer science than to artificial intelligence; however, because it has been used heavily in AI research and development, its capabilities are discussed here. The graphical editor links the two representational and manipulational capabilities discussed above (object-oriented programming and frames) with graphics. An icon, menu, or other visual representation can be associated with each frame. Relations between frames can be depicted by spatial location on the screen or with various types of interconnecting lines. Positioning the cursor on an appropriate icon will send a message to the associated object, resulting in an appropriate action being taken (Grafton, 1985; Raeder, 1985).

Graphically developing and editing the specification of the system to be simulated offers a number of advantages, both to the model builder and to the model user:

- User friendly—The user interface is perceived as being much more user friendly than one relying on the input of names and values via a keyboard.
- Efficiency—Most users can manipulate objects much more rapidly using a visual approach (assuming sufficient underlying computer capacity) than using a keyboarding approach.
- Error reduction—The graphical representation enables the user to visualize the system better, reducing oversight errors and speeding system checkout.
- Reduced training requirements—Users generally require less training to be able to use a graphical interface to a system than to be able to use a keyboard-oriented interface.

2.5 Decision Making

The various decisions made throughout a simulation have traditionally been made through procedural representations of the decision mechanism. In some cases, however, a nonprocedural representation, deriving from knowledge-based system developments, may be preferable. Consider the following three situations in which a nonprocedural representation might be an appropriate alternative:

- A poorly understood decision process—It is difficult to develop an algorithm representing the decision mechanism when the underlying process is not well understood. The user generally must rely on heuristics, which can often be captured effectively in a knowledge-based representation. The more faithful representation of the decision process results in a lesser contribution to a random variation factor and hence to a more precise model.
- Human in the loop—Some systems do not run independently of a human operator; the operator is part of the system. One approach to modeling this type of system is to include the human in the simulation rather than just a representation of the human. This technique has certain disadvantages, including longer running time, the need for human resource availability, and lack of repeatability. Knowledge-based systems, however, are intended to represent human decision making. Thus, the human in the simulation can be replaced by a knowledge-based representation, permitting a single simulation employing two types of representations to model the entire system.
- Experimental decision making—Sometimes, part of the reason for developing a simulation model is to experiment with and to understand the decision-making process in particular areas of the system. In such situations the decision-making processes are likely to be modified frequently. A knowledge-based representation can facilitate changing these processes rapidly, often more effectively than when procedural representations are being used. The nonprocedural framework can thus serve as an effective base for experimenting with different (often radically different) decision-making approaches.

2.6 Rapid Prototyping

Knowledge structures deriving from the AI community tend to have fewer and clearer interfaces that those developed by traditional means. These structures permit models to take advantage of more of the existing components. They also facilitate the assembly of those components into a model. These modular characteristics also facilitate the making of program changes, an ever-present part of the prototyping process.

In contrast, procedural models tend to have much more entwined internal relationships. Consequently, these models are more difficult to construct and change. Builders tend to think more of building the model to specification than building a prototype for experimentation.

Providing a rapid prototyping capability for simulation development has some far-reaching consequences. Rapid prototyping is much more than just a means to build a simulation model more quickly (although, of course, it does do that); rather, it provides another dimension of modeling.

Simulation programs are generally viewed as conventional programs and developed using conventional software engineering approaches. Unlike conventional programs, however, simulations generally lack good specifications before the programming begins. One purpose underlying model building then is to better understand the real system (Law and Kelton, 1982). Thus, the model development process can be considered to be part of the specification development process. The model specifications evolve with the developer's experience with the model. A rapid prototyping capability facilitates this formulate-experiment-and-modify approach.

Theoretically, the only effect of the rapid prototyping capability is on development time. Practically, however, there is a qualitative difference as well. First, because time is always limited, an approach that makes more effective use of time permits more experimentation and hence, very likely, a more effective model. Second, because humans tend to tackle easier tasks first, certain features of the model can become immutable, particularly structural choices made early in the model development process. With the passage of time, these features affect a larger percentage of the model and thus become increasingly difficult to change. A rapid prototyping capability can therefore make a significant difference in the characteristics and validity of the simulation model developed.

2.7 Data Analysis

Simulation models are often used in an optimization mode; that is, rather than executing the model once to obtain an answer, the modeler makes multiple runs, adjusting input parameters (i.e., the system configuration) between repetitions in an effort to produce results that might be judged better according to specified criteria. Thus, following the completion of a simulation run, the modeler will frequently study the simulator output data that characterize the run, trying to identify the underlying factors that limited the system's observed performance and to make system adjustments that might improve performance.

Various reasoning mechanisms can assist the modeler in this task; they can analyze the output data and suggest possible causes of observed bottlenecks for the modeler's consideration (see, for example, Prager, Belanger, and De Mori, 1989, and Raghavan, 1988). These same reasoning mechanisms can also suggest reconfigurations that might relieve the bottlenecks. The parameters to be changed must be identified, as must the degree to which the values should be changed for the next simulation run. This process can be viewed as a multidimensional, hill-climbing optimization procedure; knowledge-based procedures are well suited to estimate the degree of change to make between tests. Constructing the knowledge required to use this approach successfully can be difficult, however, for the knowledge is often both model and domain dependent.

Data from a series of simulation runs can help the modeler understand the structure of system behavior better than data from a single run; the modeler can "triangulate" on the system's behavioral characteristics and hence find a system configuration offering improved performance. A well-planned set of runs, however, will yield considerably more information than will an equal number of runs made with ad hoc parameter changes. By using a knowledge-based system to prepare an appropriate experimental design prior to the initiation of a set of simulation runs, the modeler can thereby reduce the amount of simulation required to analyze a problem. In a similar fashion, knowledge-based systems can be used to formulate input scenarios that can be used to test the dynamic behavior of systems.

The termination point of a simulation being run against an input scenario is easily determined; the end of the script marks the end of the simulation. Not so easily determined, however, is the termination point for a simulation being run to determine the steady-state behavior of a system. Determining when equilibrium behavior has been reached (and operable for a sufficiently long time for data to be statistically reliable) involves certain statistical considerations as well as a degree of pattern recognition. Developments from the AI community can assist the modeler with this latter task.

2.8 Model Modification

The need to modify a simulation model arises at several places in the life cycle. For the purposes of this discussion, consider the simulation process as involving the set of activities shown in Figure 1. Taken together, the first three activities cover model prototyping and development. Extensive modification of the model occurs during this phase of the model's life. AI-related techniques can facilitate such changes, as described previously in connection with the simulation process.

Although model modification is such an obvious aspect of the development stages, the most significant need for improving the modification process lies in the fifth stage. As shown in Figure 1, usage of a model is the final step in the life cycle; there is no iteration back through validation. Yet, as shown in Figure 2, very few models are simply "used." They undergo considerable revision and change as part of the usage process. Just as parameter changes are made from run to run, so are model changes.

Because the testing and validation activities performed during development are frequently not repeated, model revision during the usage phase can be quite dangerous. Model changes are all too often made haphazardly following the analysis of one simulation run and before the making of the next run. Modelers justify this type of change process by arguing that these changes are often small, requiring no retesting. They further argue that conducting a series of test runs to prepare for a single simulation run would be disastrously uneconomic.

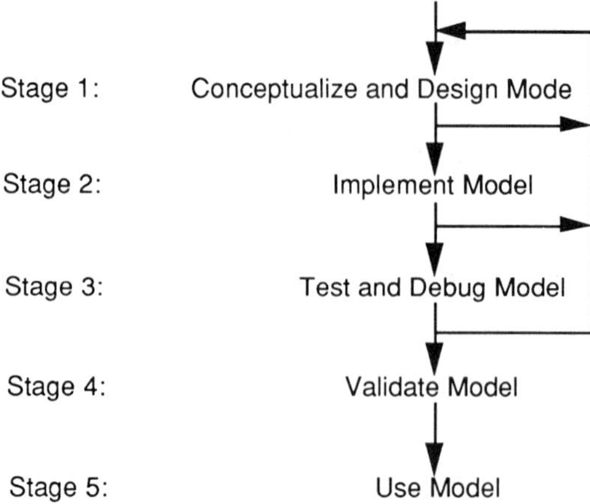

FIGURE 1. Simulation life cycle.

These arguments ignore some accuracy and reliability issues. Because mistakes frequently occur while even the smallest changes (i.e., the "obvious" ones) are made, simulated results may reflect the behavior of a system other than the one intended. Sometimes the resultant behavior is counterintuitive, and the user becomes suspicious; at other times, however, what is accepted as appropriate behavior is actually erroneous. Such problems lead many people to be skeptical of conclusions supported by simulations.

Because of the pressures not to retest and revalidate the model after small changes, expecting significant changes in user behavior is unrealistic. Mechanisms are therefore needed to reduce the frequency of error introduction during the model modification process. Two such mechanisms, involving techniques developed or enhanced by AI researchers, can contribute to this goal: graphical representations and intelligent modification.

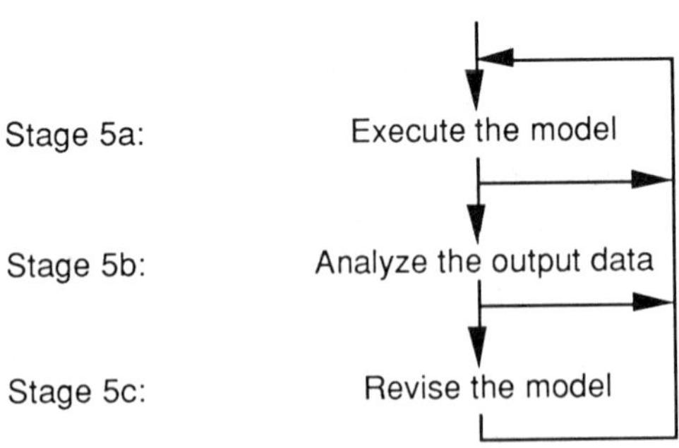

FIGURE 2. Model usage activity sequence.

Representing the system graphically (Melamed and Morris, 1985; Kramer, Magee, and Ng, 1989) enables the user to work with a representation that is closer to the mental model of the system. Not only can a graphical editor be used to modify and manipulate the system efficiently, but also the user is far more capable of detecting errors in a visual representation than in a column of words or a list of numbers. In fact, because many people tend to think in visual terms, a network specified in numerical form would most likely be converted into a mental image before the user could reason or answer questions about it. The graphical representation enables the user to "see" mistakes of omission or commission much more readily. Although this approach does not prevent human errors, it makes them more obvious, helping in their detection and elimination.

The second mechanism applies knowledge-based reasoning to the modification process, enabling users to propose changes at higher levels of abstraction than would otherwise be possible. Ideally, the user would indicate changes at a conceptual level, leaving the system to make the more detailed or derivative changes required to implement the concept. Of course, the system cannot always make every change that might be needed to install a conceptual change. Even in those circumstances, however, the system could identify the needed changes, soliciting advice or guidance from the user. In this way the system could control completeness and consistency while accepting inputs as needed from the user.

These two approaches will reduce modification errors because they divide the modification activity between the user and the computer so as to benefit from the comparative advantage of each:

- User—The user's attention is focused on higher level considerations, where humans excel. Feedback is provided in a form in which the implications of changes can be more readily assessed.
- Computer—The computer's "attention" is focused at more detailed levels, carrying out the steps necessary to implement a change strategy and thus performing those functions at which the computer excels.

These mechanisms make it possible to accomplish changes that are more nearly complete and consistent.

3 Potential Impact of AI Techniques

The adoption and incorporation of various AI-developed techniques into the simulation process can be expected to provide a number of benefits, including the following:

- Improved representational capability—Enabling the modeler to represent system aspects in ways that save space, permit programs to work with those representations more efficiently, and facilitate the modeler's understanding of the system being modeled.

- Shortened model development time—Enabling the modeler to design, construct, test, and validate a simulation in less time.
- Reduced skill level requirements—Enabling users to employ simulation capabilities effectively with a lower degree of training and experience.
- Faster model execution—Enabling programs to be developed that will execute more efficiently.
- Improved system maintainability—Enabling simulation programs to be modified more easily, rapidly, and with fewer induced errors.

Definitive answers about the degree to which these benefits are achievable do not yet exist. The continued introduction and testing of AI-developed concepts and techniques, however, are producing data to address these issues. Two experiments conducted at SRI (Nielsen, 1987; Nielsen, 1989) contribute some insight into the potential benefits.

3.1 A Model Development Experiment

SRI developed a generic control system simulator (Nielsen, 1987) for the Allen-Bradley Company, a large vendor of factory control systems. The design goals for the simulator were twofold:

1. Assist control system engineers in evaluating new factory control systems and configure specific control systems for customer plants.
2. Enable simulation analyses to be conducted by engineers having considerable knowledge about control systems but lacking expertise in computer science, simulation, or artificial intelligence.

An automated factory can be viewed as containing a mix of computer-controlled devices such as machinery to manufacture products (e.g., lathes, grinders) and equipment to move products between machines (e.g., robots, conveyors). The control of these devices is often distributed throughout a factory. A controller (i.e., computer) is attached to each device. Groups of devices (and their controllers) can be clustered into cells, with a cell computer used to sequence the work of each device. Similarly, cells can be clustered into areas under the control of an area computer, and the area computers can be connected to a factory computer, and so forth. Processors on the same or different level of the control hierarchy can be linked via a network or other communication mechanism.

As products are manufactured or assembled in the factory, a variety of messages (transactions) flow thorough the control network, triggering various processing actions as well as further control information flows. For example, routing information must be sent to controllers of material-handling equipment; status reports and alarms must be sent from device controllers to supervisory processors. Control programs to guide the manufacture of a particular part must be transferred to the applicable machine controller in synchronism with the arrival of the material at that machine.

The simulation facility (generic simulator) was expected to be able to reflect the design of an arbitrary control system under a specified workload and to provide information to assist the user in evaluating the control system's performance with respect both to factory equipment utilization and to control system utilization (processors, controllers, and network links). Design issues that the user would desire to address included:

- The number of levels that should be contained in the control system hierarchy.
- The processor power to be placed at each node in the control network.
- The data (e.g., control system programs) to be stored at each node in the network, including the possibility of redundant storage at multiple locations.
- The level in the hierarchy at which each control function should be performed.
- The bandwidth, priority mechanism, and protocol to be used on each communication link.

The goals of the simulator development effort were judged to be most appropriately addressed through an approach that relied on AI-related techniques. The modeling facility was developed using IntelliCorp's SIMKIT™. The experience of the joint Allen-Bradley, SRI, and IntelliCorp team thus provides information on the effectiveness of employing some AI techniques in a modeling effort. In particular, four aspects of the project deserve comment:

- Development time—The capabilities to be incorporated in the modeling facility implied a rather ambitious project. A modeling group within the Allen-Bradley family that worked extensively with discrete-event communication models using traditional simulation approaches had estimated that an elapsed time of 12 months would be required to develop the facility. The actual project, involving a knowledge-based approach, was completed in 4 months.
- Usage characteristics—The completed simulator enables the user to make significant configuration changes quite easily. For example, a three-level hierarchical control system can be converted to a centralized architecture in approximately 5 minutes. The process is sufficiently straightforward that such significant configuration changes can be conducted in demonstrations without the need for extensive debugging activities.
- Training—Less than 1 day of training was needed to enable a control system engineer to utilize the modeling capability effectively; however, the simulator executed on a Symbolics LISP machine, and users could not be trained on this equipment within such a short time period.
- Execution time—In comparison with conventionally constructed simulations, the simulator executed quite slowly, which is the price paid to obtain the previously described advantages. The simulator should really

be viewed as a facility for development and experimentation rather than as a facility to support long execution runs.

In summary, the impact of the use of AI techniques in the development effort was as expected from a newly applied technology. The anticipated advantages tended to be realized, but the technology could not be applied without regard to its limitations. The technology is not a panacea, but it can be advantageous if employed in appropriate circumstances.

3.2 A Maintenance Experiment

An existing simulation model (Nielsen, 1989) was taken as the basis for an experiment to assess the general applicability of intelligent maintenance techniques. This model characterized the behavior of a small telecommunications network consisting of a set of links and nodes with messages being transferred between pairs of designated nodes. The network utilized a store-and-forward protocol to transfer messages from their origins to their ultimate destinations because many nodes were not directly connected. The simulator had been designed to assist technicians in detecting, isolating, and correcting network faults and made extensive use of object-oriented programming.

Ten representative modifications were selected to serve as the framework within which the applicability of intelligent support might be evaluated. Each of the identified changes represents a class of changes of the type a user of the simulation might wish to make. (Note, though, that the change classes have not been weighted by expected frequency, so they do not represent a sample from the population of changes that might be made in the course of using the simulation model.) The classes of changes were:

1. Modify the bandwidth of a link between two specified nodes, which might be viewed simply as modifying a program parameter or adjusting a value in a table.
2. Delete an existing link from the network, which involves not only removing the link but also updating all routing tables or mechanisms to reflect the absence of the connection previously provided by the deleted link.
3. Create a new link and connect it between nodes in the network. This change involves not only creating the link and connecting it to the network but also updating all routing tables to reflect the availability of the new connection. This change also illustrates a cooperative modification. Although the system can create a link and update routing tables in response to a user request, the system must solicit user guidance as to the priorities to be assigned to each route that includes the new link.
4. Delete an existing node from the network. This change involves not only removing the node but also removing all attached links and updating all routing tables to reflect the absence of both the node and its links to the network.

5. Create a new node and connect it to the network, which involves not only creating the node but creating and attaching a link and updating all routing tables as well.
6. Modify the node queuing algorithms for message forwarding. This change might adjust the algorithms to favor messages having such characteristics as higher priority, greater age, or less size (length). It differs from the changes in classes 1–5 in that it may involve a programming change instead of (in addition to) updating table values.
7. Change a node's message routing procedure, which might, for example, adjust the procedure from a static one (e.g., based on a fixed routing table) to a dynamic one (e.g., based on a dynamically updated table based on recently observed link congestion). This change does not modify the degree of centralization of the routing procedure. Either approach can be applied on a centralized basis (complete path assigned at the time of message creation) or on a decentralized basis (path assigned incrementally, a node at a time, at each node along the route).
8. Collect message transit time data using a new metric, which can be expected to involve a cooperative man-machine effort. The system can develop data collection and summarization routines, but the user will have to indicate the points at which transit time begins and ends (e.g., from time of creation at the originating node until receipt at the destination node, but excluding the actual node-to-node transmission times, so as to provide a measure of the overhead and queuing delay added to the absolute minimum transmission time).
9. Change the measure of network congestion. This change might, for example, switch from a "link queuing delay" metric to a "time to receipt of acknowledgment" metric. It would involve an algorithmic change in that a different procedure would be used to compute the congestion measure. No change would be required, however, in any routine making use of that metric.
10. Install a congestion-avoidance message-routing algorithm, which involves creating a new algorithm, installing that algorithm in the system, and connecting it to existing code at appropriate places. Such an algorithm might cover the congestion threshold that would trigger execution of the algorithm, the congestion level on alternate routes that would suppress execution, as well as the alternate routing procedure itself.

Two levels of intelligence may be involved in the change process:

- A higher level to determine the modification strategy to be used.
- A lower level to actually make the changes dictated by the strategy.

The reasoning sophistication needed to make a specified change will depend partly on the structure of the implemented model. Consider, for example, the change of a link's bandwidth. The user would only need to change the "transmission rate" parameter of the specified link for a model having an object-oriented structure. More complicated changes might be necessary for a model having a different structure. If link transit time were embedded with message characteristics rather than with the link (rate) and message (size), the intelligent maintenance assistant would need to be able to determine how link performance parameters were incorporated in other parameters. Once this mechanism had been determined, the necessary changes would be straightforward.

Consider, as another example, the creation and connection of a new link. The connectivity pointers from the link to its end-point nodes (and from those nodes to the link) can readily be constructed and stored. A modification strategy will be needed, however, to determine the necessary routing adjustments. At a minimum, changes will be needed to the nodes attached at each end of the new link and potentially to every node, depending on the system's design structure (e.g., centralized routing). Although the same routes might be assigned to messages, regardless of the system's structure, the route characterizations to be modified might be quite different. Thus, even simple changes can require sophisticated capabilities to determine how the changes should be made.

The extent of the opportunities for applying intelligent maintenance procedures can be estimated by examining the characteristics of each type of change. Ideally, direct benefit measures such as the reduction in elapsed time to make modifications or the reduction in the number of errors introduced during the modification process would be used. The scope of the experiment, however, did not permit such measurements to be made. Instead, the error-reduction potential of an intelligent maintenance assistant was estimated by classifying each type of change according to its degree of independence: model independent, model dependent, or user dependent.

Model-independent changes are those that do not depend on the characteristics of a particular model. Capabilities for making such changes can thus be built into a modeling tool rather than into the model. Note that the tool or development system cannot provide maintenance support in a vacuum; it cannot make changes to an arbitrary program, relying only on the source code to provide information about the model's internal structure. The tool must have been used to build the model initially (e.g., graphical assembly of object-oriented modules from a library), thereby enabling the requisite structural knowledge to be obtained.

Model-dependent changes are those that do depend on the characteristics of a particular model. Capabilities for making such changes must therefore be built into the model by the developer (as opposed to being provided generically by the model development tool). The model developer must therefore anticipate the possibility of users seeking to make these types of changes and provide the requisite functionality.

User-dependent changes are those that depend on specific ideas of the user (e.g., modifications to a procedural algorithm). The details of such changes cannot be anticipated by either the tool developer or the model builder. Further, the state of the technology is such that it would not be appropriate to specify syntax and semantics sufficient to permit the system to understand a user-provided description of the desired change. Some assistance can be provided to a user seeking to make such changes, however. In fact, the system can provide information (e.g., lists of dependencies on a variable) and can check that module-to-module consistency is maintained, but the responsibility for making the desired change must lie with the user as only the user understands the implications of that change.

The ten classes of model modifications were then assigned to these three categories of independence. Changes 1–6 were assigned to the model-independent category, representing modifications for which the model-building system should be able to take responsibility. Each of these changes represents a generic type of modification that the designer of the model development tool should be able to foresee. Hence, they should be included in that tool for use in creating simulation models. Although the development tool should be able to accept responsibility for identifying all the required changes, it would not actually be able to make all the changes independently. Consultation with the user would be necessary to clarify data associated with system-proposed changes. In the case of Change 3 (adding a network link), for example, the system could create the new link and include it in routing tables, but it would need to solicit guidance from the user on the priorities to be assigned to each route that included the new link.

Changes 7 and 8 were assigned to the model-dependent category, representing modifications for which the simulation model should be able to take responsibility. Each of these changes represents a model-specific type of modification that the designer of the model should be able to foresee and hence include in that model. Again, making these changes would require a user dialog to clarify data associated with the model-controlled change process. In the case of Change 8 (new transit time metric), for example, the model would provide the necessary data collection and summarization routines, but it would need to solicit guidance from the user on the points at which transit time begins and ends.

Changes 9 and 10 were assigned to the user-dependent category because they involve modifications that neither the tool developer nor the model developer could anticipate and that the user could not easily describe. Without a rich natural language capability, the system could not readily understand the conceptual details of the changes proposed by the user. Further, without having constructed the part of the program to be changed, the system would have great difficulty understanding the structure of the relevant sections of code.

4 Conclusions

The two studies reported herein are quite limited in scope, but they do provide some evidence about both the applicability of and the benefits that can be derived from the use of AI-related techniques to support the modeling process.

The model development experiment showed that the inclusion of AI-related techniques in the developer's toolkit can result in more rapid development, improved user interfaces, and lower required skill levels for users. The experiment also demonstrated, however, that these new techniques are not without a price. The developer must cautiously determine when they might appropriately be applied.

The model maintenance experiment is encouraging, in that six of the ten identified classes of modifications should be assistable by generic intelligent support capabilities built into a model development tool. Such breadth of applicability may not only indicate the extent to which errors introduced during the maintenance process can be prevented through model-independent modification mechanisms but also may encourage vendors of simulation tools to include intelligent modification support capabilities in their products.

As a consequence of these and other experiences, the potential benefits offered modelers by AI-related techniques are beginning to be recognized. Moreover, the realized benefits will likely extend beyond those described in this chapter. New simulation tools having an "AI" content are now being developed, and older tools are being modified to provide additional capabilities. Clearly, we are at the dawn of a new age of simulation.

References

Andes, D. K., *Artificial Intelligence in SIMSCRIPT II.5*, La Jolla, California, CACI, Inc., 1986.

Bobrow, D. G. (Ed.), *Qualitative Reasoning about Physical Systems*, Cambridge, Massachusetts, MIT Press, 1986.

Cox, B. J., *Object-Oriented Programming: An Evolutionary Approach*, Reading, Massachusetts, Addison-Wesley, 1986.

Dahl, O. J., and K. Nygaard, "SIMULA—An Algol-Based Simulation Language," *Communications of the ACM*, Vol. 9, No. 9, 1966.

Fikes, R., and T. Kehler, "The Role of Frame-Based Representation in Reasoning," *Communications of the ACM*, Vol. 28, No. 9, 1985.

Fox, M. S., *Constraint-Directed Search: A Case Study of Job Shop Scheduling*, Los Altos, California, Morgan-Kaufman, 1987.

Goldberg, A., and D. Robson, *SmallTalk-80: The Language and Its Implementation*, Reading, Massachusetts, Addison-Wesley, 1983.

Grafton, R. B., and T. Ichikawa, "Visual Programming," *IEEE Computer*, Vol. 18, No. 8, 1985.

IntelliCorp, *KEE Software Development System User's Manual*, Mountain View, California, IntelliCorp, 1985b.

IntelliCorp, *The SIMKIT System: Knowledge-Based Simulation Tools in KEE*, Mountain View, California, IntelliCorp, 1985a.

International Business Machines, *General Purpose System Simulator User's Manual*, Form H 20-0163-0, White Plains, New York, IBM Corp., 1965.

Keene, S. G., *Object-Oriented Programming in Common Lisp: A Programmer's Guide to CLOS*, Reading, Massachusetts, Addison-Wesley, 1989.

Kramer, J., J. Magee, and K. Ng, "Graphical Configuration Programming," *IEEE Computer*, Vol. 22, No. 10, 1989.

Law, A. M., and W. D. Kelton, *Simulation Modeling and Analysis*, New York, New York, McGraw-Hill, 1982.

Markowitz, H. M., B. Hausner, and H. W. Karr, *Simscript: A Simulation Programming Language*, Englewood Cliffs, New Jersey, Prentice-Hall, 1963.

Melamed, B., and R.J.T. Morris, "Visual Simulation: The Performance Analysis Workstation," *IEEE Computer*, Vol. 18, No. 8, 1985.

Minsky, M., "A Framework for Representing Knowledge," in P. H. Winston (Ed.), *The Psychology of Computer Vision*, New York, New York, McGraw-Hill, 1975.

Nielsen, N. R., "The Impact of Using AI-Based Techniques in a Control System Simulator," in *Simulation and AI*, edited by P. A. Luker and G. Birtwistle, The Society for Computer Simulation, Simulation Series, Vol. 18, No. 3, July 1987.

Nielsen, N. R., "The Application of AI Techniques to Model Maintenance," *Proceedings of the 1989 AI and Simulation Conference*, San Diego, California, The Society for Computer Simulation, 1989.

Prager, R., P. Belanger, and R. DeMori, "A Knowledge-Based System for Trouble Shooting Real-Time Models," in *Artificial Intelligence, Simulation & Modeling*, Widman, Loparo, and Nielsen (Eds.), Wiley, New York, 1989.

Raeder, G., "A Survey of Current Graphical Programming Techniques," *IEEE Computer*, Vol. 18, No. 8, 1985.

Raghaven, B., "An Expert System Framework for the Management of Due Dates in Flexible Manufacturing Systems," in *Expert Systems and Intelligent Manufacturing*, Oliff (Ed.), Elsevier, New York, 1988.

Rozenblit, J. (Ed.), *Fourth Artificial Intelligence & Simulation Workshop*, 1989.

Shriver, B., and P. Wegner (Eds.), *Research Directions in Object-Oriented Programming*, Cambridge, Massachusetts, MIT Press, 1987.

Stefik, M., D.G. Bobrow, S. Mittal, and L. Conway, "Knowledge Programming in LOOPS: Report on an Experimental Course," *AI Magazine*, Vol. 4, No. 3, 1983.

Stefik, M., and D. G. Bobrow, "Object-Oriented Programming: Themes and Variations," *AI Magazine*, Vol. 6, No. 4, 1986.

CHAPTER 2

The DEVS-Scheme Modelling and Simulation Environment

Tag Gon Kim and Bernard P. Zeigler

Abstract

The Discrete Event System Specification (DEVS) formalism makes it possible to design new simulation languages with better understood and sounder semantics. The DEVS-Scheme environment is a realization of the DEVS formalism in Scheme (a LISP dialect) environment, which supports hierarchical, modular specification of discrete-event models, a systems theoretic approach not possible in conventional languages. The DEVS formalism also provides a formal representation of discrete-event systems capable of mathematical manipulation.

This chapter describes recent progress made in developing the DEVS-Scheme environment in the AI and Simulation Group at the University of Arizona. A knowledge-based modelling and simulation environment, DEVS-Scheme allows users to create models and store them in its knowledge base for reuse them as a component(s) to develop hierarchical models. The DEVS-Scheme environment has been tested on a variety of domains characterized by complex, hierarchical structures such as advanced multi-computer architectures, intelligent multi-robot organizations, and biologically-based life support systems. Thus, the DEVS-Scheme environment represents a significant step toward implementing system theory based formalisms and operations.

1 Introduction

Over the last decade, works on mathematical formalism for modelling discrete event systems, inspired by the systems theory concepts of Zadeh and Desoer (1963) and others, have been made in an attempt to cast both

---

Research reported here was supported by NSF Grants CCR 8605142 and 874148 for "Variant Families of Hierarchical Discrete Event Models: Distributed Simulation" and "Intelligent Simulation Environment for Advanced Computer Architecture."

continuous and discrete events models within a common systems modelling framework (Zeigler, 1976, 1984a, 1984b). The systems modelling concepts have facilitated development of a methodology under which simulation could be performed in a more principled and secure manner. The recent advent of high performance artificial intelligence (AI) software and hardware has made it possible to develop advanced simulation environments to implement such a modelling/simulation methodology. These environments use various AI knowledge representation schemes to express knowledge in simulation models, resulting in so-called knowledge-based simulation system (Kim, 1988; Reddy et. al., 1986; Robertson, 1986).

The compatibility between object-oriented programming paradigms and discrete event world view formalisms has been well noted (O'Keefe, 1986; Zeigler, 1987a). In such programming systems, an object, an instance of class, is a package of data structures and associated operations, usually representing a real world counterpart. These programming paradigms naturally incorporate AI knowledge representation schemes within simulation models. Such schemes can be used not only to organize information about the nature of the objects involved in the simulation, but also to model intelligent agents within components themselves (Davis, 1986; Robertson, 1986; Zeigler, 1987a).

DEVS-Scheme is an environment for specification of hierarchical, modular discrete event models and simulation in a Lisp-based object-oriented framework (Zeigler, 1986, 1987b; Kim, 1988). In contrast to other knowledge based simulation systems, DEVS-Scheme is based on the DEVS formalism, a theoretically well grounded means of expressing hierarchical, modular discrete event models (Zeigler, 1976, 1984a, 1986b; Concepcion & Zeigler, 1987). The atomic-models and digraph-models classes of DEVS-Scheme provide means of specifying basic building blocks that form the model base. Kernel-models is a generalized class in DEVS-Scheme whose subclasses provide powerful means of defining complex hierarchical structures formed by recursive compounding of basic components. Existing subclasses of kernel-models provide for broadcast, hypercube, cellular and centralized interconnections of components. Due to its object-oriented realization, new classes can be readily added. The structure of a simulation model is explicitly described in the System Entity Structure, a scheme for representing decomposition, taxonomic and interconnection knowledge. This facilitates flexible combination and amendment of the structure and/or behavior of models and makes it possible to investigate a large class of alternatives generated from the model base.

DEVS-Scheme is based on the Discrete Event System Specification (DEVS) formalism introduced by Zeigler (1976). The insight provided by the DEVS formalism is in the simple way that it characterizes how discrete event simulation languages specify discrete event systems. Having this abstraction, it is possible to design new simulation languages with better understood and sounder semantics. Indeed, the DEVS-Scheme environment discussed here is an implementation of the DEVS formalism in Scheme (a Lisp dialect: See (Abelson, Sussman, and Sussman, 1985)) which enables the modeler to specify models in a manner closely paralleling the DEVS formalism. DEVS-Scheme supports building models in a hierarchical, modular manner (successively putting systems together to form larger ones), a systems oriented approach not possible in conventional languages (Concepcion and Zeigler, 1988).

The DEVS formalism is more than just a means of constructing simulation models. It provides a formal representation of discrete event systems capable of mathematical manipulation just as differential equations serve this role for continuous systems.

This chapter reviews progress made in implementing such manipulations in the DEVS-Scheme environment. The chapter first reviews the DEVS formalism briefly, and then introduces the DEVS-Scheme environment. It also shows how to manipulate complex hierarchical structures—such as multi-level computer architectures—within the environment by employing system entity structure based knowledge representation scheme.

2 The DEVS Formalism

The DEVS hierarchical, modular formalism, as implemented in DEVS-Scheme, closely parallels the abstract set theoretic formulation developed by Zeigler (1984a). In such a formalism, one must specify 1) basic models from which larger ones are built, and 2) how these models are connected together in hierarchical fashion. A basic model, called an *atomic DEVS* is defined by a structure (Zeigler, 1984a)

$$M = \langle X, S, Y, \delta_{\text{int}}, \delta_{\text{ext}}, \lambda, \text{ta} \rangle$$

where

X is a set, the *external input event* types
S is a set, the *sequential states*
Y is a set, the *external output event* types
δ_{int} is a function, the *internal transition* specification
δ_{ext} is a function, the *external transition* specification
λ is a function, the *output function*
ta is a function, the *time-advance function*

with the following constraints:

(a) The *total state* set of the system specified by M is

$$Q = \{(s, e) \mid s \in S, 0 \leq e \leq \text{ta}(s)\};$$

(b) δ_{int} is a mapping from S to S:

$$\delta_{\text{int}} : S \longrightarrow S;$$

(c) δ_{ext} is a function:

$$\delta_{\text{ext}} : Q \times X \longrightarrow S;$$

(d) ta is a mapping from S to the non-negative reals with infinity:

$$\text{ta} : S \longrightarrow R, \qquad \text{and}$$

(e) λ is a mapping from Q to Y:

$$\lambda : Q \longrightarrow Y.$$

An interpretation of the *DEVS* and a full explication of the semantics of the *DEVS* are in (Zeigler 1984a).

The second form of model, called a coupled model, tells how to couple (connect) several component models together to form a new model. This latter model can itself be employed as a component in a larger coupled model, thus given rise to hierarchical construction. A *coupled DEVS* can be defined as a structure (Zeigler, 1984a):

$$DN = \langle D, \{M_i\}, \{I_i\}, \{Z_{i,j}\}, \text{SELECT}\rangle$$

where

D is a set, the *component names*;

for each i in D,

M_i is a *component*

I_i is a set, the *influences* of i

and for each j in I_i,

$Z_{i,j}$ is a function, the *i-to-j output translation*

and

SELECT is a function, the *tie-breaking selector*

with the following constraints:

$M_i = \langle X_i, S_i \delta_i, \lambda_i, Y_i, \text{ta}_i\rangle$

I_i is a subset of D, i is not in I_i

$Z_{i,j} : Y_i \longrightarrow X_j$

SELECT : subsets of $D \longrightarrow D$

such that for any non-empty subset E, SELECT(E) is in E.

3 Classes in the DEVS-Scheme Simulation Environment

The DEVS formalism underlies DEVS-Scheme, a general purpose environment for constructing hierarchical discrete event models (Zeigler, 1987a). DEVS-Scheme is written in the PC-Scheme language which runs on DOS compatible microcomputers and under a Scheme interpreter for the Texas Instruments Explorer. DEVS-Scheme is implemented as a shell that sits upon PC-Scheme in such a way that all of the underlying Lisp-based and objected oriented programming language features are available to the user. The result is a powerful basis for combining AI and simulation techniques.

DEVS-Scheme is principally coded in SCOOPS, the object oriented superset of PC-Scheme. The class specialization hierarchy is shown in Figure 1. All classes in DEVS-Scheme are subclasses of the universal class *entities* which provides tools for manipulating objects in these classes (these objects are hereafter called entities). The inheritance mechanism ensures that such general facilities need only be defined once and for all.

Models and *processors*, the main subclasses of *entities*, provide the basic constructs needed for modelling and simulation. *Models* is further specialized into the major classes *atomic-models* and *coupled-models*, which in turn are specialized into more specific cases, a process which may be continued indefinitely as the user builds up a specific model base. Class *processors*, on the other hand, has three specializations: *simulators*, *co-ordinators*, and *root-co-ordinators*, which serve to handle all the simulation needs.

Models and *processors* are intermediary classes which serve to provide basic slots needed by their specializations. Class *atomic-models* realizes

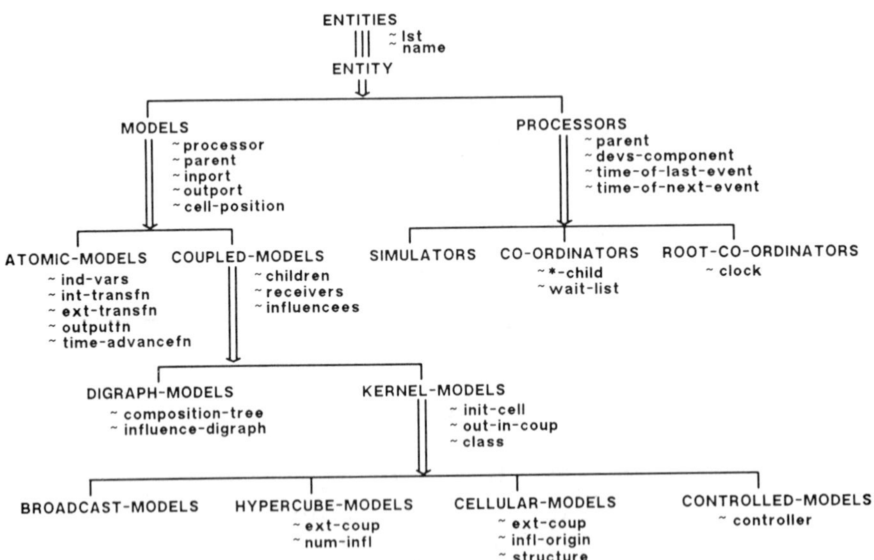

FIGURE 1. Class hierarchy in DEVS-Scheme. Uppercases are classes; lowercases are class/instance variables.

the atomic level of the underlying model formalism. It has instance variables and methods corresponding to each of the parts of this formalism. *Coupled-models* is the major class which embodies the hierarchical model composition of the DEVS formalism. *Digraph-models* and *kernel-models* are specializations which enable specialization of coupled models in specific ways. Instance variables corresponding to children and coupling relations, and methods which manipulate the variables realize model composition.

Digraph-models, a specialized class of coupled models, concern a finite set of explicitly specified children and an explicit coupling scheme connecting them. Internal and external coupling relations specify how output ports of children couple to input ports of other children, and how input/output ports of a coupled-model couple to input/output ports of its components respectively.

In contrast to *digraph-models*, instances of *kernel-models* are coupled models whose components (children) are isomorphic models. A method creates the isomorphic children which are all members of the same class, called the kernel class, stored in an instance variable. Different specialized classes of *kernel-models* realize different internal and external coupling schemes. Four coupling schemes have been defined to date: broadcast, hypercube, cellular and centrally co-ordinated coupling which are realized by the subclasses *broadcast-models*, *hypercube-models*, *cellular-models* and *controlled-models*, respectively. Constructors create models in the respective classes. Details are given in (Kim, 1988).

The *simulators*, *co-ordinators*, and *root-co-ordinators* specialization classes of processors carry out the simulation of a model in a manner following the hierarchical *abstract simulator* concepts in (Zeigler 1984a). *Simulators* and *co-ordinators* are assigned to handle *atomic-models* and *coupled-models* in a one-to-one manner, respectively. A root-co-ordinator manages the overall simulation and is linked to the co-ordinator of the outermost coupled model. Simulation proceeds by means of messages passed among the processors which carry output signals generated by the atomic models as well as data needed for co-ordination. Simulation can be interactive in "pause" or "non-pause" mode offering the experimenter ability to interrupt, save the state, modify the model, and resume at will (see Zeigler, 1987a for more detail).

4 Model Synthesis and Management Based on System Entity Structure

The DEVS-Scheme environment provides layer of objects and methods which may be used to achieve more powerful features. In particular, a second layer, ESP-Scheme, implements a knowledge representation scheme, called the *System Entity Structure*, to synthesize and organize a family of models in the model base. Complete description of ESP-Scheme is beyond the scope of this chapter. Details are available in (Zeigler, 1987b; Kim, 1988; Kim et. al., 1988; Kim, 1989).

The system entity structure represents knowledge of decomposition, taxonomic, and coupling. The model base contains models which are expressed in DEVS-Scheme as mentioned earlier. The entities of the entity structure refer to conceptual components of reality for which models may reside in the model base. Also associated with entities (as with other object types we shall discuss) are slots for attribute knowledge representation. An entity may have several aspects, each denoting a decomposition and therefore having several entities. An entity may also have several specializations, each representing a classification of the possible variants of the entity.

The system entity structure bears no relation to the Entity-Relation Database model. However, Higa (1988) has developed an approach to data base design using the system entity structure model which controlled experimentation in a classroom setting has shown to be superior to conventional schemes. Higa and Sheng (1989) are using this approach to couple knowledge bases and data bases to achieve systems capable of both inference and large data management in an object-oriented framework.

The above knowledge base framework is intended to be generative in nature, i.e., it should be a compact representation scheme which can be unfolded to generate the family of all possible models synthesizable from components in the model base. The user, whether human or artificial, should be a goal-directed agent which can interrogate the knowledge base and synthesize a model using pruning operations that ultimately reduce the structure to a composition tree. This contains all the information needed to synthesize a model in hierarchical fashion from components in the model base. Associated with aspects are coupling specifications involving their entities. In pruning, eventually one aspect is selected for each non-atomic entity. The coupling specifications associated with the selected aspects provide the information needed to carry out the hierarchical synthesis.

As suggested in Figure 2, models are synthesized from a pruned entity structure from components already residing in working memory, from models in the models base, and by synthesizing components themselves from pruned entity structures. Thus once a model has been specified, either directly in DEVS-Scheme or as pruned entity structure, it is available for reuse as a component in a larger model.

5 Manipulation of Hierarchical Structures

Since models in DEVS-Scheme may be complex, hierarchical structures special attention has been paid to replicating such structures. Isomorphic copies of existing models are needed to conveniently construct complex coupled models. DEVS-Scheme provides two main alternatives for creating

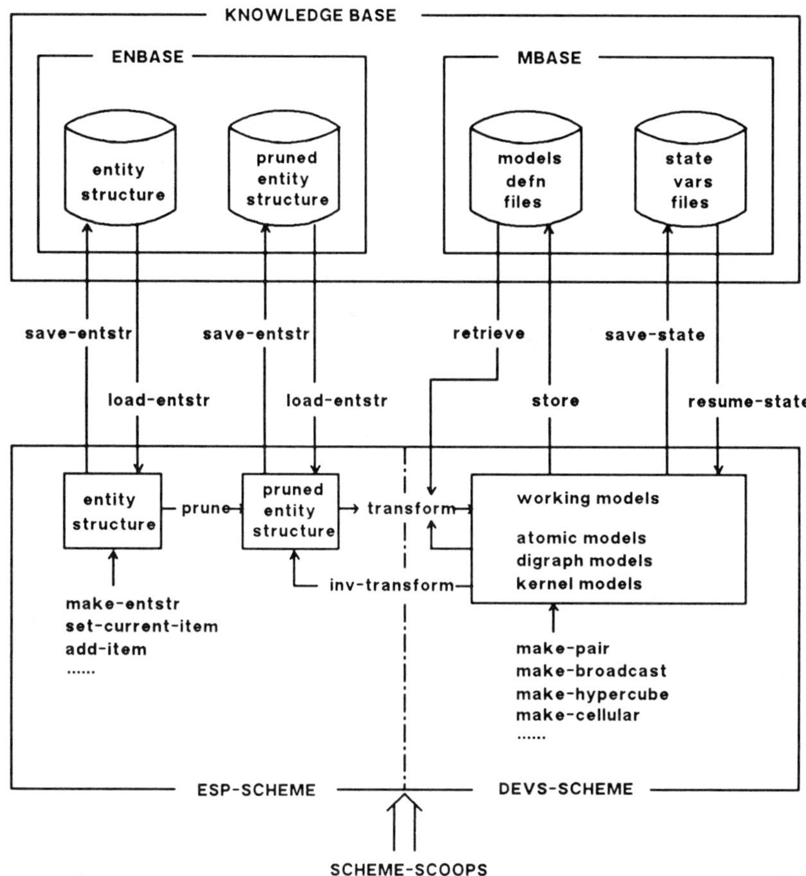

FIGURE 2. The DEVS-Scheme modelling/simulation environment.

such copies. The first method, make-new, when sent to a model creates an isomorphic copy of the original which is an instance of the same class as the original. The primary classes (*atomic-models*, *digraph-models*, and the specializations of *kernel-models*) require their own versions of the *make-new* method since each has features that are unique to itself. Since *coupled-models* instances are hierarchical in structure, the *make-new* method must be recursive in the sense that components at each level must replicate themselves with their own *make-new* methods as shown in Fig. 3. Note that two isomorphic coupled models require to have isomorphic coupling schemes and isomorphic components.

The second method, *make-class*, when sent to a model, creates a class definition with the original model as template. Instances created in such a

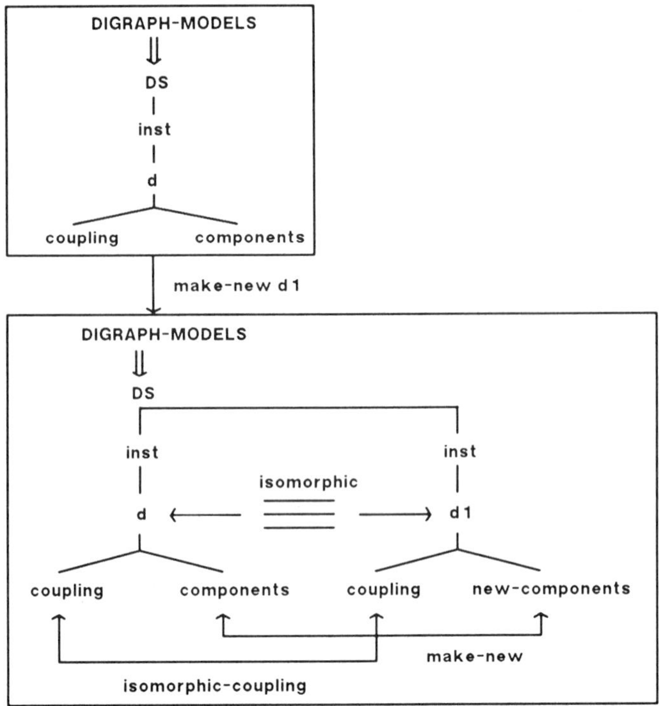

FIGURE 3. Creation of a new digraph model.

class will be isomorphic to the original. However, in contrast to the effect of *make-new*, such instances are members of a different class from the original.

Method *make-new* may be employed whenever an isomorphic copy of a model is desired. Method make-class must be employed in order to establish a class to serve as the *kernel class* for an instance of *kernel-models*. For example, to create an instance of *broadcast-models* to contain components all isomorphic to an existing model m, we require a class with m as template. Note that we can create different instances of such *kernel-models* each having a different class, but all classes having *m* as template. Details of make-class and make-new for the *kernel-models* are available in (Kim, 1988).

To test the methods for creating copies of models we employ a novel approach: we implemented a parallel set of methods for checking isomorphism between models. The criteria for correct copying are formalized in the isomorphism methods. For a copying method to be valid, a copy of a model must be isomorphic to the original as determined by the isomorphism test. Definitions of isomorphism between DEVS models and its checking algorithms within DEVS-Scheme environment are available in (Kim, 1988).

6 Hierarchical Architecture Example

The common structures already implemented as classes in DEVS-Scheme together with its support of hierarchical construction illustrate the manner in which exploration of alternative designs may be supported. The kernel models—broadcast, hypercube, or cellular—are particularly suited to model the recently introduced multi-level computer architectures for massively parallel processing. As an example, consider the multi-level hypercube architecture as shown in Figure 5. Computer models placed at the nodes of the hypercube (hc-NODES) are themselves clusters, i.e., kernel models, either broadcast or cellular. Each member of the broadcast or cellular model at a node is a processing element that consists of an active buffer and a processor.

When the hypercube model receives an incoming problem from outside, it sends the problem to all nodes (if its external coupling is *broadcast*) or the origin node only (if its external coupling is *origin-only*). If it receives a solution of the incoming problem from its nodes, the hypercube model sends the solution to the outside. When a node of the hypercube receives a problem, it send it to all processing elements in the node (if the node has a broadcast architecture) or to the specified processing element(s) (if the node has a cellular architecture).

The processor in the processing element is responsible for actual problem solving. The active buffer in the processing element accepts incoming problems for solution or retransmission. The active buffer accepts the incoming problem under certain conditions and sends it to the cascaded processor if the processor is free. If the conditions for acceptance are not met, the active buffer transfers the incoming problem to the output port *unsolved*, which takes a certain amount of time. The unsolved problem is retransmitted to other processing elements (the destination is based on the architecture of the node) in the same node where the active buffer is.

If the active buffer receives an incoming problem while transmitting a problem to the *unsolved* port, it allows itself to be interrupted and transfers the problem to the output port *interrupted*. The unsolved problem transmitted through the *interrupted* port is retransmitted to the closest neighborhood node(s) in the hypercube. However, if the active buffer receives an incoming problem while sending an unsolved problem to the port *interrupted*, the problem is lost.

The problem in designing the above parallel processing system, to be investigated with simulation, is how to take advantage of the speed in searching for free processors afforded by the hypercube with nodes broadcasting coupled, while minimizing the overhead of problems solved more than once as well as not at all.

To experiment with a model of the parallel processing system, an appropriate experimental frame needs to be specified and coupled to the model. The experimental frame module E is a digraph model containing a generator G for sending problems to the hypercube model, an acceptor A that makes decisions concerning run termination, and a transducer T, which keeps the performance statistics such as problems solution time, throughput, percentage of multiply solved problems, and percentage of lost problems.

The overall simulation model is a digraph-model consisting of the experimental frame and the hypercube-model. We specify the family of architectures of interest using the system entity structure (Zeigler, 1984; Kim, 1988) as shown in Figure 4 (a). Only a few of the alternatives are shown for illustration. By pruning this structure we select one of the alternative architectures (e.g., Figure 4 (b)). The operation *transform* compiles the structure into a simulation model employing atomic-models in the model base.

Initialization of the model then follows. It includes creating members of both hypercube and its nodes and specifying the coupling schemes of both hypercube-and broadcast-model components. Figures 5 and Figure 6 show the overall simulation model after such initialization.

As objects, DEVS-Scheme models can be executed on concurrent object-based processors; however, using the abstract simulator concepts of the DEVS formalism, more advantageous hierarchical multiprocessor systems can be designed and hierarchical models mapped to them so that maximum speed up is obtained. DEVS-Scheme provides timing measurements from the underlying "virtual multiprocessor" simulator to support analysis for optimal multiprocessor mappings (Zeigler and Zhang, in press).

7 Hierarchical Structure Modification and Model Simplification

Two hierarchical structure modification operations, *flattening* and *deepening* support structure reorganizations. One application of such restructuring is to create equivalent models with improved execution characteristics. In deepening a model, the level of the model will increase by one in the hierarchical model structure. This comes about as components of a coupled model are grouped into a new component subordinate to the original. At the same time, the couplings adjusted automatically so that the overall behavior is preserved. Flattening a coupled model within a hierarchical structure involves removing it and adjusting the couplings between its parent and children to preserve overall behavior. By repeatedly applying the flattening operation, a hierarchical model may be completely flattened, i.e., reduced to an equivalent single level coupled model.

A suite of tools for supporting simplification of discrete event models was implemented based on the simplification theory developed for DEVS formalism (Zeigler, 1976, 1984a). The criterion for valid simplification is the homomorphism of DEVS models. In the theory, a DEVS multicomponent

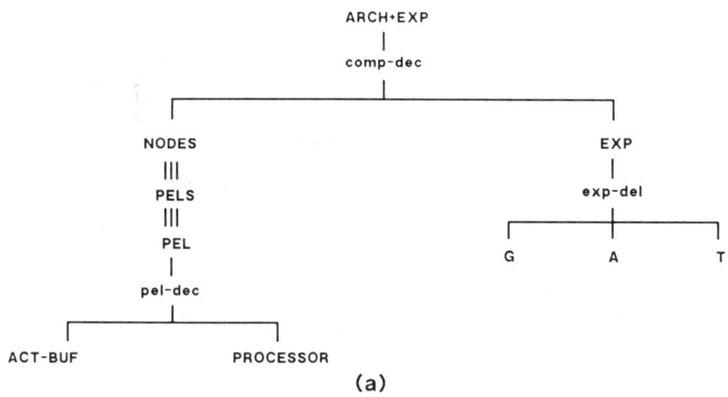

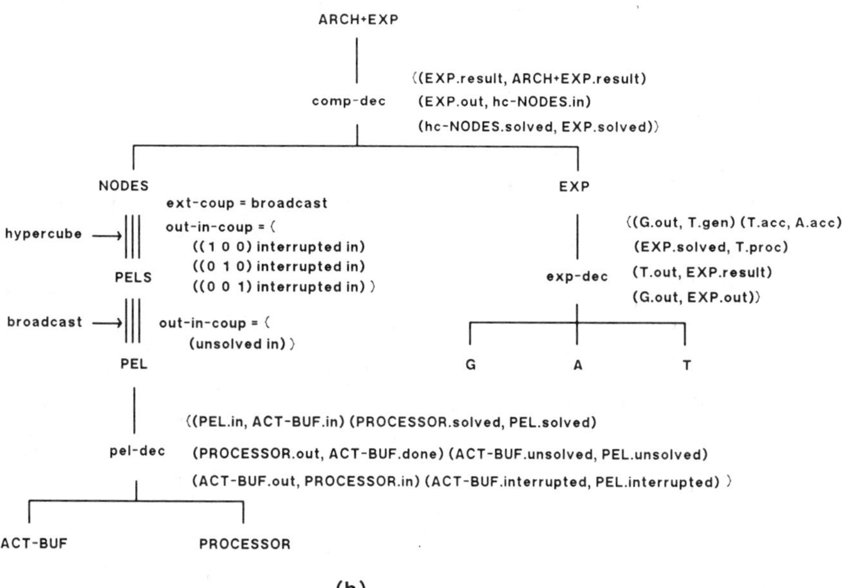

FIGURE 4. Entity structure for hypercube computer architecture. (a) entity structure; (b) pruned entity structure.

model (coupled model) is converted to an equivalent DEVS model (atomic model) for which a homomorphic relationship to a lumped model is sought. In the current approach, rather than attempt to establish such a homomorphism formally, the lumped model is generated from data gathered from simulation runs. Data is gathered in the form of output and transition lists which represent the behavior of the equivalent DEVS model as observed

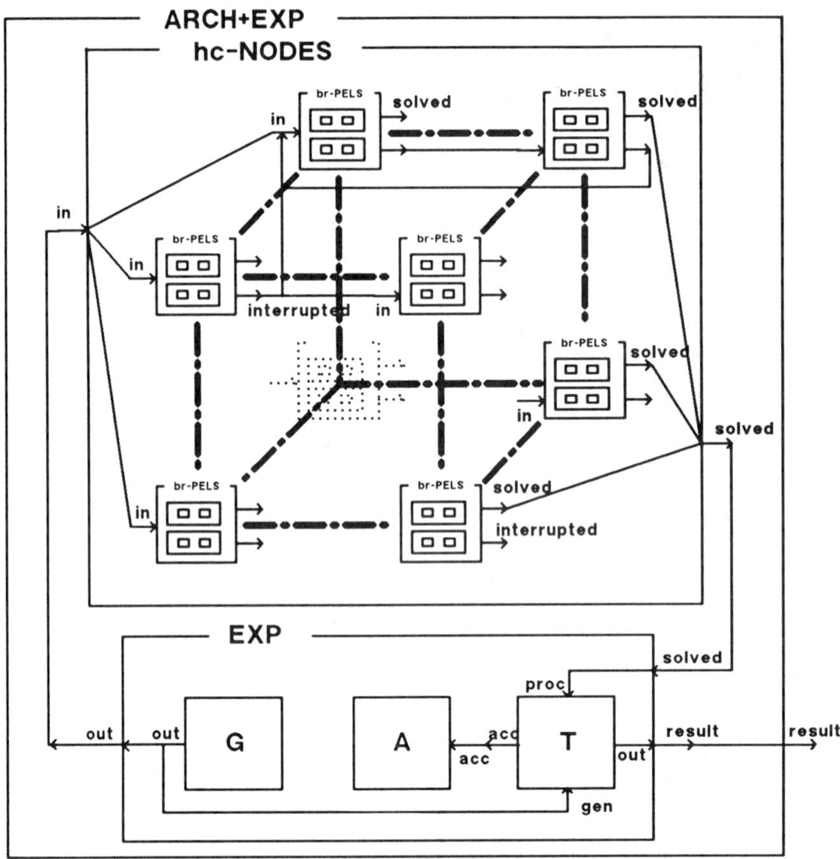

FIGURE 5. Simulation model synthesized by Fig. 4 (b).

through input, state, and output reduction maps provided by the user. The lumped model is generated in such a way that if a homomorphism exists based on the reduction maps the resulting model will be deterministic. Departures from determinism show up in randomly generated transitions and outputs. The goal in providing such simplification is less to provide completely valid (i.e. deterministic) models than to provide faster running lumped models that can replace components of a hierarchical model so that the remainder of the model can be more efficiently run and tested.

8 Further Developments

A number of extensions and enhancements to DEVS-Scheme are in various stages of completion. We shall mention them briefly.

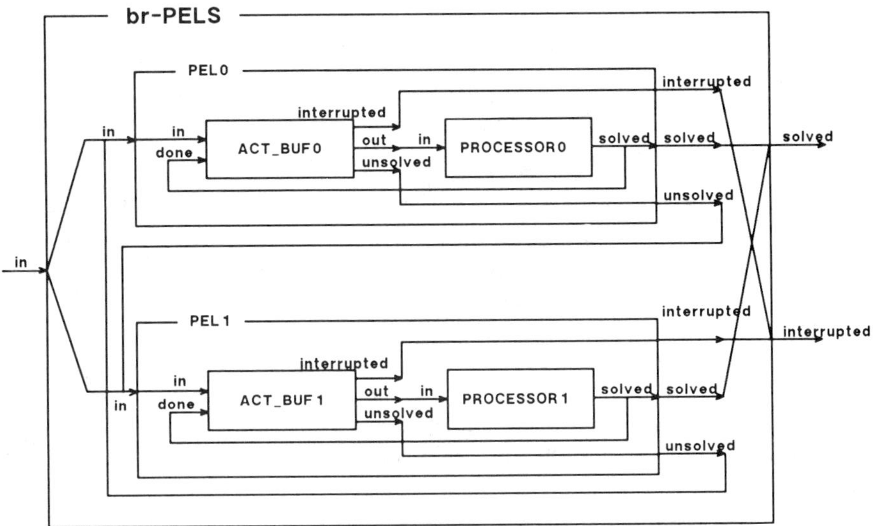

FIGURE 6. Node architecture for hypercube of Fig. 5 containing two processor elements PELs.

- Rule-based pruning and use of DEVS-Scheme in knowledge-based system design. This involve augmenting the basic system entity structure knowledge representation scheme with additional capabilities to support the system design process. See the chapter by Rozenblit in this book.
- Incorporating rule-based system as model components. The class hierarchy in DEVS-Scheme has been extended so that atomic models can be specified in a rule-based formalism. Also the symbol processing power of Scheme is being exploited by providing convenient interfaces from DEVS-Scheme to CESM, an expert system shell written in Scheme (Chi, Kim, and Zeigler 1989). The extensions facilitate embedding models of intelligent agents in simulation environment (Zeigler, Cellier, and Rozenblit, 1988; Zeigler, 1989).
- Employing the "virtual multiprocessor" simulation strategy underlying DEVS-Scheme to study various means to perform distributed simulation (Zhang and Zeigler, 1988). Porting DEVS-Scheme to a high performance multiprocessor is the ultimate goal.
- Extending DEVS-Scheme to support multi-formalism modelling. As interface is being developed to enable system entity structure management of continuous system model bases (Kim, Zhang, and Zeigler, 1988). This extension still leaves the simulation of discrete event models and continuous system models as isolated elements. Work is therefore proceeding

on designing a successor of DEVS-Scheme which will support greater freedom in combing components expressed in different formalisms.

9 Conclusions

Implementation of the DEVS formalism in DEVS-Scheme has shown possibilities for methodology-based applications of AI in modelling and simulation. The symbol manipulation and object-oriented facilities of Scheme make it relatively easy to code complex structures and operations on them. Of course, the price paid for such flexibility is execution speed.

An advantage of the developed environment over other simulation systems is that it constructs a simulation model from the structure knowledge represented by the appropriate entity structure by applying the synthesis procedure rather than employing the means provided by modelling formalism. Since the structure and behavior of the simulation model are explicitly specified, the modeller can freely change the structure of the simulation model with its behavior unchanged or vice-versa. Such explicit specification of the structure and behavior of a system allows the system designer to evaluate performance of the system with different combinations of the structure and/or behavior. The environment also serves as a medium for developing distributed simulation architectures for hierarchical, modular discrete-event models.

The model construction, manipulation, and analysis features described above have all been implemented and tested in a variety of simulation domains. Sevinc and Zeigler (1988) describe one such study for Local Area Networks. Other applications include design of hierarchically constructed rule-processing computer architectures (supported by NSF), intelligent multi-robot organizations for laboratory management in space (supported by NASA), and ecologically based life-support systems (supported by the Biosphere II project).

References

Abelson, H., G.J. Sussman and J. Sussman (1985), *Structure and Interpretation of Computer Programs*, MIT Press.

Chi, Sung Do, Tag Gon Kim, and B.P. Zeigler (1989), "Using the CESM Shell to Classify Wafer Defects from Visual Data," in *Proc. of SPIE'89*, Philadelphia, PA.

Concepcion, A.I. and B.P. Zeigler (1988), "DEVS Formalism: A Framework for Hierarchical Model Development," *IEEE Trans. Soft. Engr.*, vol. SE-14, no. 2, pp. 228–241, Feb. 1988..

Davis, P.K. (1986), "Applying Artificial Intelligence Techniques to Strategic-level Gaming and Simulation," In: *Modelling and Simulation Methodology in the Artificial Intelligence Era*, Elzas, M.S., Oren, T.I., Zeigler, B.P. (Eds), North Holland, Amsterdam.

Higa, K.H. (1988), "End-user Logical Database Design: The Structure Entity Model Approach", Doctoral Dissertation, MIS Dept., University of Arizona.

Higa, K.H. and O.R. Liu Sheng (1989), "An Object-Oriented Methodology for Database/Knowledgebase Coupling: An Implementation of the Structured Entity Model in Nexpert System", Working Paper, MIS Dept., University of Arizona.

Kim, Tag Gon (1988), "A Knowledge-Based Environment for Hierarchical Modelling and Simulation," Doctoral Dissertation, University of Arizona, Tucson.

Kim, Tag Gon, Guoqing Zhang, B.P. Zeigler (1988), "Entity Structure Management of Continuous Simulation Models," in *Proc. Summer Sim. Conf.*, Seattle.

Kim, Tag Gon (1989), "ESP-Scheme: A Realization of System Entity Structure in a LISP Environment," in *Proc. AI and Simulation, 89 Eastern Multiconf*, Tampa, FL.

O'Keefe R. (1986), "Simulation and Expert Systems—A Taxonomy and Some Examples," *Simulation*, 46:1, 10–16.

Reddy, Y.V., Fox, M.S., Husain, N. and McRoberts, M. (1986), "The Knowledge-Based Simulation System," *IEEE Software*, March, 26–37.

Robertson, P. (1986), "A Rule Based Expert Simulation Environment," In: *Intelligent Simulation Environments*, (Eds: Luker, P.A. and Adelsberger, H.H.) *Simulation Series*, vol. 17, SCS, San Diego, CA.

Sevinc, S. and B.P. Zeigler (1988), "Entity Structure Based Methodology: A LAN Protocol Example," *IEEE Trans. Soft. Engr.*, vol. 14, No. 3, March, pp. 375–383

Zadeh, L.A. and C.A. Desoer (1963), *Linear System Theory, The State Space Approach*, McGraw Hill, NY.

Zeigler, B.P. (1976), *Theory of Modelling and Simulation*, Wiley, N.Y. (Reissued by Krieger Pub. Co., Malabar, FL. 1985).

Zeigler, B.P. (1984a), *Multifaceted Modelling and Discrete Event Simulation*, Academic Press, London and Orlando, FL.

Zeigler, B.P. (1984b), "System-Theoretic Representation of Simulation Models," *IIE Trans.*, March, pp. 19–34.

Zeigler, B.P. (1986), "DEVS-Scheme: A Lisp-Based Environment for Hierarchical, Modular Discrete Event Models," Tech. Report AIS-2, Dept. of Electrical and Computer Engineering, University of Arizona, Tucson, AZ.

Zeigler, B.P. (1987a), "Knowledge Representation from Minsky to Newton and Beyond," *Applied Artificial Intelligence*, vol. 1 87–107, Hemisphere Pub. Co.

Zeigler, B.P. (1987b), "Hierarchical, Modular Discrete Event Modelling in Object Oriented Environment," *Simulation* J. Nov.

Zeigler, B.P. and G. Zhang, "Mapping Hierarchical Discrete Event Models to Multiprocessor Systems: Algorithm, Analysis, and Simulation," *J. Parallel and Distributed Computers*, (in press).

CHAPTER 3

Methods for Qualitative Modeling in Simulation

Paul A. Fishwick

Abstract

Qualitative methodology in simulation requires high level modeling constructs such as causal graphs, bond graphs, or natural language. Even though there exists a virtual continuum between qualitative and quantitative simulation methods, it is important to discuss qualitative methods since they relate to notions of process abstraction and discovery during model evolution. We will refer to the evolutionary process as *simulation model engineering*. We define the basic notions of qualitative simulation, give specific examples for a pendulum system, and finally discuss various issues and directions for future work. [Keywords: simulation model engineering, qualitative simulation, process abstraction, lumped modeling.]

1 Introduction

In a recent paper [12] we defined qualitative simulation as pertaining to simulation modeling and analysis that stresses particular high level features. Our definition of qualitative simulation differs from those present within artificial intelligence literature in that we are concerned with qualitative approaches that may or may not have a direct relationship to cognitive modeling [14]. The salient features of our definition of qualitative simulation include the capability of creating lumped models through model simplification, relaxation of system variables, and a tendency toward topological, graph-based methods for high level modeling of systems. A problem exists in that many researchers in diverse areas have attacked problems in qualitative simulation but few have strived towards a general definition

---

This research is sponsored in part by a grant from the National Science Foundation (Grant # IRI-8909152). This article originally appeared in *SIMULATION*, 52(30):95-101, March 1989.

of precisely what makes a simulation qualitative. This chapter, then, was motivated by the need to provide a general description of qualitative simulation modeling and analysis. But first, two questions need answering: 1) What exactly is qualitative simulation?, and 2) Why is it important to study qualitative methods?

Qualitative simulation and quantitative simulation can be considered to be two endpoints of a continuum. Therefore we differentiate qualitative and quantitative system approaches not to demonstrate the uniqueness of qualitative methods but rather to demonstrate the importance of considering *process abstraction* [11,15,13] and *model evolution* [10] during model development. Qualitative methods highlight the qualities of system behavior such as its asymptotic stability or the qualities of the model structure such as its simplicity in form. Specifically, we have found it appropriate to apply the adjective "qualitative" to three distinct concepts in a simulation: *input*, *model*, and *output*. Thus, we find that there is no sharp dividing line between qualitative and quantitative simulation; we simply find an interesting set of modeling and analysis concepts that can be conveniently labelled under the umbrella of qualitative simulation. The answer to the second question previously posed provides a more important reason for studying qualitative concepts. Specifically, we believe that the primary thrust for studying qualitative simulation methods relates directly to simulation model abstraction and model evolution. The evolution of simulation models leads us to study the engineering of simulation models, or *simulation model engineering*. The goals of simulation model engineering are similar to the goals of software engineering; scientists and engineers need more information on how to iteratively structure their models over time. How can we create abstract models of complex systems that attempt to preserve behavior and structure? When someone starts with observables of a system, exactly what evolutionary procedure is necessary to accurately identify the system? In this sense, we view the evolution of models from coarse grain, qualitative models to fine grain quantitative models to be equivalent to the general systems problem termed "system identification" [23]. Systems are rarely defined completely and unambiguously at first trial. Instead, many years may pass as the model becomes more and more refined.

What we are really interested in when discussing qualitative simulation is how models evolve over time and how lumped models can be created to enhance our understanding of the system structure and behavior. We may be unsure of an input $u(t)$ to a system so we might abstract the behavior of $u(t)$ by lumping, using intervals, or using fuzzy mappings of linguistic features such as "growing," "increasing," or "oscillating" to a real vector space. We may be unsure of the model that we should create to validate system behavior so we might start with a causal graph instead of a differential equation. Also, we might not want to pour through simulation output in numerical form so we opt to characterize the output using qualities. We might also be interested in the mapping between levels of abstraction in models. This last area and its relation to model evolution is discussed in more detail in [10]. Thus, we do not state that "qualitative simulation" is a completely novel concept. What we do say, on the other hand, is that the study of "qualitative methods" within the domain of simulation can help us to better understand the evolutionary timeline of the model. This, in turn, will allow researchers to 1) specify incomplete or fuzzy simulation models and view qualitative reports, and 2) use new simulation tools that contain capabilities of specifying models at different levels of abstraction. We will now further discuss the nature of qualitative methods in simulation input, modeling and output.

2 The Importance of Metaphors and Analogies

The roles of metaphors and analogies are central to the concept of qualitative simulation. When we consider, for instance, the qualitative method of system dynamics, we see the metaphor of fluid flow as applied to problems whose solution is predicated on rates and levels. Most mathematical models contain relations between state variables and their derivatives. State variables can be viewed as levels and derivatives as rates. Furthermore, one can visualize the dynamic interaction between rates and levels as relating to the process of fluid flowing into levels (which serve to "store energy") by way of valves which either attenuate or increase the flow rate. The visualization process allows us to better understand the model and its simulation. The problem of math modeling is transformed into a metaphorical equivalent, simulation is performed in this new domain and finally an inverse transform maps the result back into the original domain. Melzak [26] provides a good discussion on the transformation process; an elementary "bypass" is defined by STS^{-1} where S and S^{-1} represent the transform and inverse transform respectively and T represents the operation occurring in the middle—for our interests, this operation is simulation.

Some qualitative methods are quite explicit about the incorporation of analogies and metaphors in their frameworks: bond graphs are a prime example of this type of method. In bond graph modeling, there are explicit relationships between the concepts within different "regimes" such as the generic regime, mechanics and electronics [20]. The generic concept of momentum, for instance, is recognized as $\rho = \int edt$ (ρ = momentum and e = effort), while momentum is similar to angular momentum in rotational mechanics and to flux linkage in electronics. The analyst who works with bond graphs learns a new language and begins to think in the key generic terms of effort and flow including integrals and derivatives thereof. This "new way of thinking" creates a methodology for modeling that is easier than thinking directly in terms of mathematical expressions. One might criticize these sample qualitative methods as simply representational conveniences for the actual expressions; however, we point out that these methods are more than just simple conveniences—they promote new ways of viewing, manipulating and simulating existing expressions. In computer science, for instance, we have a plethora of high level languages, each suited to a category of problem types even though the end result (in the translation sequence) is simply machine code for the processor(s). The availability of such translational mechanisms serves to allow the programmer to "think the language." We do agree completely; however, that the representational aspect must be clear—that is, the mapping from qualitative model to mathematical model must be unambiguous.

3 Qualitative Methodology

3.1 Input and Output Methods

We first note that qualitative simulation can imply quality in two slightly different ways. One definition suggests that we define qualitative simulation as dealing with "qualities" of inputs, models and outputs. A quality in this sense would be a descriptive aspect such as "oscillating" or "quasi-linear." These words suggest mental pictures of a certain class of behavior without being so specific that they unambiguously define a unique behavior. The other definition of qualitative is something that is "not quantitative." In this sense, model structures that are topological in nature (causal graphs, pulse processes) are qualitative modeling methods although they are not necessarily descriptive—they simply stress non-quantitative system features. We will therefore identify two different types of qualitative methodology: 1) *quality-based* and 2) *abstraction-based*. In many instances, qualitative simulation of a system will not distinguish these types; however, it is possible to abstract a model, say, purely for computational reasons.

The adaption of qualitative methodology to simulation can be roughly divided into three sub-areas which reflect simulation phases: *input*, *output*, and *modeling*. We will discuss input and output first since qualitative methods are similar in both of these areas; the use of one qualitative method for input can be used inversely for output. For instance, specifying a forcing function $u(t)$ in terms of linguistic variables mapped to maxima and minima would necessitate a mapping from $\{peak, trough\} \rightarrow u(t)$. An output function $y(t)$ can simply use an "inverse" function $y(t) \rightarrow \{peak, trough\}$. Qualitative methods in modeling will be discussed the following section. Note that the choice of a modeling method might suggest qualitative methods for use in input and output. For instance, with a model based on a causal graph structure, the output would tend to be high level. In this section, we will use the standard model denoting a first order system:

$$\dot{\mathbf{x}}(t) = \mathbf{A}\mathbf{x}(t) + \mathbf{B}\mathbf{u}(t) \qquad (1)$$
$$\mathbf{y}(t) = \mathbf{C}\mathbf{x}(t) + \mathbf{D}\mathbf{u}(t)$$

There are two items that can be addressed from a qualitative perspective in eqn. 1: the parameters located in matrices A, B, C, or D and the input function (or forcing function) $u(t)$. Other variables are state variables and will be used by the model structure during simulation. Performing qualitative simulation by abstracting parameters can be viewed as a form of parameter estimation for which satisfactory methods have been defined [22]. If we choose to create a qualitative version of the input $u(t)$ we can do so in general by functional approximation or randomizing (or "shaking") the input [7,8]. We recall the distinction between quality and abstraction based qualitative simulation; many trajectories will reflect a changing quantity for u without any corresponding change in quality. This distinction is important and serves to explain why analysts tend to lump quantity variation only when they perceive quality distinctions. Let us examine the input $u(t)$. Normally this function will be defined as follows: $u : T \rightarrow U$ where $T = \mathcal{R}_0^+$ (time) and $U = \mathcal{R}$ (input variable range). Qualitative approximation can take many forms. We note, for instance, that a fuzzy $u(t)$ definition would be defined as: $u : T \rightarrow F$ where $F = \{f_1, \ldots, f_k\}$ (the set of fuzzy variables) and $\forall\alpha[f_\alpha : U \rightarrow [0,1]]$. A sample F might be defined as $F = \{small, large\}$ where *small* and *large* are fuzzy restrictions of the linguistic variable "magnitude." Another useful representation is an interval defined as: $u : T \rightarrow I$ where I is a set of intervals such as $I = \{[0.0, 3.0), [3.0, 6.0), [6.0, 10.0]\}$. Note also that calculation with intervals in interval algebra can be seen as a special case of fuzzy sets where f is a uniform distribution defined as $f(x) = c$ where $x \in U$ and c is a constant.

As can be seen, a qualitative definition of u is often linguistic in nature. One must define either mathematical methods that map linguistic variables (qualities) directly to quantitative domains or an algebra that can manipulate the qualitatively specified variables directly (QSIM [24] is an example of the latter approach where an algebra is defined containing relations such as M^+ for a relationship involving monotonically increasing variables). As far as naming specific qualitative terms, there are many that can be used. We will list only a subset of the infinite number of possibilities:

- *INPUT*—"falling, decreasing, oscillating, converging, linear, sinusoidal, pulsing." Note also that adjectives may modify any of these qualities to provide for a richer set: "strictly, quasi, semi, almost." Input segments are often characterized as "semi linear" or "strictly decreasing."
- *OUTPUT*—"steady-state, sensitivity, controllability, sensitivity, observability." The last 4 words describe the response characteristics of a system, and are often defined as qualitative attributes within systems engineering.

3.2 Modeling Methods

Perhaps the most abstract qualitative method would be using a natural language such as English to model a system. In the following section, we give an example of such an approach. For now, we say that it is possible to develop methods that translate qualitative statements such as "The car is rolling along at 55 mph" into equations that can be subsequently used as a basis for simulation models. Austin and Khoshnevis [1,2] have developed a system using DYNAMO and Beck and Fishwick [3] are studying the automatic translation of a paragraph on biological systems control present within nanoplankton respiration [27] into representative equations. We believe that the problem of translating from natural language to dynamic equations is important considering the amount of available text that serves effectively as a knowledge repository for such translators.

A slightly more structured qualitative modeling method can be loosely defined in terms of a "causal graph." In a causal graph the analyst creates a simulation by first specifying the variables of interest and then specifying the graph arcs and any weights. With respect to dynamic systems, an arc often represents some ΔT which equals the length of time for the cause/effect to take place. Causal graphs can be translated into a system of linear equations which may be either algebraic [6] or differential [29]. Examples of causal models are found in pulse processes [31], loop modeling [29] and other causal based approaches [19,5].

The term "system dynamics" is a general term which could ostensibly be attached to any simulation methodology; however, it is usually associated with Forrester's work in urban and world dynamics [16,17]. We will refer to the familiar implementation of system dynamics, called DYNAMO [32] to avoid confusion with other dynamical methods. DYNAMO is as much a discipline as a programming language since the analyst is encouraged in a step-by-step manner to create a causal graph, assign feedback designators and then finally to write down the DYNAMO code. DYNAMO graphs consist chiefly of rate icons and level icons. In this sense, DYNAMO uses the metaphor of fluidics to permit a "qualitative view" of the model; entities pass through valves an into the capacitive areas called levels. From the levels, the entity flow may pass through more valves and levels. Valves are analogs for time derivatives while levels represent state variables. Compartmental modeling is similar to the system dynamics approach in that one creates a model by visualizing flows and compartments (i.e., levels).

We discuss two more qualitative modeling methods that are of interest. Cellular modeling [9] can be viewed as a qualitative, topological method of modeling—the dynamics of a system which might be normally be modeled with partial differential equations can also be modeled with cellular automata (sometimes based on heuristics [18] instead of mathematical rules). The other method is bond graph modeling [33,34]. We view a bond graph as an important method of qualitative model specifically since the philosophy behind bond graph modeling is to present a generic modeling method that can be applied to a wide variety of domains while using the same basic universal concepts such as effort, flow, inertia and capacitance. Thus, in bond graph modeling the key notion of metaphor is explicitly defined with mappings to domains such as thermodynamics, rotational and translational mechanics, fluid dynamics and electronics. We should note that the analyst must consider only the qualitative nature of the system along with specific numeric parameters such as spring stiffnesses, etc. The study of bond graphs fosters a interdisciplinary attitude to general systems research [4] and serves as a concrete basis for qualitative system specification. Implementations such as ENPORT [21] and TUTSIM [30] greatly aid the user in developing bond graphs. ENPORT, for instance, contains a graphical user interface for editing bond graphs and viewing graphs using zoom and pan controls. Other energy based approaches have been proposed and are widely used [28].

4 Example: Pendulum Dynamics

The pendulum has been widely used to define systems because of its simplicity and the ability to add physical constraints such as extra springs or non-linear forcing functions in lieu of simple gravitational attraction. We have therefore decided to use the pendulum to demonstrate a few sample qualitative modeling methods. It is essential to note that we will be defining some fairly abstract models that reflect pendulum behavior even though, admittedly, the dynamics and physical structure of the pendulum are well known. We provide these qualitative definitions in general since there exist systems whose structure and behavior are difficult to define—such systems can be readily found in biology, medicine and economics. Therefore, we will use the pendulum as the specific system; however, we recognize the importance of viewing the qualitative modeling methods from a more general systems perspective.

4.1 Natural Language

How might we define the pendulum system at a high level of abstraction? Consider the following sentence:

`The plastic ball swings back and forth.`

This textual statement serves as a qualitative model that can be used as a basis for simulation. Our translation system first takes this sentence and parses it into the tree shown in figure 1. We see that the parser splits the sentence into workable fragments. Next the system takes the parsed fragments and considers the action verb (see fig. 2) and the object (see fig. 3) in the sentence. Figure 2 displays a section of a hierarchy which defines the semantics for action verbs—we see that "to swing" can mean either to "sweep" (i.e., to swing for half a period) or to "oscillate" (i.e., to swing many times). Furthermore, oscillation can be one of two types: SHM (simple harmonic motion) or FHM (forced harmonic motion). Since

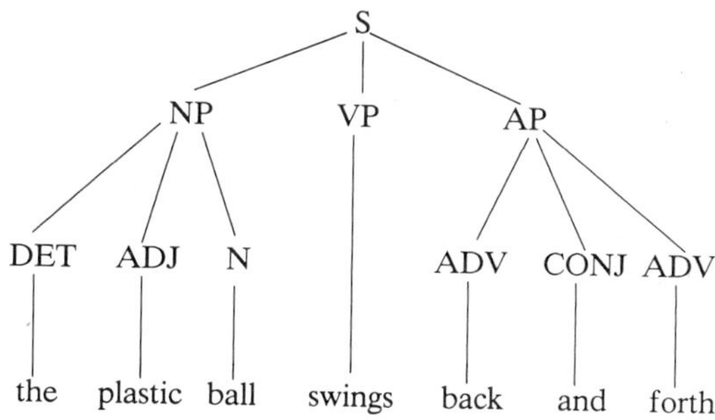

FIGURE 1. Parse tree.

the English sentence does not specify the type of motion we must create defaults within the tree (such as SHM whenever "swing" is used).

Figure 3 specifies objects and frames in an inheritance hierarchy. The frames next to objects have the following slot names: 'O' for object name, 'OT' for object type, 'A' for action, and finally 'M' for action modifier. Note that, for instance, a reference to "plastic ball" would imply rigid body motion and a reference to "rubber ball" would imply deformable body motion. Let's consider some other scenarios. If the sentence specified were "`The rubber ball moves`", the object hierarchy would fill in missing information for the object type (elastic) and action (bounces) allowing the post processor to instantiate an equation that the sentence is most likely to represent. If an action were not specified for a plastic ball then the action slot would inherit the value of "slides." Other slots could be created for items such as frictional damping or spring locations if any. Furthermore, the system can query the user for additional information if it is not available directly or via inheritance. For instance the user will have to be queried

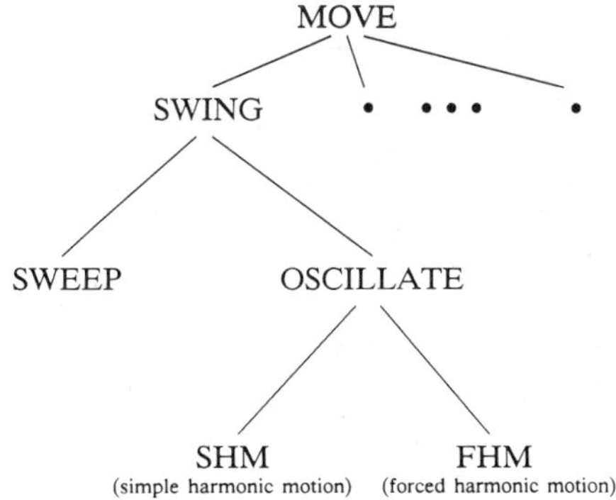

FIGURE 2. Action hierarchy.

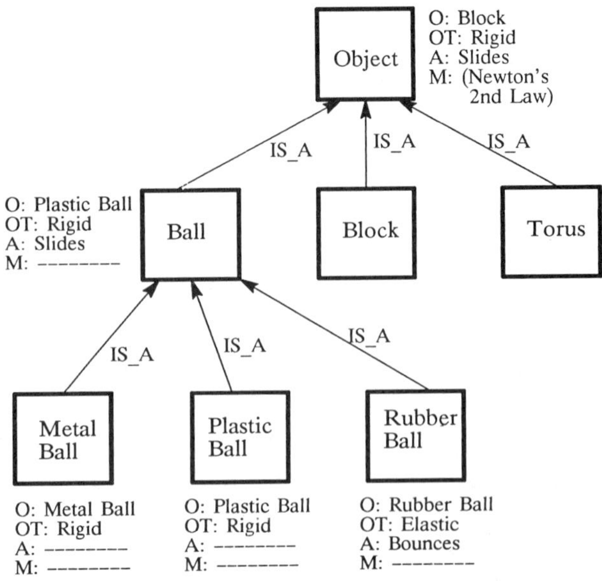

FIGURE 3. Object hierarchy.

for the damping coefficient and spring compliance if applicable. A gradual mapping from the original English sentence to the second order pendulum equation is facilitated by the action and object databases along with the extraction if additional information by querying the user. A post processor takes the information and provides a dynamic equation for simulation. With our example sentence, the system would provide an equation for a rigid plastic ball which swings according to Newton's second law of mechanics where gravity is assumed. The connection of "swinging" with the correct forces is found with the information encoded within the action hierarchy. Note the following example characteristics supplied by the object hierarchy:

- If the statement said "The thing moves" then the system would assume a sliding block (inheritance from the top node).
- If the statement said "The ball moves" then the system would assume a plastic ball with a sliding motion (inheritance from the "ball" node).
- If the statement said "The metal ball slides at constant velocity" then the system would assume a sliding metal ball (no inheritance).

Our work in natural language as a method within simulation and modeling is being investigated further [3]. One of our goals is to produce a system that cannot only receive a natural language model as input, but can also specify a natural language response. The algorithmic flow is therefore: NATURAL LANGUAGE INPUT+QUERY SYSTEM → MATH MODEL → SIMULATION → TIME SERIES → NATURAL LANGUAGE

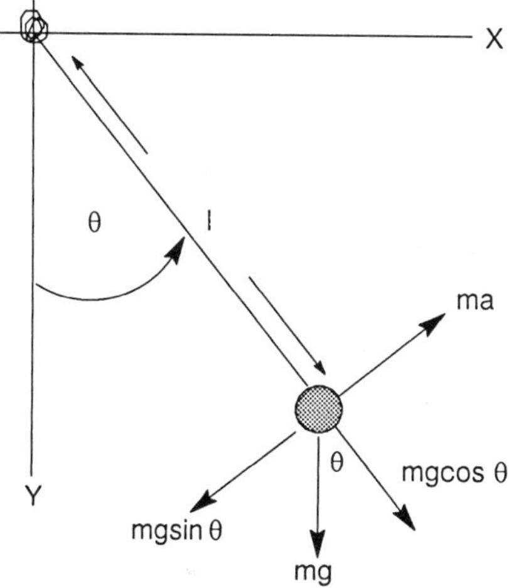

FIGURE 4. Pendulum schematic.

OUTPUT. The "QUERY SYSTEM" is used to ask the analyst about parameter values and other pertinent information that was left unspecified or ambiguously specified in the input text.

4.2 Bond Graph

Figures 4 through 6 display three graphs to represent the moving pendulum: the schematic, bond graph, and bond graph with assigned causalities.

The pendulum has a rigid body mass, a weightless arm and a spring that serves as a capacitor of potential energy. Some definitions are in order: the *SE* defines the effort source (i.e., gravity exerting a constant force on the ball mass), *TF* represents a transformation from a vertical force to an

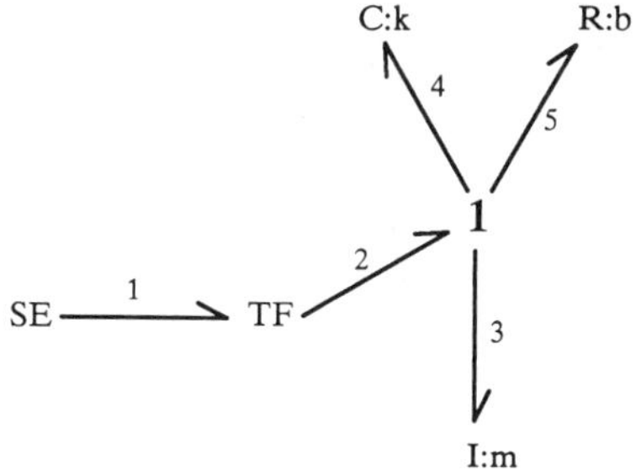

FIGURE 5. Bond graph of pendulum.

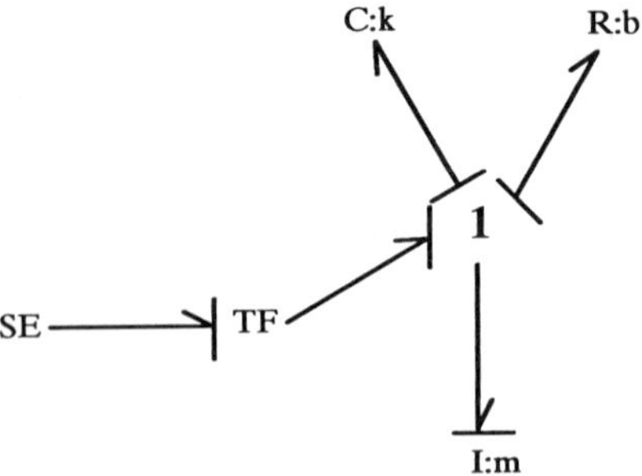

FIGURE 6. Bond graph with assigned causality.

angular force, C represents the spring capacitance with spring stiffness k, R represents spring pin resistance with damping parameter b. and finally I represents inertia for mass m. A bond graph is translatable into a block diagram which is translatable into a system of state equations. ENPORT defines state variables to be the variables associated with all of the I and C nodes since this is where power is stored. The state equations are:

$$\dot{p}_3 = -mg\sin(q_4) - q_4/C - bp_3/I \tag{2}$$
$$\dot{q}_4 = p_3/I$$

Let s be the arc length of the pendulum and θ be the angle that the pendulum forms with the vertical line. l is the pendulum length. p_3 is the momentum of the pendulum and q_4 is the angular displacement θ. Note that $s = l\theta$ (meaning that $\dot{s} = l\dot{\theta}$ and $\ddot{s} = l\ddot{\theta}$). This gives us the following relationships: $p_3 = ml\dot{\theta}$, $\dot{p}_3 = ml\ddot{\theta}$, $q_4 = \theta$, and $\dot{q}_4 = \dot{\theta}$. Finally this permits us to equate the bond graph formula of eqn. 2 to the more familiar second order equation derived from Newton's second law of mechanics:

$$ml\ddot{\theta} = -mg\sin(\theta) - k\theta - b\dot{\theta} \tag{3}$$

4.3 Finite State Machine

This example assumes a frictionless pendulum. Figure 7 shows a finite state machine with 4 states: q_1, ..., q_4 defined as follows:

1. $FSA = \langle I, O, Q, \delta, \lambda \rangle$
2. $O = \{(0, X_L, Y_L), (V_{\max}, X_C, Y_C), (0, X_R, Y_R)\}$
3. $Q = \{q_1, q_2, q_3, q_4\}$
4. $\delta : Q \to Q$
5. $\lambda : Q \to O$
6. for $i \in \{1, \ldots, 4\} : \delta(q_i) = q_{i \bmod 4+1}$

The output of each state reflects the pendulum ball speed and position (x, y). Maximum velocity, $V_{\max}$, depends on the initial height of the ball.

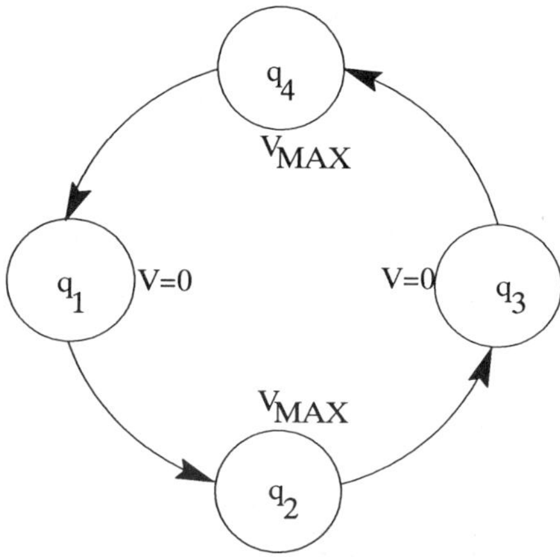

FIGURE 7. Pendulum finite state machine.

We need 4 states, instead of the apparent 3 states, since with only 3 states it would be possible for the pendulum to oscillate between neighboring states without making the full sweep. How would we use this qualitative model in a real simulation? With any continuous system, there are discrete approximations that capture only those events that can have an effect on the rest of the system. Suppose that an event is to be scheduled whenever a full sweep has occurred. It is clear that we do not have to use a continuous second order model in this instance because there are only two states that can initiate new events; all other "in between" states in the sweep continuum have no effect on the system. Thus, we can effectively model the frictionless pendulum system with the above discrete event model.

4.4 Cellular Automata

This example assumes a frictionless pendulum. The fourth and last qualitative model is based on a cellular approach. The motion of a pendulum can be approximated by the one dimensional automaton depicted in figure 8. Assuming that we determine the period T for a pendulum, then we form a one dimensional space of length k (in fig. 8(b), $k = 11$) The left-most and right-most cells contains a boundary cell that does not move (represented by a black box in fig. 8(b)). An inner cell (crossed box) represents the pendulum ball mass and moves according to the rules specified in fig. 8(c). We had to specify an auxiliary cell with an arrow so that the automaton would know the current direction of the ball. The amount of time taken for a single state change is $\Delta H = T/2(k-2)$. The cellular method models the pendulum motion from an aerial frame of reference. We should note that cellular methods are better utilized when modeling processes that contain inherent parallelism such as fluid flow around obstacles. In our pendulum

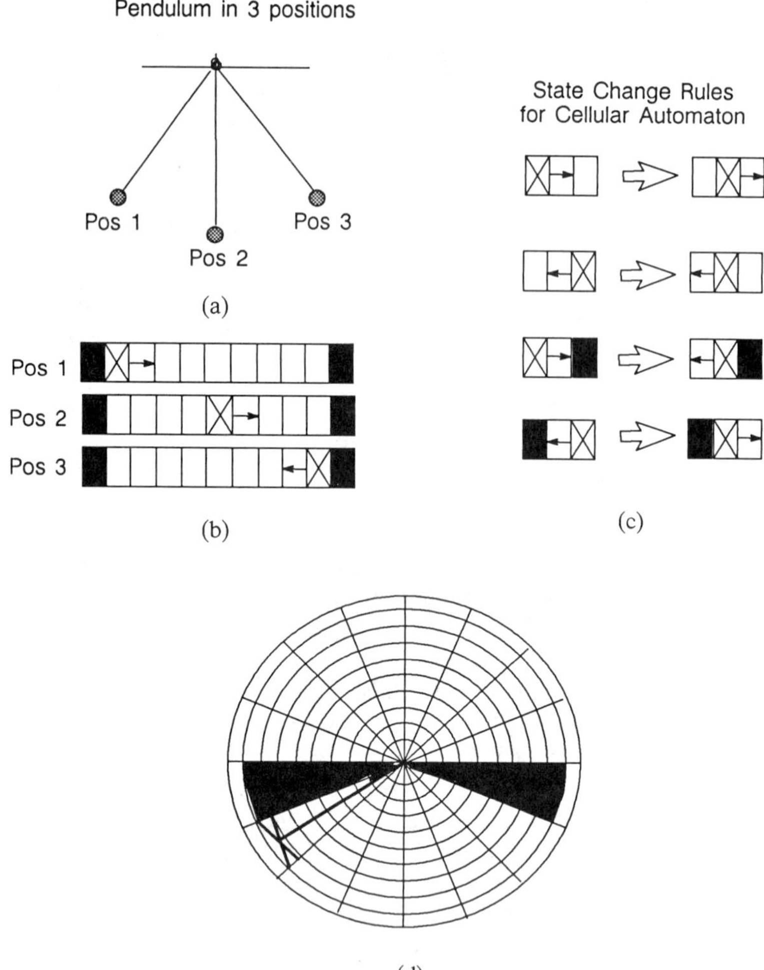

FIGURE 8. Pendulum cellular automaton.

example there is only one focus for motion—the cell referencing the position of the ball. The pendulum has a specific locus whereas a fluid flow example in two dimensions will involve less constrained motion of cells. Figure 8(d) depicts a slightly more elaborate version of the pendulum using a more typical side view ($k = 8$). The cellular rules for motion in fig. 8(d) involve the rules specified in fig. 8(c) and an additional four rules for the pendulum rod. Cells that are part of the composite pendulum rod contain a thick line. The additional four rules are the same as in fig. 8(c) with the thick line replacing the "X." We see that for motion involving a specific locus in a cellular automaton, we must create a cell space that conforms directly to the locus shape for any given view. Therefore an aerial view requires only a one dimensional automaton since the locus is a line, whereas the side view requires a circular cell space due to the arc locus from the side perspective.

5 Discussion: Key Issues and Concepts

When considering the use of qualitative methods in simulation there are a number of issues that should seriously be considered. Also there are concepts that underlie the definition of qualitative simulation. How broad is the area, and what are the limitations? Let us discuss some of these ideas.

Qualitative methodology has suggested that we can apply qualitative methods to *input*, *output*, and *modeling* for a simulation. These three methods are orthogonal—we might abstract the input, but use quantitative approaches for the output. Or, we may use a qualitative approach to modeling while keeping both input and output quantitative. Furthermore, the term "qualitative" can imply one of two characteristic types: *quality-based* or *abstraction-based* for input, output and models.

Canonical Forms are sought for most scientific applications; however, we do not see any evidence for a single canonical form for qualitative simulation. We have discussed qualitative methods in light of mathematical forms. These forms can take on a wide variety of expression—inequalities, graph structures, fuzzy sets, intervals, etc. We believe that it is important to consolidate qualitative features in many disciplines, not because we are searching for a single form, but rather because we seek to better understand the evolutionary process of simulation model discovery and creation.

Spurious qualities are qualities that are not appropriate to the system definition. The introduction of such qualities are relevant only when we are concerned with *quality-based* qualitative simulation as opposed to *abstraction-based* simulation. For instance, we might divide the forcing function $u(t)$ into a set of intervals where each interval cannot necessarily be associated with a distinct quality; if interval $[2, 10]$ does not correspond to a quality then it should not be defined. A parameter might be abstracted by associating it with one of $\{-, 0, +\}$ however if the parameter ρ has an absolute range of $0 \leq \rho < 50$ then we would be assigning spurious qualities that do not specifically relate to the application involving ρ. It might be more appropriate to classify the above numeric range in terms of the linguistic variable $amount \rightarrow \{low, medium, high\}$.

The *Instantiation vs. Constraint Propagation* issue is important when deciding on a qualitative technique. We define the instantiation approach to be one where inputs may be defined qualitatively but the input variables are instantiated prior to being placing in the model for simulation. Let us consider an example. If $u(t)$ is defined as "mostly increasing" then the instantiation approach would suggest instantiating $u(t)$ to a real function by sampling the set of trajectories identified by the quality "mostly increasing." We might, for instance, pick a linear function with a positive slope. With constraint propagation, on the other hand, we carry the qualitative constraints through the entire simulation process. This will often yield a set of possible behaviors which can be reduced by adding new information in the form, say, of new inequalities or heuristics. A classic method of set reduction is through optimization; an objective function is defined and then a unique behavior for the system is subsequently derived. If the set is left alone and given to the user as output [24,25] then the analyst may view several possible system behaviors. We will give a brief example of both approaches using the qualitative concept of interval algebra. For simplicity, this example will substitute the operation of addition for the more normal simulation operations of numerical integration. Consider the process of adding two intervals together $[2,5] + [1,9]$:

- *Instantiation*: We would first instantiate the two qualitative terms to $(2+5)/2 = 3.5$ and $(1+9)/2 = 5$ respectively and then "perform the simulation" which in this case is simple addition: $3.5 + 5 = 8.5$. We note that Monte Carlo analyses have similar approaches and goals.
- *Constraint Propagation*: Instead of instantiation, we propagate the "interval constraint" through the plus operation. Therefore, $[2,5] + [1,9] = [3,14]$. The simulation output of a highly underconstrained model will result in weak results; there must be sufficient constraints to insure meaningful results.

6 Conclusions

At this point in the chapter, we might raise our hands and state emphatically that the simulation community along with many other scientific disciplines have been doing qualitative simulation for some time. We fully support this conclusion but add that our recent research into the nature of qualitative methods in simulation is necessary for two reasons: 1) the qualitative methods in each science have not been explored to see where one might adopt a general systems perspective in characterizing and integrating the various techniques, and 2) the discussion of qualitative methods suggests the much larger research issue relating to model engineering and process abstraction. In recent work, we are investigating the concept of "simulation model engineering" which may be seen as being very similar to the area of software engineering within computer science. By studying qualitative methods and their natural progression to quantitative methods, we hope to shed some light on the model engineering problem.

In this chapter, we have described the unifying themes that bridge the gaps that exist between the qualitative methods used in different disciplines and furthermore, we have suggested methods that can be utilized in exploring the problem of model evolution. We hope that in the future we might see commercially available simulation languages that can:

- Allow for multiple abstraction levels to be constructed.
- Allow for several methods of traversing and reporting the levels.
- Allow the user to include nonhomogeneous model methods (differential equations mixed with causal graphs, say) in his simulation model.
- Allow for fuzzy and heuristic model input in addition to the usual quantitative input.
- Allow for the use of relaxation methods in constraint simulation modeling.

References

1. Wanda Austin and Behrokh Khoshnevis. Intelligent simulation environments for system modeling. In *Institute of Industrial Engineering Conference*, May 1988.
2. Wanda Austin and Behrokh Khoshnevis. A natural language interface for simulation of multistage production distribution systems. In *Second AI and Simulation Workshop at AAAI 87*, Seattle, WA, 1987. (article 3).
3. Howard Beck and Paul A. Fishwick. Incorporating natural language descriptions into modeling and simulation. (submitted to the Simulation Journal).
4. Ludwig von Bertalanffy. *General System Theory*. George Braziller, New York, 1968.
5. H. M. Blalock. *Causal Models in Panel and Experimental Designs*. Aldine Publishing Co., 1985.
6. H. M. Blalock. *Causal Models in the Social Sciences*. Aldine Publishing Co., 1971.
7. Francois E. Cellier. Qualitative simulation of technical systems using the general system problem solving framework. *International Journal of General Systems*, 13(4):333–344, 1987.
8. Francois E. Cellier and David W. Yandell. Saps-ii: a new implementation of the systems approach problem solver. *International Journal of General Systems*, 13(4):307–322, 1987.
9. Doyne Farmer, Tommaso Toffoli, and Stephen Wolfram, editors. *Cellular Automata: Proceedings of an Interdisciplinary Workshop*. North-Holland Amsterdam, 1983.
10. Paul A. Fishwick. Automating the transition from lumped models to base models. In *SCS Eastern Simulation Conference*, pages 57–63, Orlando, FL, April 1988.
11. Paul A. Fishwick. *Hierarchical Reasoning: Simulating Complex Processes over Multiple Levels of Abstraction*. Technical Report, University of Pennsylvania, 1986. Ph.D. Dissertation.
12. Paul A. Fishwick. Qualitative simulation: fundamental concepts and issues. In *AI and Simulation: The Diversity of Applications*, pages 25–31, The Society for Computer Simulation, February 1988. Part of the Society for Computer Simulation Multi-Conference (San Diego).

13. Paul A. Fishwick. The role of process abstraction in simulation. *IEEE Transactions on Systems, Man and Cybernetics*, 18(1):18–39, January/February 1988.
14. Paul A. Fishwick. A study of terminology and issues in qualitative simulation. *Simulation*, 50(11), November 1988. (to be published).
15. Paul A. Fishwick. A taxonomy for process abstraction in simulation modeling. In *IEEE International Conference on Systems, Man and Cybernetics*, pages 144–151, Alexandria, Virginia, October 1987.
16. J. W. Forrester. *Industrial Dynamics.* MIT Press, 1961.
17. J. W. Forrester. *World Dynamics.* Wright-Allen Press, 1971.
18. F. Gardin, B. Meltzer, and P. Stofella. The analogical representation of liquids in naive physics. In *Seventh European Conference on Artificial Intelligence*, 1986. (ECAI-86).
19. Clark Glymour, Richard Scheines, Peter Spirtes, and Kevin Kelly. *Discovering Causal Structure.* Academic Press, 1987.
20. P. Hezemans and L. van Geffen. *Justified use of Analogies in Systems Science*, pages 61–67. Elsevier North-Holland, 1985. Volume IV: IMACS Transactions on Scientific Computation-85.
21. Rosencode Associates Inc. Enport reference manual. 1987.
22. John A. Jacquez. *Compartmental Analysis in Biology and Medicine.* University of Michigan Press, 2nd edition, 1985.
23. George J. Klir. *Architecture of Systems Problem Solving.* Plenum Press, 1985.
24. Benjamin Kuipers. Qualitative simulation. *Artificial Intelligence*, 29(3):289–338, September 1986.
25. Benjamin Kuipers and Charles Chiu. Taming intractable branching in qualitative simulation. In *Tenth International Joint Conference in Artificial Intelligence*, pages 1079–1085, Milan, 1987.
26. Z. A. Melzak. *Bypasses: A Simple Approach to Complexity.* John Wiley, 1983.
27. John H. Milsum. *Biological Control Systems Analysis.* McGraw Hill, 1966.
28. Howard T. Odum. *Systems Ecology: An Introduction.* John Wiley and Sons, 1983.
29. Charles J. Puccia and Richard Levins. *Qualitative Modeling of Complex Systems.* Harvard University Press, 1985.
30. Walter E. Reynolds and Jinner Wolf. *TUTSIM Users Manual.* TUTSIM Products, Palo Alto, California, 1988.
31. Fred S. Roberts. *Discrete Mathematical Models.* Prentice Hall, 1976.
32. Nancy Roberts, David Andersen, Ralph Deal, Michael Garet, and William Shaffer. *Introduction to Computer Simulation: A Systems Dynamics Approach.* Addison-Wesley, 1983.
33. Ronald C. Rosenberg and Dean C. Karnopp. *Introduction to Physical System Dynamics.* McGraw Hill, 1983.
34. Jean Thoma. *Bond Graphs: Introduction and Application.* Pergamon, 1975.

CHAPTER 4

Dynamic Templates and Semantic Rules for Simulation Advisors and Certifiers

Tuncer I. Ören

Abstract

Discontinuity is conceived from a new point of view. The new causal paradigm leads to the concepts "model update" and "multimodel." Based on this new paradigm, several problem-oriented (as opposed to implementation oriented) modelling formalisms are specified as dynamic templates. The templates can be embedded in advanced modelling and simulation environments and can be automatically tailored according to the requirements of the problem. [Keywords: discontinuity, modelling paradigm, modelling formalism, model update, multimodel, dynamic templates, semantic knowledge bases].

1 Introduction

1.1 Aims

In this chapter, the aims are the following:

1. Provide a new *paradigm* (i.e., a new way) to conceive "discontinuity" in piece-wise continuous-change models. Based on this new paradigm, develop two concepts, called "*model update*" and "*multimodel.*" Show that these concepts are applicable not only to piece-wise continuous-change models, but also to discrete-change models, and memoryless models. (The concept are also applicable to other types of models such as discrete event models, process-oriented, and object oriented models). Point out that problem-oriented (as opposed to implementation oriented) modelling formalisms can be formulated based on these two basic concepts.
2. Provide "*templates*" to pictorially represent the new modelling formalisms for piece-wise continuous-change models, discrete-change models, and memoryless models. Show that these templates can be incorporated in a modelling environment to guide the user in the model

specification phase. Also show that these are dynamic templates, i.e., that they can be automatically tailored by a modelling environment according to the requirements of the problem.

3. Point out that knowledge based on the concepts "*model update*" and "*multimodel*" can be added to the knowledge base of a modelling environment to perform semantic checks on the model both at the guidance and certification modes. Provide some semantic rules based on these concepts. The semantic rules become the basis of the modelling formalism-based knowledge for the modelling environments.

1.2 Basic Terms

A *paradigm* is a way of conceiving reality. A detailed study of the concept is given by Masterman (1970). Shifts of paradigms are very important in the advancements of science. As Kuhn states it: "... the successive transition from one paradigm to another via revolution is the usual developmental pattern of mature science." (Kuhn 1970, p. 12). A shift of paradigm in simulation was proposed by Ören (1984a).

"A *formalism* specifies a class of objects under discussion in an unambiguous and general manner." (Zeigler 1984, p. 21). For example, a grammar specifies a class of programs. Similarly, a *modelling formalism* specifies a class of models in an unambiguous and general manner. In inductive approach, a modelling formalism is also the basis for abstracting a class of systems; i.e., a modelling formalism can be used to perceive and express some aspects of a class of systems.

The similarity of grammars and modelling formalisms is striking and worth elaborating on. Modelling formalisms are to models what grammars are to programs. A grammar specifies a programming language that can be used to express a class of programs. Given a grammar and a program, one can check whether or not the program is consistent with respect to the grammar. Another and more advanced use of a grammar is to have a programming environment which can assist a user in syntax directed programming according to the grammar. Similarly, a modelling formalism provides a basis for the specification of a modelling language that can be used to express a class of models. The modelling formalism can be used to check whether or not a model is consistent with respect to it to realize a computer-aided modelling and model processing environment.

There are several ways to represent a modelling formalism. For example, a finite state machine, say a Moore machine (Moore, 1964), can be represented by using a set theoretic representation, a tabular, or a graph representation. In this chapter, templates will be used for the representation of modelling formalisms that will be introduced.

"A *frame* is a sort of skeleton, somewhat like an application form with many blanks or slots to be filled. We'll call these blanks its *terminals*; we use them as connection points to which we can attach other kinds of information. For example, a frame that represents a 'chair' might have some terminals to represent a seat, a back, and legs, while a frame to represent a 'person' would have some terminals for a body and head and arms and legs. To represent a *particular* chair or person, we simply fill in the terminals of the corresponding frame with structures that represent, in more detail, particular features of the back, seat, and legs of that particular person or chair." (Minsky 1988, p. 245).

A *template* is a frame with several segments. Each segment is introduced by a keyword and contains an element or a list of elements of the model. Keywords are useful for uniform documentation of the model. They can guide a user in the specification of a model. Options in a model can easily be represented by tailoring a template automatically. This concept leads to the concept of *dynamic template* where some segments can be omitted or added automatically by the modelling environment.

The knowledge about the template elements constitutes part of the semantic knowledge of the simulation environment. (Ören and Sheng 1988).

A *modelling and simulation environment* is a computer-aided modelling and model processing system where model processing can be done for behavior generation by experiential techniques (i.e., simulation) or for other purposes such as model analysis, transformation, etc.

As an *advisor*, the simulation environment guides the user in the specification phase of a simulation study. In this mode, it provides assistance in the specifications of the model, the parameters (or parameter set), and the experimental conditions under which the (model, parameter set) pair is to be driven later by a behavior generator to generate model behavior.

To assure the integrity of the specifications of the simulation study, a simulation environment, at *certifier* mode, takes the specifications (which might have been altered using a text editor) and verifies it with respect to a knowledge base. The environment then certifies the acceptability of the specifications, if they conform to the facts and rules given in the knowledge base; otherwise, the advisor mode is entered automatically to assist the user to correct the specification errors.

1.3 Knowledge Bases

A *knowledge base* is a repository of knowledge in computer processable form. The knowledge used in the certification is also used in the guidance mode. It can consists of basically four types of knowledge:

1. Knowledge based on the *modelling and simulation methodology.*

2. Relevant *knowledge representation and processing knowledge.* A detailed taxonomy of knowledge processing knowledge, given in (Ören 1990) covers the following knowledge for:

   - knowledge *acquisition* including sensation, recognition, perception, decoding, filtering, and regulation of knowledge,
   - knowledge *dissemination* including encoding, dispatching, guidance, advising, explanation, and certification,
   - knowledge *generation* by experiential techniques (such as real word instrumentation, simulation) or by non-experiential techniques (such as computation, optimization, inferencing, reasoning, and other symbolic techniques),
   - generation of *endogenous knowledge* (such as anticipation of the future, generation of questions or hypotheses) and generation of generative knowledge (such as goal generation, model generation),
   - *organization* (such as sorting, scheduling, classification, categorization, merging),
   - *location* (searching, tracking, tracing),
   - *selection* (or decision),
   - *evaluation*,
   - *transformation* (re-formatting, re-scoping (such as generalization and abstraction), specialization, and tuning),
   - *goal-processing* and *goal-directed knowledge processing*, and
   - *adaptation* (including knowledge assimilation such as building passive knowledge bases and learning and mutation).

3. *Domain-specific knowledge* (i.e., knowledge in the application area), and
4. *Other scientific knowledge* such as basic physical laws, mathematical theorems, differentiation, integration rules, etc.

It is highly desirable to have all four types of knowledge embedded in a simulation environment to have a fully knowledgeable (or cognizant) simulation environment (Ören and Zeigler 1986). Along this line, knowledge based on the modelling and simulation methodology is being embedded in the knowledge base of the modelling and simulation environment Magest (Aytaç and Ören 1986, Ören and Tam 1988, Ören and Sheng 1988). A systematization of the knowledge bases needed in an advanced simulation environment is covered in Ören 1986).

2 A New Paradigm to Conceive Discontinuity

2.1 Piece-Wise Continuous-Change Models and Discontinuity

Systems modelled in terms of ordinary differential equations may have two types of discontinuities: discontinuity in the derivative of a state variable or in a state variable itself.

"A *discontinuous model* is, therefore, a model described by differential equations where at least one state variable and/or its derivative may assume discontinuous values." (Ören 1979, p. 38).

Discontinuity in the derivative of a state variable or *derivative discontinuity,* in short, is a sudden change of the value of the derivative of a state variable.

"Discontinuity in a state variable is a sudden change of the value of a state variable and corresponds to a re-initialization of a state variable. It can therefore be called *re-initialization discontinuity.* Since it corresponds to a sudden change of a state variable, it can also be called *jump discontinuity.*" (Ören 1987, p. 689).

Fig. 1 depicts these two types of discontinuities in piece-wise continuous-change models. At time t_1, there is a derivative discontinuity. At time t_2, a re-initialization discontinuity occurs without a derivative discontinuity. At t_3, both types of discontinuities occur.

In discontinuity problems, time of the discontinuity may or may not be known a priori. If the time of the discontinuity t_d is known a priori, an interrupt can be scheduled for the numerical integration algorithm. At time t_d of the discontinuity, necessary processing is done; i.e., an appropriate state variable, or parameter is re-initialized, or a derivative function which is used in the generation of the values of a state variable is replaced by another one. If the discontinuity is detected, the time of occurrence of the discontinuity is approximated. Integration is interrupted at this approximate discontinuity time, to perform the necessary processing.

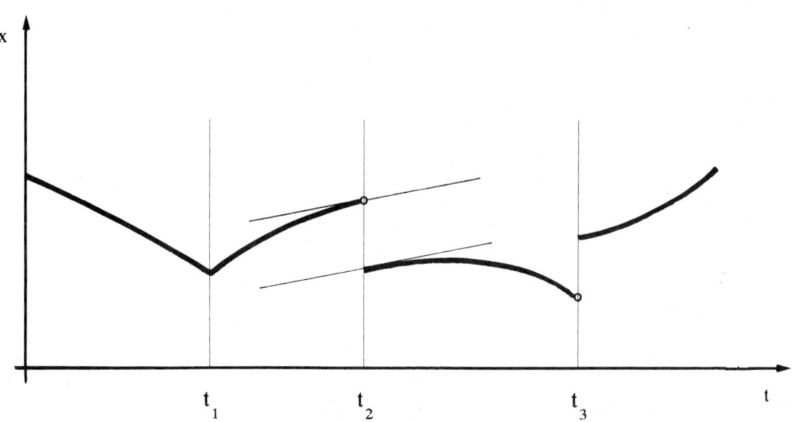

FIGURE 1. Types of discontinuities (at t_1 derivative discontinuity without re-initialization discontinuity, t_2 re-initialization discontinuity without derivative discontinuity, t_3 both derivative and re-initialization discontinuities).

Consider, for example, a model which is specified as:

$$\mathbf{x}' = \mathbf{f}_1(\mathbf{x}, \mathbf{u}, \mathbf{p}, t) \tag{1}$$

where,

$\mathbf{f}_1$ is the model represented by one or several derivative functions,
$\mathbf{x}$ is the state vector,
$\mathbf{u}$ is the input vector,
$\mathbf{p}$ is the parameter vector, and
t is the time.

At time t_d, one can change the values of one or several parameters. Then $\mathbf{x}'$, the value of the derivative of the state variable $\mathbf{x}$, will have a discontinuity at time t_d. The effect of this change is labelled "discontinuity." However, the cause of the "discontinuity" is an *update* of the value of at least one parameter. Traditionally, we are accustomed to concentrate on the *effect on* (or the change of) *the behavior* of a model. Now, we can try to concentrate on the *cause* which induces the change.

At time t_d, one can induce another change in the model. Instead of model $\mathbf{f}_1$, one can use another model $\mathbf{f}_2$, as follows:

$$\mathbf{x}' = \mathbf{f}_2(\mathbf{x}, \mathbf{u}, \mathbf{p}, t)$$

The effect of the replacement of the model $\mathbf{f}_1$ by the model $\mathbf{f}_2$ is a discontinuity in the value of the derivative of the state variable. In this case, the cause of the discontinuity is the replacement of a model by another model.

At time t_d, yet another type of discontinuity can be induced by a re-initialization of the state variable. Therefore, the cause of a re-initialization discontinuity (or jump discontinuity) is an update of the value of a state variable. We can now define model update and multimodel.

Model update is a change of the value of a parameter and/or a state variable.

A *multimodel* is a model which has several submodels. Only one of the submodels is active at any time to generate the model behavior. At the occurrence of a condition (which may depend on state vector or time or both), the currently active submodel would cease to be active and another one can become active. This fact can be viewed as a transition (or switching) from a submodel to another one and can be represented as a finite state machine where the states are the submodels of the model. Fig. 2 depicts a model with three submodels and the paths of the transitions between them. For example, while submodel 1 is active, at the occurrence of condition c_{12}, submodel 2 becomes active. Some of the submodels can be terminal. As will be seen later, a terminal submodel does not need a model selection segment for the specification of the selection of another submodel.

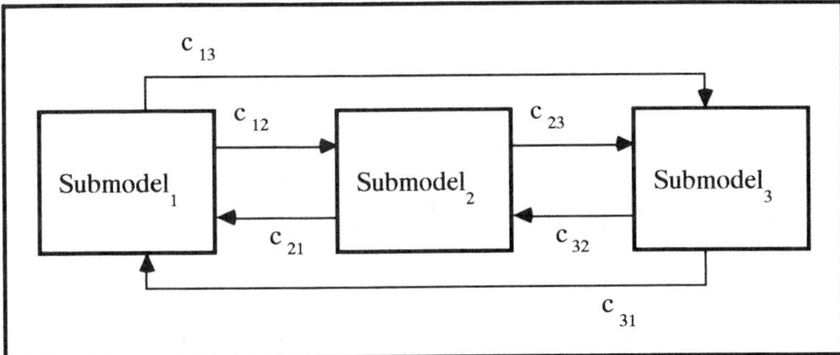

FIGURE 2. Transitions between submodels of a multimodel (c_{ij} represents the condition which triggers the transition from submodel$_i$ to submodel$_j$).

Model update and multimodel are, by definition, applicable to piece-wise continuous-change models. Therefore, two new modelling formalisms emerge for piece-wise continuous-change models. They are: continuous multimodel and continuous model with model update. To avoid cumbersome terminology, the last one can also be called updateable continuous model, or continuous model, in short, where model update can be considered as one of the options.

One would note that we shift the emphasis from the effect on the behavior of the model to the cause which induces it. These new modelling formalisms are applicable not only to piece-wise continuous-change models, but also to an important class of models including discrete-change models, memoryless models, discrete event models, process-oriented as well as object-oriented models. Fig. 3 shows the emerging modelling formalisms based on the concepts model update and multimodel.

2.2 Discrete-Change Models and the New Paradigm

The concepts, model update and multimodel are applicable to discrete-change models without any modification.

For example, let us consider, a discrete-change model where state transitions are given by the following relation:

$$\mathbf{x}_{n+1} = \mathbf{f}_1(\mathbf{x}_n, \mathbf{u}_n, \mathbf{p}_n, t_n) \tag{3}$$

where

$\mathbf{x}_n$ is the state vector at time t_n,
$\mathbf{f}_1$ is the state transition (or next state) function,
$\mathbf{u}_n$ is the input vector at time t_n, and
$\mathbf{p}_n$ is the parameter vector at time t_n.

Types of models	Modelling concepts	
	Model update	Multimodel
Piece-wise continuous[-change] model	[Updateable] continuous model	Continuous multimodel
Discrete[-change] model	[Updateable] discrete model	Discrete multimodel
Memoryless model	[Updateable] memoryless model	Memoryless multimodel
Discrete event model	[Updateable] event	Multievent
Process model	[Updateable] process	Multiprocess
Object-oriented model	[Updateable] object	Multiobject

FIGURE 3. New modelling formalisms based on "model update" and "multimodel" (attributes within [ ] are optional).

At a time t_d, model update and multimodel concepts are applicable to the discrete-change model. This means, that at t_d, one can change the value of some parameters or state variables. At the same time t_d, one can also replace the state transition function $\mathbf{f}_1$ by another function $\mathbf{f}_2$.

We notice that the concept "discontinuity" is not applicable to discrete-change models, if it is considered from the point of view of behavior induced to a model by some cause. However, the same cause (which if applied to a piece-wise continuous-change model would induce discontinuity), is directly applicable to discrete-change models. This observation is true for all the modelling formalisms discussed in this chapter.

2.3 Memoryless Models and the New Paradigm

A memoryless model is a model which does not have any state variable. It converts, instantaneously, an input into an output. Both input and output variables may be scalar or vector valued. A representation of a memoryless model is as follows:

$$\mathbf{q}_n = \mathbf{g}_1(\mathbf{u}_n, \mathbf{p}_n, t_n) \tag{5}$$

where

$\mathbf{q}_n$ is the output vector at time t_n,
$\mathbf{q}_1$ is the output function,
$\mathbf{u}_n$ is the input vector at time t_n,
$\mathbf{p}_n$ is the parameter vector at time t_n,
t_n is the current time.

In the case of a memoryless model, at a time t_d, the following changes can occur:

- One can change the values of some parameters,
- One can replace the output function $\mathbf{g}_1$ by another output function $\mathbf{g}_2$. This is replacement of a submodel by another one.

Re-initialization of state variables are not applicable in the case of memoryless models, since, they do not have state variables.

At a time t_d, model update and multimodel concepts are applicable to a memoryless model similar to the cases of piece-wise continuous-change models and discrete-change models. This means, that at t_d, one can change the value of some parameters. At the same time t_d, one can also replace the output function $\mathbf{g}_1$ by another function $\mathbf{g}_2$.

2.4 Other Modelling Formalisms and the New Paradigm

The concepts of model update and multimodel are applicable to discrete events, process models, and object-oriented modelling formalisms. Details will be available as the on-going research progresses.

3 Dynamic Templates as Modelling Formalisms

The templates used in this section are an extension of the unified graphic scheme developed to represent structured algorithms and programs (Ören 1984c). The scheme is currently being extended for object-oriented paradigms.

3.1 Dynamic Templates for Continuous Models

Fig. 4 represents the dynamic template for *updateable continuous models* (which can also be called continuous model, in short). Most segments of

ContinuousModel ...

StaticStructure

Inputs ...
States ...
Outputs ...
AuxiliaryVariables ...

Constants ...
Parameters ...
Auxiliary Parameters ...

TabularFunctions ...
Interpolations ...
MacrosUsed ...

DynamicStructure

Derivatives
...

OutputFunctions
...

Update
When ...
...
...
When ...
...

FIGURE 4. Template for updateable continuous models.

the template are optional. Therefore, if there is no appropriate entry in those segments, they can be eliminated automatically by the modelling environment. The template consists of two parts:

The first part is used to declare the static structure of a model. It consists of three divisions: (The entries are similar in nature to the elements of a component model of the Gest language (Ören 1984b). "Gest" stands for *Ge*neral *s*ystem *t*heory implementor; it is the first simulation language based on a system theory.

In the *first division*, all descriptive variables of the model are declared; these consist of the input, state, output, and auxiliary variables. If needed, for each variable, range of acceptable values as well as units can also be declared.

In the *second division*, constants can be declared and their values can be specified, and parameters and auxiliary parameters can be declared. For each auxiliary parameter, an assignment statement is given to specify the way it is related to parameters and constants. If units are declared in the first division, they must also be declared in the second division.

In the *third division*, tabular functions, interpolations using them, and any macro which will be used in the model are declared.

In the static structure the following segments are optional: input and auxiliary variables, constants, parameters (and auxiliary parameters), tabular functions (and interpolations), and macros used. Auxiliary parameters can be defined if at least one parameter has already been specified. Similarly, interpolations can be defined if at least one tabular function has already been specified. The above mentioned knowledge, in addition to other formalism-based knowledge, can be part of the knowledge base of a modelling and simulation environment which can used it both at advisor and certifier modes.

The second part of the dynamic template is used to specify the dynamic structure (i.e., the behavior generation structure) of a model and consists of three divisions:

The *first division* consists of the specifications of the derivative functions and the arithmetic statements defining the auxiliary variables.

The *second division* is used to declare the output functions of a model and the relevant auxiliary variables.

The *third division* is to specify the updates. When an update condition is satisfied, the values of some parameters or state variables can be updated. The update condition may be a function of time, state variables, input variables, or a combination of them. Several update segments can be conceived. In the existence of multiple update segments, all the update conditions have to be monitored simultaneously. As soon as an update condition is satisfied, the corresponding model update has to be performed. The model update division is optional.

In the dynamic structure, the output function is optional. If in the static structure, the output variables are declared to be a subset of the state variables, then there is no need to have output functions. This knowledge is sufficient to the modelling environment to eliminate the output function segment of the dynamic structure. If later, one would add another output variable in the static structure, depending on the case, the output function segment can be automatically inserted in the dynamic template. Model update segment is also optional.

Knowledge declared in some parts of the static structure can be used to check consistency and relevance of knowledge in other parts of the static structure as well as in the relevant parts of the dynamic structure.

Furthermore, parts of the static and dynamic structures can be dynamically tailored.

Problems where there is a change of the model during simulation, can best be formulated as an updateable continuous model. Figure 5 represents the well known bouncing ball problem expressed as an updateable continuous model.

At this point, it should be clear that the proposed template representation is equivalent to a tree representation of the components of a model. Pruning some branches of the tree corresponds to dynamically tailoring (in this case de-activating) some parts, divisions, or segments of a template. Therefore, any tree-based model management formalism can also be applied to the templates. The opposite of pruning in tree-based formalisms is re-activating some parts of a template, in the template-based formalism. In Section 4, some semantic rules are given as example of knowledge that

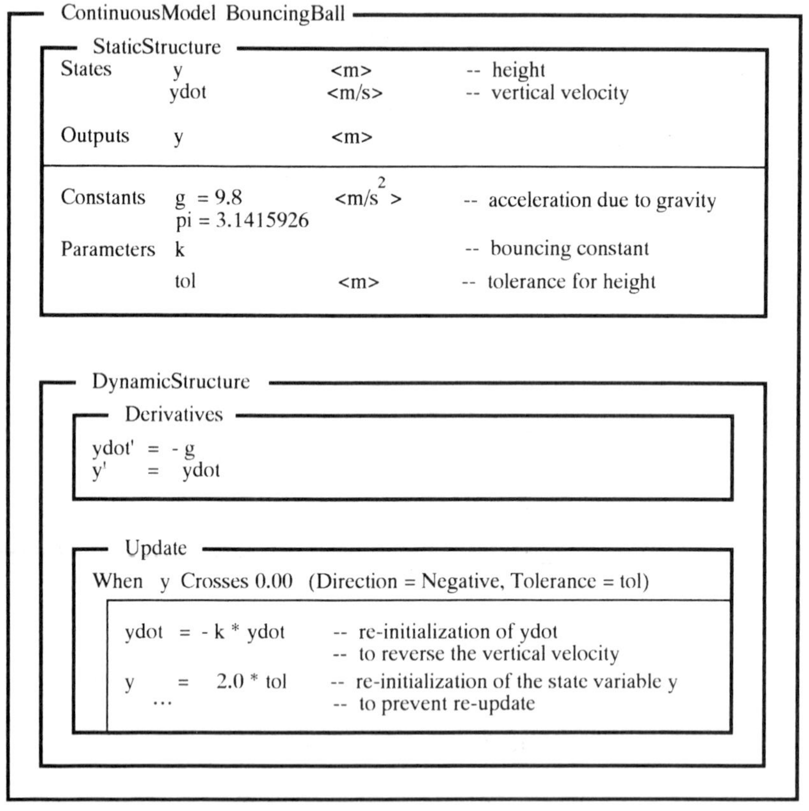

FIGURE 5. An example of an updateable continuous model.

can be used by an advanced modelling environment to dynamically tailor the templates.

Fig. 6 represents a *continuous multimodel*. A continuous multimodel has two or more submodels. The elements of the static structures of an updateable continuous model and a continuous multimodel are identical.

For each submodel of the multimodel, there is a separate dynamic structure part. Each dynamic structure of each submodel has three divisions:

The *first* and *second divisions* are used to declare the derivatives and the output functions and are similar to the corresponding divisions of the dynamic structure of an updateable continuous model.

The *third division* is used to specify model selection. Model selection condition is followed by a specification of the submodel and an optional update specification (of parameters and/or state variables). Similar to model update conditions, one can specify several model selection segments. The conditions are monitored simultaneously. When one of the conditions is satisfied, the corresponding submodel is selected and the corresponding optional updates are performed.

3.2 Dynamic Templates for Discrete Models

Figs. 7 and 8 represent updateable discrete model and discrete multimodel, respectively. They are almost identical to Figs. 4 and 6 with the following exception: In Figs. 4 and 6, the values of the next states are calculated by the derivative functions. In Figs. 7 and 8, the values of the next states are computed by state transition functions.

3.3 Dynamic Templates for Memoryless Models

Figs. 9 and 10 represent updateable memoryless model and memoryless multimodel, respectively. They are almost identical to Figs. 4 and 6 with the following exceptions: In Figs. 4 and 6, the values of the next states are calculated by the derivative functions. Since in memoryless models, there are no state variables, no derivative segments are available in Figs. 9 and 10. Furthermore, in continuous models, output function segment is optional. In the case of memoryless models, output functions are not optional.

The following dry friction model adapted from Cellier and Bongulielmi (1979) provides an example of a memoryless multimodel. As represented in Figure 11, dry friction torque (FTorque) versus angular velocity Omega consists of three branches. This memoryless model is represented in Figure 12 where the dry friction model has two inputs (Torque and Omega) and one output (FTorque).

At any point in time, the dry friction model is represented by one of the submodels 1, 2, or 3. At the beginning, the model is represented by submodel2 where Torque and Omega of the multimodel are connected to

```
ContinuousMultimodel ... with n Submodels
  StaticStructure
    Inputs ...
    States ...
    Outputs ...
    AuxiliaryVariables ...

    Constants ...
    Parameters ...
    Auxiliary Parameters ...

    TabularFunctions ...
    Interpolations ...
    MacrosUsed ...

  Submodel 1 - DynamicStructure
    Derivatives
      ...
    OutputFunctions
      ...
    ModelSelection
      When ...
        Select ... [andUpdate ... ]
      ...
      When ...
        Select ... [andUpdate ... ]
  ...
  Submodel n - DynamicStructure
```

FIGURE 6. Template for continuous multimodels.

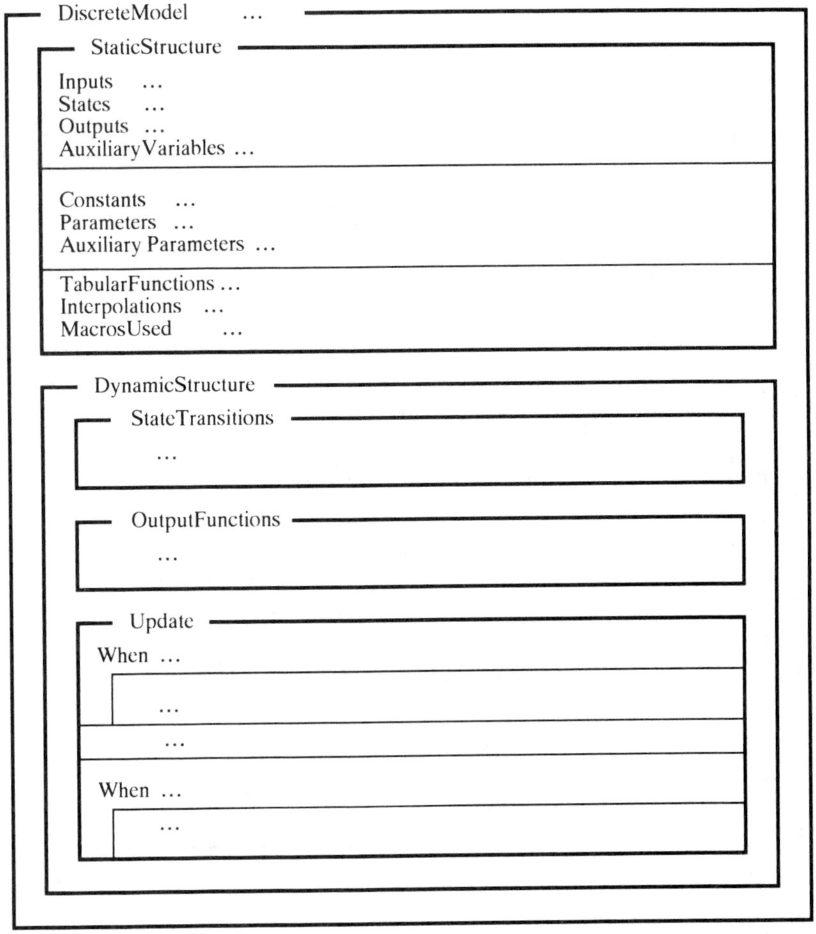

DiscreteModel ...

StaticStructure

Inputs ...
States ...
Outputs ...
AuxiliaryVariables ...

Constants ...
Parameters ...
Auxiliary Parameters ...

TabularFunctions ...
Interpolations ...
MacrosUsed ...

DynamicStructure

StateTransitions
...

OutputFunctions
...

Update
When ...
...
...
When ...
...

FIGURE 7. Template for updateable discrete models.

Torque and Omega of the submodel2; similarly, FTorque of the multimodel is connected to FTorque of the submodel2.

The output function of the submodel2 is:

$$\text{FTorque} = \text{Torque}.$$

While submodel 2 is active and used to represent the behavior of the memoryless model dry friction, the value of the input variable Torque is monitored as follows:

When Torque crosses the threshold value K2, select submodel1

When Torque crosses the threshold value −K2, select submodel3

```
DiscreteMultimodel ... ... with n Submodels
  StaticStructure
    Inputs ...
    States ...
    Outputs ...
    AuxiliaryVariables ...
    ----------------------------------------
    Constants ...
    Parameters ...
    Auxiliary Parameters ...
    ----------------------------------------
    TabularFunctions ...
    Interpolations ...
    MacrosUsed ...

  Submodel 1 - DynamicStructure
    StateTransitions
      ...
    OutputFunctions
      ...
    ModelSelection
      When ...
        Select ... [andUpdate ... ]
      ...
      When ...
        Select ... [andUpdate ... ]
  ...
  Submodel n - DynamicStructure
```

FIGURE 8. Template for discrete multimodels.

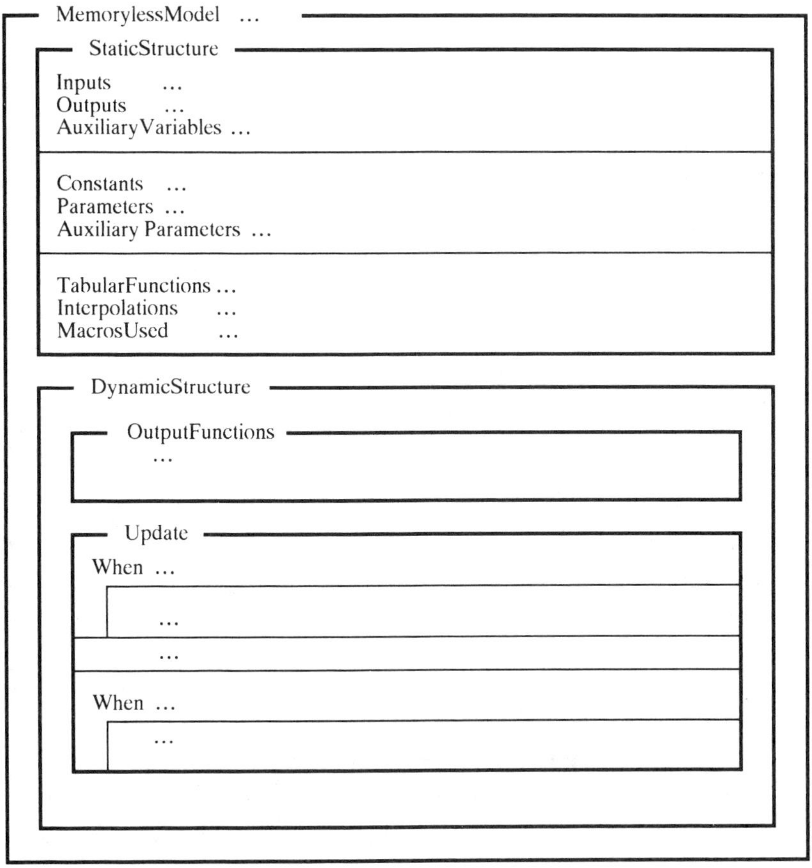

FIGURE 9. Template for updateable memoryless models.

The selections of the submodel1 or submodel3 are represented by the dotted arrows joining submodel2 to submodel1 and submodel3.

When Torque crosses K2 in the positive direction with a pre-specified tolerance, behavior generation is interrupted and submodel1 becomes active to represent the dry friction model. While submodel1 is active, the output function is:

$$\text{FTorque} = \text{K1} + \text{CM} * \text{Omega}$$

Where

K1 is a parameter,
CM = tan(Alpha), and
Omega is angular velocity.

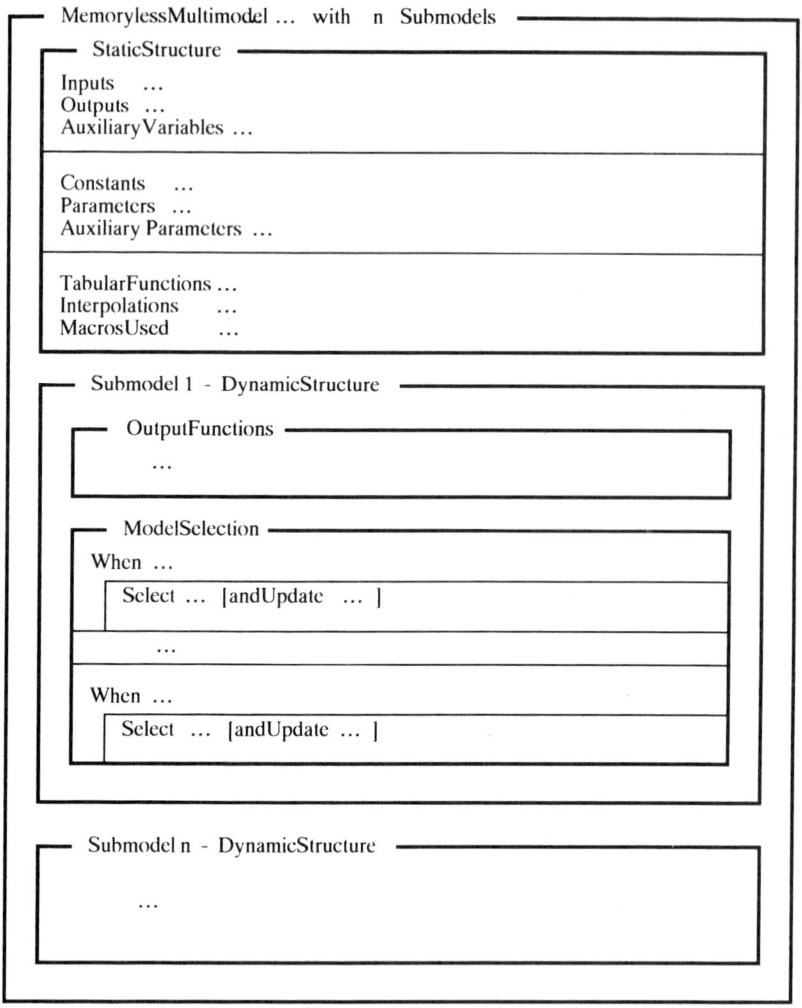

```
MemorylessMultimodel ... with n Submodels
  StaticStructure
    Inputs ...
    Outputs ...
    AuxiliaryVariables ...
    ----
    Constants ...
    Parameters ...
    Auxiliary Parameters ...
    ----
    TabularFunctions ...
    Interpolations ...
    MacrosUsed ...

  Submodel 1 - DynamicStructure
    OutputFunctions
      ...
    ModelSelection
      When ...
        Select ... [andUpdate ... ]
      ...
      When ...
        Select ... [andUpdate ... ]

  Submodel n - DynamicStructure
    ...
```

FIGURE 10. Template for memoryless multimodels.

While submodel1 is active, the necessary monitoring for submodel selection is as follows:

When Omega crosses 0.0 Select Submodel2 and update Omega = 0.0.

Similarly, while submodel3 is active, the output function is

$$\text{FTorque} = -\text{K1} + \text{CM} * \text{Omega}$$

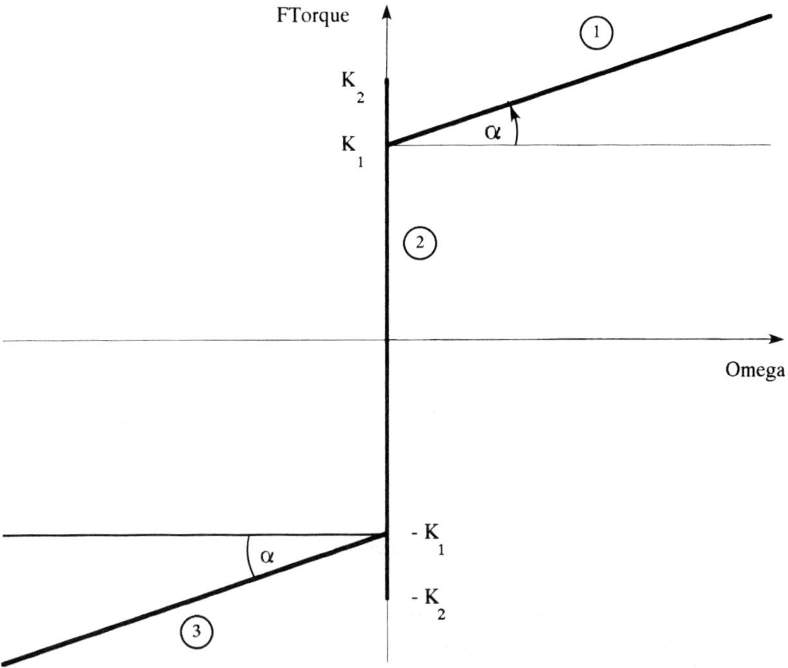

FIGURE 11. Dry friction torque (FTorque) versus angular velocity (Omega).

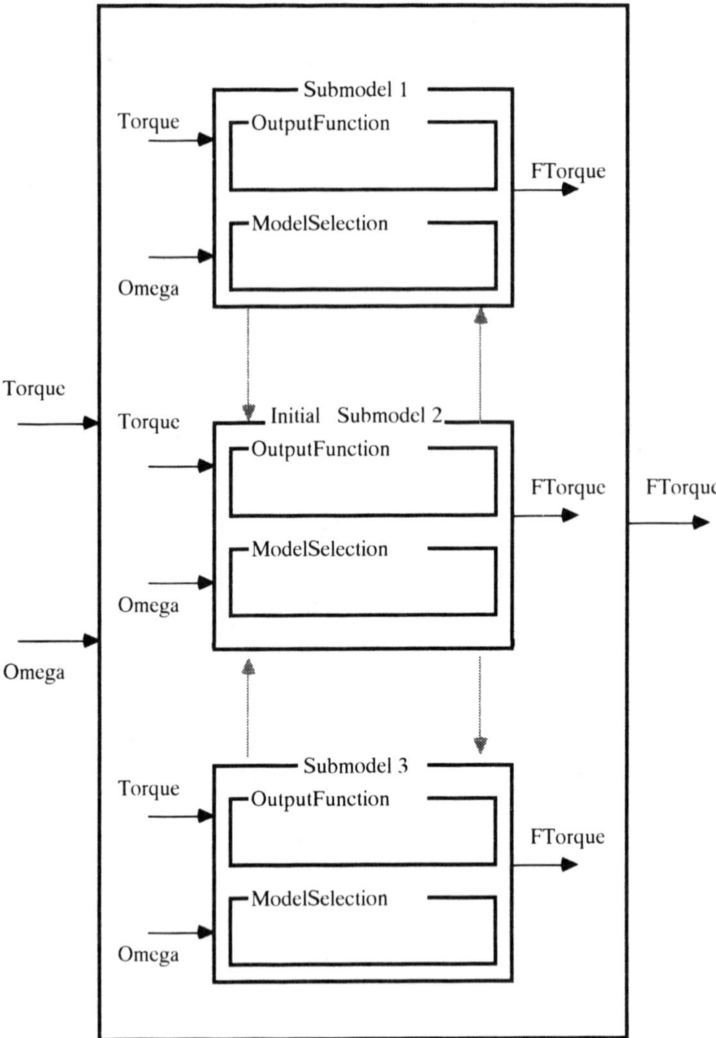

FIGURE 12. Three submodels representing the three branches of a dry friction model.

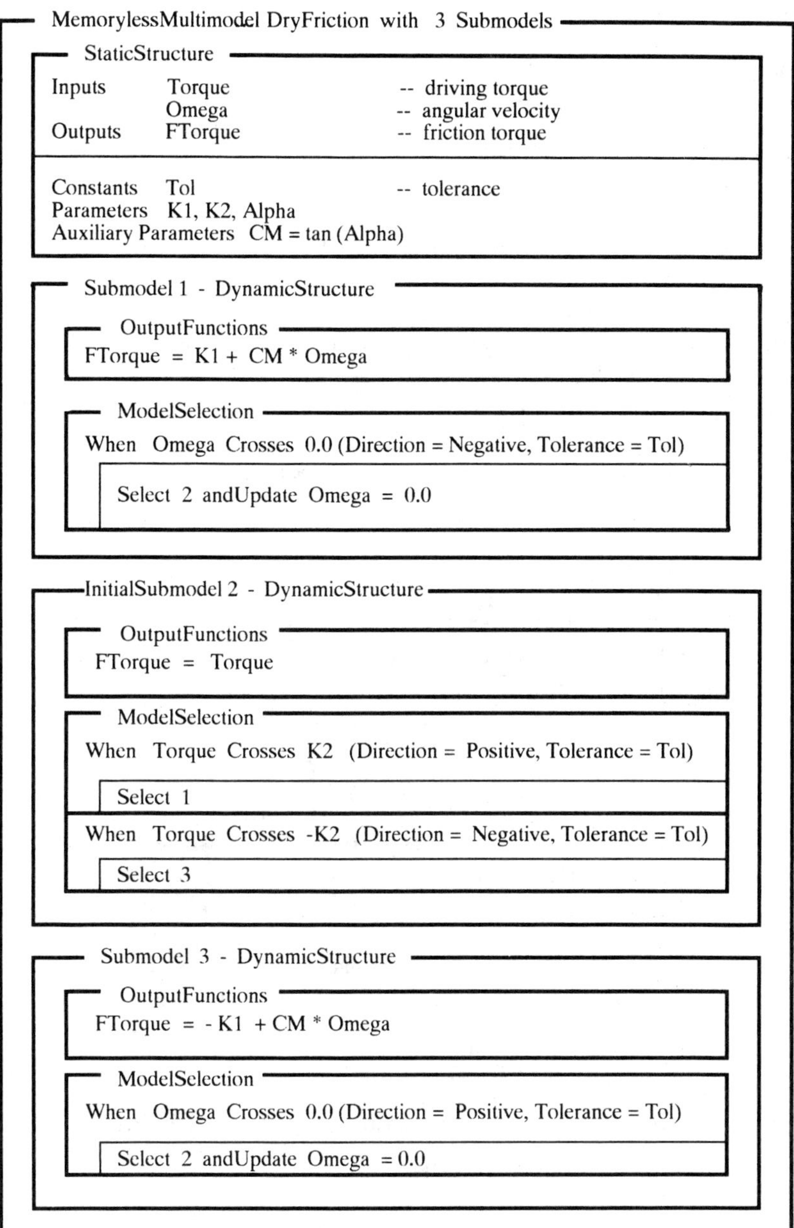

FIGURE 13. An example of a memoryless multimodel.

and the necessary monitoring for submodel selection is as follows:

When Omega crosses 0.0 Select Submodel2 and update Omega = 0.0.

Figure 13 represents the dry friction model as a memoryless multimodel consisting of three submodels.

4 Semantic Rules

The first list of model-related semantic facts and rules based on system theoretic considerations were given in Ören and Sheng (1988). In this chapter, semantic rules which affect the dynamic aspects of the templates are given. In the sequel, the terms "de-activated" and "re-activated" are used to mean "automatically de-activated and re-activated by a modelling environment." Some semantic rules that can be used to dynamically tailor the templates are given in the sequel:

Let

StaStr	be the Static Structure,
DynStr	be the Dynamic Structure,
KW	be a keyword,
list	be the list of symbols which follow a keyword, and
segment	be a segment of a template.

- **If** parameter list is empty,
  then de-activate Parameters segment in StaStr,
  & de-activate AuxiliaryParameters segment in StaStr.
- **If** TabularFunctions list is empty,
  then de-activate TabularFunctions segment in StaStr,
  & de-activate Interpolations segment in StaStr.
- In StaStr of a continuous or discrete model,
  if Outputs list is a subset of States list
  then de-activate OutputFunctions segment in DynStr.
- In DynStr of a continuous or discrete model,
  If OutputFunctions segment is not active
  & a symbol is added (& accepted by the certifier) to the Outputs list in StaStr,
  & the new symbol is not an element of the States list,
  then re-activate the OutputFunctions segment in DynStr.
- In a multimodel,
  If a submodel is an InitialSubmodel,

or there is a model selection from the InitialSubmodel leading to it,
or there is a model selection from another reachable submodel leading to it

then the submodel is reachable.

- In a multimodel,
  every submodel should be reachable.

5 Conclusion

A shift of paradigm permits us to perceive discontinuity from the point of view of the cause rather than the effect. This causal paradigm of discontinuity provides two concepts which are model update and multimodel. The concepts are applicable to a variety of types of models and lead to the following modelling formalisms: updateable continuous model, continuous multimodel, updateable discrete model, discrete multimodel, updateable memoryless model, memoryless multimodel, updateable event model, multievent, updateable process, multiprocess, updateable object, and multiobject. The formalisms can be expressed as dynamic templates which can be automatically tailored in an advanced modelling environment by using relevant semantic rules.

The templates have the following advantages: (1) For piece-wise continuous models, they provide a conceptual framework which is germane to the modelling process itself. The modeller can be freed from thinking in terms of some software engineering concepts such as case block or even some simulation concepts such as state event and time event which, being implementation details, should not be the concern of a modeller. (2) For models which are not piece-wise continuous-change models, the templates provide two new modelling paradigms which are model update and multimodel formalisms. (3) For all types of models, the templates provide a strong and flexible basis for advanced modelling environments which can function as advisors and certifiers.

References

Aytaç, Z.A., Ören, T.I. (1986). *Magest: A Model-Based Advisor and Certifier for Gest Programs.* In: Modelling and Simulation Methodology in the Artificial Intelligence Era, M.S. Elzas, T.I. Ören, B.P. Zeigler (Eds.), North-Holland, Amsterdam, pp. 299–307.

Cellier, F.E., Bongulielmi, A.P. (1979). *The Cosy Simulation Language.* In: L. Dekker, G. Savastano, and C. Vansteenkiste (Eds.) Simulation Systems. Preprints of the IMACS Congress 1979, Sorrento, Italy, Sept. 24–28, 1979, pp. 271–281.

Kuhn, T.S. (1970). *The Structure of Scientific Revolutions*, Second Edition, Enlarged. The University of Chicago Press Chicago.

Masterman, M. (1970). *The Nature of a Paradigm.* In: I. Lakatos and A. Musgrave (Eds.). Criticism and the Growth of Knowledge, Cambridge.

Minsky, M. (1988). *The Society of Mind.* Simon & Schuster, New York, NY.

Moore, E.F. (Ed.) (1964). *Sequential Machines: Selected Papers*, Addison-Wesley, Reading, Mass.

Ören, T.I. (1979). Concepts for Advanced Computer Assisted Modelling. In: B.P. Zeigler, M.S. Elzas, G.J. Klir, and T.I. Ören (Eds.) Methodology in Systems Modelling and Simulation, North-Holland, Amsterdam, Netherlands, pp. 29–55.

Ören, T.I. (1984a). *Model-Based Activities: A Paradigm Shift.* In: T.I. Ören, B.P. Zeigler, and M.S. Elzas (Eds.). Simulation and Model-Based Methodologies: An Integrative View, Springer-Verlag, Berlin, W. Germany, pp. 3–40.

Ören, T.I. (1984b). *Gest—A Modelling and Simulation Language Based on System Theoretic Concepts.* In: T.I. Ören, B.P. Zeigler, and M.S. Elzas (Eds.). Simulation and Model-Based Methodologies: An Integrative View, Springer-Verlag, Berlin, W. Germany, pp. 281–335.

Ören, T.I. (1984c). *Graphic Representation of Pseudocodes and Computer Programs: A Unifying Technique and a Family of Documentation Programs.* In: Proc. of EdCompCon-83 (First Educational Computing Conf. of IEEE Computer Society), D.C. Rine (Ed.). San Diego, CA, Oct. 18–20, 1983. IEEE Computer Society, New York, pp. 81–89.

Ören, T.I. (1986). *Knowledge-Bases for an Advanced Simulation Environment.* In: P.A. Luker and H.H. Adelsberger (Eds.) Intelligent Simulation Environments. Proc. of the Conf. on Intelligent Simulation Environments, San Diego, CA, Jan. 23–25, 1986, SCS Simulation Series 17:1, pp. 16–22.

Ören, T.I. (1987). *Model Update: A Model Specification Formalism with a Generalized View of Discontinuity.* In: Proc. of the 1987 Summer Computer Simulation Conf., Montreal, Quebec, July 27–30, 1987, SCS, San Diego, CA, pp. 689–694.

Ören, T.I. (1990—In Press). *A Paradigm for Artificial Intelligence in Software Engineering.* In: Advances in Artificial Intelligence in Software Engineering, T.I. Ören (Ed.), JAI Press, Greenwich, Connecticut.

Ören, T.I., Sheng G. (1988). *Semantic Rules and Facts for an Expert Modelling and Simulation System.* In: Vol. 2 of the Proc. of the 12th IMACS World Congress (R. Vichnevetsky, P. Borne, J. Vignes, Eds., Paris, France, July 18–22, 1988.

Ören, T.I., Tam, J.M. (1988). *An Expert Modelling and Simulation System on Sun Workstation.* In: R.C. Huntsinger et al. (Eds.). Simulation Environments and Symbol and Number Processing on Multi and Array Processing, SCS International, San Diego, CA, pp. 255–260.

Ören, T.I., Zeigler, B.P. (1986). *From Stone Tools to Cognizant Tools: The Quest Continues.* In : Proceedings of the 2nd European Simulation Congress, Antwerp, Belgium, Sept. 9–12, 1986, G.C. Vansteenkiste et al. (Eds.), SCS, San Diego, CA, pp. 801–807.

Zeigler, B.P. (1984). *Multifaceted Modelling and Discrete Event Simulation.* Academic Press, Orlando, FL.

CHAPTER 5

Knowledge Acquisition Based on Representation (KAR) for Design Model Development

Jhyfang Hu and Jerzy W. Rozenblit

Abstract

In recent years, knowledge-based systems have become one of the most popular approaches for solving engineering problems. Along with the rising complexity of the problem, knowledge management, acquisition, representation, inferencing, and refinement become increasingly difficult. Conventionally, tasks of knowledge acquisition and representation are accomplished separately and sequentially. Knowledge engineers are responsible for preparing question patterns and setting up personnel interviews with domain experts for knowledge acquisition. All acquired knowledge is then manually interpreted, verified, and transformed into a predefined representation scheme. In this chapter, a new methodology for knowledge acquisition, termed Knowledge Acquisition based on Representation (KAR) is presented. Instead of treating acquisition and representation separately and sequentially, KAR deals with acquisition and representation in an integrated manner. All knowledge acquired with KAR is verified and transformed into a representation scheme which is ready for inferencing. The major objectives of KAR are to facilitate the knowledge acquisition process, to increase its reliability, and to reduce the development cost of the model bases.

1 Introduction

Knowledge acquisition is the main bottleneck in the design of expert systems. Several methodologies have been introduced to help eliciting knowledge from experts. The most common method for knowledge acquisition is an interview [Hart 1985]. In face-to-face interviews, experts are asked questions and are expected to give informative answers. All details of the interviews must be recorded for further manual analysis and conversion so that essential knowledge can be extracted and translated into a representation scheme. Problems have been discovered with the interview approach. For example, experts are often unaware of specific details of the particular problem; experts are unable to spell out their knowledge; knowledge engineers are unable to query all the essential knowledge; experts misunderstand knowledge engineer's questions because of different interpretations of the terminology. All the above situations may result in unnecessary, duplicate, and conflicting knowledge.

Some of the interview technique problems are resolved by a more structured approach termed the protocol analysis [Waterman and Newell 1971]. With the protocol analysis, experts comment on specific examples from a problem domain. For example, experts may look at a specific design example and comment on the question: "Why is the design good or bad?". This is different from the interviewing approach which may tackle the same problem by asking question patterns such as "What made the design good or bad?". Often, it is easier to comment on a specific example in the protocol analysis rather than to answer the general questions in the interviewing process. In protocol analysis, knowledge is extracted from detecting general patterns, e.g., experts may always examine one particular characteristic first.

Computer induction [Ritchie 1984] is another technique to deal with knowledge acquisition. With induction, experts provide a set of examples of cases (called training sets) together with attributes considered in design decision making. Then a program is applied to induce rules from those training sets. The quality of the induced knowledge depends on the selection of training sets, attributes, and the use of induction algorithms.

Much of the difficulty in knowledge elicitation lies in the fact that experts cannot easily describe how they view a problem. This is essentially a psychological problem. Kelly viewed a human being as a scientist categorizing experiences and classifying his own environment. Such a description is very suitable for an expert in his knowledge domain. Based on Kelly's personal construct theory [Kelly 1955], the repertory grid technique [Boose 1988] was developed for knowledge acquisition. Given a problem domain, experts build up a model consisting of elements and constructs which are considered relevant and important. The constructs are similar to attributes except that they must be bipolar (e.g., good/bad, true/false, strong/weak). Elements are analogous to examples in induction. The grid is a cross-reference table between elements and constructs. For example, in acquiring knowledge for programming evaluation, experts may build up the grid table with a number of typical programs (elements) and attributes (constructs) such as modularity, testability, portability, meaningful variables, and readable layout. Each square of the grid table is then filled with a quality value or index. Finally, the quality of programs is determined by experts based on the summing quality index.

Although methodologies such as interviewing, protocol analysis, observation, induction, clustering, prototyping [Waterman and Newell 1971, Ritchie 1984, Hart 1985, Kessel 1986, Gaines 1987, Gaines 1988, Olson and Rueter 1987] have been proposed to help in eliciting knowledge from experts, none of them is commonly accepted. Different problem domains may require different acquisition strategies.

To reduce errors (e.g., misinterpretation of the interviewed data) caused by the human intervention, a more efficient and reliable approach for acquiring knowledge is to automate the elicitation process based on a certain representation scheme which will completely and efficiently denote all the domain traits and encompass all essential knowledge. Knowledge acquisition guided by the structure of a knowledge representation is termed Knowledge Acquisition based on Representation (KAR) [Hu et al. 1989]. To distinguish it from conventional approaches, KAR exploits the structural nature of a representation scheme to motivate acquisition activities.

2 Requirements for Design Modelling Representation Schemes

Before selecting a good representation scheme to serve as the basis of KAR, let us first examine requirements for a good design knowledge representation scheme. Reviewing the common traits in system design, structured techniques are used to reduce the complexity of the design process. Common design traits found in modern design approaches are:

Hierarchy: The use of hierarchy involves dividing a system into subsystems and then repeating this operation on the subsystems until the complexity of subsystems is at an appropriate, or desired, abstraction level.

Modularity: Modularity helps designers to reduce the complexity of system models and clarify an approach to a problem. A modular design facilitates flexibility and future modifications. The modular design approach also aids in team design.

Regularity: Employing regular structure to simplify the design process is gaining its popularity. Regularity can exist at all levels of the design hierarchy. As seen in computer system design, uniform transistors are used at the circuit level; identical gate structures are employed at the logic level. At a higher level, a multi-processor system is designed with identical processors [Weste and Eshraghian 1985].

In general, a good knowledge representation scheme for system design applications must be able to denote the above properties within its representation structure. Furthermore, the knowledge representation scheme must be able to capture both static and dynamic knowledge of the system such as:

Static knowledge:

General properties of objects.

Taxonomy/decomposition of objects.

Rules for design synthesis.

Dynamic knowledge:

Model descriptions of objects.

Procedures for generating design alternatives.

Procedures for design validation and evaluation.

A good knowledge representation scheme should also facilitate knowledge management, efficient knowledge acquisition, inferencing, and refinement. Finally, knowledge reflected by the representation scheme must be transparent to domain experts, knowledge engineers, and system users.

To qualify for KAR, a knowledge representation scheme must satisfy the following requirements:

1. The scheme is able to query (or generate question patterns automatically) knowledge about the domain.
2. The knowledge acquired from domain experts can be automatically and directly translated into an internal representation which is ready for inferencing. The internal representation of knowledge is transparent to domain experts and system users.
3. The structure of the knowledge representation scheme provides efficient and systematic mechanisms for knowledge organization, inferencing, and refinement.
4. The knowledge representation scheme must possess axioms or operations to detect conflicting information, to remind that essential knowledge may be missing, and to eliminate repeated or unnecessary knowledge.

The increasing demand on the quality of knowledge-based systems has resulted in knowledge representation becoming a major topic in AI research. Although various schemes [Quillian 1968, Minsky 1975, Schank and Abelson 1977, Nilsson 1981, Zeigler 1984, Shastri 1988] have been introduced to help representing and managing knowledge, none of these conventional representation schemes satisfies all requirements that qualifies a representation scheme for the KAR approach. We have augmented the system entity structure [Zeigler 1984] into an integrated and entity-oriented knowledge representation scheme, termed the Frame and Rule-Associated System Entity Structure (FRASES) [Hu et al. 1989]. FRASES is a scheme that combines concepts of the system entity structure, frame [Minsky 1975], and production rules [Newell and Simon 1972]. By exploiting the reasoning flexibility provided by production rules, the efficiency in representing declarative knowledge offered by frames, and the visibility and hierarchy supported by the system entity structure, FRASES is a powerful and efficient scheme for managing domain knowledge supporting design model development.

3 Structure of FRASES

FRASES is a superclass of the system entity structures that encompasses the boundaries, decompositions, and taxonomic relationships of the system components being modelled. All axioms and operations defined originally for managing system entity structures are also present in FRASES representation [Hu et al. 1989, Rozenblit et al. 1989].

Each entity of FRASES signifies a conceptual part of the system which has been identified as a component in one or more decompositions. Each such decomposition is called an aspect. In addition to decompositions, there is a relation called specialization. It facilitates representation of variants for an entity. Each specialization variant inherits properties and substructures from the parent entity to which it is related.

A typical example of FRASES for representing a tightly-coupled multiprocessor system is shown in Figure 1. As shown in the figure, each entity of FRASES is associated with an Entity Information Frame (EIF). An EIF is a generalized property list [Winston 1984] which can be divided into discrete elements called "slots". Each slot describes an attribute which may, in turn, contain one or more facets such as "value", "default", "if-needed", or "if-accessed". Every occurrence of an entity has the same Entity Information Frame (EIF) and an isomorphic substructure. During application, knowledge contained in the EIF is extracted and interpreted by the inference engine for design reasoning [Rozenblit et al. 1989]. An Entity Information Frame (EIF) is a structure:

$$\langle \mathrm{M, ATTs, DSF, ESF, CRS, CH} \rangle$$

where

M: is the name of the associated model.
ATTs: are attributes of the entity.
DSF: is the design specification form.
ESF: is the experiment specification form.
CRS: are constraint rules for design synthesis.
CH: are children entities of M.

With FRASES representation, behavioral knowledge about objects is described by simulation models stored in the model base. M represents the key to access a model of the entity to which EIF is attached. ATTs are attributes used to characterize the associated object. Attributes of an entity are partitioned into two groups, i.e., static and dynamic [Rozenblit and Hu 1988]. Static attributes are variables used to describe properties of an object that do not change over time. Dynamic attributes are related to the dynamic behavior of the models represented by entity objects.

Design Specification Form (DSF) accepts the specification of design objectives, constraints, and criteria weighting schemes. The contents of DSF define the system requirements that must be satisfied by the system being

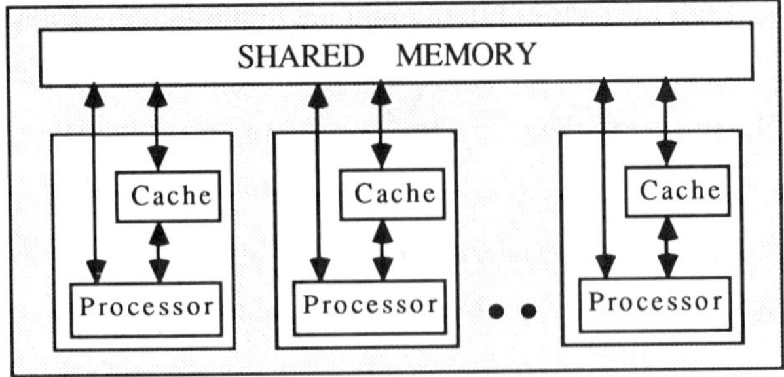

(a) Schematic representation

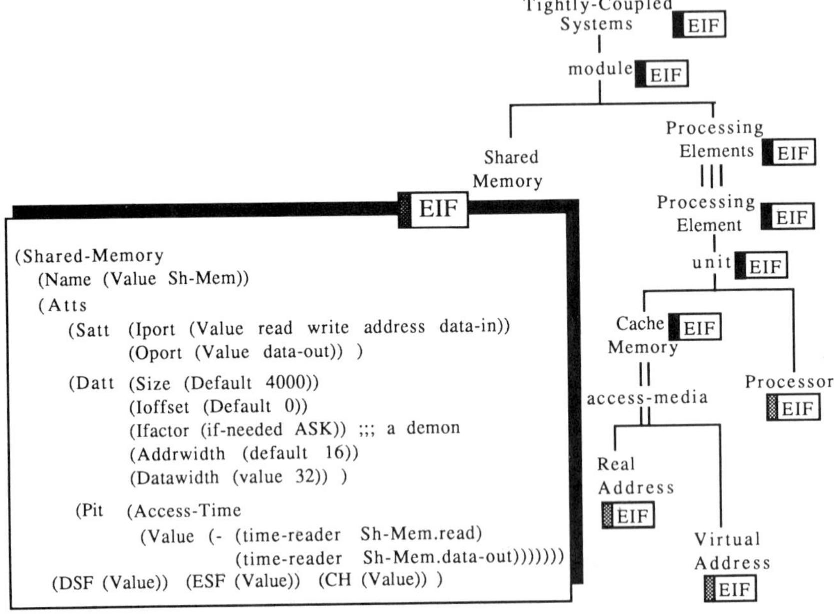

(b) FRASES representation

FIGURE 1. A tightly-coupled multi-processor system.

designed. The DSF information is used to guide the synthesis of design model structures. Each entity of FRASES has its own DSF. Once composition trees (i.e., a decomposition tree with information about the coupling schemes among model components) are generated based on the knowledge provided in the CRS (see below) slot, users are requested to define the simulation experiment in the Experiment Specification Form (ESF).

Finally, simulation is activated via automatic extraction and coupling of simulation models [Hu 1989].

Experiment Specification Form (ESF) is applied to accept the specification of simulation requirements such as an arrival process, event structure, and simulation control scheme. ESF provides information to direct the automatic generation of experimental frames [Hu 1989]. Again, ESF is placed along with entity nodes of a composition tree. For illustration, typical DSF for design of a processor of a tightly-coupled multi-processor system is shown in Figure 2. With the specified DSF, the processor should be capable of executing 10 Million Instructions Per Second (MIPS), the cost of the processor is less than 300 dollars, and the power consumption of the processor must be less than 0.5 μwatts. Figure 3 shows a simplified form of a simulation experiment for the processor. The simulation specification indicates that the input arrival rate for the first 100 events will follow the Poisson distribution with the mean value of 10. For subsequent events, the normal distribution with mean of 1 will be employed. Each event is composed of a symbolic identification and numerical workload. Simulation will be executed for 300 events. For each 50 system time units, the measurement of performance indices must be reported.

Constraint Rules for Synthesis (CRS) contains heuristic rules for configuring design model structures. Formally, selection constraint rules for pruning alternative are associated with specialization nodes, and constraint rules for synthesizing components are associated with aspect nodes. Rozenblit and Huang have defined model development driven by production rules in [Rozenblit and Huang 1987].

FRASES is a generative knowledge representation scheme which organizes the knowledge represented into an entity-based, hierarchical structure

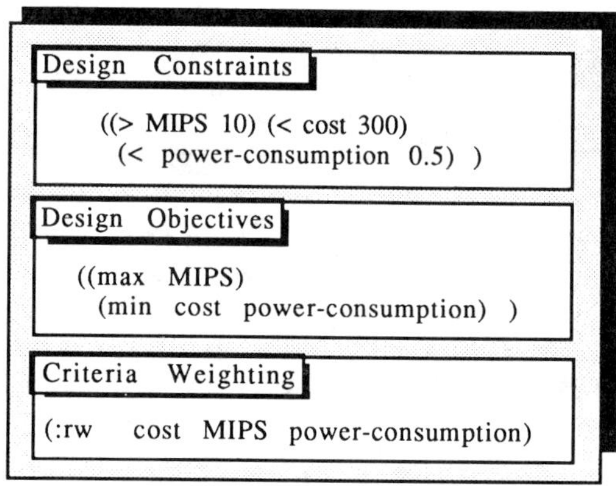

FIGURE 2. Design specification form.

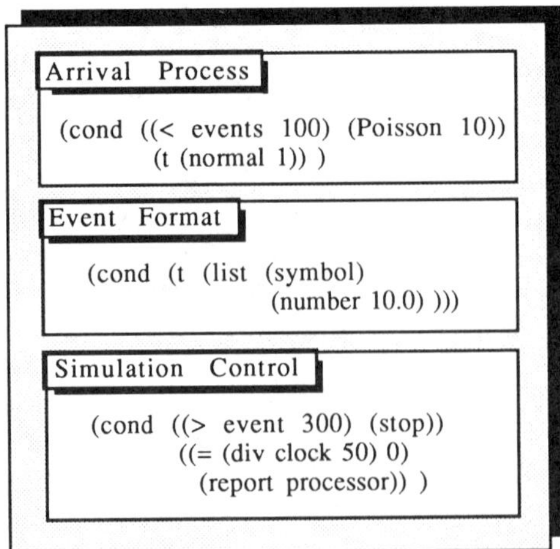
Arrival Process

(cond ((< events 100) (Poisson 10))
(t (normal 1)))

Event Format

(cond (t (list (symbol)
(number 10.0))))

Simulation Control

(cond ((> event 300) (stop))
((= (div clock 50) 0)
(report processor)))

FIGURE 3. Experiment specification form.

and allows the represented knowledge to be refined and inferred efficiently [Rozenblit et al. 1989].

4 KAR Based on FRASES

FRASES is a complete knowledge representation scheme for system design application, which conveys the declarative knowledge (structure and attributes) as well as procedural knowledge (production rules for design synthesis, verification, and evaluation). With the well- [defined axioms and operations, FRASES satisfies all the requirements of the KAR approach as follows:

1. The entity-oriented hierarchical structure of FRASES can be easily employed to represent design structures characterized by modularity, hierarchy, and regularity. By employing query rules based on the structural nature of FRASES, question patterns are generated automatically to acquire knowledge from domain experts.
2. The acquired knowledge is directly translated into an internal representation of Entity Information Frame (EIF) in the format ready for inferencing. This reduces human intervention to the minimum. Due to the graphic interface of FRASES, knowledge represented with FRASES is transparent to domain experts and system users.
3. FRASES provides an efficient scheme for knowledge representation, refinement, and inferencing by partitioning the global knowledge base into hierarchical and entity-oriented frame objects.

4. Contradiction, duplication, missing or incompleteness of essential knowledge can be detected by checking verification rules associated with each query rule. In other words, axioms and operations of FRASES are checked with verification rules to assure the consistency and validity of knowledge.

Selecting FRASES to conduct KAR, the query process can be depicted by state transitions as shown in Figure 4. The knowledge acquisition starts from querying knowledge about the problem domain. Once the problem domain is specified, the acquisition process falls into the Entity/Aspect/Specialization (EAS) loop. Component information and knowledge about determining design parameters are acquired at the "Entity" phase. Knowledge about functional decomposition, coupling, and synthesis constraints is elicited in the "Aspect" phase. Knowledge about alternatives and selection rules is acquired in the "Specialization" phase. Experts may choose the most appropriate design approach (e.g., top-down, bottom-up, and mixed) based on the characteristics of design problems by indicating processing priority between aspect and specialization nodes [Hu 1989]. At each design abstraction, the most crucial component is indicated by assigning the highest processing priority. The EAS loop will continue until desired level of abstraction is reached. After the FRASES structure is acquired, system identifies entities that require a corresponding behavior model and starts acquiring behavioral features for each entity. At each acquisition state, verification rules are automatically applied for checking knowledge inconsistency.

In Figure 5, a simple comparison between the conventional knowledge acquisition and KAR with FRASES is given. The diagram in the middle column delineates the acquisition process for developing a knowledge base. Several advantages are expected from using KAR with FRASES for knowledge acquisition:

Efficiency: Question patterns necessary to acquire design knowledge for decomposition, taxonomy, pruning, and synthesis of systems are generated automatically. Knowledge provided by users is verified automatically by applying appropriate verification rules to assure consistency of knowledge. With FRASES, verified knowledge is translated directly into a ready-for-inferencing Entity Information Frame (EIF) by a number of macros defined for managing frame objects [Hu 1989]. Once the knowledge acquisition process is completed, experts may practice a number of design applications by providing information required for Design Specification Forms (DSF) and Experiment Specification Form (ESF). By examining generated designs, experts can justify if knowledge refinement is required or if the design reasoning is performed correctly.

Flexibility: One of the problems found in conventional knowledge acquisition methods is that they only appear efficient in a specific problem

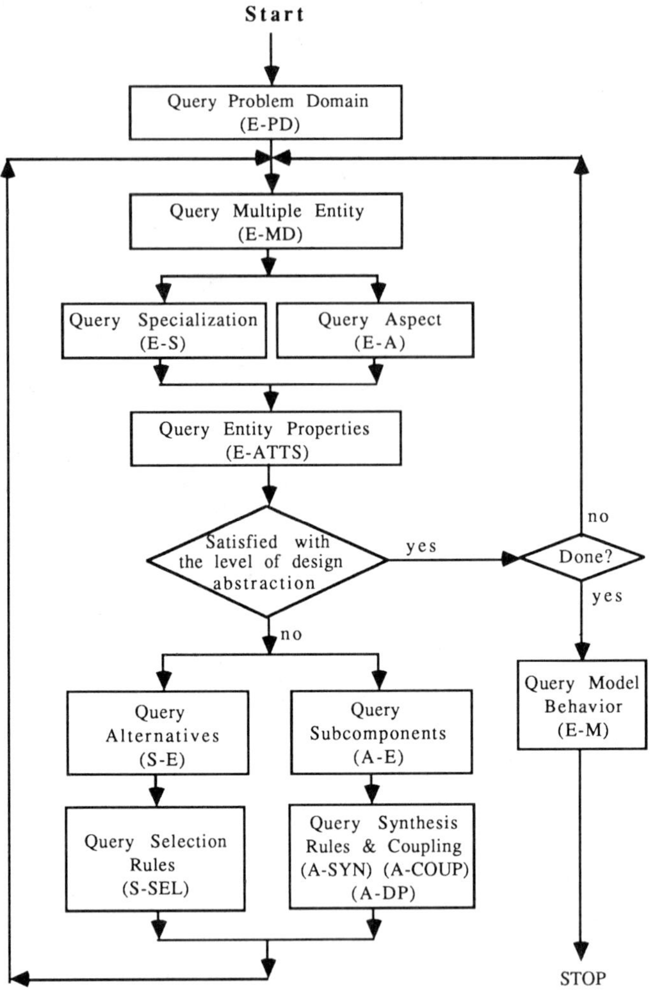

FIGURE 4. Query transition of KAR with FRASES.

domain. With the flexibility of FRASES, KAR can be used for a large class of systems exhibiting hierarchical and modular structure.

Manageability: The entity-based, hierarchical structure allows the knowledge represented to be examined and modified easily. During the knowledge acquisition process, users are allowed to modify both the structure and EIF contents of the FRASES tree.

Cost-Effectiveness: Unlike conventional acquisition approaches which require human intervention and labor-intensive preparation, interviewing, verification, translation, and organization, the complex process of knowl-

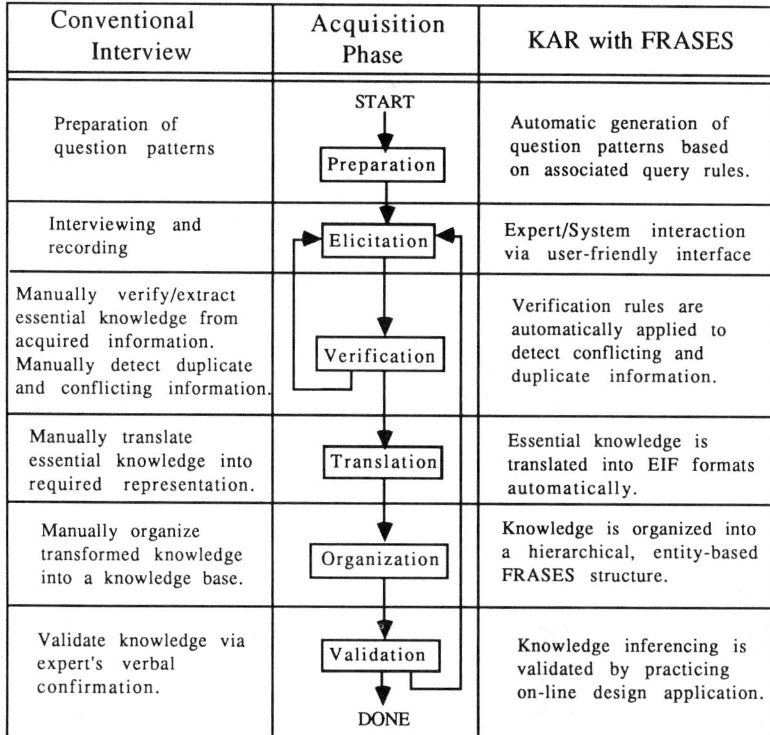

FIGURE 5. Interviewing vs. KAR with FRASES.

edge base development is automated and efficiently handled by KAR approach. The fast turnaround of knowledge base development highly reduces the cost of knowledge-based systems.

5 Query Rules of FRASES

In order to automate the generation of question patterns for constructing a FRASES tree, query rules are first defined in a database and linked to the acquisition tool. On each acquisition iteration, appropriate question patterns will be generated based on interpreting associated query rules. In general, query rules of FRASES are classified into four types:

I. Entity Query:
   A. Querying Problem Domain (E-PD).
   B. Querying Multiple Decomposition (E-MD).
   C. Querying Design Attributes (E-ATTS).
      1. Static Attributes (E-SATTS).

2. I/O Ports (E-PORTS).
3. Design Parameters (E-DPARA).
4. Performance Indices (E-PIX).
5. Processing Priority (E-PP).

D. Querying Specializations (E-S).
E. Querying Aspects (E-A).

II. Specialization Query:
A. Querying Specialization Variants (S-E).
B. Querying Selection Rules (S-SEL).

III. Aspect Query:
A. Querying Subcomponents (A-E).
B. Querying Synthesis Rules (A-SYN).
C. Querying Coupling Information (A-COUP).
D. Querying Design Priority (A-DP).

IV. Model Query:
A. Querying Model Behavior (E-M).

Each query rule is associated with three explanation patterns (e.g., WHY, WHAT, and HOW) as follows:

WHY is the question asked?
WHAT does this question mean?
HOW to answer this question?

For example, the S-SEL rule of a specialization node has three explanation rules, termed S-SEL.WHY, S-SEL.WHAT, and S-SEL.HOW, to explain "Why selection rules are required for a specialization node?", "What a selection rule means?", and "How to specify a selection rule?".

6 Verification Rules of FRASES

In order to assure the consistency of FRASES representation, verification rules based on axioms and operations of FRASES must be checked after each query rule is applied. In other words, to assure the consistency of knowledge provided by users, one or more verification rules will be applied on each query iteration. Whenever conflicting or invalid information is detected, error messages will be signaled to users so that an appropriate correction or modification can be made. For logical errors (e.g., conflicting information), the system will explain which axiom or operation of FRASES has been violated and how these problems can be solved. On the other hand, if a physical error (e.g., typos such as a missing token "IF" in the rule specification) is found, the system will correct the error by referring to the explanation rules associated with the entity (e.g., S-SEL.HOW explains how to specify selection rules for a specialization node). If the user is not satisfied with the modification made by the system, he will be requested to give a correct input.

To verify logic errors, each query has verification rules which are employed to assure the consistency of the knowledge being represented. They are:

I. Query Problem Domain (E-PD)
Verifying Domain Existence (VDE): If an old domain existed, users are allowed to use, to discard, or to save the old domain knowledge.

II. Query Multiple Decomposition (E-MD)
Verifying Variation Range (VVR): What is the maximum and minimum number of entities allowed in the system.

III. Query Design Attributes (E-SATTS, E-DPARA, E-PIX):
Verifying Attached Variables (VAV): No two variables have the same name.
Verify Inherited Knowledge (VIK): All properties and substructures inherited through a specialization (i.e., taxonomy) must be validated for the current entity. This assures knowledge consistency for future pruning operations.

IV. Query Selection Rules (E-SEL), Query Synthesis Rules (A-SYN), and Query Coupling Information (A-COUP):
Verifying Knowledge Hierarchy (VKH): Knowledge contained in an Entity Information Frame is related only to itself and its substructures.
Verifying Conflicting Knowledge (VCK): Dead-ends (e.g., none of the specialization variants is selected) and inconsistency (e.g., coupling two output ports together) should be avoided.
Verifying Concise Form (VCF): Rules which are logically related should be combined into a concise form to reduce the complexity of knowledge bases.

V. Query Specialization (E-S) and Query Aspects (E-A):
Verifying Uniformity (VUF): Any two nodes with the same labels have identical Entity Information Frames and isomorphic substructures.
Verifying Structure Hierarchy (VSH): No labels appear more than once down any path of the FRASES tree.
Verifying Valid Siblings (VVS): No two entities under the same node have the same labels.

VI. Query Subcomponents (A-E):
Verifying Uniformity (VUF)
Verifying Structure Hierarchy (VSH)
Verifying Valid Siblings (VVS)

VII. Query Specialization Variants (S-E):
Verifying Uniformity (VUF)
Verifying Structure Hierarchy (VSH)

KAR/EXPERT INTERACTION	FRASES CONVERSION
KAR> What is your problem domain (E-PD) ? => Tightly-Coupled-System	Tightly-Coupled Systems
KAR> What kind of static attributes that you want to add to the system (E-SATTS)? => (designer Jeff) (date 4/18/89) (place UA) KAR> What kind of design parameters that you want to consider at this design level (E-DPARA)? => cost size KAR> What kind of performance indices are considered for evaluating a Tightly-Coupled-System (E-PIX)? => response-time thruput KAR> Can you classify a Tightly-Coupled-System based on certain specialization (E-S)? =>why KAR> ->> This question is used to query how experts ->> classify variants of the asked entity. For ->> example, a computer network can be clssified ->> into RING, BUS, and TREE based on Topology. KAR> Can you classify a Tightly-Coupled-System based on certain specialization? => nil KAR> Can you decompose a Tightly-Coupled-System based on certain aspect (E-A)? => module	Tightly-Coupled System EIF module
• • • KAR> What are these subcomponents when you decompose a Tightly-Coupled-System based on module (A-E)? => Processing-Elements Shared-Memory • • •	Distributed Systems EIF module Porcessing Elements Shared Memory
KAR> Does the number of Processing-Elements vary with design requirements (E-MD)? => yes KAR> Specify the range for the number of Processing-Elements? => 0 64 ;;; *multiple decomposition* • • •	Tightly-Coupled EIF System module EIF EIF Processing Elements Shared Memory Processing Element

FIGURE 6. KAR with FRASES for tightly-coupled multi-processor system.

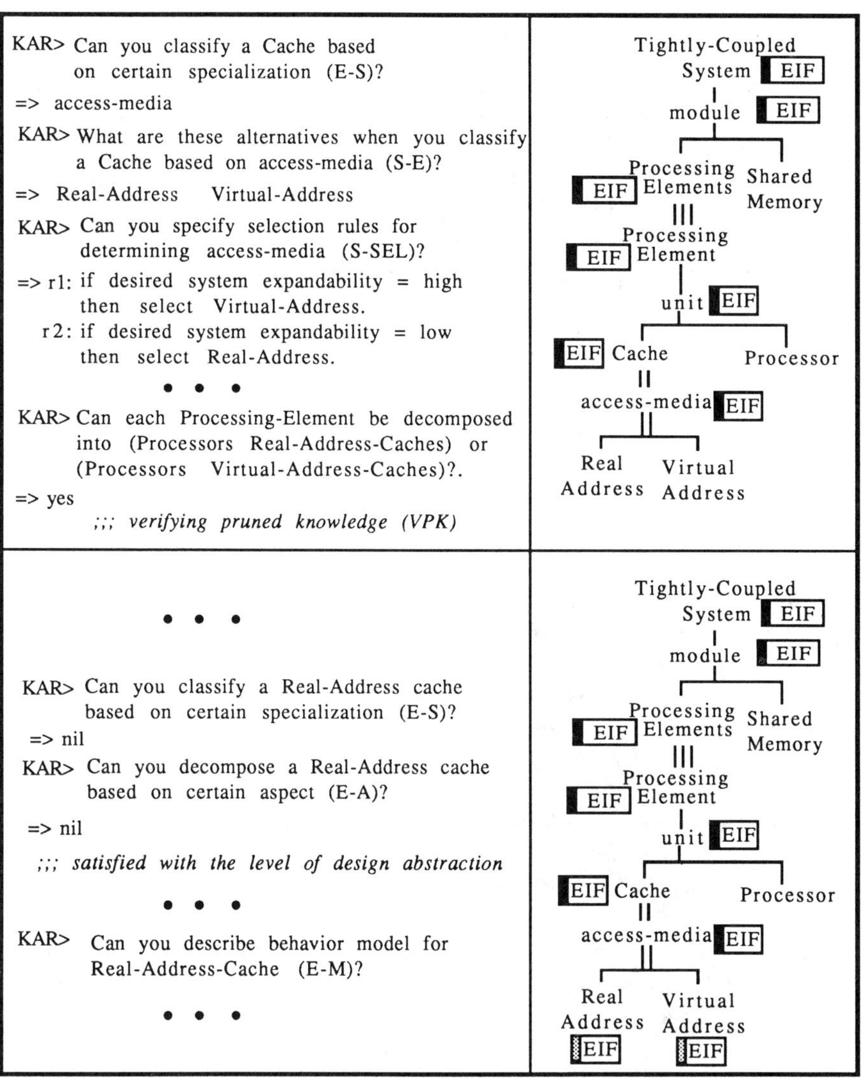

FIGURE 6. *Continued*

Verifying Valid Siblings (VVS)
Verifying Combinations of Knowledge (VCK): New knowledge obtained from combinations of multiple aspects and/or specializations of FRASES must be confirmed by the user. Constraints will be acquired to indicate invalid combinations.
Verifying Pruned Knowledge (VPK): Specialization variants should be valid for future pruning operations.
Verifying Transformed Knowledge (VTK): New knowledge transformed from the current structure of FRASES must be confirmed by the user.

With the rule base approach, verification rules defined for each query pattern can be flexibly refined by updating rules instead of reprogramming the system.

7 Example

To illustrate the operation of KAR with FRASES for knowledge acquisition, part of the query process for design of a tightly-coupled multi-processor system is illustrated in Figure 6. The acquisition process begins with generating a query about the problem domain. This query is activated by the E-PD structure incorporated in FRASES. After the answer is generated, FRASES converts it to its internal frame representation as shown in the right column of Figure 6.

The next step is to substantiate the Entity Information Frame. Relevant information is elicited through questions about the design parameters and performance indices. The Tightly-Coupled System is then decomposed in to Processing Elements and Shared Memory by answering decomposition-oriented queries (E-A). Notice that there was a negative response (nil) to a query eliciting information about a possible taxonomy of the system.

The acquisition process is carried out until a level of hierarchical specification that satisfies the modeller is reached as shown in the last section of the left column in Figure 6.

8 Conclusions and Future Research

Conventional knowledge acquisition methods require a significant human effort to prepare, verify, translate, organize, and validate knowledge. When the complexity of systems grows, conventional methods become inefficient. To improve the efficiency of knowledge acquisition and to reduce the cost of knowledge-based systems, a new methodology called the Knowledge Acquisition based on Representation (KAR) is proposed. To realize KAR we have developed a knowledge representation scheme, termed Frame and Rule-Associated System Entity Structure process by using the automatic approach via exploiting the structural nature of a representation scheme.

With the KAR approach, both the cost and time for developing a knowledge base from which a design model construction rules are derived are drastically reduced.

Topics for future research include:

1. To incorporate psychological methods in the KAR methodology for a.) developing the best query rules with which domain experts are more willing to share their knowledge; b.) determining the reason a user has asked a question so that a customized response can be generated; and c.) verify the degree of validity of knowledge with respect to the psychological factors.
2. Upgrading the KAR interface with a natural language processor for design specification and answering system queries.

References

Boose, J.H. 1988, "Uses of Repertory Grid-Centered Knowledge Acquisition Tools for Knowledge-Based Systems," *Int. J. Man-Machine Studies*, vol. 19, no. 3, p. 287–310.

Gaines, B.R. 1987, "An Overview of Knowledge Acquisition and Transfer," *Int. J. Man-Machine Studies*, no. 26, p. 453–472.

Gaines, B.R. 1988, "Knowledge Acquisition-Systems for Rapid Prototyping of Expert Systems." *Inform.*, vol. 26, no. 4, p. 256–285.

Hart, Anna 1985, "Knowledge Elicitation: Issues and Methods, Computer-Aided Design, vol. 17, No. 9, p. 455–462. Hart, Anna 1985, "The Role of Induction in Knowledge Elicitation," *Expert Systems*, 2, p. 24–28, January 1985.

Hu, Jhyfang and J.W. Rozenblit 1988, "Towards Automatic Generation of Experimental Frame in Simulation-Based System Design," *SCS AI Papers*, vol. 20, No. 1, p. 1–6.

Hu, Jhyfang, Y.M. Huang, and J.W. Rozenblit 1988, "FRASES—A Knowledge Representation Scheme for Engineering Design, " *Advance in AI and Simulation*, SCS Simulation Series, vol. 20, no. 4, p. 141–146.

Hu, Jhyfang 1989, "Towards an Integrated Knowledge-Based Design Support Environment for Design Automation and Performance Evaluation," Ph.D. Dissertation, University of Arizona, Tucson.

Kelly, G.A. 1955, *The Psychology of Personal Constructs*, New York: Norton.

Kessel, K.L. 1986, "Methodological Tools for Knowledge Acquisition and Transfer," Proceeding of the 1986 IEEE International Conference on System, Man, and Cybernetics, Atlanta, GA.

Minsky, M. 1975, "A Framework for Representing Knowledge," in Winston, P.H. (ed.), *The Psychology of Computer Vision*, New York: McGraw-Hill, p. 211–277.

Newell, A. and H.A. Simon 1972, *Human Problem Solving*, Englewood Cliffs, NJ: Prentice-Hill.

Nilsson, N.J. 1981, *Principles of Artificial Intelligence*, Palo alto, CA: Tioga Press.

Olson, J.R. and Henry H. Rueter 1987, "Extracting Expertise for Experts: Methods for Knowledge Acquisition," *Expert System*, August 1987, Vol. 4, No. 3, p. 152–168.

Quillian, M.R. 1968, "Semantic Memory," in Minsky, M. (ed.), *Semantic Information Processing*, Cambridge, MA: MIT press,p. 27–70.

Ritchie, I.C. 1984, "Knowledge Acquisition by Computer Induction," Proceedings of UNICOM Seminar, London, England.

Rozenblit, J.W. and Jhyfang Hu 1988, "Experimental Frame Generation in a Knowledge-Based System Design and Simulation Environment," to appear in: *Modeling and Simulation Methodology: Knowledge System Paradigms*, (M. Elzas et al., eds.), North Holland, Amsterdam.

Rozenblit, J.W., Jhyfang Hu, and Y.M. Huang 1989, "An Integrated, Entity-Based Knowledge Representation Scheme for System Design," The 1989 NSF Engineering Design Research Conference, Amherst, Mass., June 1989.

Schank, R.C. and Abelson, R.P. 1977, *Scripts, Plans, Goals, and Understanding*, Hillsdale, New York: Erlbaum.

Shastri, L. 1988, "Semantic Networks: an Evidential Formalization and its Connectionist Realization," *Research Notes in Artificial Intelligence*, Morgan Kaufman Publishers, San Mateo, CA.

Waterman, D.A. and A. Newell 1971, "Protocol Analysis as a Task for Artificial Intelligence," *Artificial Intelligence*, 2, p. 285.

Weste, Neil and Kamran Eshraghian 1985, *Principles of CMOS VLSI Design—A System Perspective*, Addison-Wesley Publishing Company.

Winston, Patrick H. and Berthold Klaus Paul Horn 1984, *LISP* (Second Edition), Addison-Wesley, Reading, Massachusetts.

Zeigler, B.P. 1984, *Multifaceted Modelling and Discrete event Simulation*, Academic Press.

Zeigler, B.P. (1987a), "Knowledge Representation from Newton to Minsky and Beyond," *Applied Artificial Intelligence*, 1: 87–107.

CHAPTER 6

Automatic Model Generation for Troubleshooting

Arie Ben-David

Abstract

In a typical scenario a human expert writes down a simulation model as a computer program. More demanding environments require that the computer itself will first 'figure out', or generate, the appropriate model. When the domain at hand is complicated, such a task may be non-trivial to program using conventional programing languages. Artificial intelligence techniques, and in particular expert systems, are of great assistance for achieving such goals which usually require deep on-hand experience and expertise of the domain at hand. A methodology for building such applications for the troubleshooting of processes is described through an actual example taken from the machining domain.

1 Introduction

This chapter deals with the role of automatic model generation for multiple fault troubleshooting. In particular, it demonstrates how to construct useful expert systems which support both the tasks of processes design and the troubleshooting of non-trivial process, by extensively utilizing automatic model generation. Any decent troubleshooter must resort to models of the process or the artifact at hand. Models are abstractions of reality, and as such they generally reflect simplified versions of their domains. This feature raises some difficulties while troubleshooting complex processes. For instance, a critical question which is typically to be answered deals with the validity of a process model under certain circumstances.

In many troubleshooting cases determining which is the proper model for adequately simulating a process poses a real challenge on the system designer. In particular, the task is difficult when the process at hand is not completely theoretically understood, and the relevance of the simulation model itself is questionable. Under such conditions, not only the faulty process is to be "troubleshooted", but the simulation models are to be "troubleshooted" as well.

The remainder of the chapter describes an architecture and an implementation of an expert system which copes with such difficulties. The system has been named DT, after its two major goals—the Design of a complex process, and the Troubleshooting of multiple faults, where the system criticizes its previous designs.

2 Related Work

Troubleshooting and process planning are interrelated concepts. Troubleshooting has been an important application area in AI, as can be demonstrated by the long list of applications provided by Pau [21]. Early expert troubleshooting systems for various applications have evolved from the pioneering work done by AI researchers during the sixties and seventies. Most early troubleshooters were derivatives of models such as Mycin (Shortliffe [23]), R1 (McDermott [17]) and Prospector (Duda [6]). These systems were composed of production rules. Certainty factors were attached to the rules in particular cases. Collectively, these expert systems are usually referred to as 'first generation' troubleshooters.

Troubleshooters which were solely composed of production rules drew much criticism in recent years. Furthermore, some first generation troubleshooters were found, by various researchers, to be very weak in terms of accuracy. This observation had led researchers to develop an approach which currently is being referred to as 'model based' or 'second generation' expert systems. Koton [12] suggested an alternative to the rule based approach: "model based, reasoning by using a detailed model of the object ...". He constructed two versions of expert systems using rule based and model base approaches, and observed an obvious advantage to the latter. He indicated that the second approach "created chains that are about four times longer... This results in slower execution...".

Davis [2] advocated to "reason from first principles" while troubleshooting electronic components. DeKleer [3] gave a concise definition regarding troubleshooting: "If the task is troubleshooting, then the model is presumed to be correct and all model-artifact differences indicate part malfunction. If the task is theory formation, than the artifact is assumed to be correct and all model-artifact differences require changes in the model". His approach, however, does not provide any clue regarding the handling of situations where the models are not accurate in the first place. This is the case, for example, with DT to be shortly discussed, where the domain models are empirical in nature. Herrod [10], reports a troubleshooting project for glass annealing which soon came to a dead end, and has been developed into a simulation project using domain models. The StarPlan-1 project for situation assessment of satellites, reported by Siemens [24], suffered from similar weakness until a second version, called StarPlan-2, was written using proper simulation models.

Troubleshooters differ in the degree in which they rely upon design models. In most real world applications, partial models have to be integrated into one coherent system, as has been observed by Dixon [5] and others. The need for multiple model integration has also been reported by Fink [7] and by Rychener [22]. They propose a layered integration of the various models. Different types of models are adequate for different domains and tasks, as can be seen in Fishwick [8] with respect to the Dining Philosophers Problem.

A troubleshooting environment can be defined in terms of the characteristics of the relative process design it is intended to criticize and correct. The ways in which partial models are generated and re-composed in engineering planning and design are described by Dixon [5] and Kilhoffer [11] among others. Since variables are typically shared by various sub problems, the sub models have to communicate with each other. This point has been described in detail by Pao [20] and Stroebel [25]. Many systems emphasize either a process design component or a troubleshooting task. The systems reported, for example, by Mittal [18] and Herrod [10] perform the task of planning. The systems reported by Thompson [26], Siemens [24] and others monitor and troubleshoot pre-planned processes. The tasks of design and troubleshooting are not well integrated in many of these systems. This chapter suggests some solutions in this respect.

In many cases, such as in real time embedded systems, troubleshooting must be carried out very fast (see O'Reilly [19] and Laffey [15]), as opposed to the more relaxed time constraints which are usually imposed on the design of the process. The task of many real time troubleshooters can be defined as: 'what are most reasonable actions to be tested, and possibly carried out, within a certain amount of time', rather than whether troubleshooting the process will actually eliminate all the faults. The troubleshooting algorithm of DT to be presented later fits this approach.

Dealing with multiple faults is an essential feature for some troubleshooting domains where the process variables are tightly coupled. Alleviating the severity of one fault, while ignoring the rest, usually implies that other problems may occur. A good troubleshooter is expected to be capable of solving existing problems without introducing new ones. DT has been designed to resolve multiple fault situations. Another important feature of real time troubleshooters is their ability to quickly shift focus from one fault to another, as has been indicated by Laffey [15]. The troubleshooting algorithm in DT has adopts this view. A well known difficulty while troubleshooting arises when the candidate actions have conflicting effects on various faults. in particular, when the process at hand has a high degree of variable sharing. Currently, few expert systems deal with conflicting actions.

Situations where conflicting advice (actions) is to be resolved are described by Mittal [18] and Herrod [10] among others. The latter is solving conflicting actions by rule ordering, a strategy which is not recommended for obvious reasons. The more common approach is to use explicit meta rules for resolving the conflicts as much as possible. In situations where complex, tightly coupled, processes are involved—the task of defining proper meta rules can easily evolve to a nightmare in terms of knowledge acquisition and system's response. For that reason, Kumar [14] has restricted the WAX system to deal with up to three simultaneous faults out of the ten his system is handling.

This chapter assumes that the model which synthesizes the partial results is expressed mathematically. Partial models upper in the design hierarchy are not restricted to mathematical formulation. These models can be rule based, neural nets, etc. Conflicting actions in DT are procedurally resolved as long as they are within the scope of the synthesized model.

3 A Few Words About the Grinding Domain

The knowledge base in DT is composed of two major components: design models and a causal graph from faults to potential actions. The troubleshooting algorithm works on top of them. Let us examine now these components in more detail.

Grinding, in general, is one of the most important machining operations in industry and its relative importance is continuously growing as more exotic raw materials are introduced into the market. Grinding is an attractive alternative, when compared to other machining processes, when very tough raw materials are to be processed to extremely tight tolerances. References to grinding theory and applications can be found in Malkin [16] and Kovach [13]. The latter includes the exact formulation of the empirical mathematical models used by DT.

The simplest grinding process design requires the assignment of values to about twelve process variables. Sophisticated grinding processes may involve decisions regarding more than twenty process variables. Currently, despite extensive research efforts, grinding is still one of the least theoretically understood among all machining processes. For example, up to date, not a single mathematical model which expresses the relationship among all grinding process variables is known, even for the simplest type of grinding operation.

Partial mathematical and heuristic models, however, have been developed for various grinding operations. The nature of these models is basically empirical (i.e., they have been derived by experiments rather than by a well established theory). Each partial model only can handle a subset of the process variables. Under certain conditions, these models provide relatively good predictions. In many other cases, the models fail to predict reality accurately enough.

DT, therefore, must take a skeptical approach towards the simulation models it utilizes. The nature of grinding models, for example, is unlike those which have extensively been used in qualitative physics research (see Bobrow [1] and Forbus [9]). The latter assumes that the models are essentially correct—a luxury DT cannot afford. DT aims at designing grinding processes and effectively deal with multiple fault situations. The user can select which of the two modes of operation, process design or troubleshooting, is to be activated. However, the above two tasks are tightly coupled. Any troubleshooting session follows a comprehensive process design phase. Also, the design models are updated and utilized during any troubleshooting session.

4 Process Design

A process design is done by a decomposition of the problem into smaller, hierarchical sub-problems, followed by a synthesis phase. Figure 1 shows the structure of a process design in DT. Three modules constitute the decomposition phase, while the one on the bottom represents the synthesis of the design. The module designated by 'coolant variables' determines the coolant type and its concentration. The one designated by 'wheel variables' determines the values of the wheel abrasive, wheel grit size, wheel grade, structure and its bond type. The above components are composed of production rules.

Once a wheel has been selected, a predefined mathematical model is evaluated in order to predict the system's compliance. This model does not determine any value of a process variable. Rather, its outcome, as well as the results of the previous models, are essential for the next step. Based upon the process specifications and the partial solution which has just been evaluated during the decomposition phase, DT automatically generates a non linear optimization problem (NLP) via a rule based component. The role of this particular component is to map process specifications and partial results into a synthesized mathematical model. This is one point in DT where automatic model generation is extremely important, since no expertise is required on the user's side in order to utilize state of the art grinding models. Automatic models generation is even more crucial for troubleshooting purpose.

The NLP aims at maximizing the metal removal rate, a typical target function in machining. It determines the values of five process variables:

1. Depth of cut
2. Table speed
3. Wheel surface speed
4. Dressing lead rate
5. Dressing depth

Three major soft constraint (i.e., constraints which can be violated in reality), all nonlinear, are to be obeyed in order to produce defect free products.

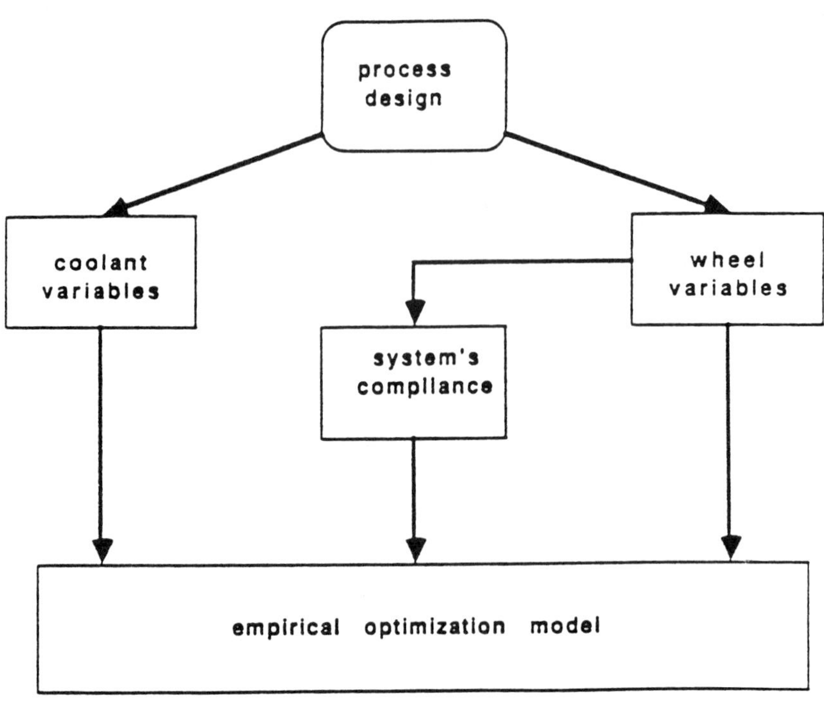

FIGURE 1. Grinding process design.

1. A burning constraint, which, if satisfied, is predicted to prevent burning related defects in the finished product.
2. A chatter constraint, which aims at preventing chatter related defects.
3. A surface finish constraint, which, if satisfied, is predicted to prevent chatter related defects.

Each of the above soft constraints is dependent upon all the above five process variables. Each process variable in the empirical NLP is also bounded by two hard constraints, usually reflecting physical limitations of the machine, such as minimum and maximum depth of cut, etc.

Once generated, the NLP problem is solved. Later, DT checks the design results via another rule based component. For instance, DT examines the feasibility of the solution and whether a local optimum makes sense within the domain. The system is capable of automatic re-design. Also, the user is free to change any parameter and re-design. The latter option is highly useful for a what-if type of sensitivity analysis. Although the designs are quite elaborate, it is expected that some of them will cause faults in reality by failing to meet the specifications. In order to attempt solving potential problems, should they occur, a process design in DT is not completed before all relevant potential troubleshooting actions are initialized in the knowledge base.

5 Troubleshooting

The task of constructing a multiple fault troubleshooter may be solved by constructing it as a production system, or by entirely relying upon various mathematical sensitivity analysis techniques. The first approach seems to be inadequate for grinding. There is no point to trade concise mathematical formulation, such as a NLP, with a (potentially) huge set of "if—then—else" type of rules. Pure mathematical sensitivity analysis of the NLP, on the other hand, is capable of solely dealing with a small subset of the process variables. Current grinding models, as has been mentioned above, are capable of dealing with five out of twelve or more process variables within a single mathematical formulation. Even that can only be done on an empirical level.

Troubleshooting actions which aim at changing the values of process variables within a mathematical model, such as the NLP, are named 'actions within the synthesized (empirical) model'. We use here the terms synthesized and empirical interchangeably when referring to DT. In general, the synthesized model may be of other nature. As has been mentioned above, there are five potential actions within the scope of the empirical model of DT—those which are within the scope of the NLP. Other types of potential troubleshooting actions exist as well. First, there are potential actions which belong to the decomposition phase of the process design mentioned earlier. We refer to this type of action as 'actions regarding other process variables'. The coolant type and the grit size, for example, belong to this category.

An action of the second type of troubleshooting action, if taken, may affect the synthesized model. Here, in DT, the NLP may be affected should such an action be considered or taken. An example of the above consideration arises while trading one coolant with another in order to evaluate its effect on a burning related problem. New types of coolant usually make the current NLP formulation inadequate. Consequently, the burning related constraint expression must be traded with another. The above observation brings us to the second point within the troubleshooting architecture where automatic models generation is crucial. We discuss this point later in the chapter. For now, it is sufficient to note that there is not only one NLP in DT during a troubleshooting session. Rather, the system continuously generates new models for simulating the effects of potential troubleshooting actions according to the specific circumstances.

Any approach towards troubleshooting processes such as grinding must also seriously consider the underlying assumptions of the models. A typical example of an important assumption in grinding modeling is the balance of a grinding wheel. An unbalanced wheel is very likely to cause serious defects in the end product. Not a single grinding empirical mathematical model even considers unbalanced grinding wheels. A troubleshooter must take such a possibility into account. Troubleshooting actions which aim at verifying the adequacy of design models by checking the existence of their underlying assumptions are called 'validity checks'.

So far we have seen three different types possible troubleshooting actions. The question which immediately arises is how to combine these actions with the design models. A qualitative level of reasoning is essential here. It is the lowest 'common denominator' for the integration of the different partial design models with the different troubleshooting actions. Some of these actions are not of mathematical nature. Rather, they are qualitative.

A table of possible qualitative troubleshooting actions which are within the scope of the empirical mathematical model of DT is shown in Figure 2. An upper arrow in Figure 2 indicates that increasing the value of a process variable is likely to decrease the severity of violating the corresponding constraint and vice versa.

Troubleshooting actions in DT are organized in a directed acyclic graph as shown in Figure 3. The qualitative level of the actions becomes apparent by observing how validity checks such as 'check if the wheel is balanced'

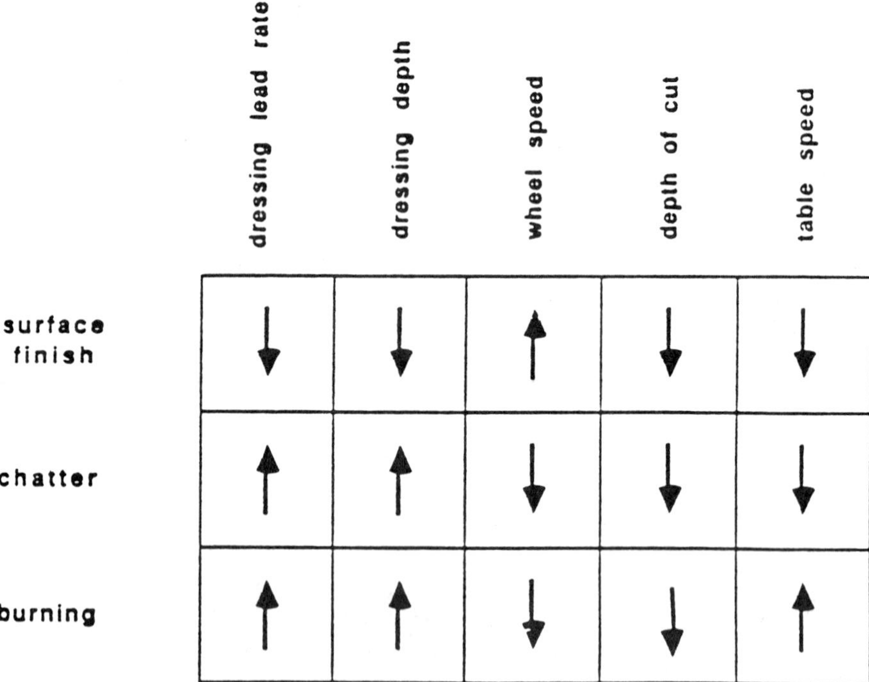

FIGURE 2. A table of qualitative actions.

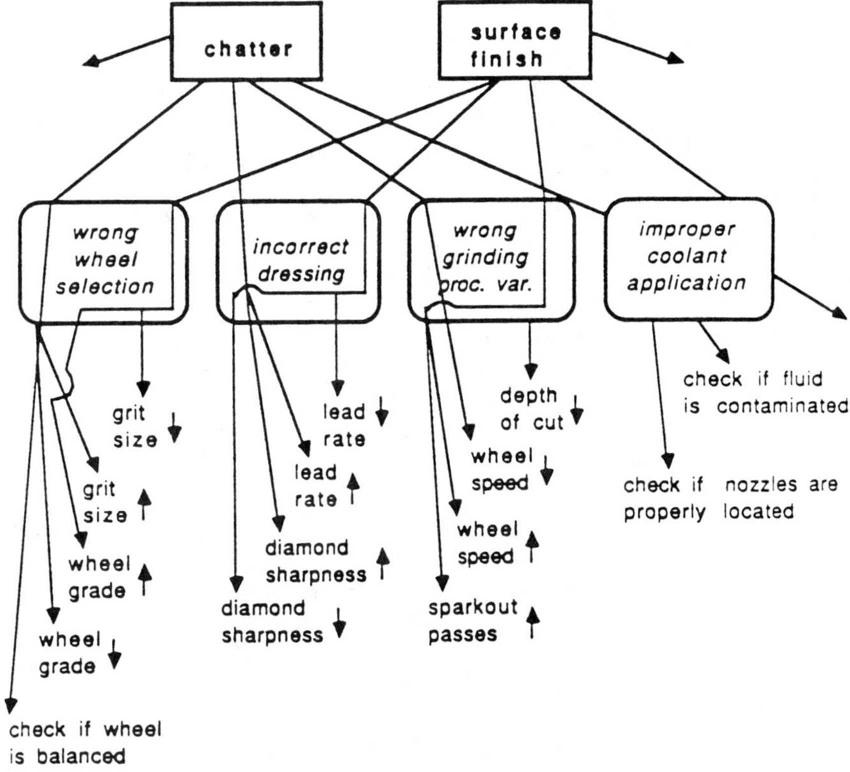

FIGURE 3. A simplified causal graph.

are mixed with actions which are within the scope of the NLP (such as depth of cut, wheel speed, etc.), and process variables which are outside the NLP's scope (e.g., grit size, wheel grade, etc.). The graph has been obtained by merging causal trees from single faults to actions and by removing all duplicates.

The causal graph in Figure 3 is an essential component in the knowledge base. It enables clear explanations why a troubleshooting action is recommended. In order to avoid traversing the graph whenever explanations are not essential, each fault is also directly connect to the relative potential actions.

6 A Troubleshooting Session

A troubleshooting session in DT begins after all potential actions to be taken are organized in the knowledge base, ready to be executed. Initialization of the knowledge base is done during the process design phase, a fact which is transparent to the user.

The system is asking iteratively for qualitative estimation of the severities of the faults. Typically, the design models predict initially that no faults will occur. The fuzzy description of the faults is matched against the predictions and qualitative corrections are made to the NLP. Faults prediction is done at this point, using the modified model. A global state criterion is updated. DT uses sum of squares of the severities predictions over all the soft constraints as a measure for the state criterion. No action within the scope of the empirical mathematical model is taken which is not predicted to improve the overwhole state.

Determining which is the next reasonable action to be tested in order to improve the state of a process is governed by the ratio between the cost of implementing an action and the potential benefit which is expected of carrying it out. Most potential actions are in qualitative form. Qualitative actions are assigned absolute values, using simple heuristic functions, also stored in the knowledge base. Typically, some easy to check, 'trivial' actions are taken before the system will suggest changing any value of a process variable. Some actions can be executed more than once and the knowledge base is updated after each candidate action is tested. The process repeats iteratively until all faults are solved or the system runs out of potential actions. The top level algorithm which is used in DT for troubleshooting is shown in Figure 4.

The troubleshooting algorithm checks sequences of actions which are predicted to improve the state of a faulty process. The troubleshooter iterates as long as at least one fault exists. Each tested sequence of actions aims at easing the most severely violated constraint. In order to decrease the response time, the troubleshooting algorithm does not fire any production

```
BEGIN

    WHILE there exist faults and there exist admissible actions
              which are predicted to improve the situation w.r.t the
              mostly violated constraint
    BEGIN
         Carry out the actions;
         Update the knowledge base;
         Get a list of all faults and their severities;
    END
END
```

FIGURE 4. Troubleshooting algorithm.

rule. Neither is it planning its next steps over a limited horizon, ready to backtrack when a path does not seem to be promising enough. Some actions may be taken several times in opposite directions such that the effect of 'bad' decisions can be later undone without explicit backtracking. Also, the algorithm does not attempt to optimize process states whenever the NLP is adapted to actual observations.

A typical troubleshooting session begins with some questions regarding the faults and their severities. To illustrate such a session suppose there is a severe surface finish problem combined with minor burning. The troubleshooter tries to resolve the more serious problem first. Assume, for simplicity, that all the possible remedies to improper surface finish are (see Figure 3 for more details):

1. "decrease grit size"
2. "increase wheel speed"
3. "check if nozzles are properly located"

Since the last potential recommendation is very easy to carry out and it cannot worsen the situation with respect to any constraint—it will be the first to be displayed. Should the user indicate that the nozzles are properly directed the troubleshooter will consider the rest of the potential actions. Increasing the wheel speed is considered next since it is also relatively easy to perform. However, using the process models this recommendation will not be issued since the situation regarding the (currently minor) burning problem is anticipated to significantly worsen. The next candidate action in our simplified troubleshooting session is to decrease the grit size, which according the process models is also in the right direction for resolving the burning problem, so the user will be asked to mount a new wheel with finer grit and to inform the system what is happening now. The troubleshooting session goes on until all faults disappear or the system runs out of reasonable advice. In the latter case the troubleshooter admits defeat.

7 Automatic Model Generation

We have already pointed out that DT automatically generates NLP simulation models. Here we briefly discuss few issues regarding this topic. The first aspect of automatic model generation in DT is speed. For comparison, process design is done by DT in about two percent of the time which was required by a grinding expert who used the same computer and the same NLP package. More importantly, working with DT does not require any prior insight into theoretical and empirical aspect of grinding research. On-hand experience with grinding (machine operator level) is sufficient in order to properly work with the system and enjoy state of the art grinding models.

As previously mentioned, the causal graph structure in DT generates potential actions for alleviating a single fault. Whenever the effects of taking an action on the empirical NLP model is known or can be estimated, it is specified with the corresponding action in the graph. For example, the wheel grit size is known to have a significant impact on the burning-related constraint in the NLP. The NLP is, therefore, updated accordingly whenever the grit size is changed during a troubleshooting session.

Consequently, there is no one unique NLP model in DT. Rather, there are a finite number (a family, if you like) of NLPs. One can abstract the model generation process in DT as a finite state machine where each state represents a unique NLP. Transitions among states are governed by troubleshooting actions, which may (or may not) bring the 'machine' into a new state, where a different NLP model is valid. We leave the formalization of this issue as an exercise for the interested reader. Should you play with the idea, please pay attention to the definition of starting and accepting states.

8 Implementation

DT has been implemented in Prolog on an IBM AT with 512K of memory. To date, the system has been tested on more than 150 cases in Ex-Cell-O metallurgy Lab by various experts. After several iterations with the experts and some 'fine tuning', the system has reached a very good level of performance. During recent tests, the system was randomly presented with about 120 surface and feed creep grinding cases. Domain experts have agreed to about 93 percent of the system's recommendations.

Process design in DT takes about two minutes using an interpreted version of Prolog and a compiled version of the NLP package. Troubleshooting recommendations are given in about 0.5–3 seconds between recommendations, depending upon the nature of the actions which are being tested (i.e., whether process models are used to simulate the effects of taking a candidate action and the outcome of that simulation). Compilation is expected to increase the speed by an order of magnitude. DT's modular architecture can be used to construct troubleshooters for other types of machining operations such as turning, milling, etc.

References

1. Bobrow G.D. (editor), Qualitative Reasoning about Physical Systems, The MIT press, 1985.
2. Davis, R. Reasoning from First Principle in Electronic Troubleshooting. International Journal of Man-Machine Studies, Sept. 1983, 403–423.
3. DeKleer J. and Brown J.S., A Qualitative Physics Based on Confluences, Qualitative Reasoning about Physical Systems, edited by Bobrow, D.G., MIT Press, 1985.
4. DeKleer D.J. Reasoning About Multiple Faults, AAAI 1986 Proc., 132–139.

5. Dixon J.R., Artificial Intelligence and Design: A Mechanical Engineering View. AAAI 1986 Proc. 872–877.
6. Duda R.O., Konolige K, Reboh R., A Computer-Based Consultation for Mineral Exploration, Technical Report, SRI International, 1979.
7. Fink, P.K. Control and Integration of Diverse Knowledge in a Diagnostic Expert System. IJCAI 1985 Proc., 426–431.
8. Fishwick, P.A. Automating the Transition from Lumped Models to Base Models, AI and Simulation Conference, 1988.
9. Forbus K.D. Qualitative Process Theory. Qualitative Reasoning about Physical Systems. (edited by Bobrow D.G), MIT Press, 1985, 85–168.
10. Herrod R.A. and Rickel J. Knowledge Based Simulation of a Glass Annealing Process. An AI Application in the Glass Industry. Proc. AAAI 1986, 800–804.
11. Kilhoffer A.R. and Kemf K.G., Designing for Manufacturability in Riveted Joints, AAAI 1986 Proc., 820–824.
12. Koton, P.H. Empirical and Model-Based Reasoning in Expert Systems. IJCAI 1985 Proc., 297–299.
13. Kovach J.A. Thermally Induced Grinding Damage in Cast Equiaxed Nickel-Based Superalloys. Ph.D. Thesis. Mechanical Eng. Dept. Case Western Reserve University, May 1986.
14. Kumar G.S., A Predictive Monitoring Architecture for Expert Systems, A Phd. dissertation, Dept. of Computer Science, Case Western Reserve University, Cleveland, OH, June 1986.
15. Laffey T.J. and others, Real-Time Knowledge Based Systems, AI Magazine, Vol. 9, No. 1, Spring 1988, 27–45.
16. Malkin, S. Grinding of Metals, Theory and Application. Journal of Applied Metalworking, Jan. 1984, 95–109.
17. McDermott J., R1: A Rule-Based Configurer of Computer Systems, Artificial Intelligence, Sept. 1982.
18. Mittal S., Dym C.L. and Morjaria M.M., PRIDE: An Expert System for the Design of Paper Handling Systems, Computer, July 1986 102–113.
19. O'Reilly C.A. and Cromarty A.S., "Fast" is not "Real-time": Designing Effective Real Time Systems, SPIE vol. 548 Application of Artificial Intelligence Proc. April 1985, Arlington, VA, 249–257.
20. Pao, Yoh-Han. Some Views on Analytic and Artificial Intelligence Approaches. IEEE Workshop on Intelligent Control Proc., August, 1985.
21. Pau L.F., Survey of Expert Systems for Fault Detection, Test Generation and Maintenance. Experts Systems, April 1986, Vol. 3, No. 2, 100–111.
22. Rychener M.D., Farinacci M.L. and others, Integration of Multiple Knowledge Sources in ALADIN, An Alloy Design System, AAAI 1986 Proc. 878–881.
23. Shortliffe E.H., Computer-Based Medical Consultation: MYCIN, Elsevier, 1976.
24. Siemens, R.W., Golden M. and Ferguson J.C. StarPlan II: Evolution of an Expert System. AAAI 1986 Proc., 844–849.
25. Stroebel G.J., Baxter R.D. and Denney M.J., A Capability Planning Expert Systems for IBM System/38. IEEE Computer, July 1986, 42–50.
26. Thompson T.F. and Wojcik R.M., Meld: An Implementation of a Meta Level Architecture for Process Diagnosis. IEEE 1984.

CHAPTER 7

From CAD/CAM to Simulation: Automatic Model Generation for Mechanical Devices

Andrew Gelsey

Abstract

Constructing an abstract model of a physical system is an important step in an attempt to analyze the system and predict or understand its behavior, but the construction of these abstract models usually requires considerable human effort. This chapter discusses the problem of automating this model-generation process, at least for certain physical systems, and describes a working program to automatically generate a model for the simulation of a machine's behavior.

1 Introduction

Constructing an abstract model of a physical system is an important step in an attempt to analyze the system and predict or understand its behavior. Depending on its complexity, the model may be used to directly predict the behavior of the physical system or at least to simulate the behavior of the system during a certain time interval.

The construction of these abstract models requires considerable human effort. I will consider the problem of automating this model-generation process. The physical systems I will focus on are machines, and in this chapter all the machines discussed will be purely mechanical devices.

This chapter describes a program to automatically generate a model for the simulation of a machine's behavior. The input for this program is a standard CAD/CAM solid model of a machine supplemented with information about nongeometric physical properties such as masses, spring constants, and coefficients of friction. The model-generation program finds state variables to represent the behavior of the machine to be simulated, and supplies a routine for calculating time derivatives of these state variables so

This work was supported primarily by the NSF through grant IRI-8610241. Some earlier portions of the work were supported by ITT.

that the machine's behavior can be simulated using a standard numerical ODE solver.

Automatic model generation has three steps:

- kinematic analysis
- partitioning
- interaction analysis

Kinematics is the study of the motion of objects without considering the forces that cause the motion. Kinematic analysis determines what motions of a given mechanism are consistent with the constraints on motion imposed by the mechanism's geometric structure. Partitioning uses the kinematic analysis to partition the mechanism into subsystems each of which has a single kinematic degree of freedom. The generalized position of each kinematic subsystem is a state variable, as is its time derivative.

During interaction analysis, the motion envelope of each subsystem is computed. This is the subset of space which might at some time be occupied by the parts of the mechanism in the subsystem. These motion envelopes are then used to determine which of the kinematic subsystems might potentially interact with which other subsystems during the simulation. These interactions would occur if a part in one subsystem collided with or pushed a part in another subsystem.

2 Kinematic Analysis

Reuleaux [Reu76] defined a number of concepts which we shall find useful, such as the *kinematic pair*—a pair of parts which constrain each other's motion. For example, in Figure 1 the crankshaft is paired with the frame in such a way that its only possible motion relative to the frame is rotation about a single axis.

Typically a part will be a member of more than one kinematic pair, so that kinematic pairs will be linked into a *kinematic chain*, as is the case in Figure 1. Reuleaux classified kinematic pairs into two categories: *lower pairs* and *higher pairs*. Lower pairs are kinematic pairs in which contact between the two elements of the pair takes place continuously at all points on a surface of contact which therefore must have the same form in both objects. Examples of lower pairs include the revolute or turning pair, the prismatic or sliding pair, and the screw. Only a few lower pairs are geometrically possible. Higher pairs are kinematic pairs in which contact between the elements takes place along lines or points of contact rather than over a full surface. The most prevalent higher pairs are gears.

Lower pairs are examples of what Reuleaux calls *complete* kinematic pairs because no other parts are needed to keep the elements of the pair together. On the other hand, the higher pairs commonly used in machinery

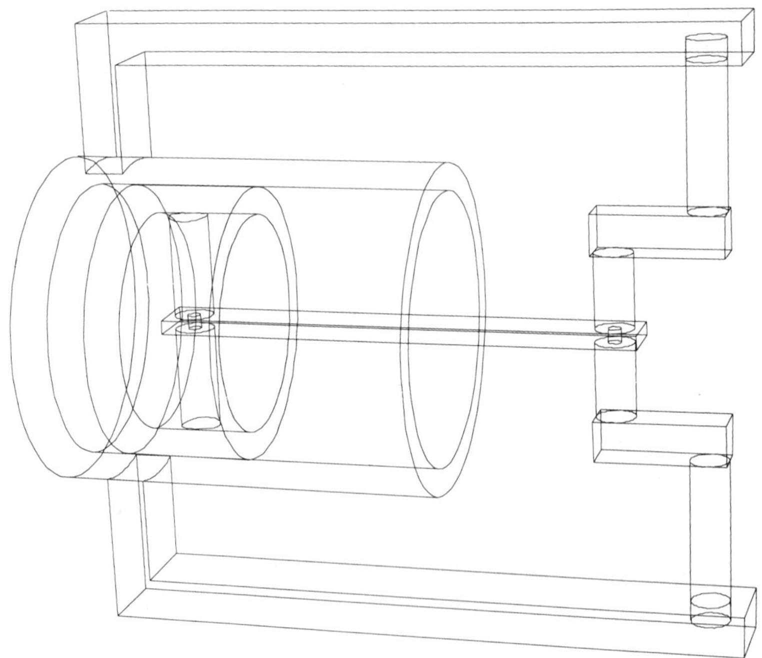

FIGURE 1. Piston and crankshaft mechanism.

are *incomplete* kinematic pairs because they only exist in the presence of other kinematic pairs. For example, two gears will only form a gear pair if they both form revolute pairs with another part, the frame on which they are mounted. It is theoretically possible to form higher pairs which are actually "degenerate lower pairs", and therefore are kinematically complete, though these don't usually occur in actual machines. In Figure 2 we see a "square peg in a round hole" which is effectively a revolute pair. However, degenerate lower pairs tend to be less useful than true lower pairs because they are harder to manufacture, wear less evenly, and are more difficult to lubricate properly.

2.1 Solid Modeling

Many CAD/CAM solid modeling systems use a representation known as Constructive Solid Geometry [Req80], which is the input representation that my program expects.* In the CSG representation, each part in a ma-

*The program makes use of the PADL-2 solid modeling system developed by the Production Automation Project at the University of Rochester.

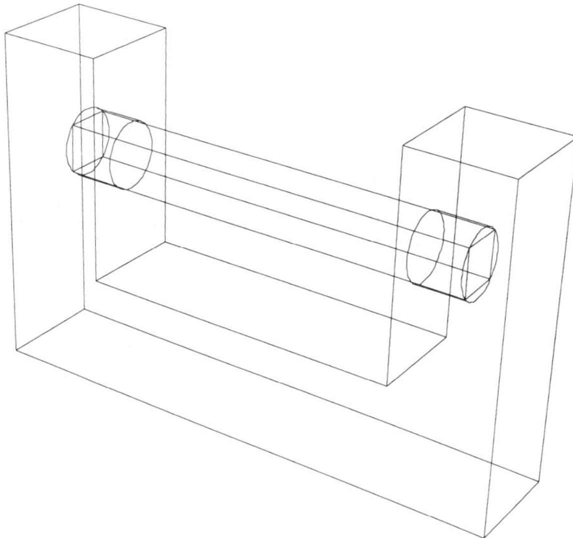

FIGURE 2. "Degenerate lower pair."

chine is represented as a closed subset of three-dimensional Euclidean space which is formed by applying the Boolean set operations of union, intersection, and difference to a small set of primitive solids. In PADL-2 the primitive solids are the block, cylinder, sphere, cone, and torus. For example, a square plate with a hole in it might be represented as the difference of block and a cylinder, where the block would be appropriately sized and positioned to represent the plate, and the cylinder would have the correct diameter and position so that the difference operation would create the desired hole in the plate. The actual representation is a binary tree whose internal nodes are set operations and rigid motions and whose leaves are primitive solids.

The CSG representation allows machine designs to be specified in a natural way, since most parts of typical machines can be specified quite simply. CSG is also convenient when symmetry is an important issue, as it is in the machine domain, because the possible symmetries of a part are easy to compute. The five CSG primitives mentioned earlier have clearly defined symmetries, and the symmetries of combined primitives may be calculated simply. For example, two solids with prismatic symmetry along parallel axes will combine to form an object with the same prismatic symmetry. The square plate with a hole in it described earlier is an example of such a combination. Both the block and the cylinder have prismatic symmetry along parallel axes and so does their combination.

2.2 Algorithms

The top-level kinematic analysis algorithm is:

- Identify lower pairs from the common symmetries of the elements of the pair
- Identify certain higher pairs
- Find constraints on positions and orientations of kinematic pairs
- Detect relationships between the motion of one pair and that of another due to relative geometric configurations of the pairs
- Compose these relationships to form new relationships

The output of this algorithm is a list of the kinematic pairs in the machine being analyzed, and a set of mutual restrictions on the positions of the pairs imposed by the kinematic structure of the mechanism. This output allows us to identify the true degrees of freedom of the mechanism. Later in the chapter when we discuss simulation, the state variables used in the simulation will be just the position-velocity pairs associated with each degree of freedom. For example, kinematic analysis shows that the mechanism in Figure 1 actually has only one degree of freedom, and therefore its state can be represented by just two state variables: a position and a velocity.

2.2.1 Lower Pairs

The kinematic analyzer finds the lower kinematic pairs of a mechanism with the following algorithm:

1. For each part in the mechanism, compute all its possible symmetries by taking the union of the symmetries of the primitive solids in the part.
2. For each pair of parts having a common symmetry, test the following requirements to see if the parts form a lower pair:
   - The primitive or set of primitives with the symmetry must be solid in one of the two parts and hollow (as a result of a difference operation) in the other. For example, in Figure 1 the CSG tree for the piston contains a solid cylinder which fits inside a hollow cylinder in the CSG tree for the frame and thus a cylindrical pair is formed.
   - The primitive or set of primitives in the two parts must be identical except for possible differences in length along the axis of symmetry, and must have the same spatial position except for a possible offset along the axis of symmetry. For example, in Figure 1 the piston and the cylindrical hole in the frame into which it fits both have the same cross section but differ in length, and their positions correspond except for a relative offset along the axis of symmetry.
   - The hollow space which forms one half of the pair must be surrounded by solid material. For example, in Figure 1 the piston and frame would

not form a lower pair if the cylindrical solid which was subtracted from the frame was not subtracted in an area where there were other solid primitives to make a hole in.

A lower pair found by this algorithm is represented as an *axis* and one or more *position variables.* For a revolute, screw, or cylindrical pair, the axis is just the axis of revolution while for a prismatic pair the axis is any line parallel to the direction of prismatic motion. For revolute and screw pairs, the value of the position variable for the pair is the number of degrees that the solid element of the pair has rotated relative to the hollow element of the pair. The zero position is the position in the initial CSG representation of the machine that was input to the program. For prismatic joints, the position is the number of distance units the solid element has moved relative to the hollow element. Cylindrical pairs have two position variables, one of each type.

2.2.2 Higher Pairs

The kinematic analyzer identifies common higher pairs which impose definite kinematic constraints on mechanisms containing them. Other higher pairs are dealt with by the simulator, which can analyze these in a very general way since the only knowledge used is the basic laws of physics. The escapement described later in the chapter is an example of such a higher pair.

The higher pairs that the kinematic analyzer is currently capable of recognizing are gears and cams. These are both incomplete kinematic pairs, so both parts in a gear or cam pair must form lower, generally revolute, pairs with a third part, normally the frame of the mechanism.

The teeth of a gear typically have a profile curve that is either a cycloid or an involute, which can't be formed directly from the simpler CSG primitives listed earlier. Gears are represented as cylinders marked with the property "gear". Gear pairs are identified by checking all pairs of gears to see if they are in contact.

Cam pairs are identified by a two-step procedure. First, parts which are elements of revolute pairs are examined to find subparts without the appropriate rotational symmetry, i.e. "suspicious bulges". The motion envelopes of these potential cams are then formed and checked to see if they intersect any part which is not known to be kinematically paired with the part containing the cam. (For example, the crankshaft in Figure 1 has suspicious bulges whose motion envelopes intersect the connecting rod, but the two parts form a revolute pair so they could not also have a cam relationship.) Typically a cam's motion envelope will intersect a part which is an element of a prismatic joint, which is then pushed when the cam is in the right position. The cam relationship may then be determined from the relative position of the cam and the prismatic pair it pushes.

2.2.3 Finding Constraints

The third step in the high level kinematic analysis algorithm is to find certain constraints on the relative and absolute positions and orientations of kinematic pairs. The constraints found at this stage of the kinematic analysis apply only to lower pairs, and are used primarily by the linkage analyzer as described in the next section to find motion relationships for linkages. These constraints are found as follows:

- For each lower pair which has the frame as one element, conclude that its axis will always have the same position.
- For each part which is an element of two different lower pairs such that in the original CSG tree the axes of those two pairs are parallel or perpendicular or a certain distance apart, conclude that this relation will hold regardless of what motions the mechanism makes, because the part is a rigid body.
- Form the transitive closure of the set of "permanently parallel axes" constraints. (For example, in Figure 1 the crankshaft/frame axis is parallel to the crankshaft/connecting rod axis and they will always stay parallel, and the crankshaft/connecting rod axis is parallel to the piston/connecting rod axis and they will always stay parallel, so therefore the crankshaft/frame axis will always stay parallel to the piston/connecting rod axis.)

2.2.4 Motion Relationships

The relationship between the position of the crankshaft/frame revolute pair and the position of the piston/frame revolute pair in the mechanism in Figure 1 is not a one-to-one function since any one position of the piston can correspond to two different positions of the crankshaft. A natural way to express this relationship is as a set of "monotonic segments" — subsets of the relationship in which both positions vary monotonically and where a precise function relating them can therefore be given. The output of the kinematic analyzer is a set of relationships between positions of kinematic pairs, expressed in terms of monotonic segments.

The fourth step of the kinematic analysis process is to find these relationships. Most of the elementary mechanisms found in typical machines are either gears, cams, or linkages [Suh1978]. They are formed from the kinematic pairs whose identification we have discussed above, and they impose the relationships we wish to find.

- The presence of a gear pair imposes a simple linear algebraic relationship on the revolute pairs which allow the gears to turn: the position of one of these revolute pairs is always be a constant multiple of the position of the other revolute pair. The coefficient is computed by comparing the diameters of the two gears.

- A cam pair imposes a relationship between the position of the revolute joint of the camshaft (i.e. the angle through which it has turned) and the position of the prismatic pair which the cam pushes. An approximation of this relationship which suffices for many purposes is a mapping taking one range of camshaft angles into the maximum displacement for the prismatic pair and the complementary range of angles into the minimum displacement.
- Transformations of frame of reference also yield relationships between the values of position variables. For example, if parts A and B form a revolute kinematic pair A:B, and parts B and C also form a revolute pair B:C which has the same axis as A:B, then the motion of C relative to A is just the sum of the motions of the pairs A:B and B:C. So if A and C also form a revolute pair then if we know the motions of any two of the three pairs we can find the motion of the remaining pair by addition or subtraction. An example of this technique appears later when we consider the kinematic analysis of the differential. Of course, this sort of transformation applies in an analogous way to prismatic pairs.
- The relationships imposed by linkages may often be found by simple reasoning about triangle geometry, since knowledge of trigonometry and triangle geometry may be applied not just to points but also to distances between sets of parallel axes. For example, in Figure 1, the three parallel axes discussed above may be projected onto a perpendicular plane, and the resulting points will form a triangle whose properties will impose additional constraints on the mechanism. This transformation is important in the analysis of linkages, because the majority are planar linkages whose revolute joints have mutually parallel axes.

2.2.5 Composition

The fifth and final step in doing the kinematic analysis is to compose the relationships found in order to form new relationships. The relationships between positions of kinematic pairs are expressed as one-to-one mathematical functions (which are split into monotonic segments if necessary). The composition of two one-to-one functions yields yet another one-to-one function. For example, if in Figure 1 a gear on the crankshaft were to drive a camshaft, then given the position of the camshaft we would know the position of the crankshaft, and given the position of the crankshaft we would know the position of the piston, so therefore by composing these two functions we would get a new function such that given the position of the camshaft we would know the position of the piston.

Thus, following classic tradition, we have reduced the problem of reasoning about geometric relations to the simpler problem of reasoning about algebraic relations. We can expect this technique of kinematic analysis to extend to complex machines with large numbers of parts, because we will use geometric reasoning to discover relationships between the motions of parts and their near neighbors, and since these relationships will be expressed as one-to-one mathematical functions we may compose them to an arbitrary extent, producing relationships between the motions of parts and far distant other parts.

2.3 Examples

2.3.1 Piston and Crankshaft Mechanism

The output from the program in analyzing the mechanism in Figure 1 appears in Figure 3. The first step of the analysis is to find lower pairs from local geometric properties using the algorithm discussed earlier. The program finds four cylindrical pairs and then uses local geometry to show three of the four are actually revolute pairs, by showing that prismatic motion of the pairs is blocked at each end. No higher pairs are found in the second step of the analysis.

The third step of the analysis looks for constraints on the interactions of the pairs. In Figure 3 the constraints applying to each pair are listed under the pair. After using transitivity to conclude that the crankshaft/frame axis will always stay parallel to the piston/connecting rod axis, as discussed above, the program uses this new constraint to conclude that the piston/frame pair is actually a prismatic pair rather than a cylindrical pair.

The fourth stage of the analysis applies basic triangle geometry to the triangle formed by the always parallel crankshaft/frame, crankshaft/connecting rod, and piston/connecting rod axes. The previous stage of analysis showed that two sides of the triangle had unchanging lengths. Therefore, if the position of the piston is known it determines the length of the third side of the triangle and thus by the side-side-side theorem uniquely determines the triangle and therefore the position of the crankshaft. Similarly, if the position of the crankshaft is known it determines an angle of the triangle and by the side-side-angle theorem (where the angle is by the shorter side) determines the triangle.

Therefore a strict relationship between the piston and crankshaft parameters has been shown to hold. The triangle inequality shows that the two extreme points of the piston's motion will occur at distances which are the sum and difference of the lengths of the other two sides of the triangle. When the extreme points are reached the three parallel axes are coplanar and their projections are colinear, at which point the triangle is no longer a triangle since one of its angles is 0 or 180 degrees. Since there are two ways to place a triangle in a plane if the positions of two of its points are fixed, there are two ways for the mechanism in Figure 1 to make the transition between its two extreme points, so the relation between the piston and crankshaft has two monotonic segments.

The precise function relating the positions of the piston and crankshaft in the two monotonic segments is a fairly complicated combination of trigonometric functions and their inverses. The above analysis gives us enough

```
Kinematic Pairs:
< LFRAME : LPISTON > (type = PRISMATIC) axis = [-3,0,0],[-4,0,0] ratio = 0
PERPENDICULAR to < LCONR : LPISTON >
PERPENDICULAR to < LFRAME : LCRS >
FIXED
< LFRAME : LCRS > (type = REVOLUTE) axis = [32,6,0],[32,7,0] ratio = 0
PARALLEL to < LCONR : LPISTON >
PARALLEL to < LCONR : LCRS >
DISTANCE to < LCONR : LCRS > = 7
PERPENDICULAR to < LFRAME : LPISTON >
FIXED
< LCONR : LPISTON > (type = REVOLUTE) axis = [-8,-0.5,0],[-8,0.5,0] ratio = 0
PARALLEL to < LFRAME : LCRS >
PARALLEL to < LCONR : LCRS >
DISTANCE to < LCONR : LCRS > = 33
PERPENDICULAR to < LFRAME : LPISTON >
< LCONR : LCRS > (type = REVOLUTE) axis = [25,-9,0],[25,-8,0] ratio = 0
PARALLEL to < LCONR : LPISTON >
DISTANCE to < LCONR : LPISTON > = 33
PARALLEL to < LFRAME : LCRS >
DISTANCE to < LFRAME : LCRS > = 7

Interrelationships:
Monotonic Segment
< LFRAME : LCRS > goes from    0 to  180
< LFRAME : LPISTON> goes from    0 to  -14
Monotonic Segment
< LFRAME : LCRS > goes from  180 to  360
< LFRAME : LPISTON> goes from  -14 to    0
```

FIGURE 3. Kinematic analysis of crank mechanism.

information about the triangle to find the exact function, but in many cases this is unnecessary, and what we really want is just the definition of the monotonic segments of the relationship in terms of their extreme points and the fact that the relationship *is* monotonic within the segment. For example, if we want to know the average turning speed of the crankshaft given a certain driving rate of the piston the precise form of the function is irrelevant as long as we know that when the piston goes back and forth once the crankshaft makes exactly one complete turn. Thus in Figure 3 the internal details of the functions in the monotonic segments are not specified.

Note that the result of the kinematic analysis process is a mathematical relationship between the position of the crankshaft and the position of the piston in the form of a mapping. This mapping is independent of what particular *motion* the crankshaft is subjected to, that is, from the parametrization of the crankshaft's position with respect to time. For example, if the crankshaft was turning at a constant speed, its position would be a linear function of time, and we could compose that function with the mapping our kinematic analysis gives us to get an expression for the piston's position as a function of time which would show that the piston was oscillating back and forth at a constant frequency.

2.3.2 Differential

Now let us consider the kinematic analysis of the differential in Figure 4. Note that in Figure 4 the gears are displayed as cylinders, due to a limitation in the CAD/CAM solid modeling program. Also note that the differential has only one pinion connecting the two half axles, rather than four as a real differential would. This simplification is irrelevant to the behavior of the program since the four pinions behave in an identical fashion, and the program would produce exactly the same analysis with four pinions as with one.

The output of the kinematic analyzer when working on the differential appears in Figure 5. The first two steps of the kinematic analysis process proceed by the standard methods described earlier and identify both the lower pairs and the higher pairs (which are all gears in this case). The constraints found in the third step of the analysis turn out to be irrelevant to the final analysis here, and the important work is done in the fourth and fifth steps. Note that the program determines that the pairs formed by the differential box and the two half axles are actually revolute pairs rather than cylindrical pairs since both the differential box and the two half axles form revolute pairs with the frame.

In the fourth step of the analysis, the local relationships are found. Each gear pair yields a simple linear relationship: the position of one revolute

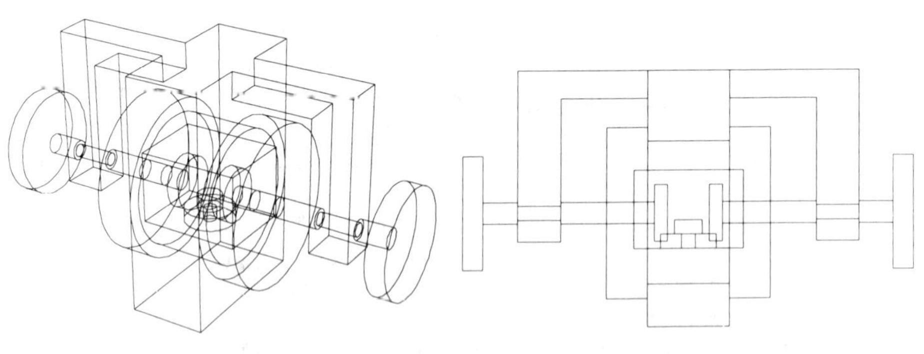

Perspective view Parallel view

FIGURE 4. Differential mechanism.

```
Kinematic Pairs:
< LFRAME : GEARR > (type = REVOLUTE) axis = [18.75,0,0],[19.75,0,0] ratio = 0
< LFRAME : GEARL > (type = REVOLUTE) axis = [18.75,0,0],[19.75,0,0] ratio = 0
< LFRAME : DBOX > (type = REVOLUTE) axis = [18.75,0,0],[19.75,0,0] ratio = 0
< GEARM : GEARR > (type = GEAR) axis = [0,0,0],[0,0,0] ratio = 1
< GEARM : GEARL > (type = GEAR) axis = [0,0,0],[0,0,0] ratio = 1
< GEARM : DBOX > (type = REVOLUTE) axis = [0,-1,0],[0,-2,0] ratio = 0
< DBOX : GEARR > (type = REVOLUTE) axis = [-12,0,0],[-11,0,0] ratio = 0
< DBOX : GEARL > (type = REVOLUTE) axis = [-12,0,0],[-11,0,0] ratio = 0

Interrelationships:
Monotonic Segment
< DBOX   : GEARL > = -1 * < DBOX   : GEARR >
Monotonic Segment
< LFRAME : GEARR > =  1 * < GEARM  : DBOX  > +  1 * < LFRAME : DBOX  >
Monotonic Segment
< LFRAME : GEARL > = -1 * < GEARM  : DBOX  > +  1 * < LFRAME : DBOX  >
Monotonic Segment
< LFRAME : GEARL > =  1 * < DBOX   : GEARL > +  1 * < LFRAME : DBOX  >
Monotonic Segment
< LFRAME : GEARR > =  1 * < DBOX   : GEARR > +  1 * < LFRAME : DBOX  >
Monotonic Segment
< GEARM  : DBOX  > = -1 * < DBOX   : GEARL >
Monotonic Segment
< GEARM  : DBOX  > =  1 * < DBOX   : GEARR >
```

FIGURE 5. Kinematic analysis of the differential (edited).

joint is always a constant multiple of the position of another revolute joint, with the constant factor being the gear ratio. Frame-of-reference transformations also yield linear relationships: for example, the angular displacement of the right gear relative to the frame is simply the sum of its displacement relative to the gear box plus the displacement of the gear box relative to the frame.

The relationships we are really interested in are generated in the fifth and final step of the kinematic analysis. Since the relationships found in the fourth step are of the simplest possible kind — just linear mappings — composing them into new relationships (which are also linear mappings) is straightforward. In Figure 5, four of the interrelationships listed are found in the fourth step of the analysis from local geometry, and the other three are generated in the fifth step by composing relationships found in the fourth step. The differential mechanism has two degrees of freedom, unlike most common mechanisms which have only one degree of freedom [Hunt59], but since our analysis works by simply composing mathematical functions it works perfectly well in this case.

The second and third interrelationships in Figure 5 are the ones that make this mechanism a differential. Consider a vehicle like an automobile. If the axle which is driven by the engine was a single rigid assembly, then when the vehicle turned, the wheels on this axle would slip since they would have different turning radii and therefore could not travel at the same speed during a turn without slipping. On the other hand, suppose the axle was not rigid but instead had a differential in the middle, and the force of the engine was used to turn the differential box. Then according to the kinematic analysis in Figure 5, the speed of the right wheel would be the speed of the differential box plus the speed of the differential pinion, and the speed of the left wheel would be the speed of the differential box minus the speed of the differential pinion. The speed of the pinion is not kinematically constrained, so the frictional force of the road on the wheels would cause the pinion to move at just the right speed to prevent slipping, since any slipping would cause an unbalanced force which would accelerate the pinion until it reached a speed at which the slipping vanished.

3 Partitioning

I will now describe the algorithm used to partition the mechanism into subsystems each of which has a single kinematic degree of freedom.

1. Let RLIST be a list of relationships between the position variables of kinematic pairs found in kinematic analysis. Let PLIST be a list of partitions, where each partition is a set of kinematic pairs. PLIST is initially empty.
2. Do until RLIST is empty:
   - (a) Initialize PARTITION to be the set of kinematic pairs referred to by the first relationship in RLIST. Delete the first relationship in RLIST.
   - (b) Do until PARTITION does not change:
     - i. For each relationship R in RLIST:
       - A. If the intersection of PARTITION with the set of kinematic pairs referred to by R is not empty, set PARTITION to the union of PARTITION with the set of kinematic pairs referred to by R, and delete R from RLIST.
     - ii. Add PARTITION to PLIST.
   - (c) For each known kinematic pair K:
     - i. If K is not a member of any partition in PLIST, create a new partition containing only K and add the new partition to PLIST.

The resulting PLIST is a list of the kinematic subsystems of the machine. Each subsystem is a set of kinematic pairs having a total of one degree of freedom between them. The mechanism in Figure 1 has only one kinematic subsystem — the entire mechanism has only one degree of freedom. The escapement mechanism whose simulation will be discussed later in the chapter has three kinematic subsystems, each consisting of just one kinematic pair. Each subsystem contributes two state variables for simulation: its position and its velocity.

4 Interaction Analysis

Interaction analysis determines which of the kinematic subsystems might potentially interact with each other during the simulation. This preprocessing is primarily an optimization, not an essential part of the model-generation process.

The first step of interaction analysis is to compute the motion envelope of each subsystem: the subset of space which might at some time be occupied by the parts of the mechanism in the subsystem. My current algorithm computes motion envelopes only for fixed-axis mechanisms, in which the axis of every kinematic pairs is fixed relative to the frame. The escapement we will discuss later is a fixed-axis mechanism.

Each kinematic subsystem of fixed-axis mechanism has one moving part. The CSG representation of this part is a binary tree whose internal nodes are set operations and rigid motions and whose leaves are primitive solids. The CSG representation of the motion envelope of the part is a tree with the same internal nodes, but with each leaf replaced by a sub-tree which is the motion envelope of the primitive solid that was in the leaf.

It is not always possible to precisely represent the motion envelope of a CSG primitive solid in CSG. However, for our purposes, it is acceptable to represent a motion envelope by a "bigger" solid, a solid which includes the true motion envelope as a subset. But the more accurately the motion envelope is represented, the more successfully the interaction analysis preprocessing will optimize the simulation.

If the axis of motion is parallel or perpendicular to an axis of symmetry of the primitive solid, then the exact motion envelope usually has a simple CSG representation. For example, if a cylinder is rotated around an axis parallel or perpendicular to its axis of symmetry, or a block is rotated around an axis parallel to one of its edges, the exact motion envelope will be the difference of two cylinders whose axis of rotation is the axis of the motion.

If the axis of motion is not parallel or perpendicular to an axis of symmetry of the primitive solid, then the motion envelope generally can't be represented precisely with CSG. This case can be dealt with in a general though not optimal way by computing the motion envelope of a more tractable primitive solid which encloses the real one.

Interaction analysis is used first to determine which kinematic subsystems in a machine can interact, and then to find out exactly which primitive solids in the subsystems could interact. This analysis reduces the amount of time-consuming geometrical computation that the time-derivative subroutine has to do for every simulation step.

After the potentially interacting subsystems and primitives have been found, we do any computations needed by the time-derivative subroutine that only have to be done once. For each potentially interacting primitive, we compute the functions of the position of the kinematic subsystem which give the ratio of the linear and angular velocities of the primitive to the velocity of the kinematic subsystem. These functions will always be independent of velocity. They may in general depend on position but for fixed-axis mechanisms they are constant.

5 Simulation

The simulation* of the machine's behavior is the numerical solution of a set of ordinary differential equations of the form

$$\frac{ds_i}{dt} = g_i(\mathbf{s}, t) \tag{1}$$

where the s_i are state variables and the g_i are their time derivatives. We will not in general be able to write an explicit formula for the derivative function $g_i(\mathbf{s}, t)$, but for a numerical solution all that is needed is an algorithm for computing the value of the function at any point.

So far, we have discussed how to identify mechanical state variables, positions and velocities of mechanical components of a machine. A machine might also have other state variables associated with, for example, its thermodynamic or electromagnetic properties. In this chapter we will limit the discussion to purely mechanical devices, so a model based on mechanical state variables will be sufficient for simulation.

I use the subroutine RKF45 [SWD76] to generate the numerical solution to the differential equations describing the machine being simulated. It is likely that any of a number of other numerical ODE solvers could be used instead. The ODE solver then calls a subroutine I supply to compute values of the time-derivative functions $g_i(\mathbf{s}, t)$.

*The simulation method described in this chapter should not be confused by readers of both papers with the considerably different method described in [GM88].

5.1 Time Derivative

My current simulator implementation is restricted to mechanisms like the escapement mechanism displayed in Figure 8 in which each kinematic subsystem has only one moving part. Consider a mechanism consisting of n kinematic subsystems. Let x_i be the position variable associated with the ith kinematic subsystem, and let v_i be the time derivative of x_i. The state of the machine at any time is specified completely by the values of the $2n$ state variables x_i and v_i, and the way the state changes is described by $2n$ differential equations of the form of Equation 1. To solve these equations numerically requires algorithms to compute the time derivatives of the state variables. For the x_i this computation is trivial since

$$\dot{x}_i = \frac{dx_i}{dt} = v_i \tag{2}$$

For the v_i

$$\dot{v}_i = \frac{dv_i}{dt} = \frac{f_i}{I_i} \tag{3}$$

In this equation I_i is the *inertia* of the moving part. If the moving part forms a prismatic pair with the frame, then the inertia is just its mass, and if it forms a revolute pair with the frame then the inertia is the moment of inertia of the moving part about the axis of the revolute pair. For a prismatic pair, f_i, the *force* on the moving part, is just the net force in the traditional sense, while for a revolute pair it is the net torque.

In my current implementation, contributions to the total force on a subsystem come from three sources: springs, friction, and contact forces. Springs are attached between the two elements of a kinematic subsystem, and the spring force is a linear function of the position state variable. Friction occurs between the two elements of a kinematic subsystem, and the frictional force is a linear function of the velocity state variable. I use a model of contact forces which greatly simplifies the physics involved but is still quite useful. Bodies are modeled as being rigid, but their volumes are allowed to overlap in space, and this overlap gives rise to a force. If o is the depth of overlap, the magnitude l of the force is defined by

$$l = \begin{cases} Eo + D\dot{o}Mo & \text{if } o \geq 0 \text{ and } E + DM\dot{o} \geq 0 \\ 0 & \text{otherwise} \end{cases}$$

The contact force is basically being modeled as a linear spring with linear damping, where E is the spring constant and D is the damping coefficient. The additional factor Mo in the second term on the right is there to make the force function continuous. The direction of the force is taken to be that of the surface normal at the point of contact.

The total force f_i on subsystem i is

$$f_i = -k_i x_i - h_i v_i - \sum_{k \in \text{contacts}} \alpha_{ik} l_k \tag{5}$$

where k_i is the spring constant of the spring, if any, attached to subsystem i, h_i is the coefficient of linear friction of subsystem i, l_k is the contact force described above between the two parts in contact at contact k, and α_{ik} is the geometric force multiplier taking the contact force l_k into a force on subsystem i. (α_{ik} is zero if subsystem i is not involved in contact k.)

A contact force contributes to $\dot{v}_i$ for two different subsystems. l will be the same for both subsystems since the force acts equally though in opposite directions on each of them, but the factors α will be different.

The equations above are incorporated into the algorithm shown in Figure 6 which is used by the time-derivative subroutine which RKF45 calls during each simulation step.

5.2 Overlap

Each time the time-derivative function is called, it must determine which potentially interacting primitive solids are currently overlapping. For each overlap, it must compute the depth of overlap, the point of overlap, and the local surface normal. This information is then used to compute the magnitude and direction of the contact force and the resulting $\dot{v}_i$.

Overlap computation is a large computational geometry problem, and I have only implemented part of the solution so far. Machines with internal collisions and/or pushing outside of standard kinematic pairs are not common, so a complete overlap computation algorithm may not be necessary.

For each kinematic subsystem i
  Set $\dot{x}_i = v_i$ and $\dot{v}_i = (-k_i x_i - h_i v_i)/I_i$
For each potentially interacting subsystem (identified by interaction analysis)
  For each pair of potentially interacting primitive solids
    If the overlap routine (described below) determines that their volumes
        overlap in space
      Let o be the depth of overlap
        $\mathbf{n}$ be the normal vector at the point of contact
      For each of the two interacting kinematic subsystems i
        Let $\hat{\mathbf{a}}_i$ be a unit vector along the axis of the kinematic pair
        If subsystem i is a prismatic pair
          then set $\alpha_i = \mathbf{n} \cdot \hat{\mathbf{a}}_i$
        Else
            Let $\mathbf{r}_i$ be the radius vector from the axis to the point of contact
            Set $\alpha_i = \mathbf{r}_i \times \mathbf{n} \cdot \hat{\mathbf{a}}_i$
        If $\mathbf{n}$ points away from subsystem i, then negate α_i
      Let $\dot{o} = \alpha_1 v_1 + \alpha_2 v_2$
        $l = Eo + D\dot{o}Mo$
      For each of the two interacting kinematic subsystems i
        Subtract $\alpha_i l / I_i$ from $\dot{v}_i$

FIGURE 6. Algorithm to compute time derivatives of state variables.

My current overlap computation algorithms work on primitive solids which have been subjected to arbitrary translations as well as rotations around a single axis, which we will call the z-axis. Generalizing the algorithms to allow arbitrary rotations should be feasible but has not yet been done. Overlap computations are currently limited to interactions between blocks and other blocks or cylinders.

The time-derivative routine calls the overlap routine for each pair of potentially interacting primitive solids. The overlap routine then projects the solids on the z-axis and checks for overlap. If there is z-axis overlap, then the solids are projected on the x-y plane and the appropriate two-dimensional routine is called. Note: in the following descriptions of the two-dimensional routines, the term "corner" refers to the corner of a block in the x-y plane projection, which is the image under projection of a line segment parallel to the z-axis in the original solid.

5.2.1 Block-Block

The block-block overlap routine looks for a face of one of the blocks which separates one corner of the other block from its other three corners, with the one corner being inside the first block and the other three corners being outside. See Figure 7a. If such a face can be found, then the depth of overlap is the distance of the one corner from the face, and the normal direction (i.e. direction of the contact force) is perpendicular to the face.

Alternatively, if one of the blocks has a face which is in a plane such that one block is entirely on one side of the plane and the other block is entirely on the other side, then the blocks do not overlap. See Figure 7b.

Otherwise the blocks do overlap, but more deeply than physically plausible. See Figure 7c. This case tends to come up when the ODE solver is adjusting its step size, and the overlap detector should return information which is a reasonable extrapolation of the results in the physically plausible range. Currently the "normal" direction returned is along the line between the centers of the containing spheres of the primitives, and the depth of overlap returned is the overlap of the containing spheres.

5.2.2 Block-Cylinder

A cylinder may contain a corner of a block, as in Figure 7d, or an edge of a block, as in Figure 7e. For a physically plausible overlap, neither solid should contain the center of the other, as in Figure 7g.

If the cylinder contains a corner of the block, as in Figure 7d, then the depth of overlap is the distance from the corner of the block to the nearest corner on the surface of the cylinder, and the normal direction is perpendicular to the surface of the cylinder.

If the cylinder contains an edge of the block, as in Figure 7e, then the depth of overlap is the distance from the edge of the block to the most

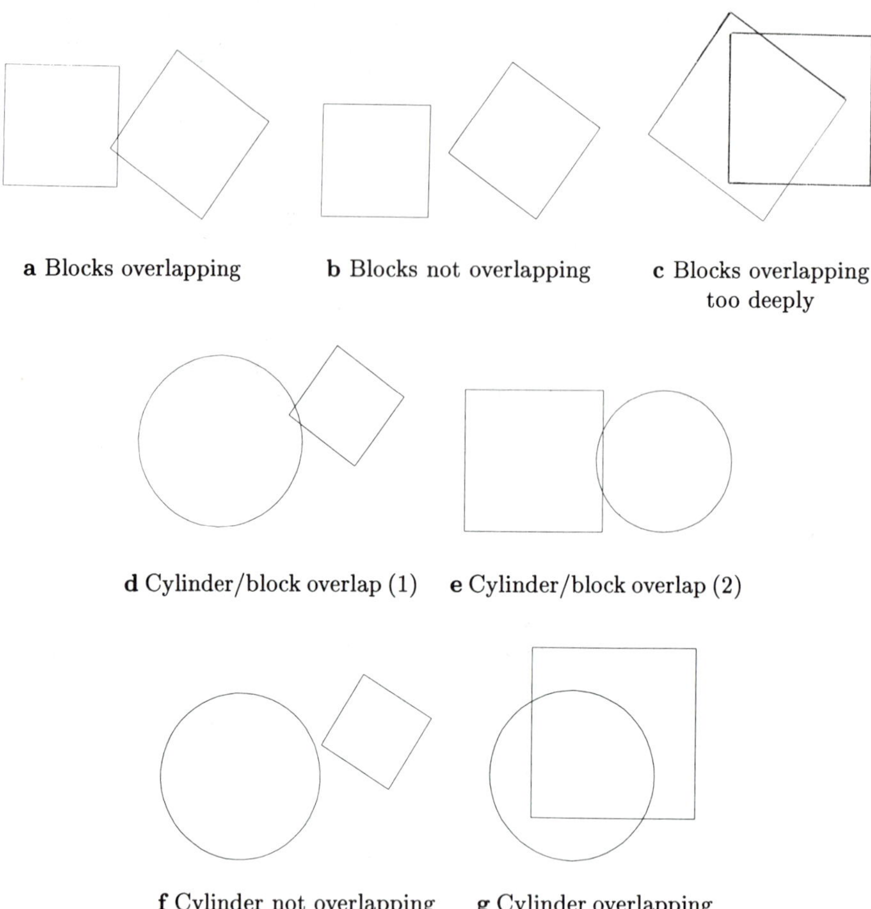

FIGURE 7. Cases with which the overlap detector must deal.

deeply embedded corner on the surface of the cylinder, and the normal direction is perpendicular to the edge of the block.

If one solid contains the center of the other, as in Figure 7g, then the solids do overlap, but more deeply than physically plausible. The depth of overlap returned is the minimum distance that one of the solids would have to move so that they would no longer overlap. The "normal" is along the line between the centers.

Otherwise the solids do not overlap. See Figure 7f.

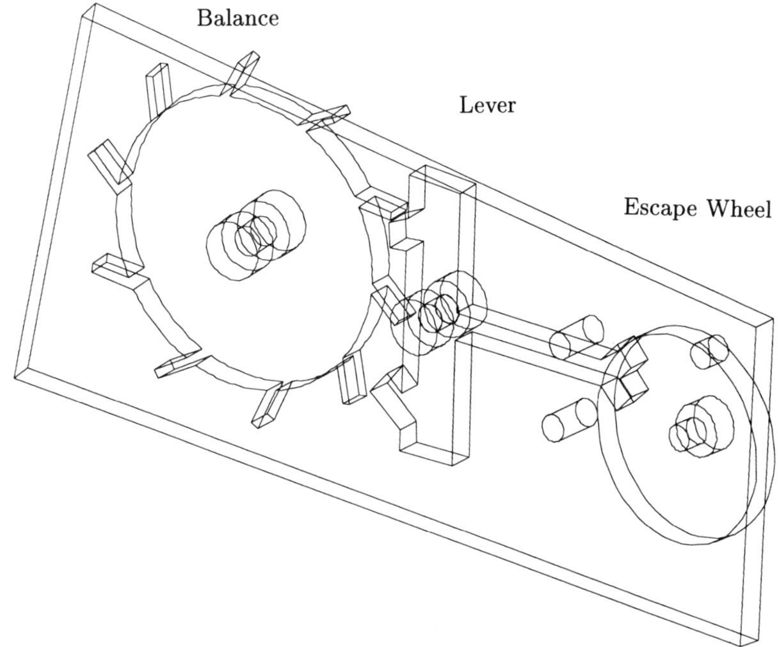

FIGURE 8. Clock or watch escapement mechanism.

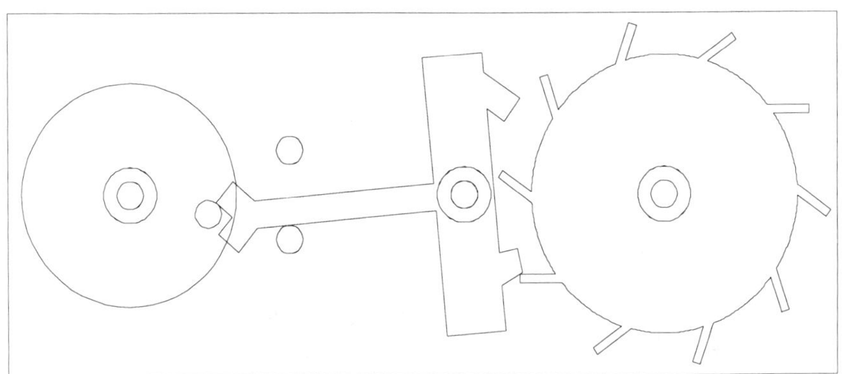

FIGURE 9. Balance collides with lever.

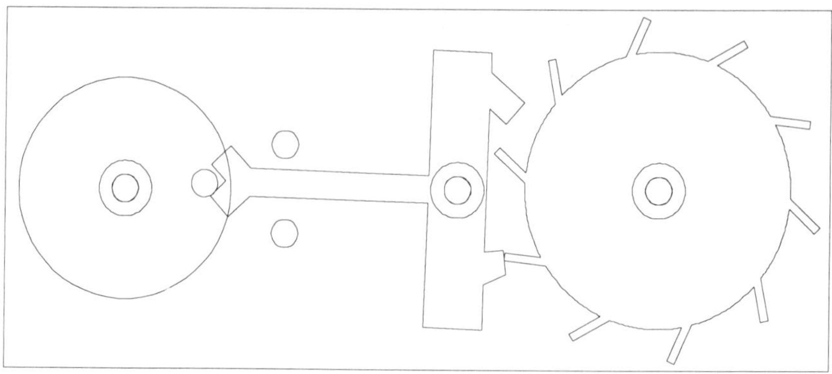

FIGURE 10. Escape wheel pushes lever and balance.

6 An Example

I will now discuss the simulation of the clock or watch escapement displayed in Figures 8 through 11. This mechanism forces the mainspring of the watch to unwind at a constant speed by allowing the escape wheel to advance by only one tooth for each swing of the balance, which is a harmonic oscillator. [Cus52] The cycle begins in Figure 8 with the motion of the escape wheel, which is attached to the mainspring, blocked by the lever, and the balance motionless at the top of its swing about to start moving towards the lever. In Figure 9 the balance has swung down to hit the lever. The momentum of the balance pushes the lever far enough to free the escape wheel, which then pushes both lever and balance as in Figure 10. Finally, in Figure 11, escape wheel and lever are once again locked, and the balance is at the top of its swing on the opposite side.

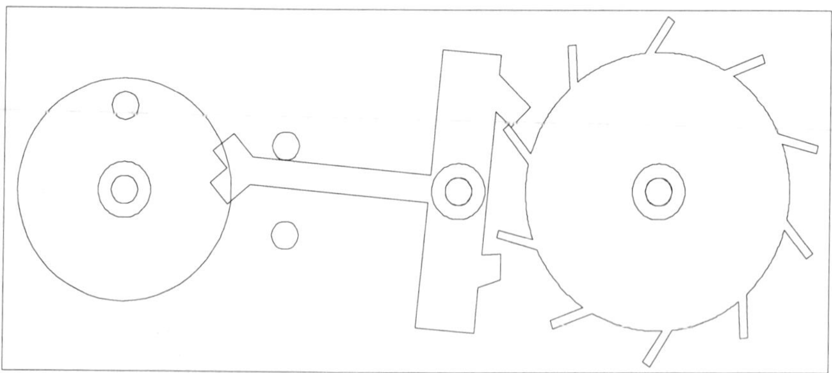

FIGURE 11. Halfway through a full cycle.

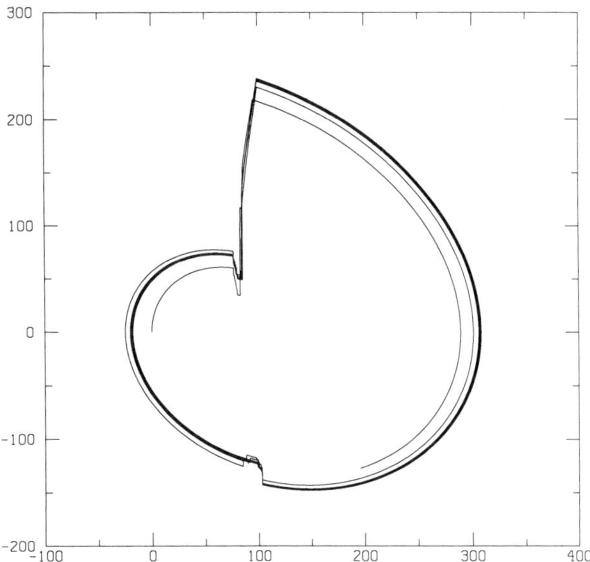

FIGURE 12. Balance phase space path.

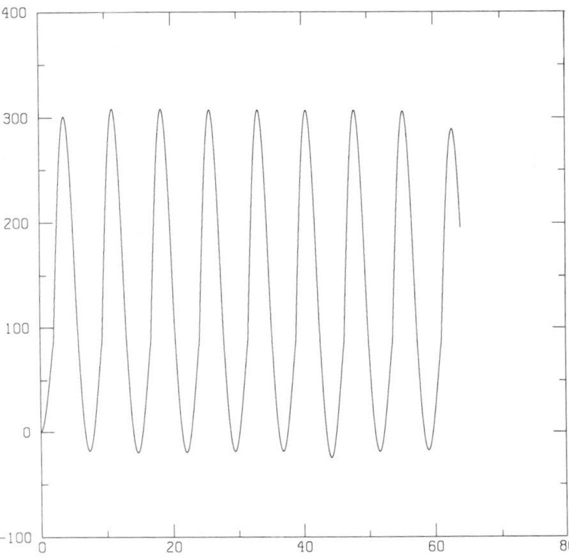

FIGURE 13. Balance position as a function of time.

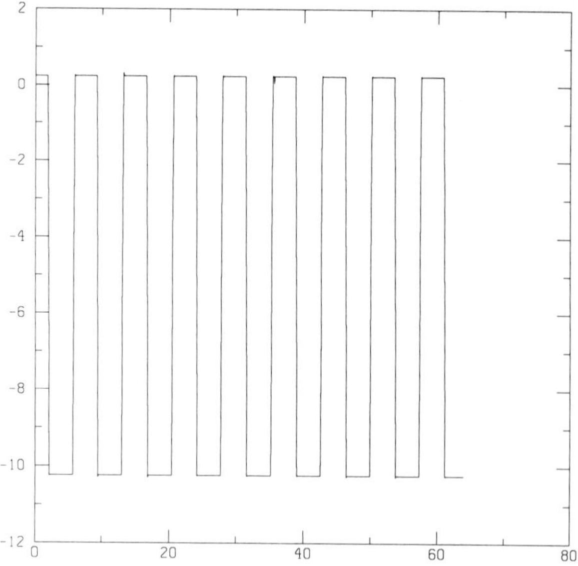

FIGURE 14. Lever position as a function of time.

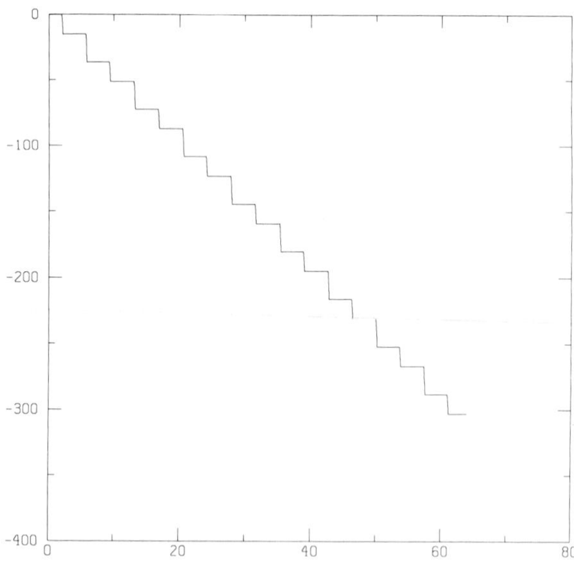

FIGURE 15. Escape wheel position as a function of time.

My model-generation/simulation program successfully simulates the behavior of this mechanism. The kinematic analyzer identifies three kinematic pairs, all revolute. No relationships between the position variables are found. Partitioning identifies three kinematic subsystems, each containing one kinematic pair. Therefore the machine has six state variables. Interaction analysis identifies three potential interactions: balance with lever, lever with escape wheel, lever with frame. It also identifies the primitive solids that might take part in the interactions.

The program repeatedly calls RKF45 to step the simulation forward in time until some desired time is reached. The inertia of each kinematic subsystem is just the moment of inertia of the single moving part in the subsystem about its axis of rotation. These inertias are all constant. The balance and escape wheel have springs attached whose spring constants are specified in the input data for the program, as are the coefficients of friction of each subsystem. The force between two kinematic subsystems in contact is calculated using the algorithm shown in Figure 6.

Figure 12 shows graphically a two-dimensional projection of the simulated path of the escapement in its six-dimensional phase space. Figures 13 through 14 show the behavior of the three kinematic subsystems as a function of time. The position of the three moving parts are measured in degrees. This simulation ran for 20 hours on a Vaxstation II.

7 Related Work

The kinematic analyzer was described previously in [Gel87]. An earlier approach to kinematic analysis was the work of Stanfill [Sta83] which is limited to simple machines consisting solely of a very small number of cylindrical parts. More recently considerable work has been done on the kinematic analysis of mechanisms by the computation of various properties of their configuration spaces. See [Fal87], and [Jos88]. Currently this work is limited to the analysis of fixed-axis mechanisms, so it could not deal with a machine like the one in Figure 1. At present, the methods for analyzing configuration space have not been successfully applied to configuration spaces with more than a small number of dimensions.

The above research was all done by researchers in artificial intelligence. For surveys of programs written by mechanical engineers to deal with various aspects of kinematic and/or dynamical analysis of mechanical systems, see [FR83] and [Hau84].

8 Conclusion and Future Work

I have presented a method for automatically generating models for simulation of machine behavior from CAD/CAM representations of the physical structure of a machine. This method has been implemented in a working program. The program was successfully used to generate a model for the simulation of the escapement mechanism of a clock or watch.

At least two directions for future research in automatic model generation seem worthwhile. The first is to extend the spectrum of machines that can be analyzed by dealing with branches of physics other than mechanics. The other research direction is test the physical models more deeply by trying to match the behavior of actual machines run in a laboratory. In the long run this sort of verification is essential to validate the simulations generated.

References

[Cus52] T.P. Camerer Cuss. *The Story of Watches.* MacGibbon & Kee Ltd., London, 1952.

[Fal87] Boi Faltings. *Qualitative Place Vocabularies For Mechanisms in Configuration Space.* PhD thesis, Dept. of Computer Science, University of Illinois at Urbana-Champaign, July, 1987.

[FR83] B. Fallahi and K.M. Ragsdell. A compact approach to planar kinematic analysis, *Transactions of the ASME Journal of Mechanisms, Transmissions, and Automation in Design*, 105:434–440, 1983.

[Gel87] Andrew Gelsey. Automated reasoning about machine geometry and kinematics. In *Proceedings of the Third IEEE Conference on Artificial Intelligence Applications*, Orlando, Florida, 1987.

[GM88] Andrew Gelsey and Drew McDermott. Spatial reasoning about mechanisms. Computer Science Department Research Report, YALEU/DCS/RR-641, Yale University, August 1988. To appear in *Advances in Spatial Reasoning*, edited by Su-shing Chen, Ablex.

[Hau84] Edward J. Haug. A survey of dynamics software. In Edward J. Haug, editor, *Computer Aided Analysis and Optimization of Mechanical System Dynamics*, pages 24–31. Springer-Verlag, Berlin, 1984.

[Hun59] Kenneth H. Hunt. *Mechanisms and Motion.* John Wiley & Sons, New York, 1959.

[Jos88] Leo Joskowicz. *Reasoning about Shape and Kinematic Function in Mechanical Devices*, PhD thesis, New York University Dept. of Computer Science, September 1988.

[Req80] Aristides A.G. Requicha, Representations for rigid solids: Theory, methods, and systems, *ACM Computing Surveys*, 12:437–464, 1980.

[Reu76] Franz Reuleaux. *The Kinematics of Machinery.* Macmillan and Co., London, 1876.

[SR78] Chung Ha Suh and Charles W. Radcliffe. *Kinematics and Mechanisms Design.* John Wiley & Sons, New York,1978.

[Sta83] Craig Stanfill. *Form and Function: The Representation of Machines.* PhD thesis, Dept. of Computer Science, University of Maryland, November, 1983.

[SWD76] L.F. Shampine and H.A. Watts and S. Davenport. Solving non-stiff ordinary differential equations—the state of the art. *Siam Review*, 18:376–411, July 1976.

Part II

Application

CHAPTER 8

Knowledge-Based Simulation at the RAND Corporation

Jeff Rothenberg

Abstract

Despite its ubiquity, current discrete-state simulation technology is sharply limited in its power, applicability, and credibility. Simulation models are typically limited to answering questions of the form *"What if... ?"* and cannot answer other kinds of questions of at least equal value. The lack of explicit knowledge in most simulations makes it difficult to verify the correctness of their underlying models and makes them hard to comprehend. Recent advances in object-oriented simulation languages, rule-oriented approaches, logic programming, automated inferencing, and interactive graphics are facilitating a new generation of "knowledge-based" simulation environments. The synergy of these techniques promises to revolutionize simulation, transforming it into something far more powerful, more useful and more believable. This chapter describes this emerging technology in the context of the Knowledge-Based Simulation project at the RAND Corporation, which has pursued research in a number of related areas, including reasoning in simulation, representing multiple relationships among simulated entities, highly interactive interfaces, sensitivity analysis, varying the level of aggregation of a model, and the modeling of "soft" concepts (such as *initiative*).

1 Overview

Discrete-state simulation is a modeling technique that is widely used for analyzing domains involving complex temporal phenomena whose interactions defy complete mathematical analysis, such as policymaking,

The research described herein is sponsored by the Defense Advanced Research Projects Agency (DARPA) under RAND's National Defense Research Institute, a Federally Funded Research and Development Center, under contract No. MDA903-90-C-0004. Views and conclusions presented here are those of the author and should not be interpreted as representing the official opinion of the RAND Corporation, DARPA, the U.S. Government, or any person or agency connected with them.

manufacturing, computer system design, and military analysis. Yet despite its ubiquity, current simulation technology is sharply limited in its power, applicability, and credibility. Simulation models typically consist of descriptions of real-world entities and "first-order" interactions among these entities; running the simulation often reveals higher level interactions and effects that were not known in advance, answering questions of the form *"What if... ?"*. This traditional approach to simulation is severely limited in its ability to answer other kinds of questions of at least equal value and in its ability to represent models in ways that are comprehensible to model builders and users.

The lack of explicit knowledge in most simulations makes it difficult to verify the correctness of their underlying models and makes them hard to comprehend. Recent advances in object-oriented simulation languages, rule-oriented approaches, logic programming, automated inferencing, and interactive graphics are facilitating a new generation of "knowledge-based" simulation environments. The synergy of these techniques promises to revolutionize simulation, transforming it into something far more powerful, more useful and more believable.

The Knowledge-Based Simulation project at RAND ("KBSim") has been engaged in research in this area for several years, focusing on:

- Reasoning in simulation
- Representing multiple relationships among simulated entities
- Highly interactive interfaces
- Sensitivity analysis
- Varying the level of aggregation of a model
- Modeling "soft" concepts (such as initiative)

This chapter describes some of the highlights of this research.

2 Background

Modeling in its broadest sense is *the cost-effective use of something in place of something else for some purpose.* Every model refers to some real-world entity (its "referent") of which it is a model; it has some purpose with respect to this referent, and it must be more cost-effective (in some relevant coin) to use the model for this purpose than to use the referent itself [60, 61]. Modeling thereby makes it possible to study phenomena that are too difficult, too dangerous, or impossible to observe directly.

One of the most common complaints among military analysts is the incomprehensibility of the models available to them. The quest for detail, the hunger for performance (to provide this detail), and the "fetish of realism" [2] conspire to create huge models, whose correctness as programs—let alone their validity—can only be taken on faith. Incomprehensibility leads to two related problems. The first is a software engineering problem: An incomprehensible program is unlikely to be *correct*, as well as being difficult to modify or maintain. The second is a modeling problem: An incomprehensible model is unlikely to be *valid*. Both the model and the program that implements it must be comprehensible in order to have any confidence that the program correctly implements a valid model.

Despite confusion in the literature about what simulation means and how it relates to modeling as a whole [31, 37, 58, 33], there is general agreement that it involves some kind of behavioral analog of the system being modeled [17, 27]. That is, simulation is concerned with modeling the unfolding of events or processes over time. It is useful to think of simulation as a *way of using* a model, i.e., the process of using a model to trace and understand the temporal behavior of its referent.

Unfortunately, simulation is often construed in its most limited sense: as the process of building a behavioral model, starting it in some initial configuration, and "running" it to see what happens. This "toy duck" view of simulation ("wind it up and see where it goes") corresponds to asking questions of the form *"What if... ?"*. While this may distinguish simulation from other kinds of modeling, it is only one of the ways that simulation can be used. Traditional simulations are generally incapable of explaining *why* a given sequence of events occurred, nor can they answer definitive questions (such as *"can this event ever happen?"*) or goal-directed questions (such as *"which events might lead to this event?"*). Answering questions like these requires the ability to perform inferencing that goes beyond *"What if... ?"*. Freeing simulation from the traditional "toy duck" view yields a powerful new approach to modeling, with vast, untapped potential.

RAND's long history of simulation research has included the development of the SIMSCRIPT language [38] and many theoretical and experimental results in game theory, Monte Carlo simulation, and military wargaming [15, 35, 29, 64, 72, 21]. A standard text on policy analysis notes that "The Rand Corporation has been the site of more important methodological work on modeling of various kinds than any other institution in the United States" [31]. Similarly, the work of Newell, Shaw and Simon at RAND in the 1950s [53, 40] was one of AI's earliest results and defined many continuing focal points for AI research. More recently, RAND's work in expert systems has produced the languages RITA [1, 3] and ROSIE [65, 36] as well as a number of expert system applications (such as LDS [74], TATR [10] and SAL [56]). Finally, RAND's research in interactive graphics has produced the RAND tablet [18], the GRAIL system [24], and fundamental ideas on the use of interactive map displays [2].

RAND began applying AI and graphics to simulation in the late 1970s and early 1980s. The development of the object-oriented ROSS language [46, 47, 48] and its use in the simulations SWIRL [41] and TWIRL [42] (as well as derivative work elsewhere [54, 32]) demonstrated the potential benefits for simulation technology. Subsequent research at

RAND has explored such areas as cooperative intelligent systems [66] and tutoring tools for simulations [49].

Object-oriented simulation as implemented in ROSS provides a rich, lucid modeling paradigm whose strength lies in its ability to represent objects and their behaviors and interactions in a cogent form that can be designed, comprehended, and modified by domain experts and analysts far more effectively than with previous approaches [39]. It hides irrelevant details of object implementation and allows model behavior to be viewed at a meaningful level. The use of objects allows encapsulating information, associating the behavior of an entity with its state definition, and modeling certain real-world entities (particularly those that are relatively dense and unstructured, such as trucks or aircraft) in a natural way. Similarly, it provides a natural way of modeling static, taxonomic relationships among objects by the use of class-subclass hierarchies, while minimizing the redundancy (and possible inconsistency) of their definitions through the inheritance of attributes and behaviors over these hierarchies. Finally, it provides a natural way of modeling certain kinds of dynamic interactions among real-world entities by the use of messages passed between objects.

Despite these achievements, however, object-oriented simulation has a number of critical limitations [60, 49]. In particular, the treatment of objects, taxonomies, inheritance, and messages in most object-oriented languages is too constraining and provides little leverage for answering the kinds of questions discussed above. More fundamentally, this approach distributes both the state of the simulation and the conditions for state transitions among the objects in the model. While this serves the software engineering goals of data hiding and modularization, it does not allow optimal comprehension of the relationships among events (since their definitions are distributed), nor does it enable inferences of the kind discussed above. Although commercial research efforts in simulation are beginning to examine some of these areas [34, 51], they have tended to consider domains like manufacturing, which are overly restrictive.

3 Military Simulation

Although much of this discussion applies to simulation in general, the focus of the KBSim effort is in military simulation. This is quite different from factory simulation, in which a relatively static collection of objects interact with each other in limited ways in a highly-structured world [28]. In contrast, military simulation typically involves a very dynamic collection of objects that are continually changing and are often created or destroyed. These have dynamic and often adversarial relationships to one another and behave and interact in varying and unpredictable ways in a highly dynamic world. In addition, many complex phenomena may have to be taken into account in a military simulation for it to be credible, including terrain, weather, command and control, and human decision making. This dynamic structure and inherent complexity make it difficult to design military simulations and to comprehend, interpret, or validate them once they have been built.

Furthermore, "military simulation" is not a single entity: There are at least three distinct potential uses of simulation in the military context, each with its own characteristics and requirements. These lie along a "continuum of stringency", as illustrated in Figure 1. The left (least stringent and least constrained) end of this continuum represents the use of simulation for analysis, for example, to explore issues and make decisions involving procurement, to evaluate tactics and doctrine, to derive requirements for new systems, etc. The middle of the continuum represents the use of simulation to provide a gaming environment for training or exercises. The right (most stringent and most constrained) end of the continuum represents the use of simulation in battle management, i.e., as an embedded decision support aid for commanders in the field. The distinctions among these different uses of simulation are important and are rarely made explicit. Since it is difficult to satisfy all possible requirements of a simulation at once, it is necessary to choose a point along this continuum and attempt to satisfy the most important requirements at that point. The focus of the KBSim project (or *any* simulation effort) can only be understood and evaluated in these terms.

For example, although analytic simulations must be valid, they need not necessarily be "realistic". Realism (especially graphic realism) is often sought for its own sake in simulation; however, what is important for analysis is the presentation of information to the analyst in an *appropriate* (i.e., easily comprehended) form, for which realism is neither necessary nor sufficient. In contrast, a gaming environment uses simulation to provide a surrogate reality in which users can hone their skills or exercise procedures

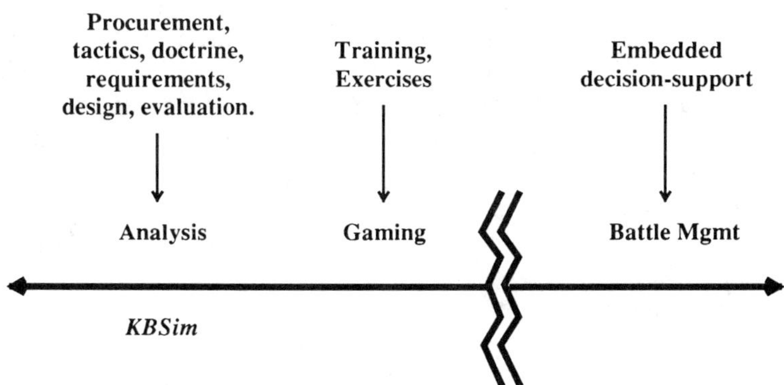

FIGURE 1. Uses of military simulation.

or tactics. Validity is typically *not* paramount in gaming, where simulation is often used to exercise procedures rather than to evaluate alternative courses of action. Here too, realism is relative to the needs of the users, who are typically support staff (often called "controllers") who interpret the results of the simulation for the trainees or participants; a realistic simulation minimizes the work required of this staff. Finally, battle management envisions the use of simulation as an embedded decision aid to be used by a commander in making tactical decisions. This is similar to the analytic case, but with critical realtime, reliability and survivability constraints added. Because immediate, critical decisions are being made, validity is crucial, as is interactive responsiveness. Realism, as in the analytic case, is subordinate to appropriateness of presentation (a commander in the field does not need the simulation to convince him of the reality of the situation).

The KBSim project has targeted its research at the analytic end of this spectrum, focusing on issues of validity, interactive responsiveness, comprehensibility, flexibility, and reusability rather than issues of performance or reliability. (One exception is the sensitivity analysis research described below, where performance can be thought of as the fundamental problem.)

4 The Problem

In most cases, a modeling effort is undertaken to explore a relatively small part of a domain. This constitutes the "model of interest", which is typically part of an "embedding" world-model that is a necessary environment for the model of interest, without itself being of particular interest. For example, an embedding model of electromagnetic propagation might be required to study communication patterns in command and control, where the communications model is the model of interest. The embedding model is itself contained in a simulation environment that allows running the model, displaying results, etc., as shown in Figure 2.

From the point of view of both the model builder and the model user, the embedding model and simulation environment are merely distractions. The mechanisms required to provide anything other than the model of interest are "artifacts" of the modeling technology that complicate and obscure the code that implements the model of interest. (Note that something may be part of the model of interest in one case and an artifact in another case.) One of the simulation builder's primary goals can be viewed as the elimination of artifacts. Even though it may not be logically possible to eliminate the embedding model and the simulation environment, their implementation should be made as invisible as possible. That is, a simulation environment should provide mechanisms for hiding the artifactual aspects of the simulation. Similarly, graphic display, user interaction, planning mechanisms, etc. must be provided transparently by the simulation environment since they are required by most simulation efforts.

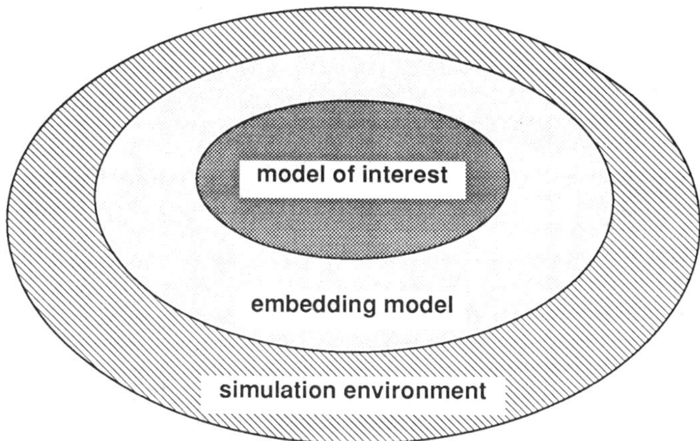

FIGURE 2. Focusing on the model of interest.

For example, a fundamental notion of "autonomy" is missing from most simulations. Objects in a discrete-state simulation interact with each other essentially by reacting to stimuli (generally represented by messages in the object-oriented paradigm). This does not capture the idea of an object that moves of its own accord: simulating this requires the introduction of artifacts in most simulation environments (e.g., having a scheduler ask each movable object to move whenever the simulation clock advances). Similarly, interaction events like collisions, intersections, and detection by sensors are difficult to simulate without additional artifactual devices.

Although object-oriented simulation languages provide a natural way of representing certain kinds of real world objects (such as tanks and airplanes), there are other kinds of entities and phenomena that stubbornly resist most current attempts at representation. For example, entities like terrain and weather and phenomena like human decision making or "soft" factors like initiative are difficult to represent in current paradigms.

In addition, users need to be able to develop confidence in the validity of a model and comprehend what it is doing and why. This requires that a simulation be able to *explain* its behavior in meaningful terms (for example, by showing chains of causality) and that users be able to view the attributes of entities and the relationships among entities in the model in appropriate ways. Users also need to be able to *explore* alternative assumptions and run "excursions" to test the model and to apply it for different purposes. Similarly, users often need to view the behavior of a model at different levels of aggregation for different purposes. Finally, users need to be able to analyze results, analyze the sensitivity of results to variations in parameters, and analyze the stability of the conclusions reached by a model.

The KBSim project has attacked various aspects of these problems, as described in the following sections.

5 Reasoning in Simulation

As discussed above, traditional simulations are severely limited in the types of questions they can answer. Users typically specify initial states of the simulated world and then run the simulation to see what happens, effectively asking questions of the form *"What (happens) if... ?"*. However, it is widely recognized [19, 25, 60] that there are many other kinds of questions that are of at least as much importance in many situations. These are questions that might be asked of a human expert in the domain that is being modeled. They include why questions ("*why* did X happen?" or "why did object X take action Z?"), *why not* questions ("why didn't X happen?"), *when* questions ("under what conditions will event Y happen?"), *how* questions ("how can result R be achieved?"), *ever/never* questions ("can X ever collide with Y?"), and *optimization* or *goal-directed questions* ("what is the highest value Z will ever reach?" or "what initial conditions will produce the highest value of Z?").

Similarly, it is important to be able to ask questions about the simulation state ("at what points in time did condition X hold?") and about explicit causality ("what events can cause event X?", "what events are caused by event Y?", or "why did event Z *not* occur?"). Finally, there are questions about the model itself ("what constraints govern the occurrence of event X?" or "under what circumstances can plan Z fail to achieve its purpose?"). We refer to the capabilities needed to answer such questions as **beyond *"What if... ?"***.

The inability of current discrete-state simulation systems to answer such questions derives from basic limitations in their representational and inferential capabilities. Representational limits include the difficulty of modeling goals, intentions, plans, beliefs and constraints. To the extent that these can be represented at all in most systems, they are usually encoded implicitly in behaviors (i.e., specified procedurally) and are therefore not amenable to inference. The kinds of inference and explanation techniques that have been applied in expert systems provide one way of extending the capabilities of simulation systems. However, simulation imposes additional requirements on these techniques: It requires the ability to represent temporal and spatial constraints and relationships as part of behavior so that inferences can be made on the basis of this information.

Solving these problems requires an ability to reason not only with simulation output, but also with the model itself. This implies that the building blocks of the model must be small and well-defined, and that there must be a powerful deductive mechanism to manipulate them. This requires formalizing precise definitions of certain primitive notions in dynamic systems, including time-varying attributes, events, and causality (i.e., scheduling and unscheduling of events). Our approach has been to use logic for this formalization: we began with a reimplementation of a subset of ROSS in Prolog and subsequently developed a new sublanguage ("DMOD"), implemented in Quintus Prolog.

The main concept in DMOD is an event. An event is said to occur when an "interesting" condition is satisfied in the world. If the sequence of events in the simulation is given, the state of the simulation at any time can be computed. A model therefore consists of two sets of rules:

(a) a set of *causality* rules specifying what other events occur, given that a particular event has occurred (and the sequence of events leading up to it)
(b) a set of *value* rules specifying how the value of a parameter changes after an event, given its value before the event occurred.

The following examples of causality and value rules are drawn from a notional air penetration model. The raw DMOD code shown would be difficult for a modeler to comprehend without a firm grasp of Prolog, but it is straightforward to define a higher-level modeling language that can be compiled easily into DMOD. The code shown here is *not* intended to illustrate the ultimate readability of the approach but rather to show that it can be implemented straightforwardly in Prolog.

(For readers who are unfamiliar with Prolog, note that variables always begin with capital letters, whereas all other terms are either the names of rules (procedures) or are uninterpreted literals; for example, the data object *penetrator(X)* is used to denote a penetrator aircraft whose name will be bound to the variable X. An underscore appearing in place of a variable name, as in *penetrator(_)*, represents an unnamed variable that need not be referred to again. The notation "[X|Y]" denotes a list whose first element is X and whose tail is Y (corresponding respectively to the LISP "car" and "cdr" of a list). The distinction between a "rule" and a "procedure" in DMOD—as in Prolog—is purely one of interpretation: both bind their uninstantiated ("output") arguments and return success or failure.)

An example of a causality rule is:

```
occurs(EventE, HistoryUptoE, EventF, HistoryUptoF) if
  EventE = flies(penetrator(X), [Px, Py], TimeT),
  EventF = detects(penetrator(X), radar(R), FutureTime),
  someRadar(R),
  entersRange(penetrator(X), [Px, Py], radar(R), FutureTime,
      [EventE|HistoryUptoE]),
  provided(EventE, HistoryUptoE, EventF, HistoryUptoF).
```

This rule says that *EventE* causes *EventF* under suitable conditions. *EventE* is an event that has just occurred. *HistoryUptoE* is the history of events up to, but not including, *EventE*, e.g., the list of events [flies(penetrator(1), [−100, 100], 0.2), takesOff(penetrator(1), 0.1)]. (Each event has a time stamp as its last argument; histories are lists of events sorted in decreasing order on their time stamps, so that the most recent event appears first on the list.) *EventF* is a variable representing a future event caused by *EventE*, and *HistoryUptoF* is a variable representing the future history up to (but not including) *EventF*. If *EventE* consists of penetrator X beginning to fly toward position [Px,Py] at some *TimeT* (given that the events in *HistoryUptoE* have occurred), then *EventF* will occur (at some *FutureTime*), wherein radar R will detect penetrator X (under suitable conditions, as discussed below). The procedure *entersRange* computes the time *FutureTime* at which the penetrator's flight path will intersect the radar's coverage, which is the time at which *EventF* will occur. Note that *HistoryUptoF* includes *EventE* and *HistoryUptoE*; the computation of *EventF* does not refer to *HistoryUptoF*, but is based purely on information about *EventE* and *HistoryUptoE*.

The condition *provided(EventE, HistoryUptoE, EventF, HistoryUptoF)* is defined by additional rules; it specifies a condition on the time period between *EventE* and *EventF*. For example, if the penetrator is destroyed or diverted from its path between *TimeT* and *FutureTime*, or if the radar is jammed at *FutureTime*, then *EventF* will not occur. These conditions are specified by the following rule:

provided(EventE, HistoryUptoE, EventF, HistoryUptoF) **if**
  EventE = flies(penetrator(X), [Px, Py], TimeT),
  EventF = detects(penetrator(X), radar(R), FutureTime),
  not occursAfter(EventE, flies(penetrator(X), _, _), HistoryUptoF),
  not occursAfter(EventE, destroys(_, penetrator(X), _), HistoryUptoF).

This is true if all of its conditions are true, i.e., if *EventE* and *EventF* are the appropriate events, and if penetrator X does not fly elsewhere and is not destroyed between *EventE* and *EventF* (that is, between *TimeT* and *FutureTime*). For example, the third condition, *not occursAfter(EventE, flies(penetrator(X), _, _), HistoryUptoF)*, says that it must not be the case that penetrator X flies to some new (unspecified) position after *EventE* in the *HistoryUptoF* (that is, between *EventE* and *EventF*).

An example of a value rule is:

value(velocity, penetrator(X), [Vx, Vy], History) **if**
  History = [flies(penetrator(X), [Px, Py], TimeT)|_],
  value(position, penetrator(X), [Mx, My], History),
  value(speed, penetrator(X), Speed, History),

distance(Px, Py, Mx, My, Hyp),

Vx is Speed $*$ (Px $-$ Mx)/Hyp,

Vy is Speed $*$ (Py $-$ My)/Hyp.

This computes a penetrator's velocity (a state parameter) by binding the pair of variables Vx and Vy to the x and y components of the velocity vector of some penetrator, X. Since *History* is in reverse chronological order, this rule matches if the most recent event (the first one on the History list) is *flies(penetrator(X), [Px,Py], TimeT)*. If this is the most recent event (i.e., the penetrator began to fly toward point [Px,Py] at *TimeT*), then the velocity can be calculated from the penetrator's speed and the distance between its current position [Mx,My] and its destination [Px,Py] (where the *distance* function is defined appropriately). The penetrator's current position and speed are in turn computed by additional value rules for these attributes (not shown here); for example, invoking *value(speed, penetrator(X), Speed, History)* binds the variable *Speed* to the current value of the speed attribute of penetrator X in the given *History.* Initial values for attributes can be specified by separate value rules; for example, the *InitialSpeed* of penetrator X after some *InitialEvent* can be specified by the rule *value(speed, penetrator(X), InitialSpeed, [InitialEvent]).*

Note that for each event that does *not* change the value of a given attribute, it is conceptually necessary to provide a rule stating that the value of the attribute is unchanged by the event; this is an instance of the "frame problem" [50]. However, this can be accomplished by a single default rule, stating that attributes never change except in the cases specified by their value rules.

Simulation in DMOD consists simply of computing the sequence of events that follow an initial event. To begin a simulation, a list of one or more events is supplied as an initial *EventQ* (written as "[InitialEvent1, ..., InitialEventN]") along with a null initial History (written as "[]"):

simulate([], [InitialEvent1, ..., InitialEventN], FinalHistory).

This is described in further detail elsewhere [62].

DMOD is a formalization of discrete-event simulation and is something of a departure from the object-oriented approach. Discrete-event simulation is based on the observation that to compute the state of a system at any point in time, it is not necessary to keep a record of its state at regular intervals of time. Instead, it is sufficient to keep a recoru of the *events* that occur in the system; from these and the initial state, the state of the system can be computed at any point in time. However, the declarative nature of DMOD allows a given model to be viewed in different ways for different purposes; for example, object-oriented views can be used wherever they are appropriate, as illustrated in Figure 3. The *object view* encapsulates those aspects of the model that adhere to objects (i.e., their states and behaviors, their relations to other objects, and the fact that they participate

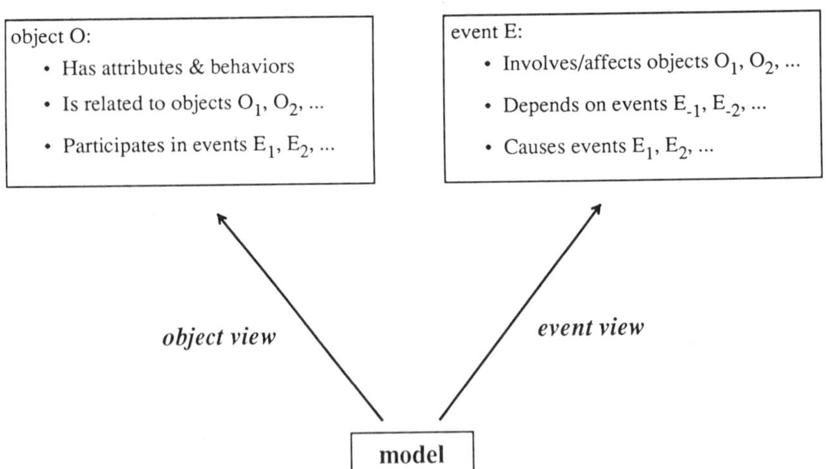

FIGURE 3. Object and event views of a model.

in certain events). The *event view* encapsulates those aspects of the model that adhere to events (i.e., which objects they affect, which other events they depend on, and which other events they cause). It should be possible for the designer or user of a model to use whichever view is most appropriate for a given purpose, deriving the information necessary to update the model and produce the complementary view on demand. This ability to derive views (as well as the underlying model itself) from other views and the full integration of object and event views is the subject of continuing research.

DMOD can currently answer certain special cases of goal-oriented questions of the form *"How can X get from A to B?"*. For example, given an event E and a history, it is possible to trace causality chains backwards and forwards from E. That is, DMOD can compute what sequence of events led to E, and what sequence of events E led to. Similarly, DMOD's causality rules can be used to determine which events *can* lead to (cause) a given event, as well as which events follow a given event. To extend this capability, we envision allowing the user to interact with the goal-directed search to give it "advice" about which paths to search. The general goal-directed simulation problem is at least as difficult as the general planning problem in AI, which remains unsolved; nevertheless, the formalized approach of DMOD provides a good starting point for attacking this problem, at least in its simpler cases.

In addition, DMOD solves two major problems that plague traditional discrete-state simulations. The first is how to simulate decision-making that requires reference to past states and events. For example, if a radar detects more than ten penetrators in a span of five minutes, it infers a major attack and informs the central command, otherwise it simply informs its fighter bases. In most discrete-event simulations, the state is destructively updated after each event. Consequently, relevant past states and events must be explicitly remembered, i.e., copied into the current state. This approach can very quickly increase the size of the current state, making it extremely unwieldy.

In DMOD the main object being computed is not the state, but the history, i.e., the sequence of events that have occurred. History is a first-class object that is passed around to procedures participating in the simulation. The state of the system at any point in time can be computed by *value* rules from the history and the initial state, solving the problem of accessing past states or events. Chains of causality can easily be inferred from history. Given an event, it is possible to trace not only what events it led to, but also what events led up to it. This is both a good form of explanation and a valuable debugging tool.

The second problem is how to ensure that events are consistently unscheduled. For example, if a penetrator takes off from an air-base and flies towards a radar, most discrete-event simulations would schedule an event for detection of the penetrator by the radar at some time in the future. If, however, the penetrator were to crash, or be diverted or shot down between the current time and this future time, the detection event must not be allowed to occur. To ensure this, the model requires explicit code to unschedule this event. As models grow larger, it becomes increasingly difficult to ensure that such unscheduling is performed consistently. In most simulation languages, unscheduling is an artifact that must be handled explicitly by the programmer, which is a source of numerous bugs.

In DMOD the notion of unscheduling is absent. Instead, when an event is scheduled, a condition is associated with it. When this becomes the first event in the event queue, the condition is evaluated in the light of the history accumulated so far. If the result is true, the event will occur, otherwise it is discarded. Since this is all done declaratively, the programmer need not even be aware of the procedural notion of unscheduling.

DMOD is already changing our thinking about issues of temporal representation appropriate for military simulation and about issues of autonomy and causality. In particular, an event-oriented view of a simulation model has certain advantages over an object-oriented view, at least for some purposes; for example, encapsulating all the state-changing side-effects of an event *as part of the event* makes it much easier to comprehend and maintain them than if they are distributed among the objects that own the state (as they would be in a strict object-oriented approach). We have therefore begun to think of a model as a database that can be *viewed* from different perspectives for different purposes (e.g., event-oriented or object-oriented).

DMOD is only a first step toward the use of reasoning in simulation. Many issues remain to be explored, including the integration of event-oriented and object-oriented approaches, the handling of stochastic behavior, and ways of taking advice from the user when attempting to answer goal-oriented queries. In addition, we believe that a suitable generalization of DMOD can serve as a formal specification language for models and as a possible way of validating scenarios (as suggested in Builder, 1983 [9]). We are continuing to explore these research areas and to develop these techniques. Nevertheless, we feel that the leverage already provided by DMOD indicates that a logic-based approach to simulation is an excellent way of answering questions that go beyond *"What if... ?"*.

6 Multiple Relations (and Extended Objects)

Complex simulations require the representation of multi-dimensional relationships among objects. For example a tank **is-a** kind of moving object, is **a-part-of** a particular tank battalion, may be **under-the-command-of** a particular "crossing area commander", may be **in-communication-with** some set of other objects, and may be *near* a (possibly different) set of objects. It is important for analysts to be able to define such relations freely, examine the state of the simulation in terms of these relations, and modify them dynamically. Traditional object-oriented systems (as well as most semantic nets, frame systems and expert system shells, with some exceptions [13]) provide strong support only for the **class-subclass** relation (also called **IS-A** and **taxonomy**). A corresponding **inheritance** mechanism is usually supplied to maintain taxonomic relationships (serving as a specialized kind of inference), but little or no support is provided for other kinds of relations. In fact, the **IS-A** relation has been pressed into service for many inconsistent purposes [7], though it is poorly suited to many of them.

Recent work in integrating relations into an object-oriented language [63] appears to ignore the issue of "inferential support" for relations. Some authors argue that the **IS-A** relation should be thought of a programming (or implementation) construct rather than a semantic modeling construct, while other relations should be accorded inferior status [16]. Our own approach is that, while implementation relations may be important, the primary responsibility of any modeling environment is to provide modeling constructs that allow representing features and phenomena of interest in the real world in natural ways (that is, to allow *modeling*). We consider multiple relations as alternative views of a model (analogous to the object and event views discussed above), which are necessary to provide natural ways of modeling alternative features and phenomena. For this reason, we feel it is important to provide a true multiple relation environment, in which different kinds of relations are supported by appropriate specialized inference mechanisms.

It is also important to note there are a number of real-world entities that are difficult to represent as traditional objects. For example, terrain, roads, rivers, weather, and electromagnetic fields defy easy representation by conventional object-oriented means. These "extended" objects or phenomena require representations and manipulations that are different from those used for more compact objects, either because they traverse or interpenetrate other objects (without actually being "part" of them), or because they are best described by continuous models (such as partial differential equations).

We have analyzed a number of important relations in military simulations, including:

class-subclass (trucks are a subclass of moving objects)
part-whole (a battalion is a part of a brigade)
command (a unit is commanded by a commander)
connectivity (two units are in-communication with each other)
proximity (two units are near each other geographically)

We have identified inference mechanisms to support these relations by analogy to the way inheritance supports the class-subclass relation. That is, for each type of relation there is some special kind of inference which is appropriate to it. In the case of a **class-subclass** relation, this inference is inheritance. However, in the case of a **part-whole** relation (for example) the appropriate inference mechanism involves distributing the values of attributes of the whole over its parts, so that the number of troops in a brigade always equals the sum of the troops in its battalions (this special case is discussed under aggregation below). In the case of a connectivity relation, on the other hand, the appropriate "inferential support" involves some form of transitivity so that if A is in communication with B and B is in communication with C, then A is (at least indirectly) in communication with C.

This is only the tip of the multiple relation iceberg: a more general approach to relations should define a framework of general characteristics (i.e., "attributes") of relations to allow defining relations in terms of these characteristics [13]. For example a relation can be defined in terms of whether it is one-to-one, one-to-many, many-to-many, onto, transitive, associative, reflexive, invertible, etc. This would allow users to define relations simply by indicating their appropriate attributes; appropriate inferential support mechanisms could then be generated automatically, at least in feasible cases.

6.1 Highly Interactive Interfaces

In the analytic military simulation domain, the designer, user, and ultimate consumer of the results of a simulation is typically an analyst who is constantly evolving and refining the simulation even while it is being run. It is important that the analyst be able to understand what the simulation does and why it does it, be convinced that it is doing the right thing, and be able to modify its behavior. This is the motivation for what we call **intelligent exploration and explanation**. One of the keys to this is the user's interface with the simulation. This must be interactive and lucid, taking full advantage of modern graphics, without falling prey to "the fetish of realism" (i.e., realism for its own sake).

In addition, since we perceive that multiple relations are ubiquitous in simulations, we feel it is important to allow a user to display relations in a perspicuous form (as an analyst would naturally draw them) and to edit them graphically. Previous work on the automated display of diagrams [70, 59] and on allowing users to define relations graphically [8] has largely ignored the problem of inferring the semantics of relations directly from drawn input.

Intelligent exploration and explanation require a highly interactive graphics environment that emphasizes the ease of manipulating simulation objects, minimizes redundant display updating, allows animation of sequences of events (such as causal chains), and eliminates graphic artifacts that have plagued previous simulations (such as ghost images of objects after they have been destroyed in the simulation).

In our attempt to separate the machinery of the simulation environment from the model of interest (as discussed above), we have eliminated the need of previous object-oriented ROSS simulations to update positions of moving objects explicitly in simulation code. This is a source of both obfuscation and potential bugs in existing simulations, since it is necessary for the programmer to remember to update the positions of objects whenever they might be affected. We have designed and implemented a **demand update** strategy for displaying the results of a simulation by computing graphic attributes of objects only when necessary. This form of "lazy evaluation" automatically updates the images of objects on the display at appropriate times and minimizes the redundant update of graphic attributes as well as minimizing graphic output. This and a number of other significant extensions to the ROSS language [11, 12] have produced an augmented language which we refer to informally as "XROSS".

7 Sensitivity Analysis

In all but the most trivial cases, it is impossible to run more than a tiny fraction of all the potentially relevant cases of a simulation. Even if cases are generated and run automatically, the computation time required is often prohibitive, and the job of analyzing the results is monumental. It is important to be able to analyze the behavior of a model in more powerful ways, such as by performing sensitivity analysis on its parameters.

A simulation can be viewed as the computation of a single top level function involving hundreds or even thousands of parameters. Sensitivity analysis attempts to show how sensitive the results of the simulation are to variations in those parameters that are of interest in a given situation. This is especially important for promoting confidence in the stability of the model (i.e., knowing that its results are independent of minor changes to its parameters) and for indicating which parameter values are the most important ones to validate (by real-world means) in order to make the model believable.

The naive approach to sensitivity analysis requires running a simulation many times, perturbing individual parameters to see how the results differ. We refer to this approach as "naive perturbation". This is prohibitive in most cases, which is why sensitivity analysis is rarely performed. The intent of our research is to provide a computationally feasible way of performing sensitivity analysis in a simulation environment. Viewing a simulation as a top level function that invokes many levels of subfunctions*, each of which is called many times (as illustrated in Figure 4), the naive approach to perturbing top level parameters executes the top level function one or more times for each parameter, each time executing each subfunction. That is, each subfunction is executed a number of times proportional to the number of parameters of its caller (where the constant of proportionality is the number of times a single parameter must be perturbed in order to approximate a partial derivative).

We have designed a new **propagative approach** to sensitivity analysis that propagates and combines the sensitivities of functions through a computation. This approach is motivated by the chain rule of the differential calculus, which defines the partial derivative of a composite function as a combination of the partial derivatives of its subfunctions (assuming these subfunctions are differentiable with respect to the parameters of interest). This propagative approach computes a representation of the sensitivity of

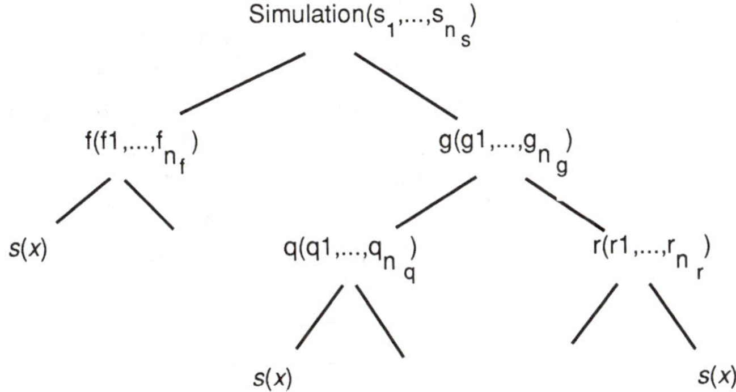

FIGURE 4. Simulation as nested function calls.

*In this discussion, we use the term "subfunction" to mean a function that is called by another function, rather than one that is defined within the lexical scope of another.

each subfunction (i.e., an approximation to its partial derivatives) the first time it is executed (e.g., by perturbing it once for each of its own parameters) and propagates that sensitivity information through the computation rather than having to recompute it each time it is needed. Since most subfunctions have fewer parameters than their callers, this approach results in their being evaluated fewer times, thereby avoiding much of the cost of sensitivity analysis. (Subfunctions that have as many or more parameters than their callers are simply evaluated as in naive perturbation.) Note that, for simplicity, this discussion focuses on sensitivity analysis in which one parameter at a time is varied; however, the propagative approach applies equally well (and has even greater potential payoff) when combinations of parameters are varied together (i.e., when higher order derivatives are required).

We have implemented a stand-alone computational environment in LISP to support the propagation and combination of sensitivities. This environment has allowed us to try our approach on a number of computations and to analyze its payoff. Not all functions in a given computation are of equal interest for sensitivity analysis. Further, it may not make sense to analyze the sensitivity of built-in functions (like the conditional function "cond" in LISP). Our computational environment therefore allows the user to designate certain *candidate* functions as those to be analyzed; these same functions are also instrumented by the environment to keep track of such things as how often they are called. The user further divides candidate functions into two groups depending on whether their return values are discrete or continuous. Each candidate function is then modified by the environment so that (among other things) it returns not only its usual return value but also a representation of its sensitivity to each of its arguments.

The sensitivity of a function is considered to be (an approximation to) the collection of partial derivatives of the function with respect to its arguments. In order to compute this, whenever a candidate function is called normally during a computation (referred to as a "primary" call), the environment causes the function to place "secondary" calls to itself recursively, perturbing each of its arguments in turn. By so doing, the function computes its sensitivity and returns this information to its caller. During these secondary invocations, the function places secondary calls to its candidate subfunctions; this approximates the return values of these candidate functions, rather than recomputing them for each secondary call. The approximation technique used is to apply the sensitivity of each called function as a linear approximation of its value (where the sensitivity of each called function is computed recursively by this same process and returned to its caller). This process hinges on the notions of primary and secondary calls, illustrated by a simple example, shown in Figure 5.

Consider a top-level function H that calls a candidate function F, which in turn calls another candidate function G. For simplicity, suppose that F calls no other candidate functions besides G and that G calls no candi-

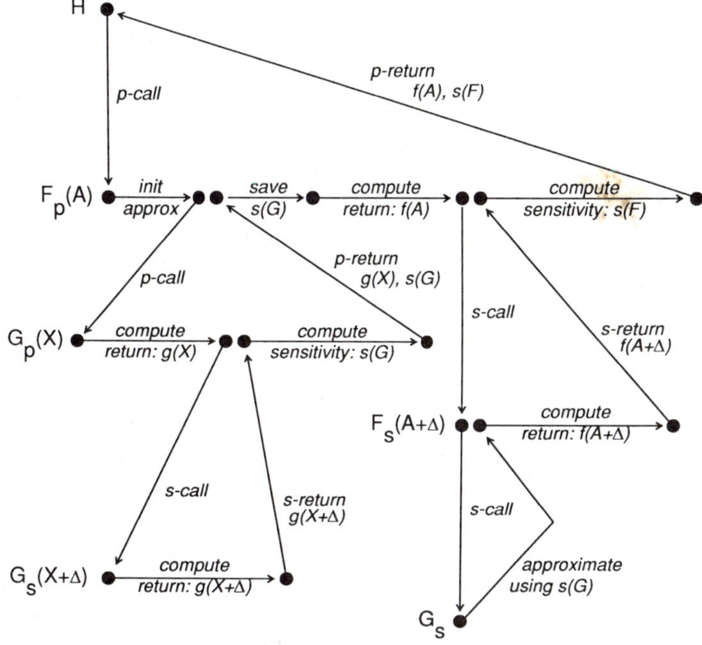

FIGURE 5. Propagative sensitivity analysis.

date functions at all. Further, suppose both F and G are continuous-valued, differentiable functions. Since F is a candidate function, the propagative environment automatically interprets H's call to F as a **primary call** (shown as "p-call" in the figure). Upon receiving this primary call, F initializes its approximation table and proceeds to compute its normal return value, in the course of which, F calls G. Since G is also a candidate function, the environment interprets this as a primary call as well. Upon receiving this primary call, G proceeds to compute its normal return value; since G calls no other candidate functions, it will have an empty approximation table. Having computed its value (and before returning from its primary call), G must compute its sensitivity (to be returned to F along with G's value, as the result of F's primary call to G).

To compute its sensitivity, G perturbs each of its own arguments in turn, placing a recursive **secondary call** (shown as "s-call") to itself for each perturbation. For example, if G has only a single formal argument, whose supplied value (in F's primary call to G) is X, then G will place a secondary call to itself with an argument of $(X + \Delta)$, where Δ provides the perturbation. This recursive secondary call to G returns the value $G(X+\Delta)$ to the primary invocation of G. Assuming, for simplicity of exposition, that a single perturbation is enough to produce a linear approximation to its "partial" derivative, G computes the Cauchy ratio $(G(X + \Delta) - G(X))/\Delta$ as its sensitivity information (shown as "s(G)"), and returns this to F along with G's normal return value, G(X). The value of the Cauchy ratio represents the sensitivity of G to its argument (in the neighborhood of the point X); it can be interpreted geometrically as the slope of the tangent to the function G at X or algebraically as a coefficient t such that $G(X+\Delta) = G(X) + t * \Delta$. This latter interpretation is used subsequently by F as a linear approximation to the value of G. (In the more general case, where G had several arguments, it would perturb each one, generating secondary calls to itself to compute a Cauchy ratio for each partial derivative, and would return the collection of the resulting coefficients as its sensitivity information.)

When the primary call to G returns to F, F separates the return value G(X) from the sensitivity information for G, which it stores as its approximation table entry for this invocation of G. F continues executing its own primary call (from H), using the value G(X) as needed to compute its own return value. Having computed its value (and before returning from its primary call), F computes its sensitivity (to be returned to H along with F's value, as the result of H's primary call to F). To compute its sensitivity, F perturbs each of its own arguments in turn, placing a recursive secondary call to itself for each perturbation. The results of these recursive secondary calls are used to compute the Cauchy ratios for F's own partials, as was done for G. However, during these secondary calls, whenever F would normally call G, it now places secondary calls to G, using its approximation table entry for G to approximate the value of G. This is the essence of the computational payoff of the propagative scheme.

To summarize, a **primary call** to a candidate function calculates its normal return value, in the course of which it places primary calls to any candidate functions it calls. The primary call then initiates a series of recursive secondary calls by the function to itself, to compute its sensitivity by perturbing its parameters. In addition, the primary call causes the function to initialize an "approximation table" for approximating the return values of those candidate functions that it calls during its recursive secondary invocations. It is the ability to approximate these return values (rather than recomputing them) that allows the propagative approach to outperform naive perturbation. Each call to a candidate function G by a given function F will generate an entry in F's approximation table. This entry will contain sensitivity information (about the called function G) that was returned to F by G (in response to F's primary call to G). This sensitivity information (which is a representation of G's partial derivatives) serves as a linear approximation for the value of the called function G. When F has completed perturbing its parameters via recursive secondary calls, it will have derived its own sensitivity to its parameters: this information is returned by F to its caller to serve as F's entry in its caller's approximation table.

A **secondary call** by a function F to a candidate function G essentially replaces the evaluation of G with an approximation, using the entry for G in F's approximation table. This entry was returned to F by G itself when F placed its primary call to G.

Our initial results indicate that this propagative approach has tremendous potential, reducing a combinatorial process to a linear one; however, additional research is needed before the approach can be integrated into our simulation environment. For example, although Boolean derivatives and a Boolean version of the chain rule can be defined [5], the general case of symbolic-valued functions requires further thought. Our computational environment allows functions of this sort, but only applies the propagative approach to those functions that are differentiable in the usual sense, performing "naive" perturbation for all others. However, even without such extension, we expect this new approach to have a major impact on the feasibility of sensitivity analysis in simulation.

8 Varying the Level of Aggregation of a Model

Current simulation models cannot vary the level at which they are aggregated: the desired level of aggregation is chosen in advance and the simulation is designed for this level. Changing this level typically requires considerable reprogramming; changing it dynamically is generally unthinkable. Dynamic aggregation (sometimes referred to as "variable resolution") would allow the user to focus attention on some aspect or area of a simulation or to run "broad brush" (highly aggregated) simulations to identify interesting cases that can later be rerun in more detail (disaggregated).

Structured, "composite" objects are poorly supported by traditional object-oriented environments. Only *ad hoc* mechanisms exist for representing part-whole relations (such as the fact that a brigade consists of several battalions), and there are no automatic facilities for maintaining attributes that are the sums of attributes of the parts of an object. Similarly, only the lowest-level objects in the hierarchy are expected to interact with other objects in a simulation. These limitations make it difficult to represent even static, uniform aggregation (where "uniform" means that all peer objects, such as brigades, are aggregated to the same level throughout the simulation), since objects at various levels of the hierarchy must maintain attributes representing summary information about their parts and must be able to interact with objects at their peer level.

Dynamic aggregation compounds these problems by requiring the ability to switch levels at runtime. For example, an aggregated object (such as a brigade) that is asked to disaggregate itself would be required to generate subordinate objects (parts, such as battalions) obeying reasonable constraints for how the attributes of the whole should be distributed among these parts. Nonuniform aggregation allows the interactions among objects to cross peer levels, so that, for example, an aggregated brigade in one sector can interact with disaggregated battalions in another sector. This allows "focusing the attention" of a simulation by disaggregating only those areas or aspects that are of particular interest. Dynamic, nonuniform aggregation requires the ability to reroute interactions to the appropriate levels dynamically.

Automatic aggregation to any arbitrary level (without a prior modeling effort at that level), requires the ability to create new models at new levels automatically. Instead, we restrict our attention to models in which a fixed set of possible levels of aggregation have been defined in advance (when building the model). That is, we expect dynamic aggregation to be performed on a model that has been constructed with aggregation in mind: the model will actually consist of a suite of coordinated models at various potential levels of aggregation.

Note that if a simulation is designed at the most disaggregated level that might ever be desired, aggregated results can be computed after the simulation is run; we refer to this (somewhat arbitrarily) as "abstraction" to distinguish it from aggregation. Unfortunately, running a highly disaggregated, detailed model may be unwarranted (i.e., unaffordable) in many cases. Furthermore, abstraction does not allow the user to interact with the simulation at different levels of aggregation (providing different "views" of the model) and is therefore a poor substitute for dynamically variable aggregation.

The fact that the level of aggregation of a model gets "frozen in" early in its design is a major impediment to the reusability of models and the utility of simulation in general. Users should be able to vary the level of aggregation (or "resolution") of a simulation and to indicate which aspects of the model are of particular interest, running those aspects of the simulation disaggregated while running peripheral aspects at higher levels of aggregation. This goal has been addressed only in very limited contexts at a theoretical level [26]. We are developing techniques for building simulations whose level of aggregation can be varied both statically and dynamically by representing "vertical slices" of objects in an aggregation hierarchy (for example, divisions, brigades, battalions) and allowing interactions between objects at different levels of aggregation.

We have taken an object-oriented approach to representing aggregation, using objects to represent each of the levels of aggregation. We associate behaviors and attributes with composite objects that simulate the behavior of their subordinates and maintain attributes representing aggregations of the attributes of those subordinates. We have successfully prototyped a scenario fragment using this approach. The fragment consists of a military company made up of several platoons; the simulation is plan-driven to provide a framework for coordinating the actions of units at various levels. Various aggregation and disaggregation functions are defined for switching among aggregation levels.

Our results to date indicate that dynamic aggregation is feasible, so long as the multi-level model is developed with certain consistency criteria held firmly in mind; this can be viewed as a semi-formal aid to developing coordinated, consistent multi-level models, which has heretofore been akin to alchemy.

9 Modeling "Soft" Concepts

Policy analysts often use simulations to try to answer qualitative questions involving intangible, "soft" concepts: factors that appear to be important but are hard to quantify. Examples in the military domain are troop morale breakdown following heavy losses, the importance of momentum in a hasty attack, or the effects of panic in chemical or biological warfare. Such factors can have major impacts on the course and outcome of a situation, but they are extremely difficult to model with metrics such as communication delays, effective force ratios or other directly quantitative criteria.

These soft concepts can best be modeled by analyzing their underlying or contributing factors and subjectively aggregating these to arrive at an estimate of the construct itself. For example, morale can be considered a "construct" composed of factors such as sleep deprivation, hunger, casualty level, weather, and bombardment level; these factors can then be aggregated to derive an estimate of morale. Because of the complexity of this process, such qualitative factors are rarely introduced into military simulations [20], and then only at a surface level.

To investigate building models that incorporate qualitative notions of this kind, we have focused on the concept of "initiative" as used by military analysts [57, 73, 23, 4]. Quotes such as the following one motivate this choice:

> The stereotypical Soviet military leader is seen in the West as being prevented from exercising initiative on the battlefield and thus unable to take full advantage of opportunities that may come his way.
>
> —Richard Armstrong, "Initiative Soviet Style," *Military Review*, June 1984

In order to submit statements like this to experimentation within a simulation, it is necessary to build a model that reflects what the term "initiative" means to analysts. Analysts seem to use the term "initiative" to mean *having the freedom and capability to plan and act independently.* A commander exercises little initiative if he simply executes detailed instructions passed down from his superior. Initiative is also absent if the commander responds to situations "by the book", invoking responses according to pre-determined rules. U.S. commanders may use "management by exception", in which subordinate units will ask for help only if they cannot accomplish their assigned objectives. The Soviets will more often give specific orders, with deviation by the subordinate allowed only after an authorization by the commander [55]. Many of the goals of AirLand 2000, such as surprise, rapid maneuver, disruption and quick reaction, should be facilitated through use of greater initiative [45, 69]. Too much initiative, on the other hand, can result in reduced coherence of overall planning and execution. The Soviets tend to concentrate on such offensive operations in their planning, while U.S. and NATO forces typically focus on defensive operations [44, 52].

In light of the above, many analysts assume that Blue force commanders possess greater initiative than their Red force counterparts; from this assumption, analysts conclude that Blue forces would be more effective than simple force ratios would suggest. This conclusion (though not the assumption on which it is based) could be verified if an appropriate model of initiative were built into the representations of commanders in a simulation.

We have identified a methodology for acquiring analysts' models of such concepts, involving a blend of expert systems knowledge engineering and an algebraic modeling technique developed for use in judgment research [71]. This methodology produces an algebraic model showing the quantitative relationship between a construct like initiative and the various component concepts and attributes that comprise it. Data from interviews with analysts and commanders and from studies of Army field manuals [67, 68], Defense Intelligence Agency publications [22], and the Soviet Military Thought series [30, 43, 14] can be used to generate possible approaches to modeling initiative. For example, to the extent that initiative consists of having greater freedom of choice in making decisions, it might be modeled by a simulation of a commander as an inferencing process having variable inference capabilities or variable access to relevant data for making inferences.

In exploring these ideas, we have become convinced that it is necessary to model commanders and the decision making process as a whole and to build simulations that are driven by plans (modeling the plans that commanders formulate and receive). Modeling decision making is also central to modeling command and control issues, which are of great current interest in the modeling community. This is an area of ongoing research, which requires further thought.

10 Summary

One of the most common complaints among military analysts is the incomprehensibility of the models available to them. Incomprehensibility is both a software engineering problem (an incomprehensible program is unlikely to be *correct*) and a modeling problem (an incomprehensible model is unlikely to be *valid*). Both the model and the program that implements it must be comprehensible in order to have any confidence that the program correctly implements a valid model.

Knowledge-based simulation attempts to bring together the best ideas of object-oriented simulation, AI, and interactive graphics to produce a new kind of modeling environment. The single most important goal of this effort is to improve the *comprehensibility* of the models produced.

The use of explicit, human-meaningful knowledge in the specification of a model can help make it directly comprehensible. To the extent that the modeling environment can draw inferences from this knowledge (for example, running a simulation) using comprehensible procedures, the entire process becomes comprehensible to the modeler and user. Our use of DMOD is an attempt to represent knowledge and inference procedures in a way that greatly improves the comprehensibility of a simulation, while still being computationally efficient. The focus on objects in object-oriented simulation has neglected the *event* as an entity in its own right. The event view encapsulates the causes, effects and side-effects of events in much the same way that the object view encapsulates the attributes and behaviors of objects. Each view has significant advantages for some purposes.

Comprehensibility must not be thought of as a purely static quality: it is equally important that the user of a model be able to comprehend the behavior and dynamics of the phenomena being modeled. We have broadened the traditional ("toy duck") view of simulation to allow the user to ask questions of the model that go beyond *"What if... ?"*. In addition, providing the user with capabilities for stopping, querying, backing up, and rerunning a simulation, as well as explanatory capabilities such as showing causal chains and the eventual ability to perform affordable sensitivity analysis will add a new dimension to the comprehensibility of the dynamics of a model.

Finally, we believe that providing multiple views of models (in terms of objects, events, multiple relations, aggregation, etc.) will make validation easier by making it more apparent what a model actually is. With this aim, we are continuing to pursue the research directions described above in order to improve the comprehensibility of models.

References

1. Anderson, R.H., and J.J. Gillogly, *RAND Intelligent Terminal Agent (RITA): Design Philosophy*, The RAND Corporation, R-1809-ARPA, 1976.
2. Anderson, R.H., and N.Z. Shapiro, *Design Considerations for Computer-Based Interactive Map Display Systems*, The RAND Corporation, R-2382-ARPA, 1979.
3. Anderson, R.H., et al., *RITA Reference Manual*, The RAND Corporation, R-1808-ARPA, 1977.
4. Armstrong, R.N., "Initiative Soviet Style," *Military Review*, June 1984, pp. 14–27.
5. Blanning, R.W., "Sensitivity Analysis in Logic-based Models," *Decision Support Systems*, Vol. 3, pp. 343–349, 1987.
6. Bowen, K.C., "Analysis of Models," (unpublished) 1978.

7. Brachman, R.J., "What IS-A Is and Isn't: An Analysis of Taxonomic Links in Semantic Networks," *Computer*, Vol. 16, No. 10, 1983.
8. Bryce, D., and R. Hull, "SNAP: A Graphics-based Schema Manager," *The Proceedings of the International Conference on Data Engineering*, Los Angeles, 1986.
9. Builder, C.H., *Toward a Calculus of Scenarios*, The RAND Corporation, N-1855-DNA, 1983.
10. Callero, M., D.A. Waterman, and J.R. Kipps, *TATR: A Prototype Expert System for Tactical Air Targeting*, The RAND Corporation, R-3096-ARPA, 1984.
11. Cammarata, S., B. Gates, and J. Rothenberg, "Dependencies and Graphical Interfaces in Object-Oriented Simulation Languages," *Proceedings of the 1987 Winter Simulation Conference* (Atlanta, Georgia, Dec. 14–16), Society for Computer Simulation, San Diego, CA, pp. 507–547, 1987.
12. Cammarata, S., B. Gates, and J. Rothenberg, *Dependencies, Demons, and Graphical Interfaces in the ROSS Language*, The RAND Corporation, N-2589-DARPA, 1988.
13. Carnegie Group Inc., *Knowledge Craft CRL Technical Manual*, Carnegie Group Inc., 1986.
14. Chuyev, Yu.V. and Yu.B. Mikhaylov, "Forecasting in Military Affairs (A Soviet View)", *Soviet Military Thought No. 16*, U.S. Government Printing Office, 1975.
15. Conway, R.W., *Some Tactical Problems in Simulation Method*, The RAND Corporation, RM-3244-PR, 1962.
16. Cox, B.J., "Objective-C: Outlook," *Journal of Object Oriented Programming*, Vol. 1, No. 1 (April/May 1988), pp. 54–57.
17. Dalkey, N.C., "Simulation" *Systems Analysis and Policy Planning: Applications in Defense*, E.S. Quade and W.I. Boucher (eds.), Elsevier, 1968.
18. Davis, M.R., and T.O. Ellis, "The Rand Tablet: A Man-Machine Graphical Communication Device," *FJCC 1964*, Spartan Books.
19. Davis, M., S. Rosenschein, and N. Shapiro, *Prospects and Problems for a General Modeling Methodology*, The RAND Corporation, N-1801-RC, June 1982.
20. Davis, P.K., and J.A. Winnefeld, *The RAND Strategic Assessment Center: An Overview and Interim Conclusions about Utility and Development Options*, R-2945-DNA, The RAND Corporation, 1983.
21. Davis, P.K., S.C. Bankes, and J.P. Kahan, *A New Methodology for Modeling National Command Level Decisionmaking in War Games and Simulations*, R-3290-NA, The RAND Corporation, 1986.
22. Defense Intelligence Agency, DDI 1150-13-77.
23. Donnelly, C., *Soviet Fighting Doctrine, NATO's Sixteen Nations*, Vol. 29 (3), May-June 1984.
24. Ellis, T.O., J.F. Heafner, and W.L. Sibley, *The GRAIL Project: An Experiment in Man-Machine Communications*, The RAND Corporation, RM-5999-ARPA, 1969.
25. Erickson, S.A., "Fusing AI and Simulation in Military Modeling," *AI Applied to Simulation, Proceedings of the European Conference at the University of Ghent*, 1985, pp. 140–150.

26. Fishwick, P.A., "Hierarchical Reasoning: Simulating Complex Processes over Multiple Levels of Abstraction," *UF-CIS Technical Report TR-86-6*, University of Florida, September 1986.
27. Gass, S.I., and R.L. Sisson, *A Guide to Models in Governmental Planning and Operations*, U.S. Environmental Protection Agency, 1974.
28. Gilmer, J.B., *Parallel Simulation Techniques for Military Problems*, The BDM Corporation, 1986.
29. Ginsberg, A.S., H.M. Markowitz, and P.M. Oldfather, *Programming by Questionnaire*, The RAND Corporation, RM-4460-PR, 1965.
30. Grechko, M.A.A., "The Armed Forces of the Soviet State (A Soviet View)", *Soviet Military Thought No. 12*, U.S. Government Printing Office, 1975.
31. Greenberger, M., M.A. Crenson, and B.L. Crissey, *Models in the Policy Process*, Russell Sage Foundation, NY, 1976.
32. Hilton, M.L., *ERIC: An Object-oriented Simulation Language*, Rome Air Development Center, RADC-TR-87-103, 1987.
33. Hughes, W.P., *Military Modeling*, The Military Operations Research Society, Inc., 1984.
34. IntelliCorp, *IntelliCorp The SimKit System Knowledge-Based Simulation Tools in KEE*, IntelliCorp, 1985.
35. Kamins, M., *Two Notes on the Lognormal Distribution*, The RAND Corporation, RM-3781-PR, 1963.
36. Kipps, J.R., B. Florman, and H.A. Sowizral, *The New ROSIE Reference Manual and User's Guide*, The RAND Corporation, R-3448-DARPA, 1987.
37. Kiviat, P.J., *Digital Computer Simulation: Modeling Concepts*, The RAND Corporation, RM-5378-PR, 1967.
38. Kiviat, P., R. Vilanueva, and H. Markowitz, *The SIMSCRIPT II Programming Language*, Prentice-Hall, Englewood Cliffs, New Jersey, 1968.
39. Klahr, P., "Expressibility in ROSS: An Object-oriented Simulation System," *AI APPLIED TO SIMULATION: Proceedings of the European Conference at the University of Ghent*, February 1985, pp. 136–139.
40. Klahr, P., and D.A. Waterman, "Artificial Intelligence: A Rand Perspective," *Expert Systems Techniques, Tools and Applications*, Addison-Wesley, 1986, pp. 3–23.
41. Klahr, P., et al., *SWIRL: Simulating Warfare in the ROSS Language*, The RAND Corporation, N-1885-AF, 1982.
42. Klahr, P., et al., *TWIRL: Tactical Warfare in the ROSS Language*, The RAND Corporation, R-3158-AF, 1984.
43. Kozlov, S.N., "The Officer's Handbook", *Soviet Military Thought No. 13*, U.S. Government Printing Office, 1971.
44. Luttwak, E.N., *The Pentagon and the Art of War*, Simon and Schuster, New York, 1985.
45. Martin, H., "AirLand Battle 2000 is Being Implemented with a High Technology Light Division," *Military Electronics/Countermeasures*, January 1983, 28–36.
46. McArthur, D., and P. Klahr, *The ROSS Language Manual*, The RAND Corporation, N-1854-AF, 1982.
47. McArthur, D., P. Klahr, and S. Narain, *ROSS: An Object-Oriented Language for Constructing Simulations*, The RAND Corporation, R-3160-AF, 1984.

48. McArthur, D., P. Klahr, and S. Narain, *The ROSS Language Manual*, The RAND Corporation, N-1854-1-AF, September 1985.
49. McArthur, D., *Building Learning and Tutoring Tools for Object-Oriented Simulation Systems*, The RAND Corporation, R-3443-DARPA/RC, 1987.
50. McCarthy, J., and P. Hayes, "Some Philosophical Problems from the Standpoint of Artificial Intelligence," in B. Meltzer and D. Michie (eds.), *Machine Intelligence*, Edinburgh University Press, Edinburgh, 1969.
51. McFall, M.E. and P. Klahr, "Simulation with Rules and Objects," *Proceedings of the 1986 Winter Simulation Conference*, Washington, D.C., 1986, pp. 470–473.
52. Naslund, W. and M. Callero, *Developing Effectiveness Relationships for Evaluating Tactical Air Command and Control: The Land Battle*, Rand working draft WD-498-AF, July 1980.
53. Newell, A., J.C. Shaw, and H. Simon, "Empirical Explorations with the Logic Theory Machine," *The Proceedings of the Western Joint Computer Conference*, 1957.
54. Nugent, R.O., and R.W. Wong, "The Battlefield Environment Model: An Army-Level Object-Oriented Simulation Model," *The Proceedings of the 1986 Summer Simulation Conference*, 1986.
55. Patrick, S., *NATO Division Commander*, Simulation Publications Pamphlet, 1979.
56. Paul, J., D.A. Waterman, and M.A. Peterson, "SAL: An Expert System for Evaluating Asbestos Claims," *The Proceedings of the First Australian Artificial Intelligence Congress*, Melbourne, Australia, 1986.
57. Peters, R., "Unmatched Spurs: A False Step in Soviet Doctrine?," *Military Intelligence*, Vol. 12, No. 1, January-March 1986, pp. 14–58.
58. Quade, E.S., "Modeling Techniques" *Handbook of Systems Analysis*, H.J. Miser, and E.S. Quade (eds.), North-Holland, 1985.
59. Reingold, E.M., and J.S. Tilford, "Tidier Drawings of Trees," *IEEE Transactions on Software Engineering*, Vol. SE-7, No. 2, 1981.
60. Rothenberg, J., "Object-oriented Simulation: Where Do We Go From Here?," *Proceedings of the 1986 Winter Simulation Conference*, Washington, D.C., 1986, pp. 464–469.
61. Rothenberg, J., "The Nature of Modeling", in *Artificial Intelligence, Simulation and Modeling*, L. Widman, et al., editors, John Wiley &Sons, Inc., 1989.
62. Rothenberg, J., et al., *Knowledge-Based Simulation: An Interim Report*, The RAND Corporation, N-2897-DARPA, July 1989.
63. Rumbaugh, J., "Relations as Semantic Constructs in an Object-oriented Language," *OOPSLA'87 Proceedings*, 1987.
64. Sharpe, W.F., *The Army Deployment Simulator*, The RAND Corporation, RM-4219-ISA, 1965.
65. Sowizral, H.A., and J.R. Kipps, *ROSIE: A Programming Environment for Expert Systems*, The RAND Corporation, R-3246-ARPA, 1985.
66. Steeb, R., S. Cammarata, S. Narain, J. Rothenberg, and W. Giarla, *Cooperative Intelligence for Remotely Piloted Vehicle Fleet Control*, The RAND Corporation, R-3408-ARPA, October 1986.
67. U.S. Army, *River Crossing Operations*, Field Manual, FM 90-13, November 1978.

68. U.S. Army, *Assault River Crossing Operations*, Army Field Manual Attachment, FM 30–102, pp. 16-6 to 16-13.
69. U.S. Army TRADOC, *The AirLand Battle and Corps 86*, Pamphlet 525-5, March 1981.
70. Vaucher, J.G., "Pretty-Printing of Trees", *Software—Practice and Experience*, Vol. 10, 1980.
71. Veit, C.T., M. Callero, and B.J. Rose, *Introduction to the Subjective Transfer Function Approach to Analyzing Systems*, The RAND Corporation, R-3021-AF, 1984.
72. Voosen, B.J., *PLANET: Planned Logistics Analysis and Evaluation Technique*, The RAND Corporation, RM-4950-PR, 1967.
73. Vorobyov, I., "Developing the Commander's Initiative," *Soviet Military Review*, May 1983, pp. 18–21.
74. Waterman, D.A., and M.A. Peterson, *Models of Legal Decisionmaking*, The RAND Corporation, R-2717-ICJ, 1981.

CHAPTER 9

An Architecture for High-Level Human Task Animation Control

Jeffrey Esakov and Norman I. Badler

Abstract

There are many problems in developing a computer-generated animation of tasks performed by a human. Sequencing actions, which may be easy to do when only a single actor is involved, becomes much more difficult as more actors and objects begin to interact. Similarly, the actual planning of a task is difficult if one considers the capabilities which are being modeled. Resource allocation also must be considered along with alternate plans of action. These types of problems imply that a knowledge base and a planner need to be involved in creating the task animation. To produce the actual motion, techniques must be used to manipulate the geometry of the scene. Three basic techniques exist for accomplishing this, dynamics, kinematics, and constraints, with no single technique superior in all respects.

Although a few systems exist which attempt to address these problems, none succeed in a general fashion. Either work is concentrated in the animation production issues ignoring difficulties in sequencing and actor capabilities, or in the task planning stage, ignoring issues involving actual scene geometry. Those which seem to achieve success in both areas use a specialized architecture designed around the particular task to be animated.

An architecture is described which addresses issues in human task performance at two levels simultaneously. The architecture demonstrates a link between the task planning stage and the motion generation stage based upon an extensible set of virtual "processors" and communication pathways between them. The types of problems which can be encountered among these processors, including nomenclature conflicts and timing synchronization, are described.

1 Introduction

The goal of this work is human-motion understanding. That is, simulating and animating "humans" performing a set of tasks for the purposes of evaluating the resulting motion and task performance. Such simulations and animations can answer basic performance questions such as whether it is possible in "real life" to perform the tasks. Furthermore, by varying parameters such as size or strength, task performance is affected. An application of such a system is simulating human-task performance in a hazardous, or prohibitively expensive, environment.

This work encompasses the areas known in Computer Science as *animation* and *simulation*. The definition of these terms, and the classification of implementations as either "animation systems" or "simulation systems," are imprecise. Historically, *animation* is what manual animators do; creation and manipulation of a set of two-dimensional images which when viewed together show objects in motion [50]. Each image in the set is called a *frame*. Therefore, "computer animation" involved the same process performed with the help of a computer. *Simulation* involves the manipulation of computer models which represent the objects (or events) on a frame-by-frame basis.

In practice, however, these definitions are inadequate. Almost every "animation system" that has been described in the literature is a simulation system, in the traditional sense of the word, with animations as output (for example, [24,21,29,49,42,53]). For the purposes of this paper, animation and simulation are distinguished as follows. Systems for which the primary purpose is ostensibly animation (or motion) output are viewed as "animation systems." The person who uses such a system is called the *animator*. Systems for which the primary purpose is to simulate a set of tasks are viewed as "simulation systems."

1.1 Animations as a Basis for Human Task Performance Analysis

There is considerable complexity inherent in computer-generated animations of human tasks. A naive approach might consider the motion of a "human" figure in the same manner as the motion of a table. However, the number of tedious details that would be required from the animator would be overwhelming; simply causing the figure to bend a knee would require the animator to maintain the connectivity of all the graphical objects representing the body! A more feasible approach is to implement a software model of the body in which connectivity is enforced [4,17,53]. With the introduction of such a model, more advanced information can be used to help guide animations. For example, restricting the movement of the limbs (joint limits) insures that the computer model can be positioned realistically; by giving the model "strength" (the ability to generate forces), the actual dynamics involved in performing a task can be correctly modeled. As more information models (such as strength and joint limits) are associated with an animation and the animator's expectations increase,* however, there is a corresponding increase in the complexity of task specification and control.

*In general, when people view animations involving human beings, expectations are considerably higher than animations involving other objects. This is because people implicitly know what looks right.

Consider the following tasks with respect to specification and control:

- Simple command processing.
- Assembling objects.
- Re-arranging furniture.
- Driving a car.

Simple command processing is a series of "simple reaches" and view changes. A simple reach is the positioning of a part of the body such that a desired position and/or orientation is achieved. In addition, it must be decided how long each reach should take. In *assembling objects* ordering of subtasks becomes an issue. Various components may need to be assembled before they are combined, but the order in which the individual components are assembled may be unimportant. *Re-arranging furniture* includes the same difficulties as the previous tasks, but also introduces the need for ordering tasks based upon the location of the movers. For example, if one mover is blocked by a couch, the couch must be moved before anything else. Of course, one mover may not be strong enough to move the couch. This implies a model for strength and a technique for resource allocation (where the resources are the three movers). Similarly, it may turn out that of three movers, one mover will only move chairs (due to labor union rules) and hence the other two must move everything else. This implies a model describing the individuals' abilities, desires, preferences and responsibilities (to name a few agent characteristics). *Driving a car* involves selecting multiple tasks to be performed depending upon a priority between tasks, as well as changing the tasks to be performed depending upon what can be seen. An example of the former is turning on the radio while waving to a friend (both can't be done at the same time since one hand must be kept on the steering wheel at all times). An example of the latter is waving to the friend only if the friend can still be seen.

The common element to each of these tasks is the increased control and data requirements of the animation. Certainly, they could be animated using conventional computer animation tools and techniques. However, with the various models that should be considered, as well as the multitude of tasks, the animator would need to make a large number of choices. It is likely that many of these decisions would be made without considering the alternatives. For example, one such decision that is routinely made is determining the order in which events should occur.

In analyzing human task performance, questions such as *Can X do the task? Could X do the task if he were left-handed? right-handed? Is X in a comfortable position? What if X were 6 feet tall? Can X see the target? Is X strong enough to lift the object?* are asked. To gain the most out of a task animation, the various models and control techniques must be accessible to the animator (although it should not be necessary to explicitly specify each in detail every time – there should be reasonable default values).

The tools needed for effective task performance analysis fall into two broad categories, control requirements and database requirements.

1.1.1 Control Requirements

Control requirements affect both task-level decisions and animation-level decisions [56]. Until now, these two aspects of task performance were not considered separately; they were combined when "generating an animation." The task level considers the tasks to be performed while the animation level deals with the techniques required to create the motion associated with a given task (see Figure 1). At this stage, the names "task-level" and "animation-level" are simply convenient handles by which one can refer to the high-level and low-level functions that need to be performed to generate an animation. As will be seen, most existing animation systems include both levels, but view "task-level" functions more as control issues for the animation rather than a separable set of functions.

We will call the control mechanism which directly affects the animation-level functions the *animation processor*. The *animation processor* specifies the motion generation technique that should be used to create an animation (kinematics, dynamics or constraints). As will be shown in Section 2.1 there are situations in which each of these techniques is superior. Therefore, to generate a realistic animation from which task performance questions can be answered, all three techniques should be accessible.

The control issues at the task-level are considerably more numerous since most task performance questions are directed to this level. Control issues which must be considered are:

1. task sequencing. In what order should the tasks be performed? The specification of tasks should not need to include explicit times for execution unless it is absolutely required that a task be performed at a

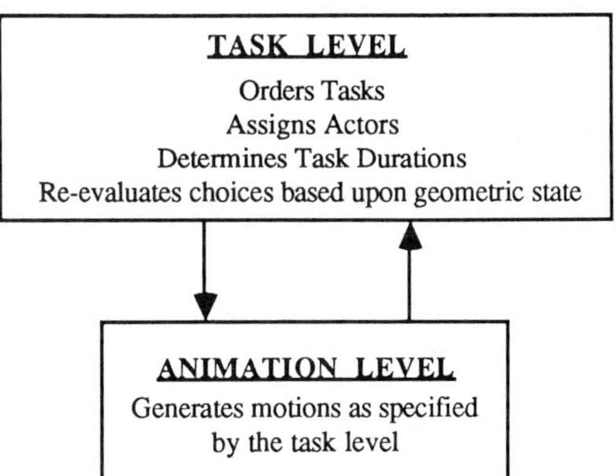

FIGURE 1. The task and animation levels.

specific time. Instead, the task specification should allow one to indicate a partial ordering of tasks.

2. task duration. How long should a task take? Clearly, less time is required to pick up a pencil when one's hand is already touching it. It should not be necessary to specify explicit durations unless it is absolutely required that a task be performed for a specific amount of time. Instead, the task specification should allow one to indicate either an approximate duration or a default duration should be assigned based upon the task to be performed.
3. task prioritization. Should one task be able to temporarily (or permanently) override the performance of another task? When there are multiple tasks to be performed and two tasks require the same agent at the same time, it must be possible to determine a relative priority between the two tasks.
4. resource allocation. Who should perform the task? When there are multiple agents available, it should not be necessary to specify explicitly who is to perform that task unless it is absolutely required that the task be performed by a specific agent. Instead, the task specification should allow one to indicate the task and allow the agent to be assigned based upon who is available, who is closer, or who is responsible for the task.

These control decisions are somewhat more complex than may first appear. There is a large body of data that must be available to facilitate making these decisions.

1.1.2 Database Requirements

Logically the task-level and animation-level functions access the same database although it will be shown in Section 5.3.1 that they need not be physically the same since there is minimal overlap. To support the control decisions required and performance questions which may be asked, a considerable amount of data must be available. This information is listed along with the type of performance analysis question which would necessitate the information model.

Task Model. This describes the tasks to be achieved. Ideally, it should be possible to specify "generic" tasks. Without this basic model, there is no "task" on which performance can be analyzed. Obviously, the components of this model have impact on the control aspects above:

- Priority Model. This relates the importance of one task to another. It is likely that priority may change depending upon the various tasks being performed at a given time.
- Resource Model. In order to perform resource allocation, the sort of resources required to accomplish a task must be known.

- Temporal Relationships. Although not explicitly part of a "generic" task model, when a task is to be performed timing relationships will need to be specified.

Body Model. This describes the body geometry and linkages. Without this basic model, there is no "human" whose performance can be analyzed. The model specifies various aspects of human perception and performance [8,9]. There are several important aspects of this model:

- Anthropometry data. *Can an average size (50th percentile height) man reach the goal? How about a 30th percentile woman?*
- Joint Limit/Comfort Model. *Can X reach the object? Comfortably (without straining)?*
- Strength/Fatigue Model. *Can X lift the object? Can X lift the object after bench pressing 200 pounds?*

This "body model" is not limited to humans. We use the generalized term "body model" when referencing robots, as well.

Agent Model. An agent model describes the characteristics of a specific agent. For example, identical twins can have different jobs and hence different responsibilities.

- Training (abilities). *How quickly can X react to an emergency?*
- Characteristics. *Will X go alone or does Y need to go along?*
- Preferences. *Can X do it left-handed? Does X favor a particular type of keyboard? Given object Y, where will X grab it?*
- Responsibilities. *Given a task and two people, who should perform the task (alternatively phrased: Is X a member of a labor union)?*

Object Model. An object model describes the characteristics of a specific object. In animation terms, an object is considered a property (in theater, abbreviated as "prop"). The details about an object are required to answer any task performance question in which the object is involved in the task (for example, a simple reach).

- Geometry (including possible linkages).
- Important features. This includes describing the "desirable" places in which the object may be grasped (*e.g.* at the top).

To a certain extent, body models and object models are the same. But for the purposes of discussion, we will continue to consider them as different types of models.

2 Animation and Simulation Techniques

Within the realm of human task performance analysis, there are basically two types of systems in use: animation systems and simulation systems.

These two types of systems approach the control issues from differing perspectives. In this section, the general techniques used in computer animation and computer simulation are discussed, and it will be shown that neither type of system in and of itself is sufficient for task performance analysis.

2.1 Animation Techniques

Given a model and the ability to manipulate it to create motion, there exist several computer animation techniques which could be used. With *key frame animation* (alternatively called kinematic specification), the individual frames which make up the animation are generated by specifying the positions, or other modeling parameters, of the objects in a minimal number of "important" (or key) frames. The remaining frames are determined through interpolation of the object position (or other parameters). *Dynamic animation* uses forces on objects to cause, or suppress, movement. The use of constraints, either in kinematics, dynamics, or as an motion generation technique by itself is based upon specification of the relationships between objects. The satisfaction of these constraints causes (or suppresses) movement.

One cannot claim that any one of these techniques is superior in all respects. There are conditions in which each is most applicable. There are also drawbacks when using each technique. Animations based upon a kinematic specification are relatively easy to control [46]. Although widely in use, a drawback to this technique is the "look" of the final animation. Unless great pains are taken by the animator, animations which use kinematics tend to look flat and unrealistic even though the path of movements depicted may be valid. This is in part due to the fact that biomechanical characteristics associated with the body are either ignored, or, due to the number of parameters (one, two or three for each joint)* involved, too difficult to specify.

Animations based upon dynamic specifications achieve greater realism at the expense of ease of control [53,23,2]. Since dynamics specifications are forces, the animator must be able to specify the forces on the objects to cause motion. Joint limits are easily modeled using springs and dampers and a strength model can be encoded directly.† There are two drawbacks with dynamics specification for animation. The first involves controlling the movement. Most of the time, an animator knows where the object is to move, not the forces required to make the move. Determining forces is not intuitive. Furthermore, a force is needed to get an object moving and

---

*An elbow is an example of a joint with one degree of freedom and hence one parameter. A wrist has two degrees of freedom and a shoulder has three.

†An example of such a model is an encoding of (maximum) joint torques to be used to establish driving or reactive forces.

an opposite force is required to cause it to stop – hence two separate sets of forces must be considered (unless the motion decay is to be equal to the attack and there are no other forces acting on the object). The second problem with dynamic specifications is that it takes a great amount of time to generate an animation (in comparison to kinematics). This time is used in setting up and solving equations with a great many degrees of freedom.

Animation by using constraints is a relatively new technique. Most notable in this area are techniques pioneered by Witkin, Fleischer and Barr [54], Barzel and Barr [7]. With this technique, the desired relationships between objects are specified and the system repositions and reorients the objects to best satisfy the constraints. The advantage to this technique is the ease at which the animation is specified. However, as with dynamics, constraint satisfaction is not a real-time process. Furthermore, constraints by themselves do not include the concept of time. In order to develop an animation, time must be super-imposed upon the constraint satisfaction algorithm (*i.e.* usually, it is the *algorithm* that is animated).

The technique of applying constraints specifically to articulated figures is addressed by Badler, Manoochehri and Walters [6]. This is considered a different problem than general constraints in that a software body model can be used to speed up the algorithm. One body model which could be implemented uses constraints themselves to represent the body linkages. This method, however, would severely effect the performance of an already costly technique. Badler *et al.* achieve near-real time satisfaction of constraints, but only consider point-in-space constraints. No one has yet considered the real-time satisfaction of general constraints, such as maintaining contact with a surface (plane) involving articulated figures although this is similar to the compliant motion problem in robotics [37].

2.2 Hybrid Animation Techniques

The variety of human movement seems to preclude any single technique of animation [52,22]. Each technique contributes to the overall goal of creating a realistic animation in a different way. Therefore, it is pointless to argue that one is superior to another; instead, they should be combined as necessary depending the task (or subtask) to be animated.

Dadamo is proposing a system, TAKE_ONE [13], which will test this hypothesis. Her technique (based upon an idea in [3]) allows one to combine the three techniques in a controlled manner. A single animation can be created from kinematic, dynamic, and constraint based animations. The technique of combining the three specifications into a single frame makes use of a weighted average of separately (in parallel) computed physical states. By moderating the weight of the combinations during the course of an animation, the frame which is generated can be preferentially based upon one or more specifications.

Regardless of which animation technique is used and the specific parameters required by the chosen technique, there are still many other parameters which must be considered when developing the animation. These parameters make up the script of the animation: who does what when. From the animator's perspective, these are not explicitly viewed as parameters of the animation. Instead, the decisions are implicitly made and a script is developed. The final animation is simply a graphical representation of the script. A considerable number of animation systems have been developed in this area (see Section 4.1), and it is along these lines that simulation techniques are applicable.

2.3 Task Simulation

For simple animations, simple control techniques are applicable. As animations become more complex, with natural, coordinated, expressive or task-oriented motions, then simulation techniques for control are more appropriate. It is logical for the animation process to be controlled at descriptive levels appropriate to the process being controlled.[30,35] An animation in which all that is required is for a person to press a button is most easily developed by specifying the kinematics (animation-level) parameters. Alternatively, if the task is to perform an "emergency shutdown," it is best viewed at a higher level; an "emergency shutdown" consists of pressing button 1 then button 2 with a delay of no more than two seconds and switch A must be toggled to the *off* position when the red light flashes.

2.3.1 Simulation Data Structures

The world model within a simulator is represented using data structures. Often the data structures are indigenous to the language in which the simulator is written. The general problem with this is that the view of the world model limits *reasoning* about the model. This type of data structure does not support a symbolic representation of the world model.

An alternative structure is to use Artificial Intelligence techniques within the simulator. AI simulation uses structures that more explicitly represent actions and their relationships. While animation systems deal directly with quantitative geometric values, AI simulation systems tend to deal with more qualitative information. Qualitative data includes relationships, interactions, and causality between events and objects. Both types of information are important as simulation systems need to perform both quantitative and qualitative reasoning. Quantitative reasoning is important where precise physical quantities are being measured whereas qualitative reasoning is important where "rule of thumb" relationships can be determined. For example, quantitative reasoning is appropriate when modeling the dynamics of a robot arm, whereas symbolic reasoning is appropriate when reasoning about the movements of an object which is being "grasped" by the robot (*i.e.* the tool will stay in the robot's hand).

Simulation systems are better equipped (than animation systems) to handle the higher-level timing relationships between motions such as concurrency, overlap, mutual exclusion, *etc.* That is, the plan of actions to be simulated (or animated) is best handled within the context of a simulator. By viewing a simulation as a system in which an overall goal is to be achieved by the application of production rules [40], the plan is simply determining which production rules to apply. This is done by starting at the goal and working back to the initial conditions. In this sense, planning can be thought of as being the reverse of simulation. The planner can uncover multiple paths (potentially an exponential growth based upon the number of rules) which lead to achieving the goal, whereas the simulator chooses one of those paths. It is not necessarily the case that all planning be completed before the simulation. In a non-deterministic simulation (for example, one involving events which occur based upon a probability function), it might be necessary to develop plans for various subgoals to be achieved at any point in the simulation.

3 Definition of the Problem

Our research involves developing an overall system architecture in which simulation and animation facilities work cooperatively.

The major issues are:

1. Existing animation systems do not include the proper task-level constructs for sufficiently complete performance analyses.
2. Existing simulation systems do not include a sufficient amount of animation constructs to allow for animation parameters to effect the course of the simulation.

Clearly, task animation and task simulation facilities do address different aspects of the *same* problem; each system provides a different level of understanding to human task performance. These facilities should work together in a "symbiotic" relationship. While animation systems can allow one to view the performance of the task (yet require one to sequence the events and specify explicit actors and actions), simulation systems can select the actors and actions to be performed.

From the animation perspective, this "off-loads" some of the difficult problems. Animation systems have only superficially solved some of the difficulties in specifying timing relationships (through the use of track-based animation, see Section 4.1.1). The difficulty in specifying parallelism and intricate timing relationships still remains for the animator. Furthermore, the animator is burdened with the choice of actors. This latter issue is important since there are several characteristics of an actor model which can affect the animation (*e.g.* the size of the figure, flexibility, the actor strength being modeled, agent models, *etc.*).

From the AI simulation perspective, a continuous simulation system (the animation system) is available to a discrete event simulator.* This allows more informed and hence realistic decisions to be made whenever a choice must be made among multiple courses of action. For example, one parameter in deciding which of two people will open a door *should* be who is closer. For a simulation system to maintain this information would require a simulation variable for each of the possible interactions. Such a method greatly increases the complexity of the simulator, making programming such a simulation very difficult and error-prone.

3.1 Goals of this Research

This research shows:

- how some of the difficult problems in specifying an animation (*e.g.* timing relationships, strength modeling, resource allocation) can be shifted to the more appropriate simulation domain.
- how tasks can be interrupted and resumed if possible. Since people are often interrupted during the performance of a task, "rules" for handling interruptions are important.
- that animations can be developed automatically which include more agent-dependent characteristics. It is not hard to visualize the need to analyze the performance of a task by both a left-handed and a right-handed person or based upon individual preferences, responsibilities, or capabilities.
- how the geometric knowledge, which is an integral part of any animation system, can be used to guide a simulation. For example, different agents may be available to move an object, with the one who is physically closest to the object chosen. Also, determining the amount of time it takes to reach an object can be estimated based upon the size of the object and the distance from the object (Fitts' Law – see Section 5.4.1).
- how the separate databases required by simulation and animation systems can be logically combined with consistency maintained without sacrificing their modularity.
- how different levels of detail can be included automatically in the generation of motion depending upon factors such as proximity to the "main action" or distance from the camera.
- that a high-level task specification (perhaps expert system-like rules or natural language) can be animated in a non-application-dependent manner.

---

*We are very careful not to use the term *embedded* as there are certain advantages to considering the two systems individually (as well as a unit).

4 Relevant Research

The work described in this paper bridges the gap between animation control systems and simulation systems. As such, it is instructive to examine existing work in both areas.

4.1 Computer Animation Control Systems

An animation control system packages, or combines, the low-level motion generation algorithms to give the animator more flexibility in specifying an animation. A representative set of animation control systems is described here.

4.1.1 Track Animation Systems

One type of animation system is a multiple track system exemplified by MUTAN [21]. The use of tracks enables the animator to synchronize various aspects of an animation. For example, the actions of two people can be synchronized by specifying that particular key frames should occur at specific frame numbers. If the synchronization is found to be inadequate, ideally, all that need be done is to change the frame numbers for the key frames.

Another such system, TWIXT (developed by Gomez [24]), is similar to MUTAN except that instead of limiting tracks to contain complete actions, individual parameters of a single object can be separated.

Dial [16] is a two-dimensional notation for specifying parallelism as well as indicating visually obvious initiation, termination, and suspension of concurrent animation events. This track system is interesting in that at each time tick, events are executed by calling back-end routines with the length of the event, the current tick in the event's execution (relative to the event's start tick) and the event's parameters. It is up to the back-end to determine how to handle events occurring over a large period of time.

These track-based systems are an improvement over basic key frame systems in that the synchronization of events are easily specified. However, since motion is kinematically specified, the problems with key frame animations remain, as do difficulties in sequencing, resource allocation, and the use of higher-level models in the control of the animation. Of course, track-based systems do not claim to address these latter problems.

4.1.2 Object-Oriented Animation Systems

Object-oriented animation systems are based upon *actors* as defined by Hewitt [25]. An actor is an object that can send and/or receive messages. All elements of a system are actors and the transmission of messages is the only operation in the system. The programming of an actor-based (object-oriented) system is merely telling actors how to interpret the various messages that can occur. There are several animation systems with foundations in actor theory [29,49,42,33]. Of those, this section describes Reynolds' ASAS [42] and Thalmann & Thalmann's CINEMIRA [33] languages.

The Actor/Scriptor Animation System (ASAS) makes full use of the object-oriented paradigm. Each actor is an instance of some object and has specific actions associated with it. If an actor needs to interact with another actor, it passes a message. It is the responsibility up the individual actor to interpret the message and act accordingly. There is a set of geometric primitives which enable an object to be animated such as basic transformations (rotation, translation, and scaling) and higher level constructs which Reynolds calls a *newton.* A *newton* allows the animator to produce curves with certain properties. For example, the *slowio* newton is one which, given starting and ending values and a time, produces a curve with zero derivatives at either end.

CINEMIRA, and its subset, CINEMIRA-2, expand upon the newton concept defined in ASAS. In its place, the user can define *laws* of animation [35]. With the ability to define subactors and timing, the user can define more complex operations such as an explosion.

It is straightforward for a system such as ASAS or CINEMIRA to model agent characteristics using accepted object-oriented programming techniques. Similarly, one can set up interactions between agents, including timing constructs such as parallelism, via the messages. However, as the user includes more agents and the timing constructs become more complex, there is a correspondingly large jump in the complexity of the programming involved. Also, there is not a clear separation between control and data as both are implicit in the methods associated with the objects.

4.1.3 Zeltzer: Motion Control Program

Zeltzer's system for the animation of walking [55] is based upon a hierarchy of motor control programs. A skill (for example, walking) invokes particular programs which in turn may invoke lower level programs. Each program proceeds based upon feedback from the programs above and below it. In this system, describing a new skill requires that a complete set of programs be developed.

This system presents a totally different way of creating animations. By encoding the tasks in a series of interconnected motion control programs, it is possible to use a form of animation feedback to effect the system. There are drawbacks, however. First, because each new skill requires a complete set of programs (rules) be developed, learning one skill does not apply directly to another skill. Secondly, it is not clear how even slight variations other than speed could be handled using the same set of control programs. For example, two people would require two sets of motion control programs to describe their different gaits, even if they were only slightly different.

4.1.4 Takashima et al.: Story Driven Animation

The Story Driven Animation System (SDAS)[48] consists of a story understanding module, a stage directing module, and an action generating module. The stories are written in a "modified" natural language. There are no pronouns, and each sentence must describe an event following the event described in the previous sentence. The story understanding module takes the events described and passes the set of active events to the stage directing module. The stage directing module divides the events into scenes and determines specific actions that need to occur. The action generation module produces the actual animation.

It seems as though this is a complete system. However, in many ways, it is less satisfactory than the ones previously described. The system is domain-dependent with rigid linkages between the various modules and input is restricted. It is not possible to represent any complex timing concepts or interrupts. The models are limited and output is developed through the selection of previously developed key frames.

4.1.5 Discussion

Clearly, the systems described thus far do not incorporate all the features desirable in a human task animation system. Neither complex timing relationships nor strength models (or even joint limits) are easily incorporated into any of these systems. Furthermore, the concept of dynamic (not preplanned) task interruptions are not considered in any of the systems. Although it might be possible to include such a concept in ASAS, certainly it would be very specific to the particular actions being performed. That is, were a different animation to be developed, it is not likely that any of the existing "interrupt" routines would be useful.

Zeltzer [56] describes a task manager for controlling his local motor programs. Of the systems reviewed thus far, this comes closest to meeting the goals outlined previously. Even so, he only considers this "knowledge-based animation" from the perspective of task decomposition, meeting preconditions, and using some default knowledge (this latter point could be considered an acknowledgment of agent models). Issues such as interruptibility, animation techniques, and strength must also be included in a human task simulation/animation environment.

4.2 AI Simulation Systems

There are a great many Artificial Intelligence simulation systems. In this section several of those systems are discussed. The systems considered are those which have function in at least one of the following areas: animation output, temporal planning, and agent modeling.

4.2.1 MIRALOGIC

MIRALOGIC [34] is an interesting approach to embedding an expert system within an animation system. The purpose of the system is to allow an artist to specify the conditions for an image using goal-directed specifications. Based upon the user input of rules, MIRALOGIC will identify possible problems as a result of the rules, identify alternative choices and propose a solution, and detect logical inconsistency among rules. For example, suppose a set of rules were entered which specified the lighting of an environment. A problem as a result of these rules could be that an important area is too dark. Alternatives could be to add another light source or increase the intensity of the existing light sources.

MIRALOGIC is being developed within the context of the MIRANIM [34] system. and is one of the first existing animation systems to use AI-like structures. Since it is an expert system, it does not deal with task interruption, task prioritization, complex timing constructs or many other of the higher-level constructs described previously.

4.2.2 HIRES

Fishwick's HIRES [19] is a rule-based process simulator which simulates processes over multiple levels of abstraction. The primary contribution of this system is that the abstraction is with respect to *processes*. By defining a hierarchy of rules, processes can be studied at a level of abstraction appropriate to the specific task. This has the advantage of increased control, computational efficiency, and selective reporting of simulation results.

HIRES can simulate both continuous and discrete systems. A set of preprocessors is implemented that automatically generate rules based upon the requirements of a particular model (*e.g.* Petri net models). HIRES provides a simple report facility through which animations can be generated. The report facility, which is implemented as a "demon" executing at certain time intervals or at the "request" of a rule, allows one to select manually created key frames.

The concepts of process abstraction and preprocessors provide great flexibility. However, the rule structure and knowledge base used by HIRES are very rigid. The knowledge base states assertions defining the current state of the world with no interrelationships. A major use of the knowledge base is for passing parameters between rules (via a variable pattern matcher). This eliminates the possibility of using agent modeling or resource allocation schemes. Although both declarative (based upon preconditions) and procedural (based upon an order) rule firing are supported, explicit times must be specified by the user, as opposed to specifying temporal relationships.

4.2.3 Robotics Simulators

A "robotics simulator" uses the physical aspects of the environment to create a continuous simulation. Such a simulator makes use of the dynamics of an environment (internally and externally generated forces, such as inertia, and their consequents). There are several such simulators [12,15,26,47,28]. Hoffman's system [26] is described here since it achieves the goals previously outlined most closely.

Hoffman developed an extensible system which simulates the behavior of physical objects from their models. The system includes an abstract modeler, a geometric modeler, a dynamics modeler, and a control modeler. The abstract modeler provides the name of the object and a property list which includes material density and color. The geometric modeler describes the object geometry. The dynamics modeler includes a set of state variables and equation schemata which summarize the relations between the changes in state variables, time-independent properties and external forces acting on the object. The control modeler represents the robotics control mechanism. For example, it might be necessary to tell the robot to grasp something or to move at a particular acceleration.

This system also includes an animation generator and event handler which drives the overall system. It includes an equation solver, an impact generation module which determines if objects collide, and tools for modifying the various models. It is this latter capability which aligns this system with our work. Hoffman's system allows feedback from the environment to affect the next state. In particular, if objects collide, the forces change and hence the dynamics model must change.

Hoffman's system is an animation system embedded in a simulation system. Issues involving separate databases are avoided by including all the models in a single database. Qualitative relationships are not encoded in any of the models – only quantitative data. This limits the reasoning that can be made about the state of the world. The system can create an animation, but based only upon the dynamics involved. A limited set of constraints can be modeled, but only by adjusting the models. For example, insuring that an object remains grasped can be done by "connecting" the geometric models – but insuring that the hand remains in a particular point in space is more difficult.

4.2.4 Temporal Planning Models

The definitive work on general planning was done by Sacerdoti [45]. His system, NOAH, uses knowledge about multiple levels of actions and generates plans which are valid over each of those levels. The concept of time within his model is limited. Actions are partially ordered, but the amount of time an action takes or the intervals between actions is irrelevant.

There have been three basic efforts to extend planning into the temporal domain. Allen [1] uses the time interval as the basic unit. Temporal information is given by relationships between intervals. With these temporal relationships events can be ordered as in "interval A occurs before interval B but after interval C"; however, durations are not considered. Another problem with this system is since only intervals are considered, there is no way to specify a precise time.

Malik and Binford [36] proposed a model based on constraints on the endpoints of intervals. Linear programming technique is used to determine the actual values for the endpoints. With this approach, durations are considered as relationships to actual time. However, this technique is very inflexible. Each constraint within the system is either satisfied completely or totally ignored. The problem with this technique is that is it quite easy to underconstrain or overconstrain the system. In an underconstrained system, not enough information is specified and a unique solution cannot be found. In an overconstrained system, too much information is given which yields conflicting results and hence no solution is found.

Vere's DEVISER [51] uses time windows to specify when events can occur. A window indicates the earliest time, the latest time, and the ideal time at which an event can occur. Also, associated with each event is a duration attribute. DEVISER attempts to meet the ideal conditions, settling for any of the other conditions in the window specified if they can not be reached.

4.2.5 Agent Planning Models

Existing AI systems such as NOAH or STRIPS [18] deal exclusively with single agents. When multiple agents are involved, planning techniques become more complex. Issues such as abilities and responsibilities should be considered. Furthermore, concepts such as *beliefs*, that which an agent believes to be true, should effect the plans. For example, agent A may act in a certain way based upon the belief that agent B has a particular object. If, in fact, A is incorrect, at some point its behavior must be adjusted. Several researchers [32,39,44] have initiated research investigating this area of planning.

Konolige [32] and Pollack *et al.* [39] predicate their work on the notion that (1) each individual agent has a task to perform, (2) the agent's beliefs may or may not be correct, and (3) events outside the agent's control may affect the agent's plans. With these conditions, an agent does only a minimal amount of planning to complete its task. It can try to predict what other agents will do based upon what it thinks the other agents believe. Pollack *et al.* developed an overall architecture in which agent beliefs and actions are "filtered" based upon the agent's sensitivities to the environment (*i.e.* how easily the agent will change it's mind).

In these systems, each agent decides exactly what it is going to do based upon the tasks it is assigned. This implies an agent-centered organization.

In fact the existing systems would lend themselves quite nicely to object-oriented programming techniques. This is different from the higher level problem of deciding which agent is to perform the task. This latter problem implies a more global knowledge, making the overall system more similar to management hierarchies where there is a manager supervising a group of workers.

Ridsdale [44] has a system for implementing theatrical characterization techniques for animating actors. His system examines the scene and insures that no action overshadows the primary action. An example of this is when a figure unintentionally moves between another figure who is speaking and the camera. This system is unlike the systems described in the previous paragraph in that, here, there is a global oracle which knows exactly what is going on and directs the action accordingly. This different architecture reflects the difference in goals of the systems. Ridsdale's system deals with a specific environment and a specific set of static rules. Also, His system deals primarily with generating animations and hence represents the director, whereas the above systems consider simulation in which there is no director.

Reynolds [43] developed a system in which the aggregate motion of a flock of birds or a herd of animals is realistically simulated. His system uses a distributed behavioral model. Object oriented programming techniques are used in which each member of the herd is an object with two basic goals; to match velocity and direction with the herd, and to avoid collisions with other members. Each member is an independent actor and navigates according to its own perception of the world. In this manner, the overall behavior of the flock is guided by the individual, distributed, behaviors of the members.

4.2.6 Discussion

None of the existing AI systems incorporates animation features to the extent needed for human task performance analysis. The "robotics simulator" described by Hoffman[26] come closest, but since only dynamics information is available for generating the animation, control is very difficult. Also, in general, robotics simulators are continuous simulators with very limited qualitative world knowledge.

However, there are features in each of the simulators that are very desirable. HIRES allows for both discrete and continuous simulation with limited kinematic output. Robotics systems have dynamics animation output (with some feedback). STEAMER has graphical interaction and allows for different views of the simulation. DEVISER performs temporal planning. Lastly, the agent-oriented systems can deal with a limited form of cooperation and interrupts. A single system is needed with all these features to achieve the most flexibility in human task performance analysis.

While such a system will be more flexible than any of the existing systems simply by virtue of its features, it is important that the organization of the components of the system is both logical and consistent.

5 Initial Implementation

Preliminary work toward realizing this architecture has proceeded in two phases. The first phase involves an implementation in which a simulation system passes reach goals to an inverse kinematics positioner. The second phase builds upon the first phase to develop a more complete simulation-animation architecture.

5.1 Initial Architecture

The goal of the initial architecture is to show that a simulation system could indeed drive an animation. Although this is intuitively obvious, implementing such a system provided insight to problems which would exist in the more complete architecture.

There are three processes in the initial architecture, linearly arranged with one-way links.

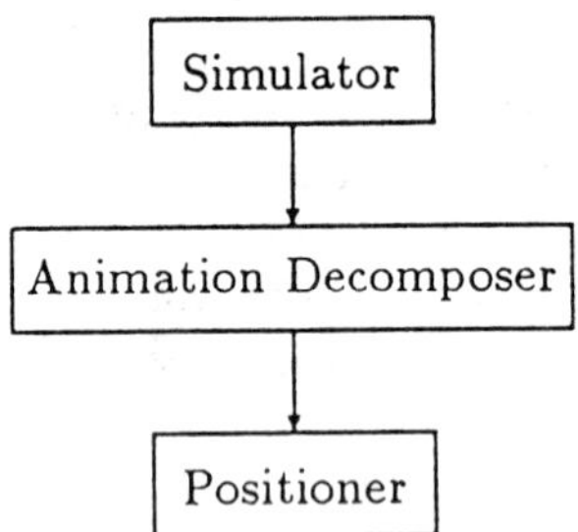

In this phase, no emphasis is placed on the simulator. Instead, effort is concentrated on the link between the simulator and animation generation. The output of the simulator is a list of "animation tasks" to be performed. The animation tasks themselves are a list of "simple reaches" to be performed by an articulated figure. The "reaches" were achieved via the positioning program.

More specifically, the "Animation Decomposer" is a program called **task**. Input to **task**, generated from an existing simulation program,* is a series of predefined animation task keywords. Using a prespecified lookup table, **task** determines which sequences of low-level animation procedures to execute. The following animation procedures were available: moving the camera, setting any number of arbitrary reach goals, solving to achieve

*The actual execution of this simulation/animation pipeline was performed at the NASA Ames Research Center.

those goals, and resetting the goals. POSIT [6] is used to achieve the goals specified.

This entire pipeline was performed in real-time as defined by the simulation program. That is, when the simulation program specifies an animation task, the **task** program interrupts POSIT (*i.e.* asynchronous interrupt causing the current reach solution algorithm to be terminated) and a new set of animation tasks to be performed is passed. Although POSIT is primarily used for generating key frames, it still allows for some visual feedback of the simulation via the "animation" of the solution algorithm. A log file of all commands passed to POSIT is maintained so that a complete set of key frames can be generated at a later date. With those key frames, a complete animation of the entire simulation can be created.

5.1.1 Example

In this example, the environment consists of a single person standing in front a control panel. The person is represented using the body model inherent in POSIT, and the control panel is comprised of a single polygon. Instead of using a simulation program to drive **task**, commands are entered at the keyboard.

The task to be performed consists of turning a series of knobs. The tables used by **task** consist of a "task table" and a "sub-task table." The entries in the task table are the high-level tasks which decompose into sub-tasks. The entries in the sub-task table are the POSIT positioning commands. The tables are as follows:

TASK TABLE:

```
initialize: sub_init
turn-knob-1: reset
turn-knob-1: reach-knob-1
turn-knob-1: reset
turn-knob-1: turn-k1
turn-knob-1: reset
turn-knob-1: move-away-from-k1
flip-knob-2: reset
flip-knob-2: reach-knob-2
flip-knob-2: reset
flip-knob-2: flip-k2
rest: reset
rest: rest
```

SUB-TASK TABLE:

```
sub_init: read_workstation panel nasapanel.pss
sub_init: move_object -33 -50 -40
sub_init: view 6 3 -5 120 0 0
reset: reset_all_goal
```

```
reset: set_goal body_root 0 0 0 1000
reset: set_goal left_foot 8 -94 0 1000
reset: set_goal right_foot -8 -94 0 1000
reset: solve
reach-knob-1: set_goal right_clav -17 48 0 50
reach-knob-1: set_goal right_hand -17 40 -35 20
reach-knob-1: solve
turn-k1: set_goal right_clav -17 48 0 100
turn-k1: set_goal right_hand -17 40 -35 100
turn-k1: set_goal right_up_arm -50 20 10 50
turn-k1: solve
move-away-from-k1: set_goal right_clav -17 48 0 100
move-away-from-k1: reset_goal right_hand
move-away-from-k1: set_goal right_up_arm -40 20 0 50
move-away-from-k1: solve
reach-knob-2: set_goal right_clav -17 48 0 100
reach-knob-2: set_goal right_hand 0 35 -30 20
reach-knob-2: solve
flip-k2: set_goal right_hand 0 36 -30 20
flip-k2: solve
rest: set_goal left_hand 18 -25 0 1000
rest: set_goal right_hand -18 -25 0 1000
rest: solve
```

The task **turn-knob-1** causes two sub-tasks to be performed: (1) the hand reaches knob-1 and (2) the knob is turned. The sub-task **reach-knob-1** is achieved using a sequence of animation goals which position the hand on the knob and insure the shoulder does not move. After that goal is achieved, the turning of the knob (subtask **turn-k1**) is simulated by moving the elbow (while insuring that the hand stays on the knob).

Partial log file output is shown below:

```
read_workstation panel nasapanel.pss
move_object -33 -50 -40
view 6 3 -5 120 0 0
reset_all_goal
set_goal body_root 0 0 0 1000
set_goal left_foot 8 -94 0 1000
set_goal right_foot -8 -94 0 1000
set_goal right_clav -17 48 0 50
set_goal right_hand -17 40 -35 20
solve
reset_all_goal
set_goal body_root 0 0 0 1000
set_goal left_foot 8 -94 0 1000
set_goal right_foot -8 -94 0 1000
```

```
set_goal right_clav -17 48 0 100
set_goal right_hand -17 40 -35 100
set_goal right_up_arm -50 20 10 50
solve
reset_all_goal
quit
```

5.1.2 Initial Results

Several observations can be made from this implementation:

- The environment in which the actions are to be performed was pre-defined, and all actions were specified in the world coordinate system. A pre-defined environment is expected, but specifying goals in the world coordinate system is very restrictive and short-sighted. Changes in the positioning of objects in the environment require that the reach goals stored in the **task** lookup tables be modified.
- Unless the animation algorithms can be completely synchronized with the simulation, immediate playback is not possible. Since the simulator did not supply information as to how long a particular task should take it could not be determined how fast to move the figure. Although not immediately useful since the particular goal-achievement algorithm implemented couldn't use this information, it would have been very useful when generating the complete animation (from the log file) as an indicator of key frame times.
- Based upon this implementation, it is obvious that interrupting an action has an impact on the speed of achievement of the next action and hence the subsequent playback of the complete animation may be different from what was viewed.
- The idea of interrupting a task is an important and necessary part of a simulation, but it needs to be evaluated further to determine exactly what an interrupt means and how (and where) it should be handled.
- This animation was limited to a single articulated figure and other objects in the environment. A more realistic environment would consist of multiple articulated figures interacting in a complex environment.
- Since this was a key frame animation system, the previously described problems with kinematic specifications pertain.

5.2 Refinement of the Initial Architecture

The first refinement of the initial architecture eliminates the need for specifying reach goals in the world coordinate system. This is achieved, in part, due to a more generally-defined geometric environment now in use in the University of Pennsylvania Computer Graphics Research Lab. The geometric environment, called **peabody** [38], is a graph of figures. A figure is an undirected graph of segments connected by joints. Important positions on segments are marked with sites. Furthermore, there is a special segment called **world** which specifies the world coordinate system. Since all these objects can be named, it is not necessary to know world coordinate positions.

The next issue addressed was the integration of this new nomenclature into the simulation environment. Consider a world consisting of a person, and a panel of switches. A panel of switches may be efficiently represented as a graphical texture map (which is a single object). Therefore, a map is needed to associate qualitative information about the various switches in the panel with their locations in the texture map. Clearly, the map between the two should be based upon the name.

A tool was developed which allows one to mark important positions on a texture map. Two files were given as output from this tool: one file is used as input into the **peabody** geometric database and the other as input into a frame-based knowledge base. With this high-level description of the environment, it is possible to develop an interface which used a subset of natural language to drive the animation.

5.2.1 Example

In this example, the environment consists of two people (one man and one woman) standing in front of a control panel. The important points (some switches) on the control panel were specified using the tool described above. The knowledge base input generated was as follows:

```
{ concept ctrlpanel from panelfig
 having (
        role twF-1 with value = ctrlpanel.panel.twf_1
        role twF-2 with value = ctrlpanel.panel.twf_2
        role tglJ-1 with value = ctrlpanel.panel.tglj_1
        )
}
```

The **peabody** file describes the actual panel with the switches represented as sites:

```
figure ctrlpanel {
    segment panel {
        psurf = "nasapanel.pss";
        site base->location = trans(0.00cm,0.00cm,0.00cm);
        site twf_1->location = trans(10.86cm,85.40cm,
            0.00cm);
        site twf_2->location = trans(45.45cm,85.40cm,
            0.00cm);
        site tglj_1->location = trans(31.72cm,85.40cm,
            0.00cm);
    }
```

```
    segment twf_1 {
        psurf = "unitpoly.pss";
        site twf_1->location = trans(0.00cm, 0.00cm,
            -.1cm);
    }
    segment twf_2 {
        psurf = "unitpoly.pss";
        site twf_2->location = trans(0.00cm, 0.00cm,
            -.1cm);
    }
    segment tglj_1 {
        psurf = "unitpoly.pss";
        site tglj_1->location = trans(0.00cm, 0.00cm,
            -.1cm);
    }
    joint twf_1 { connect panel.twf_1 to twf_1.twf_1; }
    joint twf_2 { connect panel.twf_2 to twf_2.twf_2; }
    joint tglj_1 { connect panel.tglj_1 to tglj_1.tglj_1; }
}
```

The interactive input consists of statements such as: *The man should flip tglJ-1 with his left hand.* Concurrency is achieved by using the connective "and" as in *The man should flip tglJ-1 with his left hand and the woman should move twF-1 to position 1.* A part of the script file which was generated by the positioner is shown below along with some frames created as a result of the animation:

```
point_at("ctrlpanel.panel.twf_1","man.bottom_head.between-
  eyes");
point_at("ctrlpanel.panel.twf_1","woman.bottom_head.be-
  tweeneyes");
reach_site("ctrlpanel.panel.twf_1","woman.left_fingers.
  distal");
```

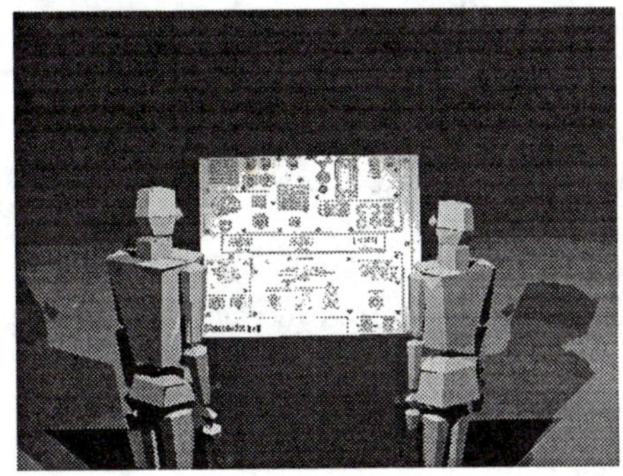

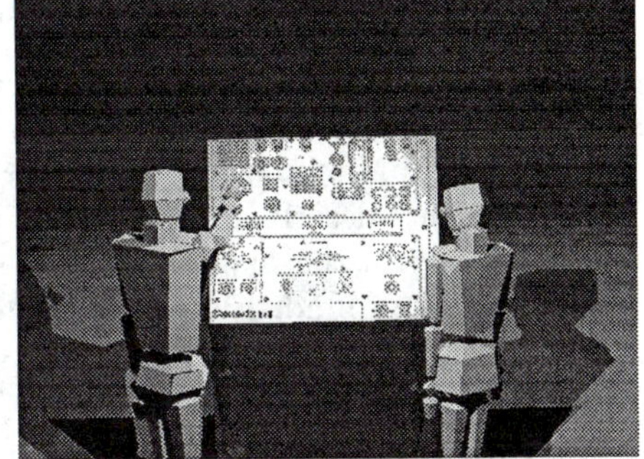

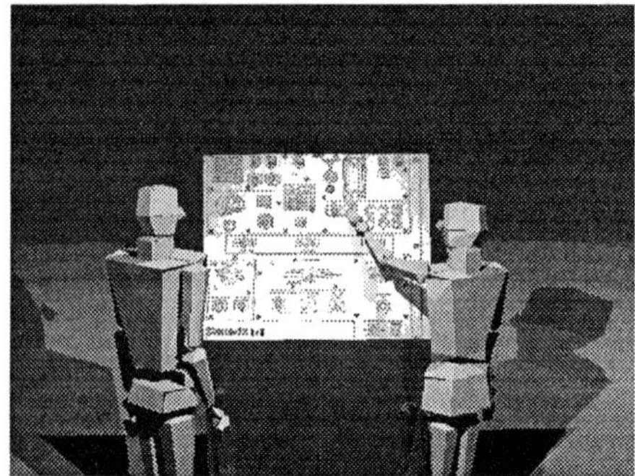

5.2.2 Refinement Results

This refinement achieved more than showing how to handle separate databases, which was the original intention. It demonstrated the following capabilities:

1. goals independent of geometry.
2. multiple figure reach goals.
3. high-level language input.
4. agent modeling (handedness).

5.3 A More Complete Architecture

These small implementations provide the groundwork for a larger architecture which includes the more interesting aspects of human task performance simulation and animation. The system architecture developed to meet the requirements described in Section 1.1 is shown in Figure 2.

Each box in the diagram represents a processor designed for a specific activity. The rounded boxes represent databases required in each environment. Although these databases are represented as being distinct, it is conceivable that an implementation can be developed in which both the

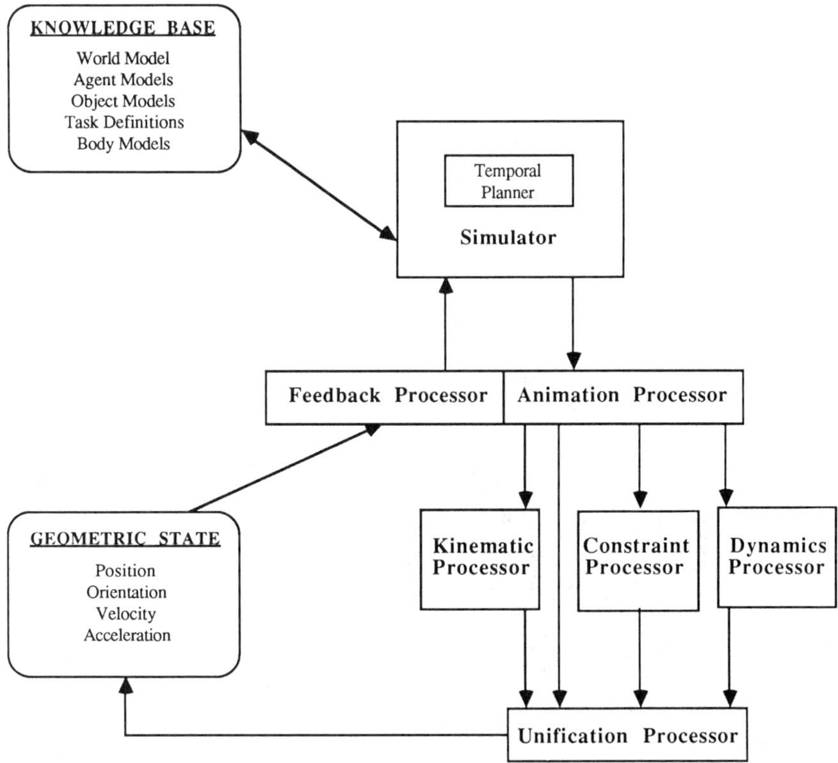

FIGURE 2. System architecture.

simulation knowledge base and the geometric data base are a single entity. Nonetheless, they can be distinguished by virtue of the type of data required.

5.3.1 Models

The world model of a simulator consists of knowledge about actors and objects. When speaking of an actor, one must consider the figure model as well as the agent model. For simulation purposes, a figure model consists of the hierarchical organization of segments which make up a body, and a strength and fatigue model. Agent models include data about agent capabilities, responsibilities and preferences. Object models include information such as object hierarchy, and part names. Ideally, no quantitative geometric information need be included. This can be supported by requiring that all path planning be done in the animation environment.

	Models	Environment Simulation	Animation
Actor	Body	•	•
	Strength	•	
	Fatigue	•	
	Agent	•	
	Geometry		•
Object	Hierarchy	•	•
	Handle	•	•
	Geometry		•
	Relations	•	
	Rules	•	

FIGURE 3. Summary of information models.

Lastly, the simulation environment requires task definitions. Task definitions can be in the form of processes (and sub-processes) and rules. Also included under task definition are rules for performing animation tasks and obtaining animation feedback.

The animation environment requires knowledge about both actor and object models as well. However, the information needed is slightly different. For animation purposes, the figure model includes the body organization, body geometry scaled according to anthropometric sizing data, joint limit and comfort models, and strength models. For object models, only geometry and hierarchy is needed. These models are summarized in Figure 3.

Thus, the two environments only overlap with the need for basic figure and object definitions.* These different environments can share a single database but this is not imposed by the architecture. This is important as it allows for placement of the various "processors" in a hardware environment most suited for the functions they perform.

5.3.2 Animation Processor

The animation processor is the gateway from the simulator to the motion-generation processors. It is responsible for interpreting the motion directives received from the simulator and passing them on to the appropriate procedure. A discussion of the exact nature of directives is deferred to the discussion of each of the motion generation processors. This processor need not maintain any knowledge or record of the type of motion being generated, except for that which is needed by the feedback processor

*Although it may seem as though the animation environment needs strength models when doing dynamics computations, the necessary information can be supplied by the simulation environment. See Section 5.3.3.

and in time synchronization. This issue is discussed more fully in Section 5.4.3.

This processor (and one or more of the motion processors) should be able to handle motion specifications involving:

1. position constraints to arbitrary *regions* in space.
2. velocity and acceleration constraints.
3. forces and torques.
4. forward and inverse kinematics.

5.3.3 Dynamics Processor

This processor computes motion given forces and torques. The input to this processor is (1) the current environment which includes location, inertial properties and current velocities and accelerations of all objects, and (2) a list of the forces to apply.

The dynamics processor has an internal clock which is not directly related to the simulation clock. When computing the motion variables (position, velocity and acceleration), a dynamics system computes the value of an integral over time. Each iteration of the computation yields a set of values for the motion variables after a small amount of time. This amount of time is independent of both the frame rate and the simulation granularity. The size of this "dynamics granularity" is determined based upon the numerical accuracy desired. For forces that are continuously changing, such as with strength models where strength depends upon joint position, new input can be given to the dynamics processor during each "tick" of the dynamics clock.

The output of this processor is generated based on an output granularity specified by the animation processor. This value can be independent of the dynamics granularity, the simulation granularity and the frame rate.

5.3.4 Constraint Processor

The constraint processor maintains relationships among objects and motion parameters. The input to this processor is (1) the current environment (same as the dynamics processor), and (2) the list of constraints to apply. Constraints can be placed on any of the motion parameters: position (*e.g.* keep your hand on the glass), orientation (*e.g.* keep the glass upright), velocity (*e.g.* keep the arm moving at a specific speed), or acceleration (*e.g.* "Floor it," but a car can only accelerate at a specific rate).

Constraints may be specified to:

- Remove degrees of freedom from the environment. As opposed to constraining an object to a specific location or orientation, any one of up to 6 degrees of freedom can be temporarily frozen in the environment. By removing degrees of freedom, subsequent dynamics and constraint equations are simplified. This improves system performance.

- Constrain objects to arbitrary regions in 6-space (position and orientation). A constraint to a region allows one to specify, for example, that the hand should remain on the desk top (as opposed to a particular point), or that keeping a glass upright so water doesn't fall out means that it can vary up to 5° along the rotation axes. This value could be specified as part of the description of the hand holding the glass and could be computed based upon the amount of water in the glass.

The output of this processor is the modified environment and motion parameters. For each input set, there is a single output set. The constraint processor is not intended to generate motion, but to clamp parameters to particular values within a specified range.

5.3.5 Kinematics Processor

This processor performs key frame animation. The input to this processor is parameter values with associated times, and an interpolation technique. The parameter data may be transmitted in the form of an environment specification (as with dynamics and kinematics) along with inverse or forward kinematic modifications. This processor then determines the in-between frames using the previously specified key frames.

This processor is inherently different from the others. With the dynamics and constraint processors, no knowledge of the future is required; each input set represented all the knowledge needed by the processor. With the kinematics processor each input set represents additional data which will be applied to future input. This has ramifications on the validity of animation feedback to the simulator.

Suppose at times $t - 10$ and t, the kinematics processor receives key frames. Now all in-between frames from time $t - 10$ to t can be computed. At time $t + 5$, some animation feedback is required (for example, current position of an object). Since the kinematic processor does not have any information for time $t + 5$, how should it respond? There are several options: (1) an "unable-to-comply" response could be given since the data does not yet exist, (2) a "request for more information" could be returned, (3) the last known values could be returned, or (4) values extrapolated from the last known values could be returned. The first two responses are unacceptable in this environment. If the first were acceptable, then the simulator would *never* get animation feedback unless it happened to request information immediately upon transmitting a key frame. The second response is inadequate for if the simulator had additional information, it would have already been given to the kinematic processor. The third and fourth responses are the best available choices. Regardless of which is chosen, it is likely that the information returned will not be an accurate reflection of what the state is going to be.

5.3.6 Unification Processor

This processor performs a weighted average computation on the animation parameters in the output of the dynamics, kinematics, and constraint processors. This processor performs the functions similar to, but in a more primitive fashion than, that described in [13]. Specifically, individual animation parameters can be weighted so that the output of any combination of processors can be favored.

5.3.7 Feedback Processor

This processor is used to supply information to the simulator about any of the animation parameters. It answers questions about the current configuration *or* a proposed configuration. For human task performance analysis, the following types of questions are expected:

- What can object X see?
- What can object X reach? (space and objects)
- How far is X from a particular object?
- How far is X from any object?
- Is X "comfortable"? (based upon some comfort index)
- What is the position, velocity, or acceleration of any segment or joint (with respect to another)?
- What is the net force or torque on any segment or joint?

5.3.8 The Simulator

The simulator is the overall animation controller. There are two forms of input into the simulator, (1) general rule templates, and (2) specific task instantiations. The advantage of using rule templates and instantiations as opposed to specifically developed rules is that properly developed templates will be applicable to more than one task application.*

Although not a requirement of the simulator from the aspect of human task performance analysis, it would be desirable to implement the simulator such that a given task may be simulated at multiple levels of detail (as in HIRES[19]). This could be done by using a partitioned frame-based knowledge base to store the rule templates where each partition represents a different level of process abstraction. To change the level of abstraction being simulated, a rule can execute the corresponding frame in the knowledge base which will start up the appropriate rule at the desired level of detail.

---

*Although it is expected that any given simulation will require some application-specific rules. Of course, having application-specific rules does not imply that the simulator is application-specific; one goal is to insure that the simulator remains application-independent.

At this stage of development, it is not necessary for the simulator to include a generalized task planner although it might be desirable in the future. Instead, a temporal planner should be incorporated which would allow for ordering of events based upon imprecisely-specified temporal relationships (as in [5]). This ordering of events would specify a procedurally-based rule firing order. There are certain tasks however, which do not lend themselves to procedurally-based firing. For example, whenever person X walks within 3 feet of a mirror, X must stop and check his hair. The firing of the task, "X checks his hair" is dependent upon the precondition, "X is within 3 feet of the mirror" which can not be temporally predicted. Therefore, the simulator must allow for declarative firing of rules as well as procedural firing.

To correctly simulate human behavior, instantiated (but not fired) rules must have a finite lifetime. This allows for the modeling of "ultimatum behavior" as in "I'll pick up the object if it's available before 3 o'clock, otherwise forget it!" Similarly, rules which have fired must be allowed to specify conditions which must remain true as long as the rule is active (operating conditions). This allows for behavior such as "I'll do this as long as you are doing that!"

Allowing the rules to have a relative priority and including the ability to interrupt (and restart) or delete a rule is also needed. This allows for more flexible resource allocation and behavior modeling. Lastly, the performance any given task may require a new set of tasks to be performed. Therefore, it is necessary for the simulator to allow new rules to be instantiated during the course of a simulation.

The control aspects of the simulator are summarized:

1. Rule-based.
2. Rules are "instantiated" from a list of rule-templates.
3. Declarative firing (based upon preconditions) is supported.
4. Procedural firing (based upon explicit or imprecisely-specified temporal relationship) is supported.
5. An instantiated rule has a potentially limited lifetime if not fired.
6. A fired rule is active for a non-negative duration.
7. New rules can be instantiated during the course of a simulation.
8. Rules can be deleted before firing or while running.
9. Rules can be interrupted and restarted.
10. Rules can specify operating conditions which must remain true throughout entire execution of rule.
11. Messages can be sent to the animation processor.
12. Messages can be received from the feedback processor.

The data requirements are as described earlier. In particular, the simulator must include facilities for effectively using the following data models:

1. Anthropometric models.
2. Strength and fatigue models.
3. Joint limits and comfort limits.
4. Agent models.
5. Resource models (resource allocation).

5.4 Preliminary Implementation Issues

5.4.1 Default Durations

The concept of having the simulator use a default value for the length of time in which a task should be performed is a natural extension to how humans specify a task to be performed. In general, one will indicate that task X is to be performed, not task X should take five seconds. Since simulator rules are how tasks are encoded, the durations associated with the rules should allow default duration specification as well as explicit values.

What should the default duration be? One possibility is to use some constant value (*e.g.* 5). Any rule which did not have an explicit duration would be performed in 5 time units. This technique is not as ill-conceived as it may seem. Since an animation will be generated, one could view the animation and determine more reasonable defaults on a rule by rule basis. This does seem inconsistent, however, with the idea of generating realistic motions and performance in an automatic fashion (as exemplified through the use of the various actor and object models).

The alternative is to use a better model for human task performance times. Several factors effect task performance times, for example: level of expertise, desire to perform the task, degree of fatigue (mental and physical), distance to be moved, and target size. Realistically speaking, all of these need to be considered in the model, yet some are difficult to quantify. Obviously, the farther the distance to be moved, the longer a task should take. Furthermore, it is intuitively accepted that performing a task which requires precision work should take longer than one not involving precision work: for example, threading a needle versus putting papers on a desk.

Fitts [20] investigated performance time with respect to two of the above factors, distance to be moved and target size. He found that amplitude (A, distance to be moved) and target width (W) are related to time in a simple equation:

$$\text{Movement Time} = a + b \log \frac{2A}{W}$$

where a and b are constants. This equation embodies a speed and accuracy tradeoff in movement. Since for any task, A is constant, to decrease the performance time, the only other variable in the equation w must be increased. That is, the faster a task is to be performed, the larger the target area and hence the movements are less accurate.

This equation (known as Fitts' Law) can be embodied in the simulation system, since for any given reach task, both A and w are known. The constants a and b are linked to the other factors (training, desire, fatigue, task type), and determining the exact values for those constants is beyond the scope of this thesis. Nonetheless, for some tasks, values for a and b have been determined [20,14,10] and a small amount of practical experience with a system embodying this equation will yield a reasonable set of values for other tasks. As a result, the simulator will give better results than if a constant value duration time were given for all tasks.

5.4.2 Temporal Planning

There are few requirements for the temporal planning phase of the simulation. Given any two of event start time, event duration, and event stop time, and a weight (relative to other events' temporal weights), it should be possible to calculate every event's start time and duration so as to best achieve the specified times. The specification of these variables (start time, duration, and end time) need not be explicit times. Instead, they can be relations to other events as in *start event A 10 minutes after event B* or *event A runs as long as event B.*

Badler, Kushnier and Kalita [5] have provided a first implementation of a system which meets the above goals. This system is different from existing temporal planners in that (1) it references an actual clock, (2) the relative importance of constraints can be specified, and (3) the system tries to satisfy the most important constraints first. With this system, it is possible to specify imprecise timing constraints which are then solved using a quadratic programming solution. The constraints are modeled using a spring analogy where the stiffness of the spring represents the weight of the constraint. This system solves for times by minimizing the following function:

$$E_{\text{tot}} = \sum_{i=1}^{n} \left(\frac{k_{s_i}}{2} (x_{s_i} - a_{s_i})^2 + \frac{k_{e_i}}{2} (x_{e_i} - a_{e_i})^2 + \frac{k_{d_i}}{2} (x_{s_i} - a_{e_i} - a_{d_i})^2 \right)$$

where:

a_s, a_e, a_d are start, end, and duration constraint vectors.
k_s, k_e, k_d are start, end, and duration constraint strength vectors.
x_s resulting vector of start times.
x_e resulting vector of end times.

5.4.3 Timing Among Processors

The ultimate reference for the passage of time is the wall clock.* Simulation clock time is directly related to wall clock time except that it is not nec-

*Actually, the sun.

essary for simulation time to pass at a constant rate (if nothing "exciting" is happening, the simulation clock can be bumped ahead). The simulation granularity is the fraction of simulation time after which rules are examined. The frame rate is related to both the simulation clock and the wall clock. For realistic motion, 24 frames (or 30, depending upon the medium) should be generated for every second of animation.

Animations need not be generated as an accurate representation of the wall clock. Instead, the simulation clock is a better reference. It is convenient to consider all processors with respect to the simulation clock. For example, the kinematics processor is told that certain positions (as represented by key frames) should be achieved at specific times. That time should be with respect to the simulation clock. The dynamics processor need not know about specific times, but instead about the passage of time (forces are active until time $t + 10$). The dynamics granularity is also dependent upon the simulation granularity. In particular, if it is known that a rule will not be examined until 10 time units have passed, it may not be necessary for the dynamics processor to compute the motion variables every .1 time units (1 time unit may be more reasonable).

At simulation time t, all motion constructs (constraints, forces, *etc.*) are known for time t. However, it is not possible to know all constructs for time $t+1$. One solution is to let the motion processors lag behind the simulation clock. Whenever feedback is required for time $t+1$, the simulator will have to wait for the motion processors to "catch up." An alternative is to let the motion processors run ahead as much as possible. This has the potential of creating frames which will be invalidated should the motion processors get ahead of the simulation clock. In a distributed environment, this extra work is inconsequential.

Using this latter technique requires a certain amount of backtracking among the motion processors and the motion database, which stores the motion variables for feedback. To place a limit on the amount of feedback (*i.e.* to essentially create "breakpoints"), the simulation clock should regularly inform the animation processor that time t has been reached. The animation processor can then indicate that the state variables within the motion data base are valid until time t. If the motion processors then continue to compute until they have reached time t_i asynchronously from the simulator, and a new set of motion constructs is received at time t_j ($t_i > t_j$), t_j becomes the new breakpoint and values generated for times in the range $t_j \dots t_i$ are discarded.

The last thing to consider is a request for feedback at a time which does not correspond to a frame generation time. Since requests for feedback can occur at any point in the simulation, based on simulation granularity, and that will most likely be finer than the frame rate, a method is needed to determine the appropriate response. There are basically two techniques which could be used: (1) extrapolate from the last known frame, or (2) modify the output granularity of the motion processors so the desired information becomes available. Since a request for feedback at time t means that the simulator has reached time t, no motion constructs are pending for times before t. Therefore, if the output granularity of the motion processors is temporarily modified, the extra variables can be stored in the motion data base and time t becomes the new breakpoint.

5.4.4 Nomenclature Conflicts Between Processors

Although there is a minimal amount of overlap of information models between the simulation and the animation environment, the overlap that does exist can introduce some problems and inconsistencies. The only data overlap is in the basic body and object descriptions. Both the simulation knowledge base and the animation database require a basic description of the environment in which the tasks are performed. Beyond the basic description, however, the two databases diverge with the animation database requiring geometric information and the knowledge base requiring qualitative (relations, causality, *etc.*) information.

References to the basic environment descriptions will be included in almost all the interaction between the animation environment and the simulation environment. It is important for a reference to person X to mean the same thing in both environments. The general solution adopted by the architecture is based upon the fact that the common information is static. Although specific relationships may change and objects may move, the *handles* by which the objects are referenced will not change. Therefore, consistency is maintained by requiring that the initial databases be set up consistently.

This does not address the problems of data consistency in a distributed data base. That problem is avoided by careful assignment of data to the individual databases. Although both databases contain dynamic information, the interface to that dynamic information is through specific processors and hence issues of concurrent update and data integrity are avoided.

6 Conclusions

It is clear that existing simulation and animation systems do not provide the necessary combination of tools and techniques to effectively simulate *and* animate the performance of tasks by humans. In this chapter, we have described an architecture which is both uniform and structured. Such an architecture allows for increased sophistication of simulations and animations through the clarification of world model semantics. With this architecture, natural language understanding systems such as those developed at the University of Pennsylvania (MVP[3] and SEAFACT[31]) can be integrated into the simulation and animation environment. These systems, by generating the appropriate rules, can create a complete animation without requiring application-dependent modifications to the architecture.

With the temporal planning stage of the simulation, no longer is an animation driven via an arbitrarily created script, but instead the script is created based upon the actual high-level requirements of the animator. Furthermore, the animation can be developed using the motion generation techniques that are appropriate for the motion being animated.

Lastly, the actual motion parameters inherent in some human performance analysis questions can be included in a simulation. With this geometric feedback helping to guide the simulations, tasks can be simulated with a heretofore unrealized degree of accuracy.

References

1. J. Allen. Maintaining knowledge about temporal intervals. *Communications of the ACM*, 26(11), November 1983.
2. W. Armstrong and M. Green. The dynamics of articulated rigid bodies for purposes of animation. *The Visual Computer*, 1(4), 1985.
3. N. Badler and J. Gangel. Natural language input for human task description. In *Proc. ROBEXS '86: The Second International Workship on Robotics and Expert Systems*, Instrument Society of America, June 1986.
4. N. Badler, J.D. Korein, J.U. Korein, G. Radack, and L. Brotman. Positioning and animating human figures in a task-oriented environment. *The Visual Computer: The International Journal of Computer Graphics*, 1(4), 1985.
5. N. Badler, S. Kushnier, and J. Kalita. *Constraint-Based Temporal Planning.* Technical Report MS-CIS-88-55, Dept. of Computer and Information Science, Univ. of Pennsylvania, Philadelphia, PA, 1988.
6. N. Badler, K. Manoochehri, and G. Walters. Articulated figure positioning by multiple constraints. *IEEE Computer Graphics and Applications*, 7(6), June 1987.
7. B. Barzel and A. Barr. A modeling system based on dynamic constraints. *Computer Graphics*, 22(4), 1988.
8. K.R. Boff, L. Kaufman, and J.P. Thomas, editors. *Handbook of Perception and Human Performance.* John Wiley and Sons, NY, 1986.
9. K.R. Boff and J.E. Lincoln, editors. *Engineering Data Compendium.* OH, 1988.
10. S. Card. The model human processor: A model for making engineering calculations of human performance. In R. Sugarman, editor, *Proc. 25th Annual Meeting of the Human Factors Society*, Santa Monica, CA, 1981.
11. D. Cebula. *The Semantic Data Model and Large Information Requirements.* Technical Report MS-CIS-87-72, Dept. of Computer and Information Science, Univ. of Pennsylvania, Philadelphia, PA, 1987.
12. M. Chace. Modeling of dynamic mechanical systems. February 1985. presented at the CAD/CAM Robotics and Automation Institute and Int. Conf., Tucson.
13. D. Dadamo. *Effective Control of Human Motion Animation.* Technical Report MS-CIS-88-52, Dept. of Computer and Information Science, Univ. of Pennsylvania, Philadelphia, PA, 1988.

14. C. Drury. Application of Fitts' Law to foot pedal design. *Human Factor*, 17, 1975.
15. S. Dubowsky and R. Kornbluh. On the development of high performance adaptive control algorithms for robotics. In *Robotics Research, Proc. 2nd Int. Symp.*, MIT Press, Cambridge, MA, 1985.
16. S. Feiner, D. Salesin, and T. Banchoff. Dial: A diagrammatic animation language. *IEEE Computer Graphics and Applications*, 2(9), September 1982.
17. W. Fetter. A progression of human figures simulated by computer graphics. *IEEE Computer Graphics and Applications*, 2(9), November 1982.
18. R. Fikes and N. Nilsson. STRIPS: A new approach to the application of theorem proving to problem solving. *Artificial Intelligence 2*, 1971.
19. P. Fishwick. The role of process abstraction in simulation. *IEEE Trans. Systems, Man, and Cybernetics*, 18(1), Jan./Feb. 1988.
20. P. Fitts. The information capacity of the human motor system in controlling the amplitude of movement. *Journal of Experimental Psychology*, 47, 1954.
21. D. Fortin, J. Lamy, and D. Thalmann. A multiple track animator system. *Proc. SIGGRAPH/SIGGART Interdisciplinary Workshop on Motion: Representation and Perception*, 1983.
22. M. Girard. Interactive design of 3-d computer-animated legged animal motion. *IEEE Computer Graphics and Applications*, 7(6), June 1987.
23. M. Girard and A. Maciejewski. Computational modeling for the computer animation of legged figures. *Computer Graphics (Proc. SIGGRAPH 85)*, 19(3), 1985.
24. J. Gomez. Twixt: A 3D animation system. *Proceedings of Eurographics '84*, September 1984.
25. C. Hewitt, P. Bishop, and R. Steiger. A universal modular actor formalism for artificial intelligence. *Proc. Intern. Joint Conf. on Artificial Intelligence*, 1973.
26. C. Hoffman and J. Hopcroft. Simulation of physical systems from geometric models. *IEEE Journal of robotics and automation*, RA-3(3), June 1987.
27. J. Hollan, E. Hutchins, and L. Weitzman. STEAMER: An interactive inspectable simulation-based training system. *AI Magazine*, 5(2), Summer 1984.
28. P. Isaacs and M. Cohen. Controlling dynamic simulation with kinematic constraints. *Computer Graphics*, 21(4), 1987.
29. K. Kahn. *An actor-based computer animation language.* Technical Report 120, MIT, 1976.
30. K. Kahn and C. Hewitt. Dynamic graphics using quasi-parallelism. *Computer Graphics*, 12(3), 1978.
31. R. Karlin. *SEAFACT: A semantic analysis system for task animation of cooking operations.* Master's thesis, Dept. of Computer and Information Science, Univ. of Pennsylvania, Philadelphia, PA, December 1987.
32. K. Konolige and N. Nilsson. Multiple-agent planning. *Proc. of the first annual conference of the American Association for Artificial Intelligence*, 1980.
33. N. Magnenat-Thalmann and D. Thalmann. *Computer Animation Theory and Practice.* Springer-Verlag, New York, 1985.
34. N. Magnenat-Thalmann and D. Thalmann. MIRANIM: An extensible director-oriented system for the animation of realistic images. *IEEE Computer Graphics and Applications*, 5(3), October 1985.

35. N. Magnenat-Thalmann and D. Thalmann. Three-dimensional computer animation: More an evolution than a motion problem. *IEEE Computer Graphics and Applications*, 5(10), October 1985.
36. J. Malik and T. Binford. Reasoning in time and space. In *Proceedings of 8th IJCAI*, IJCAI, 1983.
37. Richard Paul. *Robot Manipulators: Mathematics, Programming, and Control.* MIT Press, Cambridge, MA, 1981.
38. C. Phillips. *Using Jack.* University of Pennsylvania, 1988.
39. M. Pollack, D. Israel, and M. Bratman. *Toward an architecture for resource-bounded agents.* Technical Report CLSI-87-104, Center for the Study of Language and Information, Stanford, CA, 1987.
40. E. Post. Formal reductions of the general combinatorial problem. *American Journal of Mathematics*, 65:197–268, 1943.
41. A. Pritsker. *The GASP IV Simulation Language.* Wiley, 1974.
42. C. Reynolds. Computer animation with scripts and actors. *Computer Graphics (Proc. SIGGRAPH 1982)*, 16(3), 1982.
43. C. Reynolds. Flocks, herds, and schools: a distributed behavioral model. *Computer Graphics (Proc. SIGGRAPH 1987)*, 21(4), 1987.
44. G. Ridsdale, S. Hewitt, and T. Calvert. The interactive specification of human animation. *Proceedings of Graphics Interface 86*, 1986.
45. E. Sacerdoti. *A structure for plans and behavior.* Elsevier North-Holland, New York, 1977.
46. S. Steketee and N. Badler. Parametric keyframe interpolation incorporating kinetic adjustment and phrasing control. *Computer Graphics (Proc. SIGGRAPH 85)*, 19(3), 1985.
47. M. Takano. Development of simulation system of robot motion and its role in task planning and design systems. In *Robotics Research, Proc. 2nd Int. Symp.*, MIT Press, Cambridge, MA, 1985.
48. Y. Takashima, H. Shimazu, and M. Tomono. Story driven animation. *Proc. of Computer Human Interface and Graphics Interface*, 1987.
49. D. Thalmann and N. Magnenat-Thalmann. Actor and camera data types in computer animation. *Proc. Graphics Interface '83*, 1983.
50. F. Thomas and O. Johnston. *Disney Animation: The Illusion of Life.* Abbeville Press, New York, 1981.
51. S. Vere. Planning in time: windows and durations for activities and goals. *IEEE Transactions on Pattern Analysis and Machine Intelligence*, 5(3), May 1983.
52. J. Wilhelms. Toward automatic motion control. *IEEE Computer Graphics and Applications*, 7(4), April 1987.
53. J. Wilhelms and B.A. Barsky. Using dynamic analysis for the animation of articulated bodies such as humans and robots. In *Proc. Graphics Interface '85*, Montreal, 1985.
54. A. Witkin, K. Fleisher, and A. Barr. Energy constraints on parameterized models. *Computer Graphics*, 21(3), 1987.
55. D. Zeltzer. Motor control techniques for figure animation. *IEEE Computer Graphics and Applications*, 2(9), September 1982.
56. D. Zeltzer. Towards an integrated view of 3-D computer animation. *Proc. Graphics Interface '85*, 1985.

CHAPTER 10

The Acquisition of Cognitive Simulation Models: A Knowledge-Based Training Approach

Kent E. Williams and Richard E. Reynolds

Abstract

The production system architecture which is common to many knowledge based systems is given considerable support for its psychological validity as demonstrated by a review of empirical research in cognitive psychology. This research supports the view that knowledge bases made up of production like organizations in human memory are acquired during the learning process. A knowledge base of these productions in human memory produce a model of a systems operation. This model has been referred to as a cognitive simulation model. By conducting a cognitive task analysis of the material to be learned, these productions can be identified along with their linkages to other productions in the model. During training then exercises can be created which explicitly describe each production which makes up this model. The result of this approach provides a method for explicitly diagnosing difficulties which an individual may have in acquiring instructional material and adaptively sequencing exercises to most efficiently and effectively build up a cognitive simulation model.

1 Introduction

No doubt, the normative approach to the development of computer aided instruction (CAI) is driven by the Instructional System Development (ISD) process (Burke, 1982; Branson, Rayner, Cox, Furman, King, & Hannum, 1975). This process is essentially a systems analysis approach to the development of CAI and other training systems. With regard to courseware development and the content of the instructional material, the ISD process moves from the development of specific behavioral objectives linked to tasks which support those objectives and to performance measures, which provide an index as to whether tasks and objectives have been assimilated at criterion levels of output behavior. The instructional content and the media for presentation is derived from these task and objective specifications and constitute the knowledge which is to be transferred to the trainee. The development of the course content is usually passed on to subject matter experts who work in conjunction with training specialists in order to formulate all lesson materials. The level of analysis of the instructional content is then typically left up to the subject matter experts.

The approach developed herein follows a similar, if not identical line of methodology, however, goes considerably further when it comes to specifying the instructional content. How this approach is implemented in an intelligent computer aided instruction system is discussed in conjunction with the reasons for this approach and an exposition of research which supports the approach. This approach is typically referred to as cognitive simulation modeling or an explicit-rule formulation approach to learning.

2 Cognitive Simulation Modeling

As a compelling example of the approach, Kieras (1987a & b) surveyed a variety of material which was designed for airforce pilot training. Specifically, the instructional material was analyzed for a T38 emergency procedure when AC electrical power is lost. From this material, Kieras developed a task-goal hierarchy of how-it-works information.

This task-goal hierarchy is reproduced in Figure 1 adapted from Kieras (1987a & b). On the left side of the figure is a sketch of the explanation

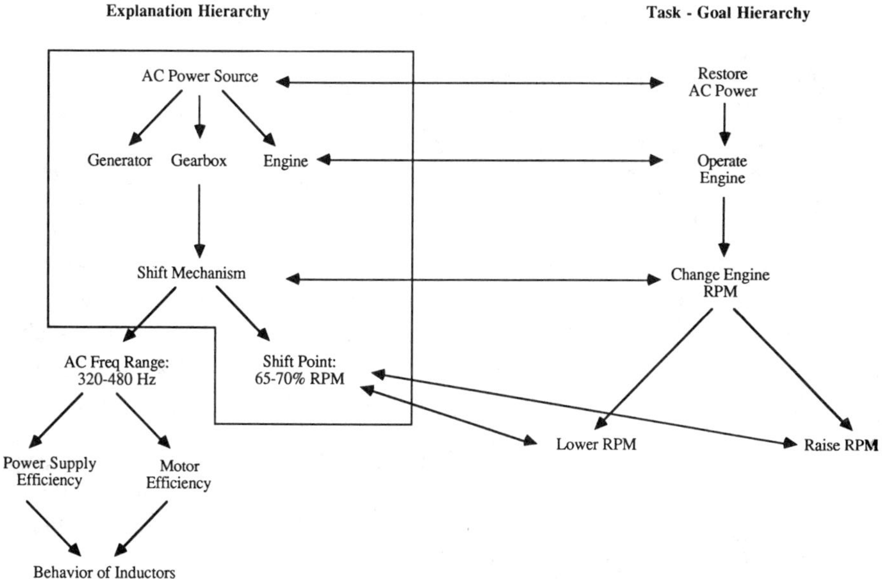

FIGURE 1. An example of the task-goal hierarchy showing the selected relevant how-it-works information (boxed in) and the links between information and tasks.

hierarchy for that portion of the aircraft, which describes the mechanisms governing the AC power of the aircraft. The AC power source is made up of the engine, a gear box, and an AC generator. In turn, the gear box includes a shift mechanism, and the explanation of the shift mechanism involves the RPM shift range and the generator output frequency range. The explanation of the generator output frequency range involves the efficiencies of the aircraft power supplies and electric motors, which in turn describes the fact that inductors are involved, and so forth. On the right hand side of the diagram is shown a sketch of the user's task-goal structure, in which the top level goal for this task is to restore AC power. This involves accomplishing the subgoals of operating on the engine and changing the engine RPM in the manner specified; namely, if it is high, make it low and, vice versa. Each of these levels in the user's task-goal hierarchy can be related to a portion of the explanation hierarchy as shown by the double-headed arrows connecting the two trees. The goal of restoring AC power can be matched up with the AC power source; the goal of operating the engine can be matched with the explanation that the engine is part of the power source, and the goal of changing the RPM can be matched with the explanation that a shift mechanism is involved. The goals of making the RPM low or high can be matched with the explanation of the RPM at which the shift occurs.

Notice on the lower left side of Figure 1, outside of the boxed portion of the explanation hierarchy that there is considerable information concerning the AC generator gear box. This explanation hierarchy describes the frequency range of the AC power as well as information about power supply efficiencies and inductors. The actual text goes on about these mechanisms. What is important to note, however, is that this information is in no way useful to the pilot for implementing the emergency procedures to get the AC power back on line. In short, this additional information is actually superfluous and not important for the pilot to know in the conduct of the emergency procedures. No links exist between the explanation hierarchy of the AC frequency range, power supply efficiency, motor efficiency, etc. and the task-goal hierarchy for user control of these systems. It should be acknowledged that there may be many good reasons why the pilots are required to learn what they do about the systems in the airplane, however, numerous examples can be found employing this kind of analysis which shows that instructional materials many times fail to include information which the pilot needs as well as, include far more information than he needs to conduct his task safely and effectively.

The problem which this raises for training or learning is that the trainee, when presented with this kind of information, has difficulty determining how it fits into the tasks which he must perform. Conversely, the trainee also spends a good deal of time trying to find information needed in order to make sense out of certain explanations. All of this makes training less efficient and less effective. The trainee is consequently left up to his own methods of discovery to determine what is unnecessary, as well as what is necessary in order for him to conduct his tasks. These kinds of problems with information content produce problems for the trainee in the learning process. This example also clearly indicates the importance of a cognitive analysis in the determination of instructional content. Therefore, the conventional ISD approach is deficient in its methods for developing logically consistent and efficient information content for instructional material. The addition of this cognitive analysis to the ISD approach, however, removes such deficiencies and will improve the efficiency of training and, as we shall demonstrate, the comprehensibility and effectiveness of training.

In order to conduct this cognitive analysis, it is necessary to develop a production model from the instructional material. When the model is assimilated by the student, it becomes what is called a cognitive simulation model and resides in the trainee's production memory. An explanation of a production system follows along with psychological evidence for the support of the isomorphic relationship between production system models or expert system models and cognitive simulation models.

2.1 Production System

The logic behind a production system model is analogous to that proposed by Post (1943). A production system model is also that which is most often employed in the design of AI systems (Nilsson, 1980). Typically, a production system consists of three interacting parts. These parts consist of a data base of facts called declarative knowledge; a set or sets of rules of the IF-THEN type which are the productions, and a control strategy which determines which subset of rules may apply on any given cycle. It may be helpful to think of a production or rule as a chunk of information which when matched with conditions in the environment trigger a specific behavior (e.g., If I see X, Y, and Z, then I should press button B.). In a production system, the data base is scanned by the set or subset of rules to determine if information in the data base matches with the IF side of any of the rules. If a match is found, the THEN side of the rule is triggered. Triggering a rule may enable an action (i.e., some behavior) or the addition of a new piece of information to this data base (i.e., new facts in the working memory of the trainee). A cognitive simulation model may be thought of as similar to a production system model and has been used in previous research to quantify the complexity of a device interface in terms of how much knowledge is required to operate a device (Polson, 1987; Kieras, 1988). For this approach, we consider a cognitive simulation model to be what is learned by a trainee during the conduct of training*. For the case at hand, trainees will be developing or learning a cognitive simulation model of the operation of a tactical console. The trainees will

*Other forms of representation such as schema have been employed to model memory organization (Marshall, 1988a, 1988b) in learning tasks.

be learning how to put facts together into chunks which are then linked to certain actions or which allow the trainee to infer a new piece of information to assist in operating the system. When these models have been developed or learned, they become an accurate representation of the operation of the console. Learning will then have been accomplished for these tasks or jobs.

2.2 Cognitive Engineering of Lesson Content

In order for this learning to take place, however, a set of rules and declarative knowledge or facts must be developed from the descriptions and explanations of how to operate the system. Given an accurate set of rules, system operation is completely defined. All of the declarative knowledge or facts, as well as, how these facts are chunked together to form rules which trigger actions will be used to create the instructional content of the intelligent computer-aided instruction (ICAI) system developed.

Each exercise of the system then will reflect or represent an underlying rule. Each rule in turn combines the relevant pieces of knowledge into a chunk. When all rules are learned, the student will have a complete cognitive model of console operations to be used for interacting with the console. Critical to this implementation is the development of the production system or set of rules which simulates system functions and operations. However, when this is accomplished the ICAI system can deliver exercise content in a most efficient manner and can diagnose any errors in the trainee's development of the cognitive simulation model in terms of which rules have not been learned properly as well as what pieces of declarative knowledge (i.e., facts or concepts) have not yet been properly assimilated or chunked in the formulation of rules. This provides an extremely powerful method for diagnosing the strengths and weaknesses of the student as he learns system operations in order to determine what lesson content should be presented to the student.

The following is a sample of some rules which were developed by the authors. These rules describe in part the logic of operating a tactical console.

Rule 14 IF the subgoal is to update a tentative track
THEN hook the track symbol
AND use your position correction variable action button (VAB)
AND complete this procedure in 1 minute and 15 seconds

Rule 15 IF the subgoal is to hook the track symbol
THEN use the ball tab
AND press the hook button

Rule 5 IF subgoal is to use the ball tab
THEN locate and press the ball tab enable button
AND manipulate the cursor with the ball tab

Rule 17 IF the subgoal is to use your position correction VAB

AND hook track symbol has been accomplished
THEN use your ball tab
AND press position correction VAB

DCLR 8 Locate and press ball tab enable button
DCLR 9 Locate and manipulate cursor with ball tab
DCLR 16 Locate and press hook button
DCLR 18 Locate and press position correction VAB
DCLR 10 Describe and identify a tentative track symbol

These rules serve to develop the production system which models how an expert would operate the tactical console in order to update a tentative track. Given this model, all relevant knowledge has been specified and related such that the operation of updating a tentative track can take place. What the student must learn is to assimilate this model such that he too can become expert at console operation. Consequently, in constructing an exercise for a training system which teaches tactical console operation, the student must first learn all of the declarative facts such as that from 8, 9, 16, 18, and 10 (or locate the ball tab enable, hook and position correction buttons, manipulate the cursor and identify a tentative track symbol). He must then learn how to compose or compile these facts such that when certain cues or subgoals are set certain actions or sequences of actions are triggered. In this example, the appearance of a tentative track sets the subgoal to update the track. This in turn requires that the operator hook the track symbol, know the proper sequence of actions to take in order to use the position correction variable action button, and to do all of this within 1 minute and 15 seconds (The time constraint is a system feature). To implement this procedure however, the operator must know how to hook the track symbol, Rule 15; know how to use the ball tab, Rule 5, and know how to use the position correction VAB, Rule 17. In order to enable the actions required of these rules he must also be knowledgeable about specific declarative facts such as DCLR 8, 9, 16, 18, and 10. In order for rules 14, 15, 5, and 17 to be learned, all of the facts making up these rules must also be learned. Consequently, a large network of exercises, each addressing each fact and each rule, would be developed from this production system. Students would then be presented with these exercises and the process of acquiring knowledge would continue until all facts and rules are learned. The trainee then must work his way through this network of exercises to acquire the required expertise.

Since each exercise created employing this methodology can be explicitly linked to pieces of knowledge in the form of facts of rules, the training software can query a trainee if he fails an exercise in such a way as to determine what rules or what facts have not been learned by the student. The system can then select another exercise for the student which addresses these unmastered facts or rules. For example, if a student fails an exercise which addresses Rule 14, the instructor can then diagnose the student in terms of the conditions or actions for which the student has weak knowledge. The diagnosis may reveal that the student doesn't understand "how to hook the track symbol". Consequently, an exercise dealing with hooking the track symbol, Rule 15 would be selected next for the student.

2.3 Components of a Cognitive Simulation Model

The explicit cognitive simulation model formulation of learning aside from having exceptional explanatory power to account for a wide variety of research in the psychology of learning has also been the impetus for considerable research. The research conducted to date has provided considerable evidence for a rule-based formulation of learning along with various components which make up a rule based system of learning. It should be mentioned that the level of description for rule-based systems is not contradictory to other formulations of learning which have focused upon neural interactions which implement the rules (Hinton & Anderson, 1981). Either formulation has sufficient explanatory power. Rules can be thought of as a higher level of description whereas neural interactions are a much lower level description. In such lower level descriptions of systems, the risk of getting lost in all of the wires is considerable (Anderson, 1983).

In general, components making up a cognitive simulation model formulation involve: processes for selecting or encoding information, processes for organizing facts into a rule-like structure, processes for organizing rules into a hierarchy of goals and subgoals, and mechanisms for directing the processing of information employing this network of rules. The evidence for these various processes making up a rule based formulation of learning shall be discussed.

3 Inclination to Process Rules

First, it is interesting to note research which attests to the facility with which the human information processing system can formulate rules and apply rules along with the limitations of this facility. Fong, Krantz, and Nisbett (1986) have conducted a series of experiments to determine if people actually abstract rules of inference as a result of their experiences. These researchers have shown that the way individuals reason about every day events can be affected by instruction in statistical rules and that once these statistical rules are acquired they can be abstracted to quite different domains. For example, test subjects were able to abstract the law of large numbers from specific examples and apply this law to making inferences in other domains. On the other hand, Cheng, Holyoak, Nisbett, and Oliver (1986) have demonstrated that teaching students the rules governing the syntax of formal logic had an extremely limited affect upon the ability of these students to apply rules of formal logic to everyday life experiences. However, if subjects were given pragmatic examples of these formal rules such that they could relate to the meaningfulness of the rules they were more likely to generalize and apply similar logic to everyday problems. Cheng et al. (1986) had a group of students receive instruction in the formal logic of conditionals such as "If p then q and p is asserted, then conclude q." Another group of subjects were given meaningful pragmatic examples of conditionals such as "If one wants to buy liquor, then one must be over 21." The subjects given the meaningful examples were most likely to abstract the modus ponens rule and apply it correctly to other arbitrary problems. Those given only presentations of the logic in a course which emphasized syntax, truth tables, and the construction of proofs, showed very little generalizations of such rules to solving or reasoning about everyday problems. What this series of experiments demonstrates is that people are very good at abstracting rules from examples as long as those examples involve naturally occurring events (i.e., events to which they can relate). It also appears from the work of Fong et al. (1986) that people do well in applying statistical rules when modeling everyday life problems, perhaps due to the inherent variability of everyday life events. Nisbett and Kunda (1985) have demonstrated that subjects are quite good at estimating dispersion and distribution shape as well as central tendency.

3.1 Categorization and Covariance Detection

Research involving the psychological phenomenon of categorization has provoked the development of numerous theories or accounts of categorization (Smith & Medin, 1981). Categorization and rule encoding are essentially the same. A category can be thought of as a set of attributes or preconditions which signify that some object or concept belongs to a specific category. What is common to the diversity of explanations of categorization is the fact that humans naturally encode categories and assign property values representing several attributes to alternative categories. Brooks (1978) and Fried and Holyoak (1984) demonstrated that people can form categories in the absence of any feedback or instruction to do so. Subjects in these experiments were simply told to watch patterns carefully as they were presented. Following presentation of the patterns, they were told that the patterns could be categorized into a number of alternatives (i.e., two) and were then told they would see new patterns which they would have to categorize. Subjects in these experiments learned readily to categorize the new patterns in accordance with properties which they abstracted and used to categorize the initial set of patterns.

Humans, therefore, seem to be very adept at detecting covariation in stimuli encountered in everyday life. Such covariation detection is fundamental to the development of rule structures to form knowledge. But how does the individual learn to encode and identify the relevant properties form the excess of features and cues which bombard the system? Billman (1983) proposes that humans will use what they find to be predictive to guide subsequent encoding. Billman called this focused sampling. The learner faced with the need to encode a large amount of information will encode those properties already involved in predictive regularities. Billman has demonstrated in an artificial language learning experiment that multiple, inter-related associations between properties was learned more readily than single associations. That is, when the artificial language regularities were grouped together, language learning was better than when regularities were presented in isolation as single associations. This evidence indicates that encoding is dependent upon groups of relationships or groups of regularities established from experience.

In conjunction with the covariation detection research and categorization research summarized above, the human information processing system seems inherently motivated to encode regularities in the environment at peripheral levels in pattern classification, as well as at more abstract levels in applying pragmatic reasoning schemes. In the absence of regularity necessary to predict a specific outcome, that is, where a needed predictive regularity cannot be retrieved from memory or where the regularity does not exist in memory, the individual will fail to understand and predict an outcome. In this case Siegler (1983) found that if practice were given to subjects on the needed regularity, they would quickly learn to predict an accurate outcome. Explicit practice in observing specific regularities can then assist the learning processes, particularly when embedded in a context of other necessary regularities required to produce a specific outcome. Consequently, in building an instructional system, learning will progress most efficiently if the rules to be learned can be explicitly observed by the individual and can be grouped or coupled to form multiple associations in a meaningful way.

4 Goals

In addition to encoding information consistent with IF-THEN rules, a rule-based formulation of learning also emphasizes the importance of goals and subgoals in a hierarchy of rules.

The importance of goals in information processing is evident in production models or rule-based models of cognition (Newell and Simon, 1972; Anderson, 1983; Holland, Holyoak Nisbett and Thagard, 1986; Klahr, Langley and Neches, 1987). (These models also address the importance of a hierarchical goal structure which guides processing.) The importance of a goal in directing attention and processing has been demonstrated in a variety of priming experiments. Priming, in essence, is the setting of goals. La Berge (1973) conducted experiments in which subjects had to recognize familiar letters or pseudo letters under conditions where subjects either had been primed to expect a letter to follow or had not been primed. When the pattern following a stimulus was familiar, priming had no effect on recognition of the pattern over the non-primed group. When the subject was primed to expect an unfamiliar pattern, the priming or goal setting had a distinctive effect upon recognition time over the non-primed condition. Consequently, goals can set the speed of successful perceptions as well as what is perceived (Posner and Snyder, 1975).

Almost all of human behavior can be characterized in terms of goals. Goals establish end points toward which sequences of action are linked. These sequences of action are referred to as plans. Large networks of goals and plans describe the structures of memory and organized knowledge. The importance of goals and plans to human behavior is a significant insight of modern cognitive psychology that was first pointed out by Miller, Gallanter, & Pribram (1960). Most of the evidence supporting goal-plan representations of information has come from studies of human memory of stories and the understanding of story text. Episodes in a story can be analyzed into separate goals and plan action segments directed toward the acquisition of the goal. Black and Bower (1979) tested the assumption that goals and plan actions existed as independent chunks in memory. These investigators manipulated the lengths of episodes (i.e., goal-plan unites) and found that the length of an episode affected the recall of the actions in the episode but not recall of actions in other episodes. For example, one story used had an overall goal of trying to find a book on a university campus. The story consisted of two episodes: One episodes described trying to find the book in the library while the other described trying to find the book in the university bookstore. Black and Bower created a short version of each episode by including three actions in support of attaining a goal (entering the library, looking in the card catalogue, and finding the book location) and the goal or outcome (the book was not there). They also created a long version of each episode by including five other actions (e.g., asking the librarian about the book, etc.). Adding the five actions in a given episode increased the recall of the original goal, the outcome, and the actions for that episode, but had no effect on the recall of statements from the other episode. Consequently, the goal plan episodes showed independence in recall and adding more stages in the episode increased recall in the episode.

4.1 Goal Hierarchy

Other evidence points to the notion that these goal-plan episodes are basic building blocks for memory which are linked together to form a hierarchy of goals such that when one goal is evoked, other goals (subgoals) which have to be attained first are also evoked. In brief, the episodes of the overall goal are integrated with episodes for subordinate goals in a hierarchical structure. Black and Bower (1980) and Graesser (1980) have found that the more the subordinate goal-plan episodes—that is, the lower they are in a hierarchy—the worse they are recalled. The lower in the hierarchy an item is, the more likely the item is to be irretrievable. This evidence fits well with that of Anderson (1986), who has found that it is difficult for experts to recall old procedures which they employ early in their training. As experts acquire their knowledge, these early learned procedures are built upon and form higher level goal-plan segments. At this point it becomes difficult for experts to retrieve their lower level procedures, from which the higher level procedures were formed, even thought when they are reminded of the lower level procedures they readily recognize and recall how important those were in the development of their expertise.

It has also been found by Siefer, Robertson, and Black (1985) that when readers were asked to read story episodes where a specific goal or plan statement was left out, it took longer to read the story than when the goal or plan statement was explicitly stated. They also found that these readers later claimed that they actually read statements similar to those which were left out. For example, given these statements—He wanted to be king; He was tired of waiting; He thought arsenic would work well—readers would recall the statement; He killed the king with arsenic; even thought it never appeared. This is what would be expected if readers were making inferences during the comprehension of a story in order to construct a complete goal-plan memory representation of the story.

In addition to the importance of a goal in guiding and directing attention and actions, a hierarchy of goals also plays a prominent role in memory organization. Aside from story episodes, and more to the case at hand, Anderson (1983) has demonstrated the importance of a hierarchy of goals in guiding the development of rules or productions and the creation of new rules by combining existing rules. Jeffries, Turner, Polson, and Atwood (1981) and Anderson (1986) have further shown that problem solving episodes are organized as a hierarchical goal structure. As Anderson (1986) has noted, by establishing a goal tree, one can predict what rules are likely to be composed by students. This has been validated by Anderson's LISP tutor, which instructs students to program in LISP.

As a result, in an instructional environment compatible with a rule-based learning system, goals and subgoals related in a hierarchy of rules are an important design principle for structuring to-be-learned information. The goal hierarchy, in turn, assists in guiding the relatedness of the to-be-learned information consistent with a rule-based system of learning and information processing. As Kieras (1987a & b) has shown with his task-goal hierarchy, this methodology is critical to determining instructional content and advancing training systems in terms of their efficiency, effectiveness, and their ability to diagnose student difficulties in learning.

5 Lesson Content Design Guidelines

As a result of the literature review presented in the above, considerable evidence points to a set of high level guidelines for the development of an instructional system based upon empirical research from cognitive learning. These guidelines shall direct a generic structuring of information which can be applied to any domain. The structuring of information, which will drive the construction of exercises, shall consist of developing a hierarchy of goals and subgoals related to the tasks to be learned and performed by the potential user. These goals and subgoals once identified shall be structured in an AND/OR graph hierarchy. The analysis of the goals and subgoals into this AND/OR hierarchy requires a detailed cognitive analysis of the domain knowledge. Having identified the task goals and subgoals, all responses required of the individual in order to perform the to-be-learned tasks must be identified. These responses must then be associated with each task goal and subgoal in the task-goal hierarchy. For task goals or subgoals which require a sequence of responses, the sequence or order of responses must be specified. Next, all stimuli or conditions associated with each individual response must be identified and linked to that specific response. This requires the identification of all declarative knowledge (i.e., names, locations, symbols, etc.). The result of this cognitive task analysis will be a hierarchy of rules or IF-THEN statements associated with each goal and subgoal in the AND/OR graph of the task-goal hierarchy. In essence, this process is consistent with that which is required in knowledge engineering when developing an expert system knowledge base. The specification of these IF-THEN statements in the AND/OR graph structure is also consistent with Anderson's (1983) cognitive architecture, what Kieras' (1987a & b) calls a cognitive simulation model or mental model and what is also referred to as a production system model. Developing exercises as a result of this knowledge engineering process would specify explicitly the model of system operations which the trainee must acquire.

Associated with each rule and declarative fact in the hierarchy is an exercise which is constructed to represent all of the corresponding rule knowledge and fact knowledge. Each exercise shall also explicitly describe the subgoal or goal states which are associated with the underlying production represented by the exercise. These exercises shall be tightly related to the rules and facts which they represent. Each exercise shall consist of a packet which will include an exposition of the information represented by a rule, an example which requires a response from the student to test the student's ability to use the knowledge addressed by the exposition, and a diagnostic which will determine what part or parts of the rule (represented by the exposition and its example) has not yet been mastered by the student. A typical sequence for any production to be learned by the student would then consist of presenting the exposition part of the exercise, followed by the problem or example created to elicit some behavior by the student and if the behavior is incorrect or inappropriate, the student will be presented with the diagnostic to isolate the error or errors in his knowledge which produced the incorrect response to the example problem. Given that the error or errors in the trainees' knowledge concerning a production have been identified, the system can automatically employ the instructional approach which will be defined in the following section to select other appropriate exercises for the trainee. This will enable the trainee to overcome his difficulties in acquiring a working cognitive model of console operations. It should be noted that the hierarchical structure of exercises, the specification of goals and subgoals, and the derivation of exercises from underlying productions are all consistent with empirical evidence from cognitive learning experiments. The structuring of exercises and the information content is consistent with the way humans organize and acquire knowledge. The problem segment of each exercise provides the student with the opportunity to practice (Rosenbloom & Newell, 1986) what he has learned from the exposition segment, as well as provide feedback dependent upon success or failure. If failure, the diagnostic will localize the error or errors, providing more specific feedback (Hayes-Roth, Klahr, & Mostow, 1981) to the student and guide the system in its selection of the next best exercise for that particular student. Both practice and knowledge of results are obviously characteristics which support the learning process. This courseware development process is completely consistent with the learning process.

5.1 Instructional Strategy—Adaptive Exercise Sequencing

Having viewed the evidence in support of a rule-based formulation of learning, it is evident that cognitively engineering instructional exercises, in accordance with the research results described, shall improve the efficiency of learning over that which currently exists. The instructional approach is based upon the heuristic that one learns from what one almost already knows. To phrase this another way, new rules must be related to what one already knows if they are to be learned effectively and efficiently. The new rules to be learned by the trainee must therefore be related rule sets which exist in part or in whole in the trainee's knowledge base. The importance of relating to existing knowledge and of overlapping new knowledge with old knowledge is critical to guiding lesson sequencing. Evidence for the approach shall now be presented.

5.2 Empirical Evidence Supporting Instructional Strategy

Billman (1983) has demonstrated the importance of learning rules in association with other rules in his focused sampling experiments. In these experiments, Billman demonstrated that when individuals were required to learn rules in isolation as compared to those which were required to learn the same rules in clusters or as a group of rules, those in the grouped or clustered condition learned the rules better. Also, the results of the experiments which have investigated the effect of instruction in formal physics on the ability to apply formal physical principles to solving problems about physical motion have indicted that such instruction does not have a profound impact because it cannot relate to existing intuitive rules (i.e., beliefs), which people have about physical motion. McClosky (1983) found for some problems that there appeared to be no effect of participation in a physics course on a student's ability to apply what he/she had learned to everyday life problems involving physical motion. Research conducted by Champagne, Klopfer, and Anderson (1980) made the distinction between the accurate rules of physics and some basic rules which subjects intuitively held about physics. These intuitive rules held by students were, however, incorrect about the nature of the physical world. It is assumed then that since the intuitive physics held by the college level students who participated in these experiments are so strongly developed and counter to the physics of the actual world, that the students had difficulty in learning how to relate these principles to solving the test problems presented to them. The lack of effectiveness of instruction in physics can then be accounted for by the lack of associative strength between the incorrect intuitive rules held by the students and the rules of actual physics.

Consistent with the above, Cheng, Holyoak, Nisbett, and Oliver (1986) found that instruction in formal logic emphasizing syntax, truth tables, and the construction of proofs in accordance with this syntax has very little, if any, impact upon the way in which students reason about everyday life problems. However, if these formal rules were presented in a semantically pragmatic context (e.g., IF you want to drive a car, THEN you must pass a course in drivers education.), students learn to generalize such modus ponens reasoning to other problems outside the domain of the examples given. Surely these results can be inferred to support the notion that instruction is most effective when the to-be-learned information is related to the clusters or rules extant in the belief system of the learner. Even the ubiquitous capability of people to classify and categorize seems to support the notion that rules are clustered. Without such clusters of rules with their associated attributes, classification and categorization would be difficult to explain.

Kieras and Bovair (1986) have shown that reading time is expedited if the sequence of procedures describing how a device works has rules in common or conditions in common between the rules describing device operations. Consequently, efficiency in terms of the time required to read procedures about the device operations was improved by ordering the productions making up the procedures in such a way that overlap between conditions of productions was maximized. Kieras and Bovair (1986) in the same study also demonstrated that training time (i.e., the time required to learn a procedure correctly) was also dependent upon the number of new rules which were added to a procedure. When examining the amount of time required to train subjects on a transfer task, these investigators found that training time could be predicted based upon the number of new rules added to the transfer task as compared to the initial task.

Consistent with the Process of Induction (PI) model of Thagard and Holyoak (1985) as well as the evidence presented, learning best takes place when input rules can be related to strong existing rules. In accordance with the PI model new rules have a better chance of entering the system when they can be associated with strong existing clusters of rules. Existing strong rules can then be used to assist in the generation of new rules and the recombination of old rules to produce improved predictive power as in adaptation to the new task environment. This being the case, the sequencing of to-be-learned lessons should be made dependent upon the strength of old rules and that one should avoid transition to new information until specific rules related to that new information are strengthened.

In our conceptualization of instruction as a hierarchy of related facts and rules, lower level lessons in this hierarchy should first be strengthened to assist in new rule assimilation and generation. Sequencing of exercises plays a very important role in this process. The strengthening of lower level rules in the hierarchy will spread its effect to other related rules in the hierarchy of lessons, thus, giving new inputs a better chance to compete against any existing incorrect rules which may interfere with new rule coupling to existing clusters. This notion also predicts that when students are having difficulty with the insertion of rules (i.e., learning new rules and strengthening new rules), old incorrect rules of considerable strength are interfering with new rule insertion. This prediction has been validated by Black, Kay, and Soloway (1987) who have found that when naive subjects were asked to rate the similarity of some identical pairs of commands from several text editors, the ratings of similarity of commands clustered around their knowledge concerning the command terms. For example, CODE and MESSAGE were related as being similar commands as well as CANCEL and DELETE. After the subjects had trained on the different systems, however, similarity ratings concerning these test editing commands changed sharply. In order to overcome this problem, additional practice on an exercise would be required until its predictive strength surpasses that of the old interfering rule.

Consequently, by developing exercises based upon a cognitive level analysis of task requirements and selecting appropriate sequences of exercise such that overlap between the productions represented by each exercise is optimized, training time can be influenced positively. That is, training time can be optimized relative to currently employed instructional technologies and learning can be accelerated. In order to optimize training time and comprehensibility of the instructional content, one must also capitalize on the prior declarative knowledge and production knowledge which for whatever reasons a trainee possesses or for which a trainee has a natural inclination to assimilate rapidly. This, however, requires that the system be capable of selecting exercises in a manner which is most compatible with the strengths and weaknesses of a particular individual.

5.3 Structure of Exercise Content and Diagnostic Tests

Figure 2 depicts an AND/OR graph which shall contain the instructional content for each exercise. This instructional content in turn will

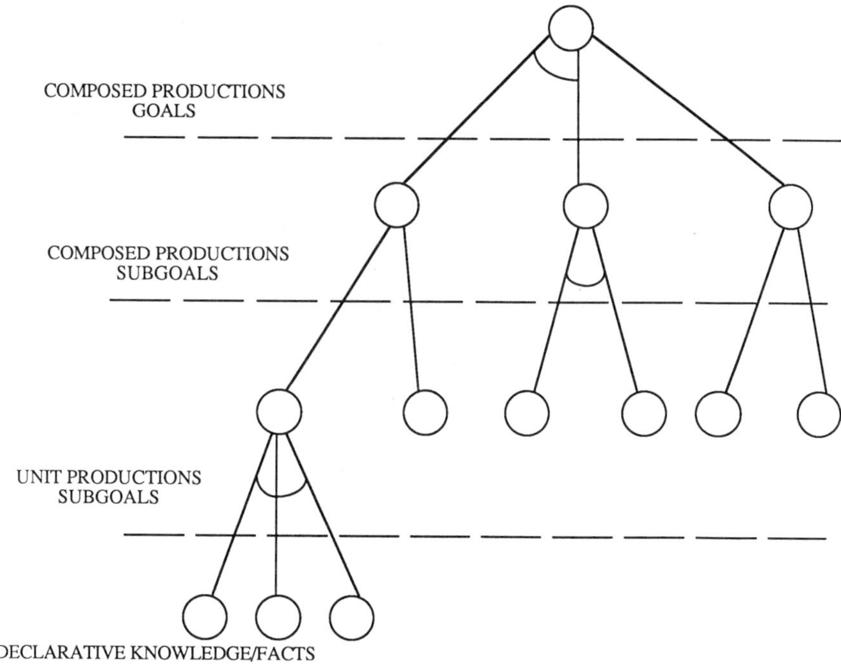

FIGURE 2. AND/OR graph of productions representing the instructional content.

have been identified as a result of developing a cognitive simulation model of device operation. Associated with each exercise is a diagnostic test(s). These diagnostics are designed to assess the trainees strength of knowledge and performance relative to the conditions and actions of the production represented by the exercise. For example, in Figure 3; A, B, and C; can be thought of as diagnostics associated with declarative level knowledge exercises. Diagnostic A may query the trainee about his ability to identify the meaning of a specific symbol or his ability to identify the specific location of a control input. Diagnostic A then will represent a measure of how well the trainee knows the material associated with exercise A. Exercise A, in turn, represents information about a specific declarative. At a higher level, exercise D will represent the information of a specific production which is composed of the declarative knowledge from exercises A, B, and C. A diagnostic for exercise D will test the individuals ability to respond in a specific way following instruction on exercise D. This process continues until all productions in the network have been represented by an exercise and diagnostics for each particular exercise. The task for the trainee then becomes working through his problem space of exercises until all productions of the underlying cognitive simulation model have been acquired.

It is not sufficient for the student simply to master all productions in a haphazard or random fashion since such a strategy would not capitalize upon the trainee's prior knowledge and, as Kieras and Bovair (1986) have shown, would not be conducive to training efficiency and effectiveness. What is implemented, therefore, is a capability to select a set of exercises which overlap with the exercise which the student has failed. The system can then select a specific exercise from this set of overlapping exercises which shows the greatest overlap in partial knowledge with the elements mastered by the student and the fewest new elements of knowledge which were failed by the student. With this approach, the system can implement

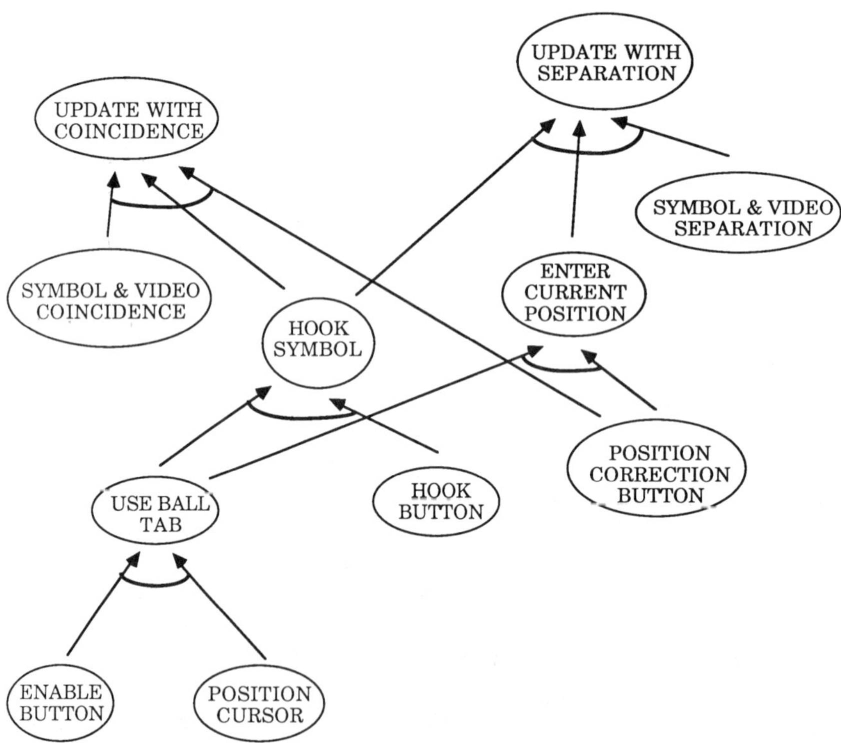

FIGURE 3. A partial network of exercises for learning computerized tactical console operations.

the strategy that one can learn only from what one almost already knows, or exploit partial knowledge to guide learning.

As an example, referring back to Figure 3, if the problem example associated with the exercise packet in Node "M" is failed, the appropriate diagnostic will be presented to the student. This diagnostic will determine what lower level production, J or K or both, that the student is having trouble with. If the student is having trouble with J, then the system will select an exercise with elements F and G in it along with some of the failed elements of J (i.e., D or E). This would result in the selection of exercise K. The exercise with the most overlap of mastered knowledge elements and the fewest unmastered knowledge elements would then be selected for presentation to the student. If none can be found except for the exercise which was just failed, then that exercise would be presented again along with some feedback or additional hints from the instructor.

6 Exercise Selection Heuristic

This exercise selection heuristic is made up of three techniques: (1) to handle selection procedures in the event of exercise failure (2) to handle the apportionment of credit and (3) to handle procedures in the event of exercise success.

6.1 Exercise Failure

The exercise selection heuristic is enabled following two consecutive failures on an exercise. Two consecutive failures are allowed in order to be forgiving of inadvertent errors in responding. Upon the second consecutive failure the heuristic searches and selects an exercise in comparison to the current active exercise (that exercise which was last failed) which shares the greatest number of productions or preconditions which were correctly responded to in the current active exercise and the greatest number of productions or preconditions which were not correctly responded to in the current active exercise. The exercise selected shall be further constrained in that it cannot represent an exercise which has productions or preconditions that are not included in the current active exercise. Additionally, the exercise selected cannot be the current active exercise. The exercise meeting these criteria shall be the next exercise to be presented.

If an exercise cannot be found which meets these criteria, the second cycle of the search is directed to find an exercise which has the greatest number of productions or preconditions which were correctly responded to in the current active exercise and the greatest number of productions or preconditions which were not correctly responded to in the current active exercise and the fewest number of productions not included in the current active exercise which have the highest predictive strength and the highest frequency of coupling.

If an exercise cannot be found which shares correctly responded to productions with the current active exercise then select an exercise which has the greatest number of shared productions with the current active exercise which were not correctly responded to and which does not include any new productions not included in the current active exercise.

If an exercise cannot be found then select an exercise which does not have any shared correctly responded to productions with the current active exercise and has the greatest number of shared productions which were not correctly responded to in the current active exercise and which includes the lowest number of productions not included in the current active exercise which have the highest predictive strength and highest frequency of coupling.

If an exercise cannot be found then select an exercise with the fewest productions not included in the current active exercise which has the highest predictive strength and the highest frequency of coupling. This would be a new exercise at the lowest level of the AND/OR graph. To summarize, cycle one and cycle two find exercises which share strong knowledge and weak knowledge with the failed exercise. If these tests fail then cycle three and four looks for exercises which have only weak knowledge in common with the failed exercise. If these tests fail then select an exercise which has indirectly related knowledge with the failed exercise. Indirect knowledge gets coupled with direct knowledge through predictive strength and coupling frequency which is defined in the following description of the apportionment of credit.

6.2 Apportionment of Credit

Apportionment of credit involves identifying rules which contribute to successful learning and assigning a strength value to those rules. For the case at hand, it is assumed that productions or preconditions which assist in learning are those which have been associated with a successful outcome or a correct response. A correct response, therefore, increases the predictive capability of the rule. Consequently, each time an exercise is visited, its visitation frequency shall be incremented by one. Each time the exercise is successfully completed, its frequency of correct response shall be incremented by one. The inverse of the ratio of frequency of visitation to frequency of correct response will define the predictive strength of the production(s) represented by the exercise. The higher this value, the higher the predictive strength of the productions represented by the exercise. The lower the value, the lower the predictive strength of the exercise. It is also assumed that if a rule made up of composed productions (i.e., where productions are coupled together) is visited, that the experience with this rule also implies experience with the rules component productions. Consequently, each time such a composed rule is visited, a frequency count should also be added to its component productions. This count shall be propagated throughout the network. This frequency shall be called a rule's "coupled frequency". Predictive strength applies to a rule being directly visited in an exercise. Coupled frequency applies to a rule being visited indirectly. It is a measure of the associative experience that the trainee has had with rules which are coupled with other rules in the network or a measure of relatedness of a production with other productions. If a rule has a high predictive strength and a high frequency of coupling then it is a strong rule with a high degree of relatedness to the cognitive simulation model. Predictive strength and coupled frequency thus can be used by the exercise selection heuristics in determining the selection of an exercise which will contain information about a production not included in the current active exercise. It is felt that these measures of visitation and coupling will assist in implementing the heuristic that you only learn from what you almost already know and that learning must take advantage of strong prior knowledge.

6.3 Exercise Success

If an exercise is successfully completed by the trainee, the next exercise on the goal stack shall be selected. If the goal stack is empty, then select an exercise which shared the greatest number of productions correctly responded to in comparison with the last exercise and the fewest number of productions which have not yet been visited and which have the highest coupling frequency.

If none can be found; that is, if only exercises with shared productions with the last exercise can be found without any new productions which have not yet been visited, then select an exercise with the fewest productions which have not yet been visited and which have the highest coupling frequency.

If none exist then all exercises have been successfully completed.

7 Goal Stack and Success Sequence Stack

Two other components of the system consist of a Goal Stack which orders the sequence of exercises *to be completed* after a failure and a Success Sequence Stack which orders the sequence of exercises *which have been successfully completed.* Each time an exercise is selected for presentation it is be placed on the top of the Goal Stack. After successful completion of an exercise it is removed from the top of the Goal Stack and placed on the top of the Success Sequence Stack. The next exercise to be selected is the exercise on top of the Goal Stack. If no other exercises can be found, the training session will have been completed and the sequence of skill development shall be the bottom to top order of the exercises on the Success Sequence Stack.

7.1 Conflict Resolution

Any conflicts which arise as a result of the exercise selection process shall be resolved by placing each exercise in conflict on the Goal Stack on a first come basis. That is, if two or three exercises meet the heuristic search criterion for the exercise selection they will be placed on the Goal Stack in the order in which they were found. It should be interesting to note that any exercises found to be in conflict may also be considered potential candidates for interference among rules depending upon their degree of similarity. Consequently, all exercises found to be in conflict are flagged and identified such that their potential for interference can be examined during later analyses of the sequence of skill development as determined by the order of exercises from the Success Sequence Stack.

8 Summary

In summary, what we have described is an intelligent computer-aided instruction system which makes empirically valid assumptions about knowledge representation. Employing this representation scheme, student diagnosis can provide inputs to a teaching tactic or teaching strategy which in turn can form a modifiable plan of instruction for the individual. This technique is similar to what Ohlsson (1987) has referred to as his principle of "teaching plans" where the tutor is able to generate a plan (i.e., sequence of instruction) based upon its representation of the subject matter, the current goals of instruction, and knowledge of the student. The plan is continually subject to revision.

References

Anderson, J.R. (1983). *The architecture of cognition.* Cambridge, Massachusetts: Harvard University Press.

Anderson, J.R. (1986). Knowledge compilation: The general learning mechanism. In R.S. Michalski, J.G. Carbonell, and T.M. Mitchell, (Eds.). *Machine learning an artificial intelligence approach volume II.* Los Altos, California: Morgan Kaufmann.

Billman, D. (1983). Inductive learning of syntactic categories. Cited in Holland, J.H., Holyoak, K.J., Nisbett, R.E., and Thagard, P.R. (1986). *Induction processes of inference, learning, and discovery.* Cambridge, Massachusetts: MIT Press.

Black, J.B., & Bower, G.H. (1979). Episodes as chunks in narrative memory. *Journal of Verbal Learning and Verbal Behavior, 18*, 309–318.

Black, J.B., & Bower, G.H. (1980). Story understanding as problem-solving. *Poetics, 9*, 223–250.

Black, J.B., Kay, D.S., & Soloway, E.M. (1987). Goals and plan knowledge representations: From stories to text editors and programs. In J.M. Carroll (Ed.), *Interfacing Thought: Cognitive aspects of human-computer interaction* (pp. 36–60). Cambridge, Massachusetts: The MIT Press.

Branson, R.K., Rayner, G.T., Cox, J.L., Furman, J.P., King, F.J., & Hannum, W.H. (1975). *Interservice procedures for instructional systems development: executive summary.* Tallahassee, FL: Florida State University, Center for Educational Technology (DTIC/NTIS No. ADA 019 486).

Brooks, L. (1978). Nonanalytic concept formation and memory for instances. In *Cognition and categorization*, E. Rosch and B.B. Lloyd (Eds). Hillsdale, New Jersey: Lawrence Erlbaum.

Burke, R.L. (1982). CAI Sourcebook: *Background and procedures for computer assisted instruction in education and industrial training.* Englewood Cliffs, New Jersey: Prentice-Hall, Inc.

Champagne, A.B., Klopfer, L.E., and Anderson, J.R. (1980). Factors influencing the learning of classical mechanics. *American Journal of Physics, 48*, 1074–1079.

Cheng, P.W., Holyoak, K.J., Nisbett, R.E., and Oliver, L.M. (1986). Pragmatic versus syntactic approaches to training deductive reasoning. *Cognitive Psychology, 18.*

Fong, G.T., Krantz, D.H., and Nisbett, R.E. (1986). The effects of statistical training on thinking about everyday problems. *Cognitive Psychology, 18.*

Fried, L.S., and Holyoak, K.L. (1984). Induction of category distributions: A framework for classification learning. *Journal of Experimental Psychology: Learning, Memory, and Cognition, 10*, 234–257.

Graesser, A.C. (1980). *Prose comprehension beyond the world.* New York: Springer-Verlag.

Hayes-Roth, F., Klahr, P., & Mostow, D.J. (1981). Advice taking and knowledge refinement: An iterative view of skill acquisition. In J.R. Anderson (Ed.), *Cognitive skills and their acquisition* (pp. 231–253). Hillsdale, New Jersey: Lawrence Erlbaum Associates.

Hinton, G.E., and Anderson, J.A. (1981). *Parallel models of associative memory.* Hillsdale, New Jersey: Erlbaum Associates.

Holland, J.H., Holyoak, K.J., Nisbett, R.E., and Thagard, P.R. (1986). *Induction processes of inference, learning, and discovery.* Cambridge, Massachusetts: MIT Press.

Jeffries, A., Turner, A.A., Polson, P.G., and Atwood, M.E. (1981). The processes involved in designing software. In J.R. Anderson (Ed), *Cognitive Skills and Their Acquisition.* Hillsdale, New Jersey: Lawrence Erlbaum.

Kieras, D.E. (1988). Towards a practical GOMS model methodology for user interface design. In M. Helander (ed.), *Handbook of human-computer interaction.* North-Holland: Elsevier Science Publishers B.V.

Kieras, D.E. (1987a). *The role of cognitive simulation models in the development of advanced training and testing systems.* Office of Naval Research Technical Report No. 23 (TR-87/ONR-23).

Kieras, D.E. (1987b). *What model should be taught: Choosing instructional content for complex engineered systems.* Office of Naval Research Technical Report No. 24 (TR-87/ONR-24).

Kieras, D.E., & Bovair, S. (1986). The acquisition of procedures from text: A production-system analysis of transfer of training. *Journal of Memory and Language, 25*, 507–524.

Klahr, D., Langley, P., & Neches, R. (1987). *Production system models of learning and development.* Cambridge, Massachusetts: MIT Press.

La Berge, D. (1973). Attention and the measurement of perceptual learning. *Memory and Cognition, 1*, 268–276.

Marshall, S.P. (1988a). *Schema knowledge for solving arithmetic story problems: Some affective components.* Office of Naval Research, Cognitive Sciences Programs Contract No. N-00014-K-85-0661.

Marshall, S.P. (1988b). *Assessing schema knowledge.* Office of Naval Research, Cognitive Sciences Programs Contract No. N-00014-K-85-0661.

McClosky, M. (1983). Intuitive physics. *Scientific American, 24*, 122–130.

Miller, G.A., Galanter, G, & Pribram, K.H. (1960). *Plans and the structure of behavior*, New York: Holt, Rinehart and Winston.

Minsky, M. 91975). A framework for representing knowledge. In P.H. Winston (Ed.), *The psychology of computer vision.* New York: McGraw-Hill.

Newell, A., and Simon, H.A. (1972). *Human problem solving.* Englewood Cliffs, New Jersey: Prentice Hall.

Nilsson, N.J. (1980). *Principles of artificial intelligence.* Palo Alto, CA: Tioga Publishing Co.

Nisbett, R.E., and Kunda, Z. (1985). Perception of social distributions. *Journal of Personality and Social Psychology, 48*, 297–311.

Ohlsson, S. (1987). Some principles of intelligent tutoring. In R.W. Lawler & M. Yazdani (Eds.), *Artificial intelligence and education volume one* (pp. 203–237), Norwood, New Jersey: Ablex Publishing.

Polson, P.G. (1987). A quantitative theory of human-computer interaction. In J.M. Carroll (ed.), *Interacting thought: Cognitive aspects of human-computer interaction.* Cambridge, Massachusetts: The MIT Press.

Posner, M.I., and Snyder, C.R. (1975). Attention and cognitive control. In R. 2. Solso, (Ed.), *Information processing and cognition.* Hillsdale, New Jersey: Erlbaum Associates.

Post, E. (1943). Formal reductions of the general combinational problem. *American Journal of Mathematics, 65*, 197–268.

Rosenbloom, P.S., & Newell, A., (1986). The chunking of goal hierarchies: A generalized model of practice. In r.S. Michalski, J.G. Carbonell, & T.M. Mitchell (Eds.), *Machine Learning: An artificial intelligence approach volume II* (pp. 247–288). Lost Altos, California: Morgan Kaufmann.

Seifert, C.M., Robertson, S.P., & Black, J.B. (1985). Types of inferences generated during reading. *Journal of Memory and Language, 24*, 405–422.

Siegler, R.S. (1983). How knowledge influences learning. *American Scientist, 71*, 631–638.

Smith, E.E., & Medin, D. (1981). *Categories and concepts.* Cambridge, Massachusetts: Harvard University Press.

Thagard, P. and Holyoak, K.J. (1985). Discovering the wave theory of sound. In *Proceedings of the Ninth International Joint Conference on Artificial Intelligence.* Los Altos, California: Morgan Kaufmann.

CHAPTER 11

Strategic Automatic Discovery System (STRADS)

Colleen M. Oresky, Douglas B. Lenat, Albert Clarkson, and Stephen H. Kaisler

Abstract

Today, intelligence analysts spend most of their time determining the significance and implications of each new event as it occurs: in short, "strategists" still are largely reacting creatures. Few tools have been developed to assist in exploring contingencies. This chapter describes the Strategic Automatic Discovery System (STRADS) which uses knowledge-based simulation to generate scenarios (plausible long chains of actions-reactions) of world actors responding to given events.

1 Overview

The Strategic Automatic Discovery System (STRADS) is a knowledge-based simulation system for generating and analyzing alternative scenarios in geopolitical military situations. Given an event (or set of events), STRADS simulates the responses of various actors (countries, leaders, radical groups, etc.) in the context specified by the particular scenario. These responses, in turn, generate new events which cause the process to repeat. A STRADS simulation continues until no new events can be generated or until the termination criteria of the simulation are met.

STRADS is intended to become a tool that aids intelligence analysts by evaluating the likely consequences of critical events. The basic need arises from the many documented human limitations, cognitive and institutional, which constrain strategic analysts from recognizing and anticipating potential situations. For example, these limitations engender "mirror-imaging", which prevents analysts from viewing a situation from the perspective of the countries being analyzed (consider the way we made deals with Iran, mistakenly believing that would make them feel indebted to us, rather than viewing it from their perspective of Koran-sanctioned cheating and stealing and lying to infidels). Or, as another example, they may cause analysts to predict future situations based on past occurrences which are only superficially similar to the current situation (consider the Mayaguez

Crisis, when everyone thought of the Pueblo, just because both ships had Spanish-sounding names). These cognitive short falls are classic sources of strategic surprise.

In sum, because of time and human limitations, analysts are not always able to review important factors relating to their region of interest; and in many cases they are not able to perform detailed analysis of how events in their region might be related to events in other areas. Yet our era more and more requires a global strategic perspective. Successful analysis will increasingly require labor-intensive efforts to generate and analyze contrasting outcomes of multiple situations.

In more specific terms, STRADS aids analysts by generating several plausible scenarios that take into account multiple actor viewpoints (what X believes that Y believes ...). By varying the starting conditions, analysts are able to explore hypothetical situations such as "What if Kim Il Sung dies?" or "What if Israel gives up the West Bank?" or "What if the U.S. military solidarity were much higher than it is today?". Analysts could evaluate how changes in current foreign and domestic policies would effect the United States in the future. The objective is to support analysts, planners and decision makers by promoting strategic readiness.

The longer term goal, but perhaps an even more significant objective of STRADS, is to generate a large number of scenarios from which STRADS can automatically learn new general heuristics (rules of thumb), new strategic insights. The STRADS design is at a frontier in artificial intelligence. At the same time, the signs are increasing for the first groundswell of interest in machine learning, reminiscent of the earlier period of new interest in expert systems a few years ago. The technical importance of the STRADS architecture is both that it points the way to future designs and represents one of the pioneering design projects in applied machine learning.

The remainder of the chapter provides a description of how STRADS benefits the intelligence analyst, a brief introduction to Automatic Discovery Systems, a description of the STRADS implementation, and an overview of an example scenario successfully generated by STRADS.

2 The Strategic Intelligence Analysis Environment

There are two important fundamental concepts to define at the outset: the *strategic analyst* and the *strategic analysis problem.* In an earlier book on the application of information technology to strategic analysis, Clarkson (Clarkson, 1981, pp. 7–9) provided this profile of the strategic analyst:

> The strategic analyst watches some part of the world—an economy, an industry, a foreign country. He receives information of many kinds and levels of credibility from many sources on events and situations in his sphere. He researches problems and prospects of leaders, countries, economic sectors, alliances, and regions. Perhaps he has visited his assigned part of the world. If responsible for a foreign

activity, he may have learned one or more of the languages of the area. He has undergone selected training.

The strategic analyst is supposed to do no less than this: understand the dynamics and prospects of change in the area he watches; recognize signs of change, particularly threatening change; assess its significance; make projections; and carry out warning as appropriate.

He strives for literal realism but properly acts on the basis of probabilities.

Through modern communications technology, he encounters on the job (and off the job, too) an unprecedented, growing, vast amount of information, much of it individual facts, isolated events. He is one of the people most caught up in the information revolution. The myriad data provides diverse, sometimes conflicting views of parts of reality.

He is within the realistic tradition of philosophy. He is an empiricist. His operational epistemological assumption is that in some sense "reality" is objective; it is knowable. There are at least some correspondences between his experience and the facts of reality. Moreover, the world in its change has an order, governed by sets of laws, some of which are now known and can be understood and recognized by humans in their perception of reality.

His chief impulse is interpretive. The strategic analyst will be seeking to order the chaos of experience, much of that experience being secondhand, its objects removed like echoes from the scene of his interest. He will seek to discover as much certainty and necessity within the reality he watches as possible. To some extent, he must believe that changes are comprehensible in terms of explainable cause and effect. If change is perverse, it is also consistent within some bounds; it is similar to some degree across different times and places. This basic logic of change derives from the assumptions of purpose and of reality governed by laws recognizable by the rational mind operating on current and past information. Hence factual data are taken as reliable cognitive elements.

Perhaps most fundamentally, he will believe implicitly in the authenticity of models organized by "plots"; models in which experience is ordered in chronological, causal forms. This is not to exclude other perceptual and analytic modes such as mosaic techniques.

Analyzing input data with his models and analytic techniques, perhaps he can be said to have two modes of interpretation:

To extract a pattern of significance from information.
To impose scheme of meaning on reality.

Clarkson (Clarkson, 1981, p. 10) goes on to define the problem of strategic analysis as follows:

Strategic analysis is a rigorous cognitive process by which possible crucial realities of the future are first imagined and then modeled systematically to delineate their conditions, dynamics and potential outcomes, every effort being made to achieve realism and verisimilitude; with various inferential strategies procedurally employed to develop comparative probabilities; with the models and probabilities continuously reviewed and modified appropriately on the basis of new data; with *post mortems* conducted systematically to measure performance and to simulate learning; and the entire process oriented toward decision making and policy formulation.

In sum, then, the intelligence analyst is faced with the problem of interpreting sequences of events in a larger model of both a geographic region (e.g., the Middle East) and an analytical discipline (e.g., Political Instability). Obviously, an analyst's model is often constructed over many years of study and immersion in a variety of subject areas such as geography, religion, economics, etc. associated with a particular region. Using this model, an analyst projects forward in time to determine the impact of current events on future occurrences. Based on this projection, the analyst may prepare a variety of products which alert managers to the significance of the event and its likely outcomes. Using this information, national decision makers can determine what responses, if any, to make to the event.

As a growing body of research and publications indicate, human cognitive limitations can seriously constrain the effectiveness of strategic analysis (Clarkson 1981). Although we cannot here explore in depth the complexities and subtleties of the cognitive and epistemological dimension of the strategic analysis problem, we can analyze the process of strategic analysis in terms of the characteristics amenable to machine learning.

2.1 Mindset

A major problem affecting the strategic analysis process is mindset, the tendency to perceive what you expect to happen rather than what actually happened. In many cases, the two perceptions coincide; but in some cases, they diverge dramatically, often with catastrophic results. Specifically, mindset leads an analyst to develop patterns of expectation; patterns which are sometimes biased by the analyst's point-of-view and background. Mindset also results because analysts have limited time to review all factors relating to their region of interest, and in many cases they are not able to perform detailed analysis of how events in their region might be related to events in other areas.

Success in the past serves to reinforce views of the future. For example, the overthrow of the Shah of Iran by Shi'ite fundamentalists in the face of military neutrality and secular resistance illustrates how analysis is seriously affected by mindset. It was unexpected that a grass roots religious upheaval would succeed in a country with a powerful secret police (the SAVAK) and a disciplined, well-armed military. What analysts tended to overlook was the powerful *political* role of the clergy in the situation: the phenomenon of the "clerical junta." The mindset that developed among several analysts can be succinctly stated as:

> "A totalitarian government enjoying the support of effective military and security organizations cannot be overthrown by fundamentalist popular opinion."

Contributing to this preconception were two other ideas:

1. "When the position of a dictatorial ruler is threatened, he will defend his position with force, if necessary."

2. "The principal threat to friendly governments comes from the left, not the right."

Many analysts shared this view of the situation in Iran in late 1978 and early 1979. Very few believed the Shi'ite clergy could muster popular opinion and political strength to force the abdication of the Shah.

The overthrow of Ferdinand Marcos in the Philippines is another example of analyst mindset. Although analysts successfully predicted a deterioration of the government, the event sequence was accelerated because of the statements about the Marcos government by the Catholic clergy. While the influence of religious leaders may have been discussed by analysts, it was discounted by a great extent. In retrospect, the involvement of the religious factors and the dissatisfaction of such groups is an integral part of geopolitical analysis, especially in those countries where the populace is predominantly of one religion. Those analysts who experienced the impact of religion on a government have added a new mindset to their analytical data bank.

2.2 Why STRADS?

Of course, the above examples are only two of many such cases. General awareness of these problems led us to realize there was a lack of adequate tools to properly assist analysts in overcoming mindset, and in exploring the ramifications of current events in a model of a geopolitical situation. STRADS was developed to fill this gap. It aids analysts by: exploring responses to specified events, suggesting alternatives for analysts, stimulating analytical thought, assisting in expansion and retention of strategic knowledge for analysts, and providing inputs for various reports. Specifically, STRADS aids analysts by:

1. Simulating sequences of events arising from a given event. This permits the analyst to quickly establish a wide range of plausible outcomes. One very important factor is that it is far easier for analysts to critique a large number of scenarios than to generate all of them themselves.
2. Varying the initial assumptions, the analyst can explore alternative outcomes for a situation. During scenario generation, the user is primarily interested in conducting a specific and predetermined analysis that is intended to answer some specific question(s). Typically, this takes the form of problems posed as "what-if" questions (i.e. given certain initial conditions, what events are likely to occur).
3. Explaining the interactions among complex sequences of events.
4. Providing a browsing capability for exploring a large knowledge base of facts about the world.
5. Promoting the discovery of new insights through the use of the STRADS automatic discovery component.

3 Introduction to Discovery Systems

Machine Learning is a major field of Artificial Intelligence (AI). STRADS employs automatic discovery techniques, a form of machine learning based on the EURISKO concept developed by Lenat (refer to 8–13). This concept has been successfully applied to a diverse set of experimental applications, including the design of Naval fleets for a national wargame against human opponents, VLSI design, and the discovery of mathematical concepts. For example, for the naval fleet design task, EURISKO was given two hundred pages of rules and constraints for designing ships and a simulator to be used to test one fleet against another. EURISKO spent many hours designing fleet after fleet, before ultimately generating the winning naval fleet. EURISKO accomplished this by analyzing the differences between the designs and in particular the differences between the individual ships that make up a fleet. These differences might include noticing that one fleet was more heavily armored or that one fleet had a fewer number of ships.

After a while, EURISKO noticed another kind of regularity. For almost all parameters (e.g., the number of weapons, the amount of armor), the optimal value seemed to be almost, but not quite, an extreme value. This regularity was formed into a heuristic rule that enabled EURISKO to very rapidly discover a winning fleet design. The new heuristic said:

IF designing either an individual ship or a fleet for Traveller TCS, and a certain parameter is having its value changed, THEN change it to a nearly but not quite extremal value. (Lenat 1982)

This is just one example of many heuristics that EURISKO used to design its naval fleet. The final fleet contained a large number of ships, each was fairly small, each had nearly as many weapons as allowed, each was nearly as heavily armored as possible, each was nearly as slow as possible, etc. The fleet won the national (Traveller TCS Origins) tournament by winning seven consecutive battles. The next year, the tournament rules were changed. In response, EURISKO was modified and again it won more easily, generating the winning fleet design in two days (the first year it took several weeks). So in exchange for being made an honorary admiral, Lenat has agreed not to enter any future tournaments.

The Traveller TCS Naval Fleet design task is one example of how EURISKO was successfully used to discover new heuristics within a domain. The remainder of this section describes the EURISKO concept in more detail and provides a brief introduction to STRADS, the latest application of the EURISKO concept.

3.1 The EURISKO Concept

EURISKO applications provide some critical advantages over more traditional AI expert systems. There are two serious problems facing expert system developers and users: knowledge acquisition and range-of-application. The literature contains several case studies and anecdotes detailing the bottleneck associated with knowledge acquisition. Many expert system developers have experienced the difficulties of interfacing with experts to acquire the "right" knowledge for making their system act intelligently.

The second problem, range-of-application, is not as well documented; however, many users have experienced the dilemma that once the domain of expertise is exceeded, the usefulness of the expert system diminishes rapidly. The dilemma remains that considerable time is expended in developing systems which are comparatively narrow and simplistic.

One response to these problems has been to use natural language understanding techniques. The basic idea is to provide an automatic way to "read" large portions of knowledge from textual sources into the knowledge base. Unfortunately, the past three decades have shown serious, persistent difficulties which appear to strongly preclude widespread near-term solutions via that approach. Problems of semantics, context, and ambiguity have proven to be extremely formidable barriers. An alternative solution is to develop machine learning to the point where the machine itself, using built-in expertise, can discover and generate further expertise. EURISKO applications provide through automatic discovery techniques the ability to develop new designs, to generate novel scenarios, to structure new solutions, and to discover new heuristics. For certain kinds of problems, such as those where the present state of expertise is relatively limited and/or not well formalized, EURISKO can be extremely useful.

To summarize, systems modelled after the EURISKO concept operate as follows. Steps 3, 4 and 5 are the heart of the automatic discovery (machine learning) process.

1. It is necessary to symbolically represent a sizable domain such as VLSI or Naval Fleet design. This means that the system maintains a sizable data base of factual and estimative knowledge which represents the "world."
2. EURISKO seeks to expand its data base by simulating data about the "world." The simulation capability allows EURISKO to produce significant amounts of additional data (designs or scenarios), guided by "heuristics". The heuristics operate to avoid combinatorial explosions while searching the large knowledge base; yet, they allow extremely robust and productive exploration of alternative possibilities. This open-ended exploratory capability distinguishes a EURISKO application from the typical expert system that is attempting to find the "correct" answer in response to a well-defined question.
3. EURISKO focuses on narrowing the population of data (designs or scenarios) by using heuristics to notice regularities and irregularities in the populations of system-generated data. The goal is to use a set of heuristics for generating plausible new concepts out of old ones. These

include both "fleshing out" heuristics for filling in details, and "defining" heuristics for creating brand new concepts. Some of these heuristics are domain-specific, but many are more generally applicable such as "Look at extreme cases."

4. To test the newly discovered hypotheses, EURISKO conducts directed experiments. These experiments evaluate what to keep and what to forget, how interesting or useful the new discoveries are and why. As in step 3, domain-specific and general sets of heuristics are used for judging the discoveries' interestingness. They may need to refer to the current goals of the system, and to a model of the user and his/her goals and constraints.
5. EURISKO updates its knowledge base upon confirmation from the users that the newly discovered heuristics are valid. These new heuristics, when properly validated, contribute to increasing the knowledge base content and the analytical capability of the application built upon EURISKO.

3.2 EURISKO Concept Applied to Strategic Analysis (STRADS)

STRADS which is currently being developed at ESL, Incorporated, is the latest application of the EURISKO concept, essentially incorporating major design features from the past and enhancements based on additional research (illustrated in Figure 1). Based on the steps outlined in the previous section, STRADS operates as follows:

1. STRADS symbolically represents knowledge about the world (e.g., countries, organizations such as OPEC and OECD, factions within a country, leaders of organizations). The STRADS knowledge base contains detailed information about many political, economic, military, cultural, and environmental aspects of these actors who interact in various geopolitical situations.
2. STRADS produces numerous scenarios to explore strategic possibilities using a program guided by search heuristics. These heuristics, together with some constrained randomness, facilitate the intelligent generation and interconnection of individual events to efficiently discover plausible and instructive scenarios. STRADS also provides explanations of its decisions by allowing analysts to review why and how specific events occurred in a given scenario.
3. To achieve strategic learning, STRADS would begin to learn by using heuristics to inspect the large population of generated scenarios to notice interesting patterns. It must narrow the population of scenarios to interesting sets of scenarios which are then reviewed by analysts. To do the "front end" filtering, STRADS uses heuristics designed to perform operations such as grouping scenarios by criteria possible criteria being similar outcome (e.g. scenarios in which a military conflict occurs), similar patterns of actor activity (e.g. scenarios which illustrate an actor responding to certain events in the same manner), and cases exhibiting

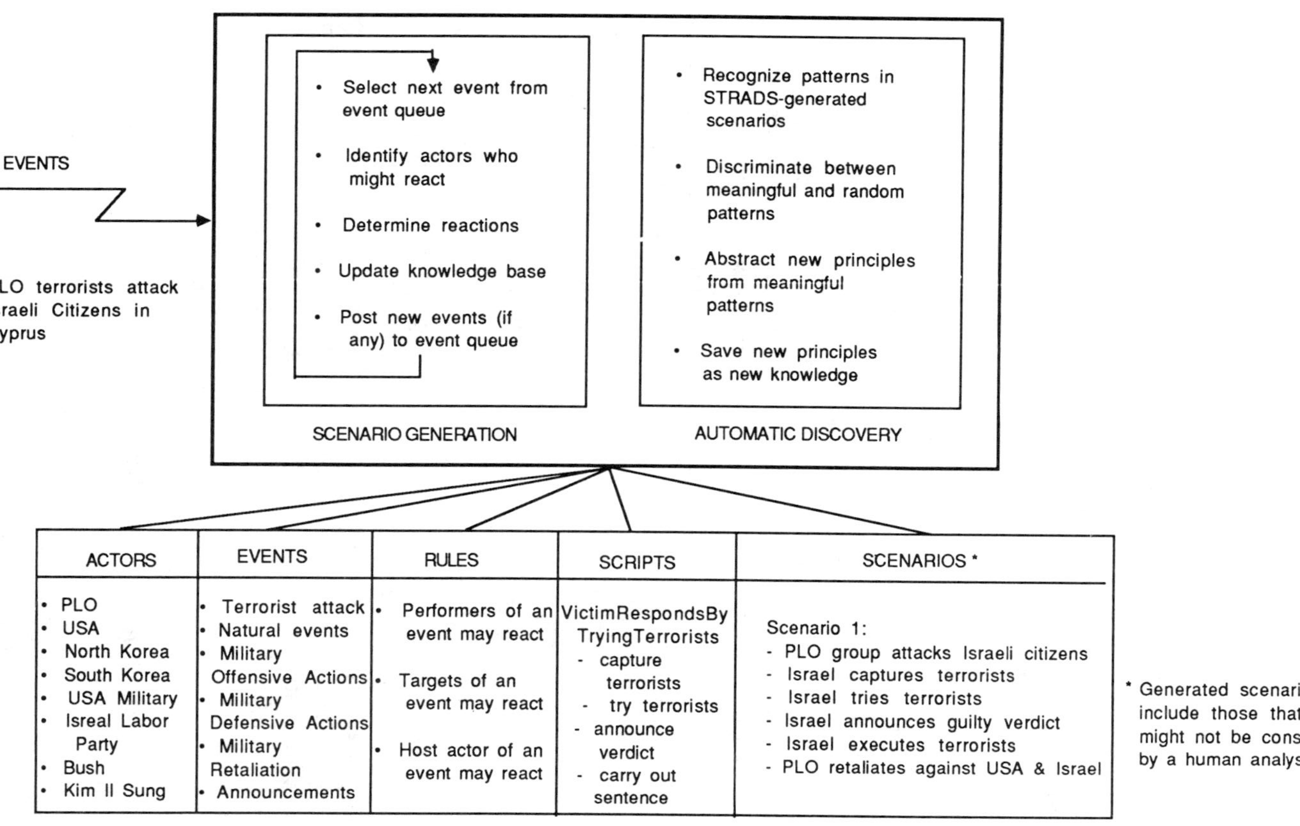

FIGURE 1. STRADS overview.

exceptions to typical behavior (e.g. scenarios which illustrate why goals were thwarted when it was expected that they would be achieved, scenarios in which unusual actor alliances were formed). Interesting scenarios are analyzed in depth, and expected behavior is used to troubleshoot unexpected behavior.

4. Using the scenario generator, STRADS would then conduct directed experiments to test whether the regularities, patterns and irregularities are meaningful or simply coincidental. These experiments involve describing several real and hypothetical situations, and then running the STRADS scenario generator. The scenarios would be reviewed by "experts" to determine the plausibility of the scenarios and to evaluate the results of the experiments. In essence, STRADS "challenges" its findings to determine the validity and applicability of the discovered patterns. It seeks to establish the limits of its own discoveries. For example, STRADS may discover that certain actor alliances disappear in peculiar situations. A country which regularly provides economic and political support to certain terrorist groups may be unwilling to do so in cases when those terrorists are threatening a nation that the country depends upon economically.
5. After the newly discovered heuristics have been validated by analysts, STRADS would update the knowledge base to reflect these changes. The new heuristics would be used to guide future scenario generation.

To perform the above mentioned functions, STRADS employs a large domain-specific knowledge base, a flexible but complex control structure, and a (so far) simplistic man-machine interface. Sections 4, 5 and 6 describe each of these components in more detail.

4 STRADS Knowledge Base

The STRADS knowledge base contains symbolic descriptions of the various components (actors, events and scripts) that represent the simulated world, along with a small number of rules that guide the generation of plausible scenarios. All elements of the STRADS knowledge base are described by a data structure referred to as a *unit.* A unit is a frame that consists of a set of slots (e.g., military readiness, GNP, government stability). Slots are used to store values for the various characteristics describing the knowledge base element (e.g., a country).

The knowledge base is structured into five taxonomic hierarchies (actor, event, script, rule and slot) that allow for inheritance of default values, and describe the interrelationships among its elements. Within each hierarchy, there are single entries (e.g., United States, Bush, PLO), and class entries that combine single entries into groups (e.g. Western Actors, Democratic Society, Actors Allied to the U.S. Politically) based on several criteria. Knowledge base elements are members of several different classes within their respective hierarchies. For example, actors are divided into various classes based on geographic, economic, political, military, religious, cultural and other criteria. The United States is a member of several classes including NorthernHemisphereActors, WesternActors and SuperPowerActors.

There are several advantages for using the representation scheme described above:

1. Taxonomic hierarchies using inheritance of default values simplify and reduce the knowledge entry and maintenance tasks. Values for attributes that are common to all members of a class are placed at the highest, most general level; low level elements inherit the information based on their class memberships. Exceptions can be recorded within appropriate elements, as required.
2. Class definitions reduce the number of slots needed to describe knowledge base elements, again making the knowledge base entry and maintenance tasks easier. Information can be retrieved based on the defined classes within the hierarchies.
3. Scenario generation is faster and more efficient. The script hierarchy minimizes the number of invalid options that are considered when reacting to a particular event. Also, actor responses can be simulated at the most general and appropriate level (i.e. the country versus an individual) based on the evolving situation. Sensitivity analyses on the resultant scenarios would indicate if more detailed reasoning is required.
4. The control structure is simplified. Because the representation of all knowledge base elements (static and dynamic) is similar, the underlying control functions are general and can be used to process all types of data.
5. Frames and hierarchies are a natural way for representing the appropriate domain knowledge. Analysts naturally converse about categories of actors and responses. This simplifies the knowledge acquisition and knowledge engineering tasks.

The following sections provide a brief discussion of each of the five hierarchies (actors, slots, events, scripts and rules).

4.1 Actors

STRADS *actors* represent real world entities that could respond to events depending on the current situation. Actors can be thought of as having beliefs about themselves and other actors, and as having specific goals that they are actively trying to achieve. An actor may be an individual (e.g., Margaret Thatcher, George Bush), a group (e.g., PLO, International Red Cross, British Government), a country (e.g., Israel, Libya), a class of actors (e.g., Western Actors), or a mechanical object (e.g., aircraft, ships).

An actor may have several subactors which also represent independent decision makers. Subactors of a country might include its military, government, and civilian population. Each subactor can act independently or in concert with any other actor or subactor. For example, Libya's subactors include the Libyan population, Libyan Rebel Groups, and the Libyan Government. Since the Libyan people often take a less radical stance towards certain issues than does the Libyan Government (chiefly, but not wholly, represented by Muammar Qhadafi), in those situations different responses would be simulated for the Libyan people than for the Libyan government.

Actors are organized in the hierarchy based on several criteria such as superpower allegiance, military and political orientation, economic stability, geographic location, and religious affiliations and traditions. There are currently several hundred representative actors contained in the STRADS knowledge base including: several class actors such as Western Actors and Authoritarian Societies, several Middle East countries, the United States, the USSR, North and South Korea, Japan, the government, civilian population, military and major leaders of all included countries, the PLO and some of its splinter groups, and some types of military equipment. Figure 2 illustrates a small portion of the full actor hierarchy. Ultimately, several tens of thousands of actors would be included in the hierarchy.

Several hundred slots are used to describe various characteristics (political, military, cultural, economic, and geographic aspects) about all actors. This includes factual information such as GNP, the morale level of the army, the form of government, population, religious affiliations, its border territories, and the number of monsoons, earthquakes, etc. Figure 3 illustrates some representative slot values for the actor, United States.

Values for actor slots are themselves complex structures used to store not only the present value (ActualValue), but also what the actor believes the present value to be (CurrentValue), an actual count for slots such as GNP or Population, or a list of numbers for slots such as those referencing equipment inventories (ActualNumberValue), what the actor wants the value to be (GoalValue), how important it is to the actor that that value be achieved (ImportanceOfGoalValue), and what all other actors want the value to be an how important it is to them that that value is achieved (OtherActorsGoals). This is necessary to accurately model the beliefs, goals and strength of goals for each actor.

In addition to goals, actors respond to events in part based on their beliefs about other actors. For each attribute of each actor, there exists values that represent what other actors believe the values to be. Specifically, the slot, *Beliefs*, attempts to capture the image an actor has about other actors.

4.2 Slots

Slots are used to store values for various characteristics about knowledge base elements (actor, event, rule, script or slot). The large set of slots describe a major portion of the STRADS representation language. As can be seen in Figure 4, slots are classified in a hierarchy primarily based on their domain (what types of units are allowed to have this kind of slot).

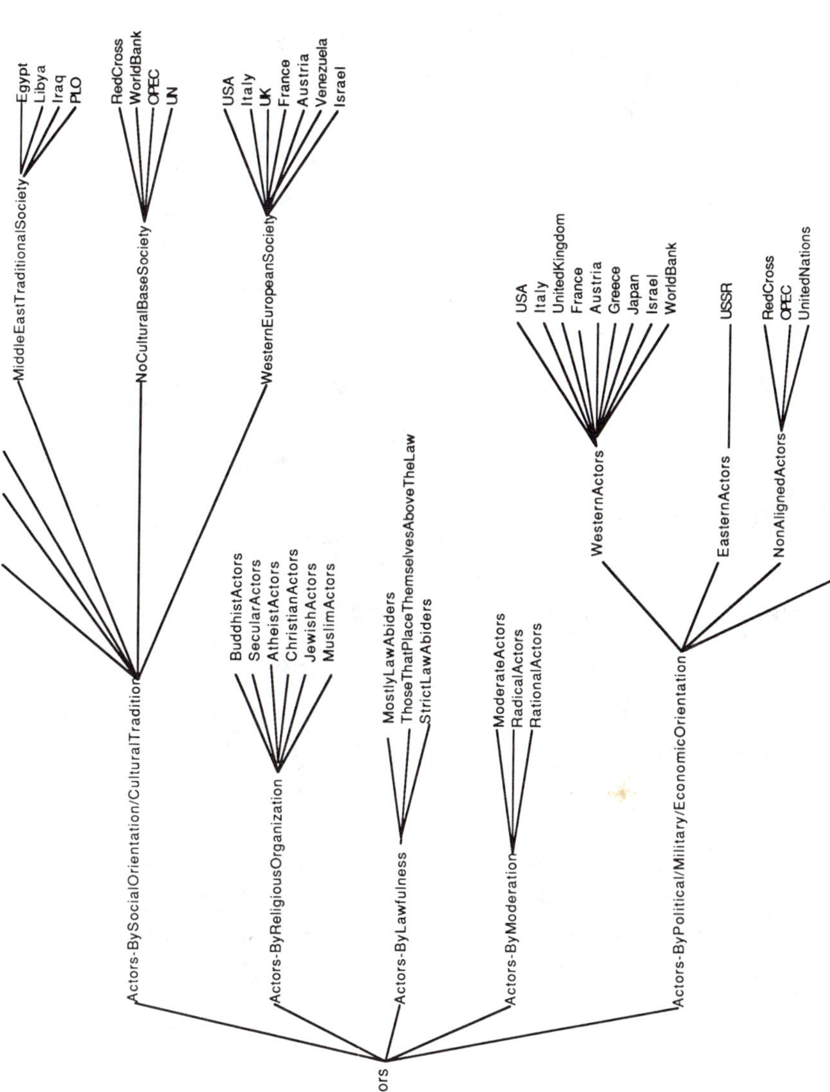

FIGURE 2. Subset of STRADS actor hierarchy.

ActorModeration:	ActualValue	High
	CurrentValue	High
	GoalValue	(>= High)
	ImportanceOfGoalValue	VeryImportant
	OtherActorsGoals	NIL
ActorTrustworthiness:	ActualValue	Moderate
	CurrentValue	High
	GoalValue	(>= (^ ActorTrustworthiness USA))
	ImportanceOfGoalValue	VeryImportant
	OtherActorsGoals	((WesternActors (>= (^^ ActorTrustworthiness USA)) Important) (USSR (>= (^^ ActorTrustworthiness USA)) Important))
AmountOilProduced:	ActualValue	High
	CurrentValue	High
	GoalValue	(>= High)
	ImportanceOfGoalValue	Important
	OtherActorsGoals	((WesternActors (>= High) Important) (ThirdWorldActors (>= Low) Important))
CulturalAllies:	ActualValue	(WesternActors)
	CurrentValue	(WesternActors)
	GoalValue	(= (WesternActors))
	ImportanceOfGoalValue	Important
	OtherActorsGoals	NIL
ImageInMiddleEast:	ActualValue	Moderate
	CurrentValue	Low
	GoalValue	(>= (^^^ ImageInMiddleEast USA))
	ImportanceOfGoalValue	Important
	OtherActorsGoals	((WesternActors (>= High) VeryImportant) (USSR (<= Low) Important))
Population	ActualValue	High
	CurrentValue	High
	ActualNumberValue	240000000

FIGURE 3. Representative actor slots for the United States.

4.3 Events

An *event* corresponds to an action that occurred in the world at a particular time and place. A STRADS event would describe who was involved, what action was performed, how the action was performed, when it took place, where it took place, why it took place, and who knows and believes the event took place. Events are organized in a hierarchy based on action type (e.g., planning, attack, announcement) as illustrated in Figure 5.

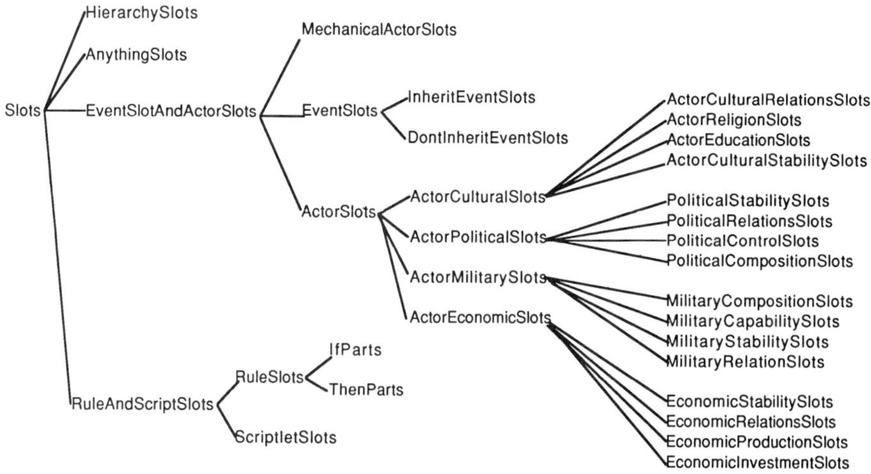

FIGURE 4. Subset of STRADS slot hierarchy.

4.4 Scripts

A *script* represents an option for how an actor might respond to a particular situation. Specifically, it describes the set of events (represented in the event hierarchy) that might take place if an actor chooses to respond to an event in a certain way. This response of actors largely corresponds to those actors attempting to achieve goals; in other words, a script describes the set of events that would aid the actor to achieve a goal. To use a highly simplified example, a government wants to respond to a terrorist attack against its citizens. If the government's goals include demonstrating that the perpetrators must pay for violent crimes against its citizens and the government is not afraid to use military force whenever necessary when dealing with terrorists, one response might be for the government to (1) identify the perpetrators, (2) plan to forcibly retaliate, and then (3) retaliate by attacking a headquarters location of the responsible party. In the present simplified example, these three events would comprise one script. Other options might describe different retaliatory methods or non violent methods for dealing with the terrorists.

Scripts are organized in a hierarchy base on the event type being react to. The larger the number of scripts, the larger the number of options that can be considered and therefore, the larger the search space from which plausible scenarios can be generated. Figure 6 illustrates a subset of the current STRADS Script Hierarchy.

FIGURE 5. Subset of STRADS event hierarchy.

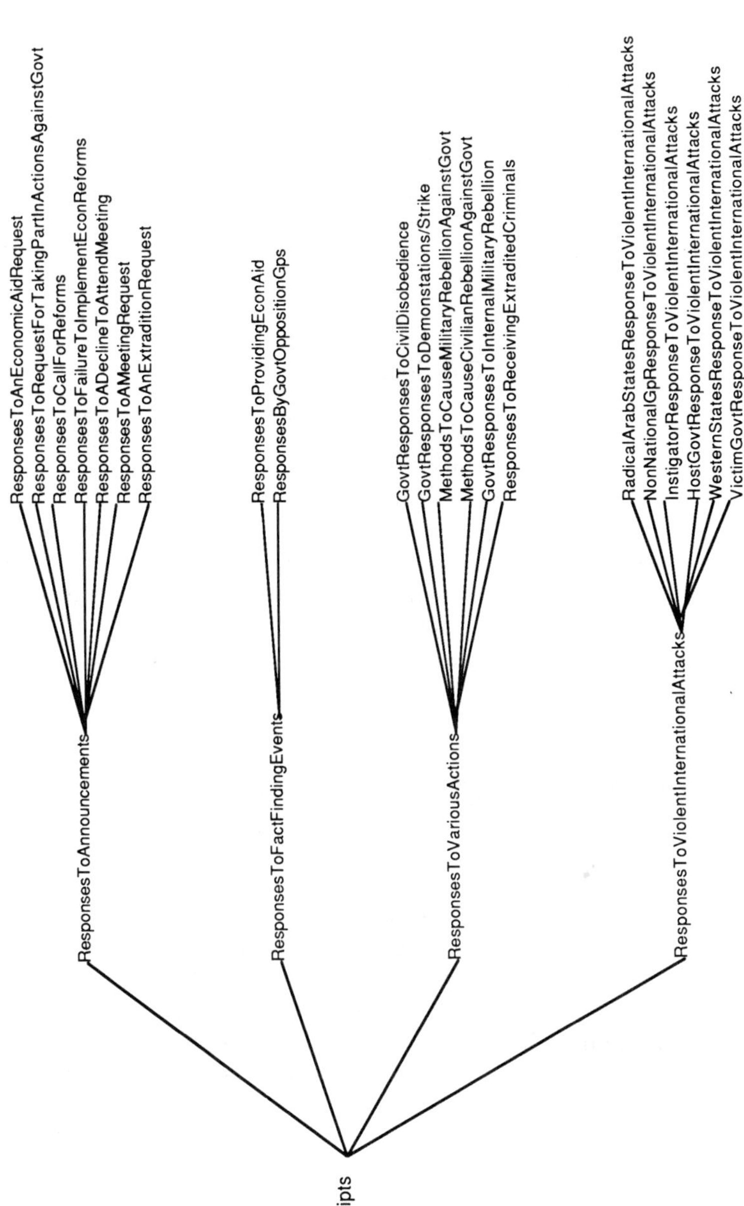

FIGURE 6. Subset of STRADS script hierarchy.

4.5 Rules

Rules are a very small part of the STRADS knowledge base. At a very high level, rules control the generation of scenarios and represent the procedural knowledge for stopping a simulation. Specifically, STRADS rules contain general information to govern the use of the details which are contained within the slots of various actors, events and scripts. The search space is increased with the addition of new scripts and events; however, the rule base remains relatively small and may even decrease in size based on knowledge base design changes. Figure 7 illustrates a subset of the current rule hierarchy.

4.6 STRADS Knowledge Base Dimensions

The STRADS knowledge base is constantly being updated and expanded. Table 1 lists its current size by unit type. Since everything in the STRADS knowledge base is represented by a unit, the number of units changes as new actors, slot, events, rules, slots and scripts are created. The number of kinds of slots has remained relatively stable; new scenario types occasionally require new descriptive slots to be added. The number of actors will change with the introduction of new geographic areas. Current efforts are being expended to increase the depth of the knowledge base by adding more events and scripts.

5 STRADS Control Structure

STRADS captures a model of a situation through use of a scenario. As noted above, a scenario is a set of progressive events which describe actor reactions to evolving situations. These events may either be generated by actors behaviors and reactions (e.g., declaration of war, imposition of tariffs, announcement of economic problems), or caused by natural conditions (e.g., earthquake, monsoons). New events occur when actors respond to previous events that they know or believe took place. The set of events that comprise a scenario varies depending on the number and type of actors involved, the starting conditions as stated by the user (i.e. to simulate "What If" conditions), the simulation time period, and the depth of reasoning that is employed.

To be realistic and plausible, scenarios must account for the diverse viewpoints and beliefs of each of the actors. Actors will act based on aspects such as their beliefs about themselves and other actors (actors do not always have an accurate view of the world), their goals, and their understanding of the current situation.

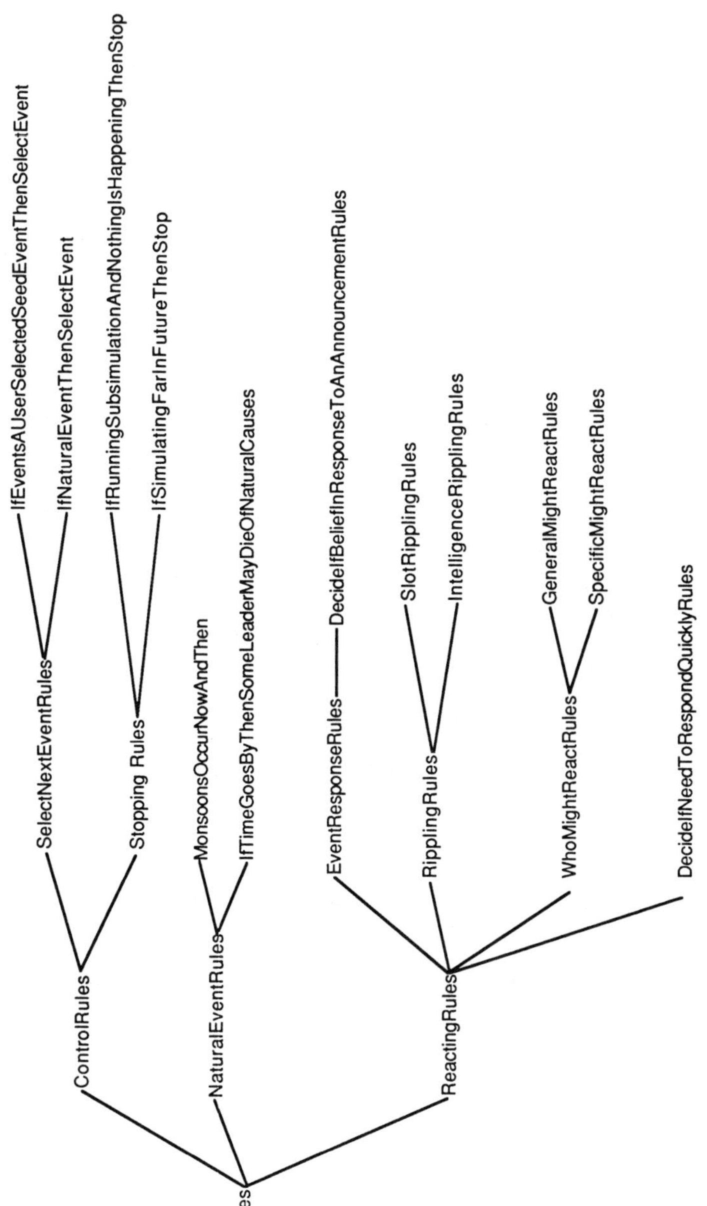

FIGURE 7. Subset of STRADS rules hierarchy.

TABLE 1. STRADS Knowledge Base Size

Unit Type	Number of Units
Actors	492
Events	281
Scripts	253
Rules	225
Slots	560
Total	1811

5.1 Scenario Initialization

Scenario generation begins with the creation of a Seed World. This can be the current world, or one in which some slots of some units have been changed. Also, the Seed World can contain any number of *seed events.* A seed event is a trigger that describes the starting condition and sets the context for the resultant scenario. Like other events, all seed events describe what actions were performed, who was involved, where and when the actions took place, why the actions took place, and who knows and believes the event took place. Optimally, several hundred seed events from various problem areas would be accepted by STRADS.

The user-selected seed events are placed on the *Global Event List* (i.e., the agenda). At any time during the simulation, the Global Event List contains events, sorted in ascending order according to expected start time, that are *expected* to take place sometime in the future. (An initial start time for an event is determined when the event is created and place on the Global Event List). Even though an event is added to the list, it may not necessarily happen or it may happen at a time much different than originally expected. As a result of other events running, certain events may be delayed (the event is moved to a different position by adjusting its starting time) until their appropriate preconditions have been satisfied. Other events may be removed from the agenda entirely because the actions they represent have been superseded by previously executed events.

5.2 Scenario Generation

During scenario generation, events are systematically removed from the Global Event List and actor reactions are determined. The basic control cycle is to select the first event from the Global Event List, determine its status, determine any actor responses (which may add new events to the Global Event List), and repeat until the scenario termination criteria are satisfied (e.g., simulation time period is exceeded). Depending on what is happening, the time interval between events varies radically. Whenever the

Global Event List is empty, STRADS jumps a larger time interval to see if anything interesting occurs (i.e. a conflict situation is resolved, economic conditions worsen within a country).

In order to react to an event, an actor must first know or believe, that the event took place. To know an event took place, an actor must be a participant in the action represented by the event. If an actor does not participate in the event, his belief about the event is based on his evaluation of the reporting source and when he found out about it (e.g., immediately or one week later). Occasionally actors tell other actors incorrect information solely for the purpose of misleading them. Future reactions by the misled actors may seem irrational to third-party observers, since those reactions are based on misinformation.

5.2.1 Scenario Generation Control Cycle

To determine an actor's response, different scripts might be considered depending on the event type and the actors involved. Specifically, the scenario generation process consists of the following control steps:

1. Consult Global Event List. Select the topmost event from Global Event List and determine its status. Events can either be aborted, delayed or run. An aborted event is removed from the event list, and the time and reason for aborting the event are recorded. For a delayed event, a new start time is calculated and the event is then reposted on the Global Event List. In both cases, repeat step 1.
2. For an event that runs:
   (a) Adjust STRADS System Clock. Set STRADS system clock to time of selected event. The time interval between events varies radically depending on what is happening. When the Global Event List is empty, STRADS jumps a large time interval to see if anything interesting would occur (i.e. a conflict situation is resolved, economic conditions worsen within a country).
   (b) Determine belief. Determine which actors know or believe the event took place. Based on this, determine which actors might consider reacting to this event. This does not identify reactions; the purpose is to prune the list of potential reactors.
   (c) Determine responses. Determine responses for all appropriate actors identified in "b." A decision to react on the part of an actor is based on his beliefs about himself and other actors, perception of the current situation, and decision making policies and style.

   To determine an actor's response, STRADS dynamically computes probabilities that the actor would select each of the potential options based on its beliefs, goals, strength of goals and other characteristic information. The actual selection of the "best" option is based on generating a random number that is weighted according to actor type and the calculated probabilities. For example, only in very extreme cases does a rational actor select anything but the most likely option. A moderate actor follows expected behavior patterns most of the time, but not as religiously as a rational actor. On the other hand, a radical actor can not be expected to conform to any behavior pattern and therefore its response could be viewed as being random. In each of these cases, the random number generator is given different constraints to work within and the various options are weighted accordingly. Since actors do not follow their policies 100% of the time, the use of constrained randomness insures that the effects of choosing the least likely options are evaluated. Nine times out of ten, an actor would respond in a particular way, but STRADS must also account for the tenth time when he responds differently than expected.

The events that comprise an actor's response are posted on the Global Event List in time-ordered sequence.

(d) Determine additional outcomes. Determine whether any other events would result from this event executing. For example, as a result of a revolution or internal coup, the national leader(s) may die. This death event would be added on the Global Event List so that other actors could react to it in the future.

(e) Update knowledge base. Update the system state to reflect the occurrence of the event (execute actor slot change routines), and ripple changes to related actors. For example, if the just-executed event was a successful internal coup, then the "government stability" slot for the target actor might decrease causing neighboring country slots, such as the Cost of Intervening Politically in the target actor, to also decrease.

3. Test simulation termination conditions. Test to see if any terminating conditions are satisfied. If the stopping conditions are satisfied, execution halts and the user is free to browse the generated scenario and the knowledge base. Ultimately, additional explanation capabilities and report generation capabilities will be added to STRADS to make post-mortem analysis easier.
4. If execution continues, consider creating pseudo-random natural events. These include weather conditions (e.g., droughts, monsoons), the deaths of leaders due to natural causes, and actors pursuing their goals.
5. Go to step 1 and repeat the cycle.

5.3 Processing Modes

Scenario generation can be performed in one of two modes: *Recursive Mode* and *Quick Select Mode*. Depending on the amount of detail required and the time available, one mode may be more appropriate than the other. Actor perceptions and beliefs are considered during both; however, depending on the mode selected, how these views are simulated is very different.

In Recursive Mode, STRADS simulates in great detail the effects of choosing each available option in response to the current event. As a simplified example, the host actor, in response to a terrorist attack in its territory, might select one of four options: (1) follow the set of protocols of its legal system; (2) release the instigators to the custody of the victim country's officials; (3) release the instigators to the custody of their parent organization; or (4) try to ignore that the event took place. In such a case, STRADS would initiate four subprocesses to simulate, from the host actor's point of view, what the other actors would do in response to the host actor selecting options 1–4 respectively. A subprocess allows STRADS to evaluate what the host actor thinks actor Y will do if he selects option 1, option 2, etc. respectively. Each subprocess would initiate a different recursive run of STRADS with the "seed world" being the host actor's model of the world at that time, plus the first event the option as a seed event. Beliefs of the host actor would be used when making all decisions during the recursive run.

Once all the subprocesses have completed, an analysis of the results would be performed. A comparison between the host actor's goals and the subprocesses can take a varied amount of time depending on the scenario type, the amount of activity, and how many decisions are considered.

In contrast, Quick Select Mode is much faster; however, not as much information is available to help decide which option to choose. In this mode, the results of executing various function, which access values from the actor knowledge base, are used to decide the "best" option. The function results vary depending on the script, the event being responded to, and the actors involved. The important point is that these functions do not use a detailed analysis of what an actor thinks other actors will do in response to the same event or in response to the actor selecting each available option.

5.4 Strategic Learning

A long term objective of STRADS is to complete development of an automatic discovery component that identifies novel situations and alternatives. The primary difference between scenario generation and learning is that in the former mode the user looks at alternatives and draws conclusions, whereas in the latter mode STRADS uses the results of running the scenario generator to automatically discover new concepts which can then be used to generate other scenarios. The goal is to reduce the number of implausible scenarios generated by STRADS.

To perform learning, many scenarios will be analyzed by STRADS to notice patterns and regularities. Once patterns are discovered, test cases will be created, and experiments will be run (using the scenario generator) to determine if the results correspond to expectations. These experiments may confirm hypotheses (resulting in the identification of new knowledge), or contradict them (meaning the noted patterns are meaningless and/or invalid). Specifically the learning component will consist of functions to:

1. Select a scenario to be analyzed.
2. Note which actors reacted in different situations and what their reactions were.
3. Note what changes were made to the knowledge base after an event or events were processed.
4. Note groups of events which appear together. These events could comprise a new script. Note where pre-established scripts were *not* followed.
5. Note where recursion (detailed simulation of effects of choosing options) was used. Evaluate the advantages and disadvantages of using recursion in different situations.
6. Repeat steps 2 through 5 for all relevant and "interesting" STRADS-generated scenarios.
7. Analyze results from several scenarios for commonalities or irregularities among them. Based on this analysis, test cases would be created.

An initial learning capability is currently being developed. Functions are being developed to analyze several scenarios to notice event patterns, knowledge base changes, and actor reactions. For the time being, test cases are manually created based on the results of this analysis.

6 STRADS Man-Machine Interface

Through the use of menus, windows and the keyboard, the user controls and operates STRADS. Menu options allow the user to browse and modify the knowledge, to print simulation results, and to print knowledge base structures. The keyboard is used to set various systems parameters and to enter certain commands. Currently STRADS can be used in one of two modes: (1) knowledge base browsing and editing, and (2) scenario generation. The following sections describe how a user interacts with STRADS in each of these modes.

6.1 STRADS Screen Layout

The STRADS screen is divided into several windows, each having a specific purpose (illustrated in Figure 8):

Window	Window Function
Chronology of Events	Shows events and changes which have occurred since the start of the simulation. Entries are shown in chronological order based on simulated time of occurrence.

Event Graph	Shows all events that were created during the simulation including aborted, delayed and events that were not considered because the simulation ended before they were set to run.
Events on the Queue	Shows the current state of the Global Event List.
Lisp Executive	Used to initialize system parameters and to display system trace information. This is the standard Lisp input window.
Prompt	Used to display knowledge base entries as the user browses or edits the knowledge base.
Logo	Contains the STRADS logo. Currently, it has no interactive function within the STRADS system.
Options Menu	Allows user to select various ways to browse or edit the knowledge base, and to set scenario generation control parameters.
Scenario Control Menu	Allows user to control the overall scenario process (e.g., Start).

6.2 Knowledge Base Interface

To allow the user to review and edit domain-specific information contained in the knowledge base, the analyst uses one of two different methods:

1. Selecting elements from one of the many graphs that illustrate the relationships represented within the respective hierarchies (e.g., actors, events).
2. Selecting unit-slot pairs from various menus.

Most slots can be modified because a particular analyst disagrees with the currently stored value. STRADS also contains functions to print on the screen or in hardcopy format the contents of a knowledge base element (e.g., a specific actor or event).

6.3 Scenario Generation Interface

To initiate the scenario generator, the user establishes a base state which would be used as the seed world for several scenarios. Setting the base state is done by entering various starting conditions including selecting a seed event(s) from a menu, and entering a starting date and time, and the simulation time period via the keyboard. The user may also modify several actor slots, using several menus and the keyboard, to reflect a hypothetical situation such as an actor being stronger or weaker then actually is the case. Once the base state has been entered, the system generates plausible scenarios. It should be noted that several different scenarios could be developed from the same set of starting conditions because of the occurrence

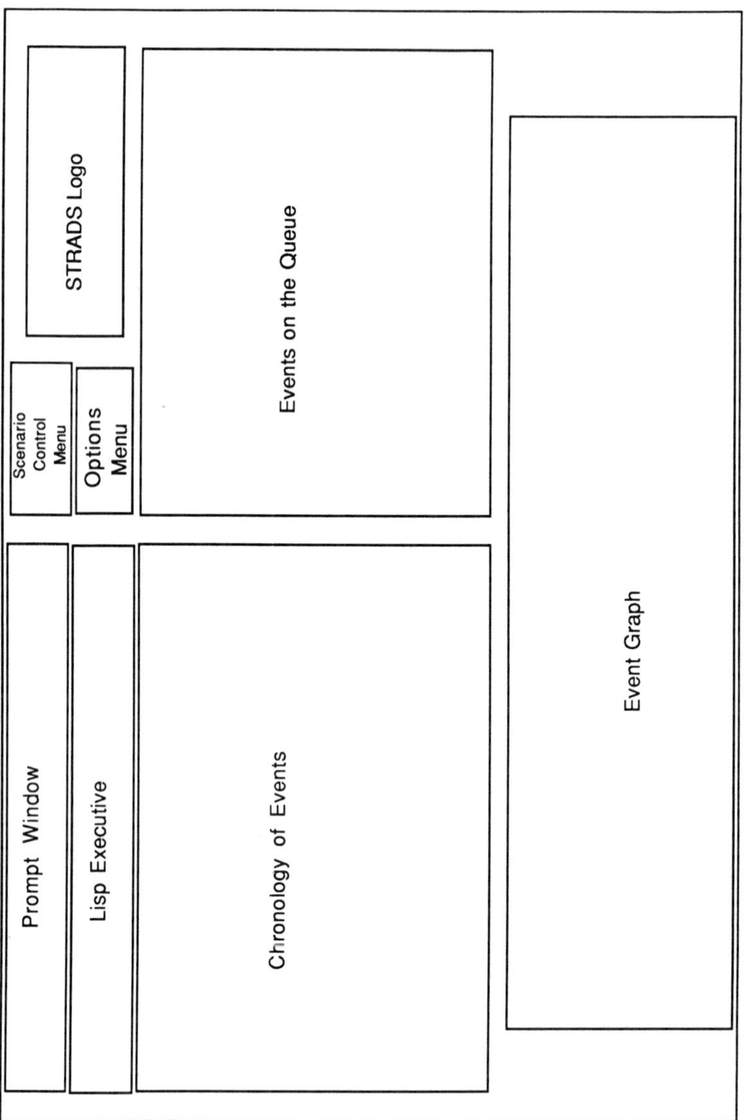

FIGURE 8. STRADS display layout.

of natural events and as a result of using constrained randomness during response selection. To review alternative situations, the user would modify attributes associated with selected actors, describe the seed event(s), set system control parameters, run the scenario generator, and then analyze the generated scenarios.

During scenario generation, trace information is displayed on the screen. Since STRADS is not designed to be used as an interactive system, most of the displayed information is meant to alert the user that something meaningful is happening. The user need only be concerned with the events displayed in the Event Graph window, the length of the Global Event List displayed in the Events on the Queue window, and the short one-line descriptions displayed in the Chronology of Events window.

A completed STRADS scenario is displayed via a graph which illustrates cause and effect between events in the scenario. Events to the left of a line caused the creation of the events to the right. Event names at the left-most border of the graph represent either seed events or natural events, (e.g., earthquakes, leaders dying of natural causes, and actors pursuing certain goals). Event names in boxes appear multiple times in the graph. Event names surrounded by square brackets represent aborted events. Event names in italics represent events which have been added to the Global Event List, but have yet to be processed. Time information is not visibly displayed on the graph.

To get an overall view of how the scenario evolved, the user browses the events in the graph, looking at various event slots such as Performers, Targets, TimeOfEvent, ScriptCreator and RuleCreator. To do this, the user selects from the graph. By viewing several events, the user is able to review criteria used to create and execute them thereby gaining an appreciation for how the system generated its conclusions.

7 Example STRADS Scenario

To better understand how STRADS generates scenarios, let's examine how simulation would proceed. The events discussed below are only some of the events created during a *single* STRADS run. If different random numbers had been generated during the simulation, the generated scenario (from the same seed world) may have been different.

A start date of 18-FEB-90, a start time of 9:00, a simulation time period of 30 days, the seed event *PLOGroupAttacksIsraeliCitizens*, and Quick Select Mode were chosen for this example scenario run. The seed event represents the shooting of three Israeli Citizens in Cyprus by members of the PLO Splinter Group, Force 17. At the time the event takes place, the targets (the three Israeli citizens), the instigators (Force 17), and the host actor (Cyprus, who essentially finds out about the shooting immediately) are the only actors who know about the event.

To start the simulation, the seed event is removed from the Global Event list, and it's determined that, since the event was a user-selected seed event, it will run. Since the target, performer and host actors of an event usually react, STRADS determines that the Force 17 and Cyprus may react in some manner. Since the target actors are dead, it is unlikely they will react; the Israeli government can not react until they find out about the shooting.

The system must now determine if and how these actors would react. The instigators (Force 17) have two options: (1) announce responsibility for the attack and (2) do nothing. Because the goal of a PLO group is to bring world attention to their political/religious cause (i.e. the need for a Palestine homeland), it is likely they would want to announce responsibility for the attack (option 1) unless the attack were unsuccessful. Using the goals, beliefs and description of the Force 17, STRADS dynamically computes a 77% chance the Force 17 will select option 1, and a 23% chance they will select option 2. Using a random number, STRADS determines that the Force 17 will respond by announcing responsibility for the attack and the appropriate event is added to the Global Event List.

The host actor (Cyprus) has four options:

1. Follow the set of protocols of its legal system (try the instigators within their own legal system);
2. Release the instigators to the custody of the victim country's officials (Israeli Government);
3. Release the instigators to the custody of their parent organization (PLO);
4. Try to ignore the event took place and hope the world does not find out about it.

Cyprus is most likely to try the Force 17 members within its own legal system because (a) it is a law abiding nation, (b) it want to maintain a high world image, and (c) it does not want to be a victim of retaliatory actions by either Israel or the PLO. Using this and other goal, beliefs and status information about Cyprus, STRADS dynamically calculates a 59% chance Cyprus will select option 1, a 21% chance they will select option 2, a 13% chance they will select option 3, and a 7% chance they will select option 4. STRADS determines that Cyprus will indeed try the instigators within its own legal system (option 1). Four events (the capture and interrogation of the instigators, an announcement about the attack, the trial of the instigators and the sentencing of the instigators) are added to the Global Event List.

Since other actors have yet to learn of the attack, and there are no other outcomes that result from this event running, the StoppingRules and NaturalEventRules are run. At the end of the first cycle, the updated STRADS display is illustrated in Figure 9; the Global Event List now contains five events in time-sequenced order (each having its own estimated date and time of occurrence displayed next to the event name):

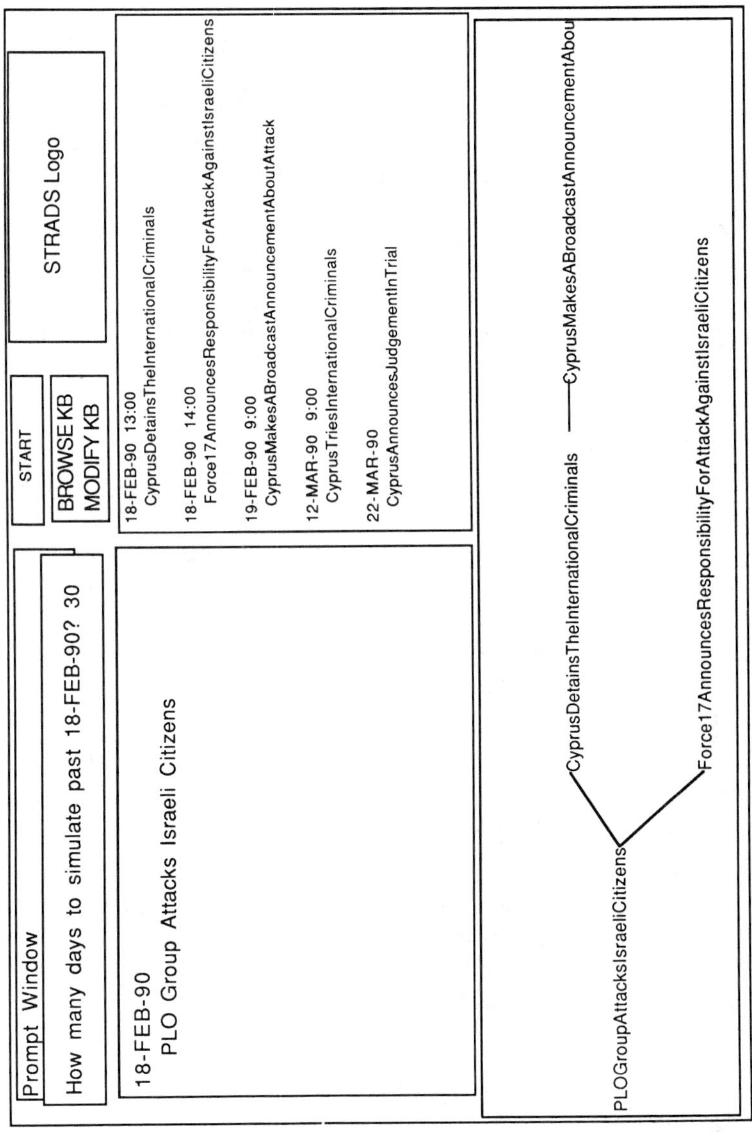

FIGURE 9. Snapshot of STRADS display during scenario generation—1.

CyprusDetainsTheInternationalCriminals
Force17AnnouncesResponsibilityForAttackAgainstIsraeliCitizens
CyprusMakesABroadcastAnnouncementAboutAttack
CyprusTriesInternationalCriminals
CyprusAnnouncesJudgementInTrial

The simulation continues with Cyprus apprehending the attackers and interrogating them about the shooting. No new events are added to the Global Event List, but Cyprus reiterates its decision to try the attackers within their own legal system. The Global Event List remains the same as above, except the event *CyprusDetainsTheInternationalCriminals* has been removed.

Force17AnnouncesResponsibilityForAttackAgainstIsraeliCitizens is the next event to run. Other actors suddenly become aware of the attack when Force 17 members make their announcement proclaiming responsibility for the attack. Because most actors are not sure whether to believe this report, they wait to respond until they have more evidence about the attack. The Global Event List now contains only three events:

CyprusMakesABroadcastAnnouncementAboutAttack
CyprusTriesInternationalCriminals
CyprusAnnouncesJudgementInTrial

Once Cyprus announces to the world they have captured the attackers and they plan to try them, many actors respond based on their allegiances to Cyprus, Israel and the PLO respectively. In particular, Israel, the United States, the United Kingdom, PLO PNC, Syria and Libya all responded to the announcement about the attack.

Israel, being the victim country, has two options:

1. Denounce the attack and vow revenge against the attackers (PLO);
2. Denounce the attack and request extradition of the attackers to Israel so they can be tried in Israeli courts.

Israel has vowed to protect its people and therefore, if they are able to identify the perpetrators they are most likely to retaliate forcibly. Using this and data from the knowledge base, STRADS computes a 87% chance Israel will select option 1, and a 13% chance they will select option 2. Option 1 is selected, and four events (Israel identifying the perpetrators, denouncing the attack, planning a retaliatory strike and performing the strike) are added to the Global Event List.

Western actors or actors friendly to Israel (United Kingdom and United States) have two options:

1. Denounce the actions of the attackers and urge Israel not to respond forcibly;
2. Denounce the actions of the attackers and condone any retaliatory strike by Israel against the instigators.

The United States currently maintains the policy whereby a victim country may conduct retaliatory strikes against an attacker if the perpetrators can be positively identified. Because of this policy, it is likely that the United States would condone a retaliatory strike by Israel if they were able to accurately identify the perpetrators. Using this and other information, STRADS computes probabilities: 37% option 1 and 63% option 2, generates a random number and selects option 1: urge Israel not to respond violently at this time. The selection of the least likely option is a direct result of the use of constrained (weighted) randomness to simulate the effects of unexpected behavior. Two announcement events, one directed to the PLO and the other directed to Israel, are added to the Global Event List.

The PLO/PNC, the ruling body of the PLO, is currently striving for legitimacy as a government in exile. Therefore, if they condone such a use of violence, it would only serve to discredit the PLO as nothing more than a terrorist organization. Therefore, the PLO/PNC has two options:

1. Denounce the terrorist action and request extradition of the instigators to them;
2. Support the attack since it is perceived that the PLO is losing support of the Palestinian people or that the peace process is not progressing as rapidly as possible.

Using the calculated probabilities: 73% option 1 and 27% option 2, option 2 is selected. As in the case of the United States, the unexpected response was selected. One event, an announcement supporting the attack, is added to the Global Event List.

Radical Arab actors such as Libya and Syria are likely to support any type of terrorist attack against a Western actor unless they perceive that there would be massive retaliation, in which case they may publicly denounce the activity but privately support it. STRADS dynamically calculates a 91% chance Libya and Syria would support the attack and a 9% chance they would denounce the action. Using the random number generator, option 1 (support the attack) is selected for both Syria and Libya. Two events, one for Libya's announcement and one for Syria's announcement, are added to the Global Event List.

Since other actors are not active participants at this time and there are no other outcomes that result from this event running, the StoppingRules and NaturalEventRules are run. At the end of this cycle, the updated STRADS display is illustrated in Figure 10; the Global Event List now contains the following events in time-sequenced order:

IsraelDenouncesActionsOfForce17
IsraelTriesToIdentifyInstigators
UnitedStatesDenouncesActionsOfForce17
UnitedKingdomDenouncesActionsOfForce17
PLO/PNCSupportsTheAttackByForce17

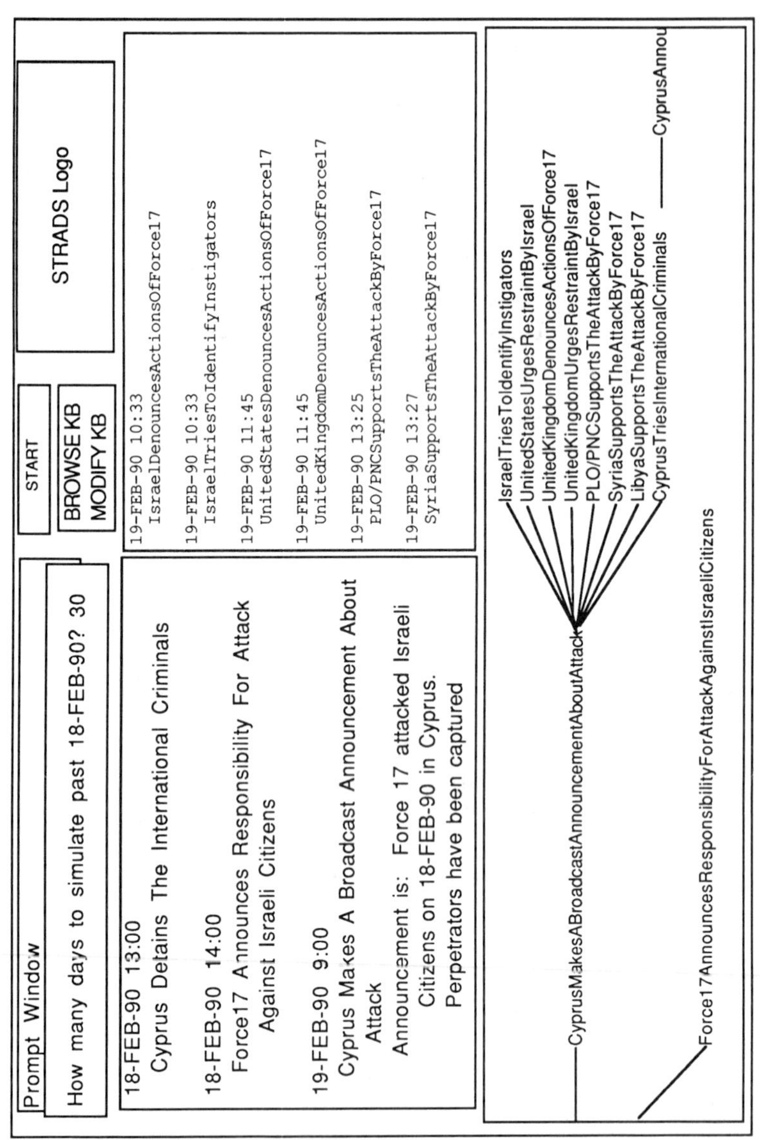

FIGURE 10. Snapshot of STRADS display during scenario generation—2.

SyriaSupportsTheAttackByForce17
UnitedStatesUrgesRestraintByIsrael
LibyaSupportsTheAttackByForce17
UnitedKingdomUrgesRestraintByIsrael
IsraelPlansRetaliatoryStrikeAgainstInstigators
CyprusTriesInternationalCriminals
IsraelStrikesInstigators
CyprusAnnouncesJudgementInTrial

The simulation continues with several actors denouncing the Force 17 attack and several supporting the attack. Once Israel identifies the instigators, they actively pursue a plan to retaliate. During all this, Cyprus is holding the attackers in jail and the trial is proceeding. Figure 11 shows a subset of the complete scenario graph.

8 STRADS Application

For the past two years STRADS has been in use at a military intelligence analysis center. The two STRADS modes, knowledge base browsing and editing and scenario generation, support analysts in their daily activities. Knowledge base browsing and editing support analysts by providing background information on a domain of interest, aiding new analysts in learning about a new domain, and helping in the analysis of current geopolitical situations. Scenario generation allows the analyst to automatically generate many possible future scenarios based on current or hypothetical situations. The results of these scenarios are then used as direct inputs into topic and point papers, and as indirect inputs into the analyst's thought process.

8.1 Knowledge Base Editing and Browsing

Analysts are frequently called upon to provide short term analysis products known as brief items. These brief items are generated to fulfill requests by senior decision makers, usually in response to a geopolitical situation in the world that is of interest or concern to the United States. For example, in response to an increase in tensions between a country where U.S. forces are stationed and the country's principal enemy, the analyst would be asked to provide up to date information on the enemy country's order of battle. This information includes the number of, type, current location, and current readiness of specific units of the country's military forces.

An analyst would use STRADS to gather this information by browsing the knowledge base for the slot values that detail information about the enemy country's military forces. For aircraft, for example, the STRADS knowledge base contains specific slots concerning number of aircraft available, the readiness of these aircraft, their current locations, the type of aircraft, the weapons these aircraft can carry, the capabilities of these

FIGURE 11. Example scenario graph.

weapons, and the capabilities of aircraft. Similar sets of slots describe other military equipment and military manpower.

The STRADS knowledge base also contains information about a country's military capability at a higher level. Some specific slots that would be of use in this situation include level of military readiness, military alert level, number of reserves, state of civil defense, and level of military stability. The analyst would combine these subjective values with the specific equipment characteristics to make an assessment of the enemy's military capability.

8.2 Scenario Generation

The scenario generation capability of STRADS would be used by the analyst to aid in the generation of brief items, as well as longer analysis products, such as point papers or topic reports. In the latter cases, the analyst would be writing about a particular problem area or situation, where the situation may be either an actual current situation or a hypothetical situation. The goal is to present a scenario that reflects the analyst's opinion of how the situation will develop. In the process of generation such a report, the analyst would bring together many sources of information, such as past experience with similar situations, knowledge of how the parties involved are predicted to react based on the circumstances at hand, and the expertise of other individuals.

Scenarios generated by STRADS are intended to be one more information source that the analyst would consult during the report generation process. The purpose of using STRADS is to generate a set of plausible scenarios, based on the given situation, that provide the analyst with possible situations that he may not have considered based on the traditional information sources he relies upon. For example, there may be a large number of cause-event chains which lead to outcome X, even though there is no one highly plausible scenario leading there. As a result, analysts may initially discount the possibility of X occurring, even though the sum of all those unlikely routes deserves consideration. After a review of the STRADS data, the analyst may be convinced that outcome X will occur, and that at a higher level how X occurs is not the really important issue but rather what happens after X.

Specifically, STRADS is used by analysts in several different ways. In one instance, an analyst considering a situation of unrest in a country of interest to the United States concluded that the current situation would develop in a similar fashion to many previous situations of unrest—that the government in power would use force to suppress the unrest and return the country to a state of stability. This assessment was based on his personal knowledge and expertise of the country, and on many previous similar situations. In this case, however, the government agreed to the demands of the demonstrators, a situation that the analyst never anticipated.

In this case, STRADS generated several scenarios for how the government would end the crisis: (1) the government suppresses the demonstrations through the use of police and military force, (2) the government institutes martial rule and curfews, and (3) the government meets with the demonstrators and makes concessions. The first two are very familiar and the analysts felt were extremely plausible. The analysts were skeptical about scenario 3. The last scenario was generated because STRADS views scenarios in a more generic sense, using information from many similar situations over a long period of time and in different countries. To aid in convincing the analyst that the third scenario is also plausible, STRADS provides the reasoning chain used to generate the events within the scenario. The analyst can choose to include the last scenario in the product (with supporting data), or ignore the last STRADS scenario and discuss only the first two methods for ending the unrest.

A slightly different use of STRADS scenario generation is to explore how the events in one country might be affecting events within an analyst's country. For example, an analyst may be responsible for country X. The analyst suspects that events in country Y are strongly affecting various aspects of country X, but the analyst is not very familiar with country Y. The analyst would set up STRADS simulations describing the situation to explore possible interactions between the countries. This information would aid the analyst in learning more about country Y and in more accurately reporting events within country X.

The analyst is also interested in longer term issues such as "What if the leader of country Z dies?" or "What if country A increases its military force by 50%?" To help investigate these questions, STRADS can be used to generate "What if?" scenarios. To accomplish this, the analyst would set up the hypothetical world, and STRADS generates appropriate scenarios. Once the analyst sets up his hypothetical world, scenario generation and analysis proceeds in the same fashion as when scenarios are generated based on real world situations. Again the analyst chooses which scenario inputs will be included in the submitted report.

9 Conclusions

STRADS research to date has primarily centered on the development of an intelligent scenario generator. It has been installed at an operational military intelligence analysis center in order to evaluate its utility to the intelligence analysis process. As analysts identify problem areas, additional knowledge is added. This approach is based on our "build a little, test a little, deliver a little" philosophy which allows for direct analyst feedback and interaction to grow STRADS into a functioning analyst tool.

Now that the scenario generation capability has been successfully demonstrated and STRADS is expected to be integrated into other analytic environments, emphasis is being shifted towards providing more technical capabilities (e.g. automatic discovery) and easier user accessibility. This involves identifying short-tern goals (such as an improved man-machine interface, and a more flexible and generalized scenario generator and learning component), as well as long term goals (such as providing a network of distributed analyst workstations which would interface to existing data bases and message processing systems).

Acknowledgments

Numerous people have contributed to the development and success of the STRADS Program. Funding was partially provided by the Defense Advanced Research Projects Agency for the development of STRADS. In addition, Dr. Richard Steinheiser served as COTR and provided substantial guidance in orienting the program towards helping intelligence analysts. Ms. Andrea Davis provided the sponsorship for the program at the Intelligence Center Pacific (IPAC), the Intelligence Arm of the Commander-in-Chief, Pacific (CINCPAC), and is instrumental in enlisting analysts to investigate its capabilities. Mr. Michael Livingstone did much of the analysis necessary to construct the knowledge base for the first few scenarios.

References

1. Clarkson, Albert. *Toward Effective Strategic Analysis.* Westview Press, Boulder, Colorado 1981.
2. Clarkson, Albert. "Applying Automatic Machine Learning to National Security Problems." *Technically Speaking*, Sunnyvale, CA: ESL Incorporated, September 1987.
3. ESL, Inc. *Project STRADS 2: Final Report.* 495 Java Drive, Sunnyvale, CA 1988.
4. ESL, Inc. *STRADS 1 Final Report.* 495 Java Drive, Sunnyvale, CA 1985.
5. ESL, Inc. *STRADS Concept of Operations.* 495 Java Drive, Sunnyvale, CA 1987.
6. ESL, Inc. *STRADS Programmer's Manual (Draft).* 495 Java Drive, Sunnyvale, CA 1988.
7. ESL, Inc. *STRADS Users Manual.* 495 Java Drive, Sunnyvale, CA 1987.
8. Greiner, Russell, and D. Lenat. "RLL: A Representation Language Language." *Proceeding 1st AAAI Conference, Stanford*, pp. 165–169, 1980.
9. Lenat, Douglas B. "AM: An Artificial Intelligence Approach to Discovery in Mathematics as Heuristic Search." Stanford Artificial Intelligence Laboratory Memo AIM-286, Computer Science Department Report No. STAN-CS-76-570, 1976.
10. Lenat, Douglas B. "EURISKO: A Program that Learns New Heuristics and Domain Concepts." *Artificial Intelligence 21*, pp. 61–98, 1983.
11. Lenat, Douglas B. "The Nature of Heuristics II: Background and Examples." *Artificial Intelligence 21*, pp. 31–59, 1983.

12. Lenat, Douglas, J.S. Brown. "Why AM and Eurisko Appear to Work." *Artificial Intelligence 23*, pp. 269–294, 1984.
13. Lenat, Douglas B., W.R. Sutherland, J. Gibbons. "Heuristic Search For New Microcircuit Structures: An Application of Artificial Intelligence." 1982.
14. Oresky, Colleen. "Strategic Automatic Discovery System." *Technically Speaking*, Sunnyvale CA: ESL Incorporated, December 1987.

CHAPTER 12

Uncertainty Management in Battle-Planning Software

Ben P. Wise and Richard B. Modjeski

Abstract

Many types of uncertainty can arise in computer simulation modules which model command and control for battle planning. This chapter treats the issue of computer simulated planning for battle planning experiments. Computer simulation of attrition, movement, and logistics are not included. Techniques for computer simulated battle-planning are reviewed. Implications of resolving conflicting planning methodologies and their effects on program design are discussed. It is the authors thesis that the model logic of current combat simulation models lacks the capability for reasoning ahead of its current state (i.e. look-aheads). This provides future combat simulation models a tremendous opportunity for "smart" command and control (C2) logic to reflect the knowledge of the commander rather than the "geometry" of the battlefield. Since perfect knowledge of battle-planning may not be attainable an effective trade-off is to adapt a less extreme position in which foresight is introduced into the models. These notions require a fundamental restructuring of combat simulations driven entirely by physical entities in order to economically address the different types of questions which arise in C2 planning.

1 Introduction

The domain considered in this paper is that of planning maneuvers within a software-driven simulation of mid to high intensity combat in the European theater. The domain is similar to the thrust of fighting which stopped the battle in World War I and World War II. This domain was also chosen because it clearly raises many of the same problems of real combat, such as limited material resources and limited information, while being a simplified, abstracted model of real-time, real world battle management. Choosing this domain avoids the social, psychological, and political issues of low intensity conflict in third world nations. The problem of theater-level war in Europe not only involves chance but also competition, which adds to the uncertainty of the total problem.

Uncertainty may be defined as whatever cannot be computed in advance, regardless of whether or not it is deterministic. For example, in any given chess position, exhaustive search suffices to determine whether it is a win, loss, or draw for white and what the optimal strategy is. Thus in the abstract mathematical sense, there is never any doubt as to the outcome—even before a single piece is moved. In practical terms there is still considerable uncertainty. In this case a well-defined algorithm does exist; it simply happens to be impractical. Similarly, while there may or may not exist algorithms capable of accurately predicating the outcomes of past and future battles, it is clear that those algorithms are not yet widely known, that sufficient data is not available on each possible battle, and hence that the outcomes are not precisely predictable in practice. In making useful predications in real-time any algorithm would be further hampered by the various components of the "fog of war." Hence the uncertainty which we refer to arises not only from the intrinsic structures we are handling, but also from our limited capabilities to gather data as well as to design and execute algorithms.

2 Major Sources of Uncertainty

Uncertainty may be characterized by many possible sources: stochastic processes, linguistic vagueness, and subjective belief. A review of the concept of uncertainty and approaches to reasoning under uncertainty was published by Wise and Modjeski (1987). Stochastic uncertainty holds when we consider false alarms of a sensor, accidents among vehicles in a supply network, or any other situation where our expectations are based on the statistics of past experience. In stochastic situations, probability is universally accepted as the "gold standard" which specifies what answers one should get in a simulation. Controversy arises when considering methods intended as fast approximations to probability, or as extensions to non-stochastic situations. Linguistic uncertainty arises from fuzzily-defined phrases like "strong position" or "tall man." The word "tall" shades off into "medium" and "very tall" on either side of a semantic differential. Because there is no crisp dividing line among the meaning of phrases such as "tall," Zadeh (1978) invented the concept of the fuzzy set, where each height is assigned a number between 0 and 1, its "degree of membership" in the set "tall." Subject beliefs are prominent in one-of-a-kind situations, or wherever accurate statistics are not available (e.g. "will the red side attack at A or at B, and will red try to divert me away from the attack at A or at B?"). Proponents of all systems of inference reviewed by Wise and Modjeski (1987) cite subjective beliefs as the type of uncertainty that is most difficult to bring under logical control. Bayesian statisticians, for example, argue that it is the only type (Scherish, 1983), as one cannot avoid subjective judgments when deciding how relevant past data are to the current situation, or what someone else's words meant.

In computer simulation models of combat the major sources of uncertainty are many. Among the sources of uncertainty that affect computer models predictive power for future events are:

Psychological. It is a simple fact that leadership, morale, exhaustion, and other human factors exert a strong influence on the direction, tenor, and outcome of battle. Yet no satisfactory model methodology exists to capture human factors in a computer simulation. Dupuy (1979) suggests that a quantified judgment model may be useful in projecting future combat. Schank and Abelson (1977) suggest that script-based theories of understanding presume the process is knowledge-based and adaptable. For example, extreme effort may produce either debilitating exhaustion or a boost in morale from shared achievement. Such human factors yield substantial and as yet unreduced uncertainty about how a conflict would really turn out. Most computer simulations probably would exclude such factors since there is not accepted modeling methodology yet available to capture these effects within the simulation.

Physical Parameters. Parameters such as the firepower, range, speed, accuracy, and reliability of weapon systems are imprecisely known in the real world, on both sides of a conflict. These uncertainties could also appear inside a model. Shephard, Hartley, Haysman, Thorpe and Bathe (1988) suggest that even using deterministic Lanchester equations there is uncertainty between the different direct-fire weapons systems that constitute weapon mixes of opposing forces in battle. For example, the Blue decision logic in a force-on-force combat model does not need to know about the fuel situation of the opposing Red units in order to yield an answer from a deterministic algorithm. Knowledge about whether an opponent was running out of fuel or was freshly resupplied could make a major difference in deciding whether or not to engage an enemy using a quick strike.

Doctrine Employed. Doctrine is a summary expression of an Army's approach to fighting campaigns, major operations, battles, and engagements. Doctrine is the root source of tactics, techniques, procedures, organizations, support structure, equipment and training. The U.S. Army outlines its doctrine in field manual 100-5 (1986). Soviet doctrine is asymmetric to that of the United States (Ivanov, Savelyev, Shemanskiy, 1977). Doctrine provide the theoretical concepts that are used to guide battle planning. A good example of Doctrine is the effort to infer exactly what an opponent is planning to do even if one can see exactly what he is currently doing. Even knowing what is happening, there may be multiple interpretations, or the enemy may simply be following a script which is unknown to the observer.

Context Dependence. Brewer and Shubik (1979) have suggested that context is an important variable in mathematical models, manual games, man-machine games, and machine simulations. A given move in any game may mean one thing in one context, but quite another when the context changes. The classic chess example is the difference between the situation in which a move threatens one piece, and a slightly different situation when it also threatens a second. Similarly, in combat, a sudden increase in radio traffic may mean one thing when it occurs in isolation, and something quite different when there is also a large influx of combat supplies. This problem is closely related to foresight.

Stochastic Variations. Variations in weather dramatically affect the availability of aircraft, the mobility of ground units and the efficiency of combat service support. Clausewitz (1976) repeatedly suggests that combat has strong stochastic elements. The issue of interest to simulation modelers in whether these stochastic variations average out (i.e. atomic motions in a gas) or amplify (amplify like the lucky/talented individual who rallies his troops). Many researchers argue that "evenly balanced force" are best defined not as a situation in which both sides eventually diminish to zero at the same moment in time and space, but as one in which each side has a 50% chance of victory. Simulation results by Dockery (1988) and Wise (1988) suggest that even under the "evenly balanced forces" condition, the winner of a two-sided battle has a substantial fraction of his forces left after the other side is totally annihilated. Hence, the situation has less than an even probability of two similar outcomes, (where one side has zero and the other side is negligible), but even probability of two very different outcomes.

Maneuver. There is a well-formalized body of theory (Taylor, 1980, 1983a, 1983b) about the computer modeling of opposing forces which are pushing on either side of a well-defined Forward Edge of the Battle Area (FEBA). This formalism can represent and predict the behavior of large-scale combat units (e.g. tank divisions) without having to resort to detailed modeling of exactly how each soldier, tank, or plane moves, finds targets, communicates, etc. Many of those interactions can be summarized into sets of parameters which can be plugged into the theoretical equations. With variations, this formalism is embodied in many well-known simulation programs. However, the concept of the continuous FEBA breaks down when there are breakthroughs, envelopments, infiltration (i.e. the effects of maneuver). While there are many discussions and much thought devoted to understanding such situations, little has been reduced to mathematical formulae or computer-usable formalisms called algorithms (short of detailed physical modeling). Therefore Maneuver, a critical feature of modern warfare is ill-defined except by historical analogies of World War II. Prediction of the consequences of a breakthrough of the FEBA is difficult with most formal theories although human experts can often make confident informal estimates from the data.

Foresight. In battle planning (i.e. force deployment) software, foresight is perhaps the most important category of uncertainty. First, it has a large effect. Second, there are some techniques under development for dealing with it (unlike psychological factors). Some good examples are the classic perfect information games like chess or go (the national game of Japan in which two players compete to secure territory on a board of squares). While the players have perfectly accurate, complete information about the entire situation displayed on the board in front of them at all times, there is still considerable uncertainty as to exactly what the patterns mean. In the context of writing software that is supposed to handle competition combined with uncertainty, as in battle planning, it is useful to compare the situation of chess and go.

The most efficient computer chess programs work by very fast brute search over all possible future sequences of moves out to a certain depth (Berliner, 1988). While this form of search does achieve enough foresight to soundly beat the average human, it does not generalize to more complex games which in turn require more complex search. For example, in chess there are typically around 30 legal moves to choose from at any given moment. This makes brute-force search feasible. In go, there are typically two or three hundred moves available at any given moment. At this level of complexity brute force search is infeasible. Thus, a go-playing program has to rely more on "intelligence" than speed. At this time, no one has been able to program a computer to play go well enough to beat a novice with more than a few months exposure to the game. The uncertainty about the meaning of patterns, and hence about the game's future is too great.

2.1 Thresholds Versus Look-Aheads

A typical way to make choices in a software module for C2 is the use of thresholds in decision logic. For example, the issue might arise as to whether or not to use reinforcements, when a Blue combat unit B1 was attacking a Red combat unit, R1. A simple way of deciding might be to simply look at the ratio of Blue strength to Red strength. Consider the following rule for attacking prepared defenses, with purely notional numbers. "If the force ratio is above the threshold, where the threshold equals 3, do not use the reinforcements. If it is below the threshold, use the reinforcements (Metzger, Bates, & Womack, 1986)."

Unfortunately, this rule may produce worse overall behavior with a force-ratio of 3.01 (it rashly attacks when it is barely able to), than with a force ratio of 2.99 (the unit gets the needed reinforcements). The most obvious problem is the discontinuous, binary response to a continuous variable, but the real reason is that the force-ratio is being used as a predictor of the desirability of the outcome, and it is simply not a very precise indicator. The outcome is too context dependent to be summarized by the presence or absence of a simple pattern like x is greater than 3. What is needed is an acknowledgment that extreme values of the force-ratio do indicate a fairly predictable outcome, justifying a quick threshold-driven decision. But intermediate values indicate that the decision can not be made on the base of a force ratio alone. Recourse to other information must be available, and the decision must be deferred until that information is processes. That information might be obtained by trying to match more complicated patterns onto the current situation, or by searching over some of the future possibilities by a look-ahead process.

Clearly, one wants to defer the issues which really can not be resolved quickly, but for efficiency's sake one should not defer those which can be resolved quickly. A series of 300-way branches in a decision tree would quickly stop any computer planning program. This is equally true for both domains of go and maneuver planning. In the force-ratio example, an obvious approach toward a solution is to establish a "gray zone" around the value 3. Special measures will be taken to resolve the uncertainty inside the zone, while the decision is made quickly outside the gray zone. While this does produce an improvement, it introduces new threshold effects at the two new thresholds. What is really needed is to defer the decision until sufficient information becomes available, whenever that might be. When several decisions get deferred in this manner, the net effect is that issues get addressed only when they outrank other issues which are also outstanding. Hence, there is a double uncertainty: one cannot say in advance which decisions will be deferred rather than addressed immediately, and even among those which were deferred, the order in which they are actually executed depends on the entire set, not on any particular one.

The fundamental point is that the flow of the program logic must be able to radically shift depending on what data is received. This is uncertainty about how the program will actually execute, which can not be resolved in advance of observing the data (i.e. actually running the simulation). The exact time at which a module will be executed can not be determined by examining the model itself. This is a strong contrast to traditional programming languages, where a function is performed immediately when it is called. Therefore there are quite significant programming issues involved with being able to defer processing, as will be discussed later.

In the force-ratio example, a simple way to resolve the uncertainty is to simply run the simulation once with reinforcements, and once without them, and observe which outcome is more desirable. This is how humans do what-if analysis, and it is a small-scale version of how chess-playing computer programs run. There is a clear trade-off here: the less look-ahead it does, the "smarter" a program must be in order to perform well. Conversely, the faster a program is, the less "smart" it need be.

It should be noted that both human and machine chess do look-aheads with a simplified model. People simplify the problem by using a mental model rather than full-scale trial and error exercises. Computer chess programs simplify the problem by taking a short-sighted approach and only consider the next N moves. In order to make this approach work, the computer program must be able to do several things: (1) set up during a simulation run, a well-formed simplified model of the current sub-situation, (2) run the simplified model quickly to observe what happens, and (3) return from the simplified "thought experiment" to the original detailed simulation which must not have been disturbed in any way. And, as there are at least two decision makers, one Red and one Blue, it must be possible to set up multiple simplified models at various points in the simulation and run them.

2.1.1 Look-Aheads Under Uncertainty

There is a fundamental problem in setting up simplified models, when the phenomenon being modeled is stochastic. One "simplified model" used to predict the likely outcomes of a battle is to simply sum up the combat worth of the opposing units, and compare the force-ratio (U.S. Army Command and General Staff College Student Text ST 100-9, 1988). While that is just a start for a human decision-maker, it is frequently the critical step for software. Consider the problem of attacking a line of defenders at several points simultaneously in a Forward Edge of the Battle Area (FEBA). Consider that the opposing forces are evenly distributed over a linear FEBA, and the attackers are just under the critical threshold of evenly balanced forces (taking into account armament, numbers, force postures, etc.). One might estimate, from force balance alone, that the attacker has a 40% chance of breaking through the defenders FEBA. But does that mean 40% in one large breakthrough of the front as a whole or 40% chance of a small breakthrough in each of several smaller segments of the front? If one considers a 40% chance of breakthrough in each of the quarters, then there is only a 13% chance that no breakthrough will occur anywhere. But if an initial rupture does appear than all the well-known and dramatic events will happen—reinforcements rush in, the attackers can spread out and turn on both sides, defenders rush to control the situation, and so on. Losing an entire quarter of the front would probably lead to disintegration of the whole FEBA, giving an estimated probability of a general breakthrough that is much higher than the initial 40%.

The current literature on combat modeling (Battilega & Grange, 1984; Brewer & Shubik, 1979; Hughes, 1984) is inconclusive on the question of how to estimate the chances of a simultaneous breakthrough. Yet the essential issue in the above scenario is that, while each segment is likely to hold, it is very unlikely that the defending forces will all hold. Any simple logic based on thresholds would come to the same conclusion, either holding or breaking, for each segment, failing to take into account the probabilistic interactions of several events. The real situation is neither that bad nor that good because the defenders will not all withdraw simultaneously, nor will they all defend in place. Hence, many military planners on defense would hold a mobile defense back to catch the inevitable leaks, and planners on offense would hold forces back to exploit these leaks. This presents the problems of concentrating the mobile forces so as to be sufficiently strong, while also keeping these forces mobile and/or dispersed enough to rapidly move to any of several possible breaks in the FEBA quickly. While this notion is hardly novel to humans, any software for planning, critiquing, or aiding in maneuver planning would have to address this issue in some manner, and hence must be able to perform some analog to probabilistic reasoning sketched above.

There are at least two alternative approaches to the scenario above. One is to estimate the 40% probabilities for each segment, then use an explicit probability computation to arrive at the 13% figure, and try to place mobile reserves so as to get the best expected results. While this mathematical, optimizing approach may have the attraction of intellectual coherence and a firm basis in formal decision theory, it has several severe drawbacks. First, not everyone accepts that all the relevant criteria can be captured in statements about probabilities and a general utility function. Second, it rapidly becomes intractable. For example, to get the "best expected result", it is necessary to compute the probable outcome for each different stochastic expected event. This is a significantly complex computation for the initial placement of forces—i.e. one combination per mini-scenario. An initial inspection of the problem focuses on the task of 300-way branches that was mentioned earlier in this chapter. This task makes the problem solution prohibitively slow, even if the mini-scenarios were not allowed to use further branching, and sophisticated algorithms used to restrict the solution search, such a branch and bound of A* search with alpha-alpha pruning (Koff, Flann & Dietterich, 1988).

An alternative approach is to have the software recognize a very broad range of fuzzy patterns (e.g. "wide, almost even front"), and also have stored in computer memory a few suggestions about what to do in each case. The problem of a general utility function is at least partially addressed by having the different suggestions specify what particular goal and defeat mechanism they aim for and rely upon (respectively). One complication of this notion is that any given situation will match many patterns, particularly when the patterns mix tactical and operational levels. Which pattern should the software react to first, in attempting to determine what a specific configuration of forces signifies and what to do about it? Second, there are very many patterns that would need to be stored, demanding a very flexible formalism both for defining them and for matching them onto a given situation. This approach enters the whole area of using pattern-directed software, with patterns at different levels of abstraction, to interpret a block of data. A particularly successful approach has been the use of computer software "blackboards" as will be discussed later.

Fundamentally, we argue that current combat simulation models are all clustered at the end of the spectrum where there is very little look-ahead, and hence tremendous pressure for "smart" command and control logic. Simultaneously, the traditional simulation languages do not readily support the sophisticated "smart" pattern-matching required to dispense with search. As with most tradeoffs, it may be more effective to adopt a less extreme position, in which more foresight, and more flexible pattern-matching are both introduced into the models. However, as mentioned above, this requires some rather radical restructuring of the physical combat simulation, so as to be able to economically answer the different types of questions which arise in command and control planning.

2.2 Problems of Programming Under Uncertainty

Having described some way in which uncertainty arises, and suggesting some approaches to dealing with it, we must consider which programming techniques are appropriate to implementing these approaches. The first step is to clearly lay out the issues.

Depending on the data encountered, processing steps may or may not be performed. A decision may be so obvious that it is made immediately; the functions designed to handle ambiguous cases go totally unused. Also depending on the data, processing steps may occur in very different orders under different circumstances. As mentioned earlier, this represents a radical change from the traditional style of programming, which is succinctly described by standard computer flowcharts.

The approaches of deferring processing steps and of setting up and running sub-simulations both involve quite a bit of bookkeeping. That is, both processes require that large and complicated data-structures be created, used, modified, and finally destroyed at run-time. This places a strong speed requirement on the software, because it must be possible to initialize and run multiple simulations quickly. It is well-known that human decision makers want this capability so as to do their own "what-if" analyses (Hosmer, 1988). The point here is that even software for analyzing courses of action needs this capability, providing another reason for the development of quick "workbench" types of modeling systems.

Consider for a moment the sequence of steps: (1) a combat simulation is run, with a command and control module inside it; (2) issues arise which call for a simpler sub-simulation to be run, with another command and control module inside it; (3) issues arise .... Clearly, this is a recursive process which threatens to become an infinite regress. However, there are several ways out of the regress, depending on exactly how it was started. If the problem is to determine the plausible outcomes of a course of action, then the sub-simulation will be a simpler representation of the current situation. Clearly, it will be reduced to some version which is simple enough to be directly evaluated. This translation can be done all in one step by immediately summing up all the combat worths—but this high degree of aggregation has many well-known flaws. What is needed is some intermediate levels of aggregation.

If the problem is one of determining whether or not a particular pattern is present, than one approach is to individually determine whether or not each sub-pattern is present. This search process proceeds until very detailed patterns are obtained which can be read directly off the data. Because it works by starting at high-level features and trying to determine whether or not the lower-level features support them, this is often called backward chaining or goal-directed search. The reverse of backward chaining is to look at all the simple patterns present, and determine what higher level features they support. This process of forward chaining is data driven rather than goal driven.

2.2.1 Static Versus Dynamic Patterns

There is great freedom in how the tip-level, general features are defined. They may be defined as some range of spatial position (e.g. a Soviet divisional headquarters has X components, arranged like Y), or some range of force ratios. Thus, one might define a general feature like "strong defensive position" as one which has at least a 1-to-3 strength ratio, or which has its avenues of approach well-covered, etc. These are essentially static definitions, because they refer to what the situation is at a given moment. Alternatively, one might define a general feature like "strong defensive position" as "one which can not be broken using typical plans." This is an essentially dynamic definition because it refers to how the situation can change over time. The dynamic definition is, in a sense the more fundamental definition, as it directly reflects the issue of how strongly it resists attack, and indirectly reflects the dependence on doctrine. Immediately prior to World War II, the fortress Eben Emael was considered to be quite strong. It was expected to resist standard, large scale attacks by tanks and infantry for a week or more. In reality, it fell in one day to the airborne attack of seventy seven soldiers. Thus what looks quite strong at one point may suddenly be revealed as quite vulnerable by the introduction of new techniques and tools. The static definition fails to capture this variability, while the dynamic definition does so quite robustly.

This example also points out some novel features of the dynamic definition. First the state definition really just uses static features to estimate (under implicit assumptions about what tools and techniques will be used) what outcome will be. They are, in a sense, compiled versions of the dynamic rule. If the dynamics change, the static definitions must be "recompiled," while the dynamic one does not. Second, the dynamic definition points out that the processes of situation assessment and planning are not totally distinct. While this is explicitly emphasized when discussing how people think (U.S. Army Command and General Staff College Student Test ST 100-9, 1988), the two processes are usually treated as totally separate by software. The attempt to lay out a plan may reveal unexpected opportunities or problems, changing the situation estimate, which may lead to further revisions of the plan. The static definitions do not capture this interaction, while the dynamic definition does. In fact, the dynamic definition forces this interaction to occur, which complicates the task of programming. That is, to determine whether a plan will work, one must check certain features, but to do that requires determining whether other plans will work.

While mixing situation assessment and planning adds some obvious complications to the former, there are some indirect benefits. For example, the use of dynamic patterns enables some of the static definitions to be eliminated and could reduce the need for rewriting them whenever new weapons, scenarios, or tactics are introduced. It is a continual problem in modeling that the patterns may be carefully tuned to work in one set of situations, but are then promptly applied to a very different set of situations (e.g. a model built for a war in Europe being used in a Southeast Asia scenario). Using more dynamic definitions may help control the undesirable consequences of such changes. Second, mixing the two stages has some definite benefits for the planning, because there will be a large collection of fragmentary plans left over from the assessment, which can be used to develop a firmer plan.

Again, there is the potential for infinite regress, because there is not a clear division between (1) backward chaining from high-level problems down to low-level problems, and (2) forward chaining from low-level data up to high-level data. Because things do not partition so neatly, it becomes necessary to mix forward and backward chaining in an island driving software strategy (i.e. a parsing strategy that begins at a random point and systematically processes adjacent chunks of information of greater and greater size in a decision-tree). The blackboard model of computation is designed to simultaneously deal with all these problems.

2.3 Combining Plan Fragments

As mentioned earlier, an advantage of integrating the situation-assessment and planning stages is that the process of interpreting patterns also yields preliminary ideas about what to do. However, this leads to a style of planning which is not typical in the artificial intelligence research domain. Charniak and McDermott (1986) suggest the usual planning problems start with a given state, a set of operators for changing that state, and a goal-condition. The idea is to find a series of operations which can change the current state into one satisfying the goal-condition (e.g. which moves a military unit to its goal while destroying any opposing enemy forces). However, the second approach described above presents a slightly different problem because the rules contain suggestions about plans to achieve a goal. Rather than a set of operators, the planning software is given a current situation, a set of goals to be satisfied, and a set of partial plans for achieving some of those goals. Genesereth and Nilsson (1987) suggest that planning tasks involve reasoning about the plans. The goal is to combine the plans into one big plan which achieves as many goals as possible. In general, it is not possible to satisfy all goals. For example, a plausible general goal for combat units would be "don't waste resources", so that if two plans both achieve the same purpose, the plan with lower attrition would be preferred. A specific goal might be to defend a specific area, and a third might be to break out toward an objective and seize the initiative. A standard plan to defend an area is to place a light screening force of soldiers along the perimeter with mobile forces held back in the center. A standard plan to break out might be to mass soldiers at a point, attack, then exploit and enlarge any small breaks. The conflict between these two plans is classic because one can not be strong everywhere on defense while concentrating to attack.

The only way out of the dilemma is to reduce one's expectations for one of the plans. One may retain a defensive posture and pay the price of sacrificing initiative. Alternatively, one may adopt the offensive, and pay a price in the form of increased risk in the defensive positions. But there is no magic sequence of maneuvers to achieve both goals simultaneously. Hence, the classical artificial intelligence planning paradigm would fruitlessly search forever, or at best give up. The real problem is to decide which goal to sacrifice, how much, and to formulate a plan which does just that (running the necessary risks, but not the foolhardy ones). Using multi-attribute utility theory (MAUT) provides some structure for addressing such tradeoffs, but does not provide help in formulating plans. That is, MAUT helps in selecting options from a given list (perhaps with adjustment of continuous parameters), but it does not give any guidance in the structural reasoning necessary to add new items to the list.

The development of techniques to combine plan-fragments is on-going, but the work of Wilensky (1983) and the various case-based reasoning projects (Kolodner, 1988) are quite relevant to planning in combat simulation models. Recent research (Simmons, 1988; Dean and Boddy, 1988) has suggested that in reconfiguring plans it is essential to have a reasoning mechanism whose special domain is handling goal interactions, synergisms and conflicts.

3 The Blackboard Model of Uncertainty Management

The literature on, and experience with, the blackboard computer software architecture is rich and varied; the interested reader is referred to Nii (1986a, 1986b) and Englemore and Morgan (1988) for a basic introduction.

The blackboard architecture takes its name from a simple metaphor. Imagine a group of experts standing around a blackboard, cooperatively working a problem. Each one, when he sees something he know how to handle, writes down what he thinks it might imply, or what additional data he might need to very his guess. Of course whatever an expert writes immediately becomes available for all the others to read. For programming the blackboard architecture consists of (1) a global data structure called the blackboard, (2) a collection of program modules called knowledge sources (KS's), each one of which is "watching" a specific region of the blackboard, and (3) an agenda of requests from KS's to do their computation, called knowledge source activation records (KSAR's). The fundamental action of a computation is to either erase a piece of old data from the blackboard, or to compute and post a new datum. Notice that is one KS sees several interesting things appear on its region of the blackboard, then it may push several KSAR's onto the agenda at once. Alternatively, if a piece of data has two contradictory interpretations (e.g. our example of deciding either "attack with reinforcements" or "attack without reinforcements") it is perfectly free to post multiple KSAR's, each of which tries to verify one interpretation. Also there is no predetermined interval between a KSAR entering the agenda and its actually being executed in the program.

Conceptually, the whole system works in a simple cycle. All the KS's examine their region of the blackboard, looking for something they know how to process. All the KS's which find something produce and prioritize KSAR's. All the KSAR's are pushed onto the agenda, which is then sorted to bring the highest-priority KSAR to the top. That KSAR is executed, and it is allowed to modify the blackboard. Then the cycle repeats.

The issues of matching are of great importance, particularly with regards partial matches. For example, if one KS needs to observe X, Y, and Z so as to conclude A, but only observes X and Y, then it might post two different KSAR's—either a request that someone confirm A (causing backward chaining), a tentative suggestion that Z may hold (uncertain forward chaining), or both. It is evident that the "island driving" strategy is easy to implement because firmly established facts will provide firm matches, and the islands of certainty can be made to slowly spread out over the whole blackboard. Of course, the blackboard is analyzing a dynamic situation, then it will track the situation, without ever fully resolving every uncertainty.

The issues of agenda maintenance are still areas of active research. For example, two different KS's might propose different interpretations of an observation, contingent on the status of a second observation. They post their respective KSAR's on the agenda. If there is already a KSAR on the agenda, which might resolve the status of that second, pivotal observation, then its priority should be raised even if it was initially given a low priority. Conversely, if several KSAR's all deal with ways to determine a particular important fact, then they will go onto the agenda with high priorities.

But as soon as one of them establishes the fact, all the others should be permanently dropped in priority (in practice, they are completely deleted from the agenda).

As compared to the usual computation model of function calls and procedures, the blackboard architecture represents a radical departure. Nevertheless, several general blackboard utilities are available, such as BB1 and GBB (Johnson, Gallagher, & Corkill, 1987). They are essentially large LISP language programs which compile "blackboard language" programs down into LISP code, just as large assembly language programs compile FORTRAN language programs down into assembly language. The choice of LISP is driven by the very simple criterion of ease and consequently cost. The reasons why LISP is so easy to use is given in detail by Abelson and Sussman (1986). An interpreter for the SIMSCRIPT language was given by Modjeski (1987) in just six pages of LISP code. Considering the probable length of a SIMSCRIPT interpreter written in FORTRAN, PASCAL, or ADA, it is obvious that LISP is the language of choice to implement the blackboard language. It is noted that other languages are capable of implementing the blackboard concept only at greater size, cost and maintainability.

4 Conclusions

One can start at some very simple examples of the uncertainties which arise in battle planning and quickly come to some strong implications about how to structure programs. The three most fundamental implications are:

1. There is a need for some form of look-ahead, to simulate a human commander's foresight, and to trade-off searching against pattern matching. While lots of search of not adequate to outperform human game players in simple games like chess, pure pattern matching is worse. For games too complicated to be fully searched, what seems to work best is a combination of pattern-matching and search.
2. To support the look-aheads, there is a need for a combat simulation which can be rapidly reconfigure under software control to run different scenario, at differing levels of detail, over differing time spans. Moreover, it must be possible to partially run one simulation, stop it, run a more detailed sub-simulation to resolve a sub-issue, then resume the original simulation.
3. The blackboard architecture provides a structured way to explicit whatever certainty does currently exist in a problem, while flexibly choosing the most appropriate ways to reduce what uncertainty remains.

References

Abelson, H. & Sussman, G.L. (1986). *Structure and interpretation of computer programs.* Cambridge, MA: MIT Press.

Berliner, H. (1988). HITECH report: HITECH becomes first computer senior master, *AI magazine, 9* (3), 85–87.

Brewer, G.D., & Shubik, M. (1979). *The war game: a critique of military problem solving.* Cambridge, MA: Harvard University Press.

Battilega, J.A., & Grange, J.K. (1984). *The military applications of modeling.* Wright-Patterson Air Force Base, OH: Air Force Institute of Technology Press.

Clausewitz, C. (1976). *On war.* In M. Howard & P. Paret (Ed. and Trans.), *Carl von Clausewitz on war.* Princeton, NJ: Princeton University Press.

Charniak, E. & McDermott, D. (1986). *Introduction to artificial intelligence.* Reading, MA: Addison-Wesley Publishing Company.

Dean, T., & Boddy, M. (1988). An analysis of time-dependent planning. *Proceedings of the seventh national conference on artificial intelligence (pp. 49–543).* San Mateo, CA: Morgan Kaufmann Publishers.

Dockery, J.T., & van den Driessche, J. (1984). *Use of artificial intelligence and Psychology in the analysis of command and control.* (Technical Memorandum STC). The Hague, Holland: Supreme Headquarters Allied Powers Europe (SHAPE), Technical Center.

Dockery, J.T., & Santoro, R.T. (1988). Lanchester revisited: progress in modeling C2 in combat. *Signal magazine*, 41–48.

Dupuy, T.N. (1979). *Numbers, predications and war: using history to evaluate combat factors and predict the outcome of battles.* New York: Bobbs-Merrill Co.

Genesereth, M.R., & Nilsson, N.J. (1987). *Logical foundations of artificial intelligence.* Los Altos, CA: Morgan Kaufmann Publishers.

Harris, Corporation (1985). *Interactive theater wargame FORCEM Gaming Evaluator (FORGE): program specification.* (Contract MDA 903-84-C-0509 Phase I Report). Melbourne, FL: Harris Corporation.

Hosmer, B.C. (1988). Operational art: the importance of the operational level of war. *Bulletin of Military Operations Research: Phalanx, 21* (3), 1–6.

Hughes, W.P. (1984). *Military modeling.* Alexandria, VA: Military Operations Research Society, Inc.

Ivanov, D.A., Savelyev, V.P., Shemanskiy, P.V. (1977). *Fundamentals of tactical command and control: a soviet view* (translated). Washington, DC: United States Government Printing Office.

Johnson, P., Gallagher, K., & Corkill, D. (1987). *GBB reference manual and GBB source code* COINS Technical Report 87-120). Amherst, MA: Computer and Information Sciences Department, University of Massachusetts, Amherst.

Koff, C.N., Flann, N.S., & Dietterich, T.G. (1988). An efficient ATMS (automated truth maintenance system) for equivalence relations. *Proceedings of the seventh national conference on artificial intelligence* (pp. 182–187). San Mateo, CA: Morgan Kaufmann Publishers, Inc.

Kolodner, J. (1988). *Proceeding of the DARPA workshop on case-based reasoning.* Palo Alto, CA: Morgan Kaufmann.

Metzger, J.J., Bates, C.B., Womack, F.E. (1986). *Command and Control (C2) enhancements for FORCEM* (CAA Study Report CAA-SR-86-5). Bethesda, MD: United States Army Concepts Analysis Agency (NTIS/DTIC Number ADF86077).

McQuie, R. (1987). What good is a man in the loop? *Bulletin of Military Operations Research, 20*, (2), 10–11.

Modjeski, R. (1987). *Artificial intelligence study (AIS)* (CAA Research Product CAA-RP-87-1). Bethesda, MD: United States Army Concept Analysis Agency.

Nii, P. (1986). Blackboard systems: the blackboard model of problem solving and the evolution of blackboard architectures, *AI Magazine, 7* (2), 38–53.

Nii, P. (1986). Blackboard systems: blackboard applications systems, blackboard systems from a knowledge engineering perspective, *AI Magazine* 7 (2), 82–106.

Shank, R. & Abelson, R. (1977). *Scripts, plans, goals and understanding.* Hillsdale, NJ: Lawrence Erlbaum Publishers.

Shephard, R.W., Hartley, D.A., Haysman, P.J., Thorpe, L., & Bathe, M.R. (1988). *Applied operations research: examples from defense assessment.* New York: Plenum Press.

Simmons, R.G. (1988). A theory of debugging plans and interpretations. *Proceedings of the seventh national conference on artificial intelligence* (pp. 94–99). San Mateo, CA: Morgan Kaufmann Publishers.

Sweet, R., Metersky, M., Sovereign, M. (1985). *Proceedings of the Military Operations Research Society Command and Control Evaluations Workshop.* Monterey, CA: Navel Postgraduate School.

Taylor, J.G. (1980). *Force-on-Force attrition modeling.* Arlington, VA: Military Operations Research Society of America.

Taylor, J.G. (1983a). *Lanchester models of warfare* (Vol. 1). Arlington, VA: Military Operations Research Society of America.

Taylor, J.G. (1983b). *Lanchester models of warfare* (Vol. 2). Arlington, VA: Military Operations Research Society of America.

United States Army Command and General Staff College (1988). *The command estimate* (Student Test ST 100-9). Fort Leavenworth, KS: United States Command and General Staff College.

United States Army (1986). *Operations.* (Field Manual 100-5). Fort Monroe, VA: United States Army Training and Doctrine Command.

von Mellinthin, Stolfi, & Sobick (1984) *NATO under attack.* Durham, NC: Duke University Press.

Wilensky, R. (1983). *Planning and understanding.* Reading MA: Addison-Wesley.

Wise, B.P. (1988a). *Simulation experiments in command and control.* Unpublished manuscript, McDonnell Douglas Research Laboratories, Saint Louis, MO.

Wise, B.P. (1988b). Experimentally comparing uncertain inference systems to probability. In J.F. Lemmer, & L.N. Kanal (Eds.) *Uncertainty in artificial intelligence.* New York: Elsevier Science Publishers.

Wise, B.P. (1986). *An experimental comparison of uncertain inference systems.* Unpublished doctoral dissertation, Department of Engineering and Public Policy, Carnegie-Mellon University.

Wise, B.P., & Modjeski, R.B. (1987). Thinking about AI and OR: uncertainty management, *Bulletin of military operations research, 20* (4), 8–11.

Biographies

Norman I. Badler
Department of Computer and Information Science
University of Pennsylvania
Philadelphia, PA 19104-6389
USA
EMAIL: badler@central.cis.upenn.edu

Norman I. Badler is Professor of Computer and Information Science at the Moore School of the University of Pennsylvania and has been on that faculty ksince 1974. Active in computer graphics since 1968, his main areas of work include computer modeling, manipulation, and animation of human figures, interactive system design, and the application of artificial intelligence techniques to graphical problems. He is the author or co-author of over 75 technical papers and has given over 50 professional presentations to groups in industry, academia, and government.

Badler is a Senior Editor of *Computer Vision, Graphics, and Image Processing*, and will become a Co-Editor of the new Journal *Graphical Models and Image Processing* when *CVGIP* splits in 1990. He is also the Associate Editor of *IEEE Computer Graphics and Applications*. He has served on the organizing and program committees of several major conferences, including the annual SIGGRAPH conference. He has also been a Vice-Chair of ACM SIGGRAPH. He currently directs a Computer Graphics Research Facility with two full time staff members and about 40 students.

Badler received the BA degree in Creative Studies Mathematics from the University of California at Santa Barbara in 1970, the MSc in Mathematics in 1971, and the Ph.D. in Computer Science in 1975, both from the University of Toronto.

Arie Ben-David
Information Systems Department
School of Business Adminstration

The Hebrew University of Jerusalem
Mount Scopus, Jerusalem 91905
Israel
Phone: 972-2-883235, 883449
Fax: 972-2-826249
EMAIL: kbuba@hujivm1.bitnet

Arie Ben-David heads the Information Systems Dept. of the Business Administration School at the Hebrew University of Jerusalem. He earned his Ph.D. in Computer Science at Case Western Reserve University (1988). His main interests are in Artificial Intelligence, in particular in Machine Learning and in Expert Systems. His current research concerns the development of new machine learning paradigms.

Albert Clarkson
ESL Incorporated
Advanced Intelligence Analysis Technology Laboratory
495 Java Drive
Sunnyvale, CA 94088-3510
USA

Albert Clarkson is a novelist, Director of the Advanced Intelligence Analysis Technology Laboratory at ESL, Incorporated, and a consultant on computer-based C3I applications. He is currently working on the theoretical foundations for a new knowledge-intensive machine art. He has worked for the past several years with Dr. Lenat and other colleagues on a series of projects to develop early prototype scenario-generation systems exploiting Lenat's automated discovery technique in machine learning. This work has led empirically to some of his current ideas of machine storytelling. Among his publications are *Toward Effective Strategic Analysis: New Applications of Information Technology* (Westview, 1982), and a novel, *The Old World* (Alchemy Books, 1988).

Jeffrey Esakov
Department of Computer and Information Science
University of Pennsylvania
Philadelphia, PA 19104-6389
USA
EMAIL: esakov@cis.upenn.edu

Jeffrey Esakov is a Ph.D. candidate a the University of Pennsylvania. His areas of interest include computer graphics and animation, object-oriented languages and software engineering. He is co-author of the book *Data Structures: An Advanced Approach Using C.*

Esakov received the BS degree in Computer Science from Union College in 1982 and the MS degree in Computer Science from the University of Illinois at Urbana-Champaign in 1983. Prior to returning for his Ph.D., he worked at AT&T Bell Laboratories in 1983.

Paul A. Fishwick
Department of Computer and Information Science
University of Florida
Building CSE, Room 301
Gainesville, FL 32611
USA
EMAIL: fishwick@cis.ufl.edu

Paul A. Fishwick is an Assistant Professor in the Department of Computer and Information Science at the University of Florida. He received the BS in Mathematics from the Pennsylvania State University, MS in Applied Science from the College of William and Mary, and Ph.D. in Computer and Information Science from the University of Pennsylvania in 1986. He also has six years of industrial/government production and research experience working at Newport News Shipbuilding and Dry Dock Co. (doing CAD/CAM parts definition research) and at NASA Langley Research Center (studying engineering data base models for structural engineering). His current research interests are in computer simulation modeling, systems science, artificial intelligence, and scientific visualization. He has published a number of journal articles in the topics of process abstraction in modeling, the use of natural language as a simulation modeling medium, and qualitative simulation. He is a member of IEEE, IEEE Society for Systems, Man and Cybernetics, IEEE Computer Society, The Society for Computer Simulation, ACM, AAAI, and IMACS. Dr. Fishwick is chairman of the IEEE Computer Society Technical Committee on Simulation (TCSIM) which has one thousand members worldwide and publishes *Simulation Digest* in conjunction with ACM SIGSIM. He is a member of several editorial boards including *ACM Transactions on Modelling and Computer Simulation* and the *Transactions of the Society for Computer Simulation.*

Andrew Gelsey
Department of Computer Science
Yale University
P.O. Box 2158 Yale Station
New Haven, CT 06520-2158
USA
EMAIL: gelsey@cs.yale.edu

Andrew Gelsey is a graduate student at Yale University. Ph.D. degree expected May 1990. Dissertation Title: Automated Reasoning about Machines.

Recent Publication: Andrew Gelsey. Automated Physical Modeling. In "Proceedings of the 11th International Joint Conference on Artificial Intelligence", Detroit, Michigan USA, August 1989.

Jhyfang Hu
Department of Electrical Engineering
Tulane University
New Orleans, LA 70118
USA
Phone: (504) 865-5785
EMAIL: hu@bourbon.ee.tulane.edu

Jhyfang Hu is an assistant professor in the Department of Electrical Engineering at Tulane University. He received his M. S. and Ph.D. degrees in Electrical and Computer Engineering from University of Arizona in 1986 and 1989. His research interests are in the areas of artificial intelligence, modeling and simulation, distributed systems, and design automation. He is a member of Eta Kappa Nu and IEEE Computer Society.

Steven H. Kaisler
DARPA/NTO
1400 Wilson Boulevard
Arlington, VA 22209
USA
Phone: (202) 694-1703
EMAIL: kaisler-s@a.isi.edu

Stephen H. Kaisler is currently Chief Scientist for Analytics Corporation where he is responsible for guiding advanced technology development as well as overseeing the technology planning for the corporation. Prior to this, he was a program manager at the Defense Advanced Research Projects Agency. In this role, he managed the Fleet Command Center Battle Management Program and several parallel processor projects. Mr. Kaisler initiated the STRADS II project as a vehicle for exploring the application of machine learning technology to intelligence analysis and strategy assessment. Mr. Kaisler has a B. S. in Physics and an M. S. in Computer Science from the University of Maryland, College Park. He is currently working on a Ph.D. at the George Washington University.

Tag Gon Kim
Department of Electrical and Computer Engineering
University of Kansas
Lawrence, KS 66045
USA
EMAIL: TKIM@UKANVAX

Tag Gon Kim received the BSEE and MSEE from Pusan National University, Korea and Kyunpook National University, Korea, in 1975 and 1980, respectively. He received his Ph.D. in EE from University of Arizona, Tucson, AZ, in 1988. From 1987 to 1989, he worked as a research staff engineer in the Environmental Research Lab of University of Arizona. Since August 1989, he has been an assistant professor in the Telecommunications and Information Sciences Lab, Department of Electrical and Computer Engineering, The University of Kansas, Lawrence, KS. He also held a faculty position in Department of Electronics, National Fisheries University of Pusan, Pusan, Korea. His research interests include AI for advanced simulation methodology, computer systems modelling, and object-oriented software environment. Dr. Kim is a member of IEEE, ACM, AAAI, SCS, and Eta Kappa Nu.

Douglas B. Lenat
Microelectronics and Computer Technology Corporation
P.O. Box 200195
Austin, TX 78720
USA

Douglas B. Lenat is Principal Scientist of Microelectronics and Computer Technology Corporation (MCC) in Austin, Texas. The CYC program, his major research project at MCC, is a ten-year project that began in 1984 to develop a huge knowledge base of real-world facts, problem-solving methods, and heuristics. In essence, it is the equivalent of encoding all of the explicit and implicit facts that are found in, or which one would need to know in order to understand, one-volume enCYClopedia.

Dr. Lenat's 1976 Stanford thesis was a demonstration that certain kinds of "creative discoveries" in mathematics could be produced by a computer program. This work earned him the biannual IJCAI Computers & Thought award in 1977. He was named one of America's 100 brightest scientists under the age of 40 in the December *1984 Science Digest.* He has been a professor of computer science at Carnegie Mellon University and Stanford. He is also a cofounder of Teknowledge. Dr. Lenat has published more than 50 papers and books, including *Knowledge Based Systems in Artificial Intelligence* (McGraw Hill, 1982), and *Building Expert Systems* (Addison-Wesley, 1983). He has also designed and built many large knowledge-based systems (PUP5, AM, Eurisko) and representation languages (BEINGS, RLL, CYCL).

Richard B. Modjeski
United States Army
Operational Test and Evaluation Agency
Technical Support Directorate
Policy and Review Methodology Division
Park Center IV, 4501 Ford Avenue
Alexandria, VA 22302-1458
USA

Richard B. Modjeski is an Operations Research Analyst for the United States Army. He has a BS degree with honors from the University of Wisconsin–Oshkosh, two Masters degrees from the University of Hawaii, and a Ph.D. in Measurement Theory from the University of Southern California. He has worked for the Army Research Institute, the Advanced Research Projects Office at the Army Concepts Analysis Agency, and the Army Operational Test and Evaluation Agency. He has published over 100 articles in basic research, military testing, training, and artificial intelligence. He is editor of the Advanced Technology section of the Bulletin of Military Operations Research (Phalanx). His current research focuses on the application of AI to public policy.

Norman R. Nielsen
Intelligent Systems Laboratory
SRI International
333 Ravenswood Avenue
Menlo Park, CA 94025
USA
EMAIL: nielsen@kl.sri.com

Norman R. Nielsen is Associate Director of the Information Technology Center at SRI International (formerly Stanford Research Institute). He has long been involved in the modeling of computer systems and has more recently been applying knowledge-based reasoning capabilities to the simulation process. Much of his work has involved applied studies for computer system vendors and commercial organizations having large-scale, advanced computer systems installations. He is a co-editor of *Artificial Intelligence, Simulation & Modeling* (Wiley, 1989) and will be serving as the chairman of the AI and Simulation Workshop at the 1990 AAAI national conference.

Dr. Nielsen received his Ph.D. from Stanford University in operations and systems analysis.

Tuncer I. Ören
Simulation Research Group
Department of Computer Science
University of Ottawa
Ottawa, Ontario, K1N 6N5
Canada
EMAIL: tiosl@uottawa.bitnet

Tuncer I. Ören is a professor of Computer Science at the University of Ottawa. His current research interests include applications of artificial intelligence in modelling, simulation, and software engineering. He has published over two hundred thirty documents, and has been editor or co-editor of eleven books. He has been active in over one hundred twenty conferences and seminars held in twenty countries.

Dr. Ören has been the first chairman of the National Executive Committee of the Canadian Computer Science Departments Chairman. Since 1980, he has been the representative of the Canadian Information Processing Society to Atomic Energy of Canada on the nuclear fuel waste management program.

He is an ex-chairman of the special group on simulation of the Association for Computing Machinery and an ex-editor of the quarterly of the group. He is an associate editor of Simulation, San Diego, California as well as of the System Analysis, Modelling, and Simulation, the quarterly by Akademie-Verlag, East Berlin.

Colleen M. Oresky
ESL Incorporated
495 Java Drive
P.O. Box 3510
Sunnyvale, CA 94088-3510
USA

Colleen M. Oresky is a senior engineer at ESL, Incorporated (a subsidiary of TRW). She is both the principal engineer and the current STRADS Program Manager. Since completing a year-long knowledge engineering training course at Teknowledge, Inc., she has designed and developed several knowledge-based systems. As part of the development, she has worked directly with users to define system requirements and to extract and formulate representations for various types of knowledge. She has worked closely with Dr. Douglas Lenat for the past several years during all phases of the STRADS design and development. She has published technical papers on various aspects of the STRADS research.

Richard E. Reynolds
Naval Training Systems Center
Human Factors Laboratory
Orlando, FL 32826
USA

Richard E. Reynolds received his Ph.D. from Miami University, Oxford, Ohio in experimental Psychology. Dr. Reynolds is a Research Program Manager for the Naval Training Systems Center, Human Factors Laboratory, Orlando, Florida. Dr. Reynolds is currently involved in the development of knowledge-based techniques for applications to embedded training and simulation systems.

Jeff Rothenberg
The RAND Corporation
1700 Main Street
P.O. Box 2138
Santa Monica, CA 90506
USA

Jeff Rothenberg is a Senior Computer Scientist at the RAND Corporation, where he is principal investigator for the Knowledge-Based Simulation project. He performed his graduate work in Artificial Intelligence at the University of Wisconsin, Madison, from 1968 to 1973. Since then, he has been involved in various simulation, graphics, and intelligent tutoring applications at USC Information Sciences Institute, Clear Systems, TRW, and Uniform Software. His work at RAND has included developing criteria for evaluating expert system tools, developing graphic user interfaces for simulation, and developing requirements for high-level languages. His current research interests include model-based teaching, designing new simulation languages, and extending the power and comprehensibility of object-oriented simulation using knowledge-based techniques.

Jerzy W. Rozenblit
Department of Electrical and Computer Engineering
University of Arizona
Tucson, AZ 85721
USA

Phone: (602) 621-6177
EMAIL: ROZENBLIT%EVAX2@ARIZONA.EDU

Jerzy W. Rozenblit is an assistant professor in the Department of Electrical and Computer Engineering at University of Arizona. He received his Ph.D. in Computer Science from Wayne State University in Detroit, in 1985. His research interests are in the areas of modeling and simulation, system design, and artificial intelligence. He is a member of ACM, IEEE Computer Society, and The Society for Computer Simulation.

Kent E. WIlliams
Institute for Simulation and Training
University of Central Florida
P. O. Box 25000
Orlando, FL 32816-0544
USA

Kent E. Williams received his Ph.D. from the University of Connecticut in Cognition Human Learning, and Memory. Dr. Williams is the Research Manager for the Institute for Simulation and Training, University of Central Florida. Dr. Williams is currently involved in a variety of projects applying principles of cognitive science to simulation technology for training and education purposes.

Dr. Kent E. Williams is currently at the University of Central Florida's Institute for Simulation and Training, Research Pavilion, Suite 300; 12424 Research Parkway, Orlando, Florida 32826. Dr. Williams holds a Ph.D. in cognitive psychology from the University of Connecticut. He has been involved in cognitive science research for application to training systems since 1976. He is currently designing a classroom of the future which shall implement a variety of cognitive science technologies to enhance learning for the individual in the public school classroom.

Ben P. Wise
McDonnell Douglas Research Laboratories
Department 225, Building 105
P. O. Box 516
St. Louis, MO 63166
USA

Ben P. Wise is a Senior Scientist at the McDonnell Douglas Research Laboratories in Saint Louis, MO. He has a BS in physics from the MIT and a Ph.D. in Engineering and Public Policy from Carnegie Mellon University. He has taught graduate courses in AI, optimization, decision analysis, and probability/statistics in the Thayer School of Engineering and the

Computer Science Department at Dartmouth College. His current research focuses on AI techniques for planning under uncertainty and competition.

Prof. Bernard P. Zeigler
Department of Electrical and Computer Engineering
University of Arizona
Tucson, AZ 85721
USA
EMAIL: ZEIGLER%EVAX2@ARIZONA.EDU

Bernard P. Zeigler received the Ph.D. degree in Computer/Communication Science from the University of Michigan, Ann Arbor, in 1969, and the preceding degrees from McGill University, Montreal, P.Q., Canada, and MIT, Cambridge. He is a professor in the Department of Electrical and Computer Engineering at the University of Arizona. He is the author of *Multifaceted Modelling and Discrete Event Simulation*, Academic Press, 1984, and *Theory of Modelling and Simulation*, John Wiley, 1976. His research interests include AI, distributed simulation, and expert systems for simulation methodology.

Index